HISTORY OF THE RUSSIAN THEATRE

(Seventeenth Through Nineteenth Century)

WORKS TRANSLATED UNDER THE RUSSIAN TRANSLATION
PROJECT OF THE AMERICAN COUNCIL OF
LEARNED SOCIETIES, AND PUBLISHED BY
THE MACMILLAN COMPANY

W. CHAPIN HUNTINGTON, EDITOR

TOLSTOY AS I KNEW HIM
My Life at Home and at Yasnaya Polyana
By T. A. Kuzminskaya, sister-in-law
of Leo Tolstoy

THE LAW OF THE SOVIET STATE
By Andrei Y. Vyshinsky, Deputy Minister
for Foreign Affairs of the USSR

HISTORY OF EARLY RUSSIAN LITERATURE
By N. K. Gudzy, member, Academy of
Sciences of the USSR

ECONOMIC GEOGRAPHY OF THE USSR
Edited by S. S. Balzak, V. F. Vasyutin,
and Y. G. Feigin

HISTORY OF THE NATIONAL ECONOMY OF RUSSIA
TO THE 1917 REVOLUTION
By P. I. Lyashchenko, member, Academy of
Sciences of the USSR

NATURAL REGIONS OF THE USSR
By L. S. Berg, President, All-Union Geographical
Society of the USSR

RUSSIAN FOLKLORE
By Y. M. Sokolov

HISTORY OF THE RUSSIAN THEATRE
Seventeenth Through Nineteenth Century
By B. V. Varneke, Philologist and Theatre Historian

HISTORY OF THE RUSSIAN THEATRE

**SEVENTEENTH THROUGH
NINETEENTH CENTURY**

B. V. Varneke

Original Translation by BORIS BRASOL

Revised and Edited by BELLE MARTIN
Associate on Russian Programs
American Council of Learned Societies

THE MACMILLAN COMPANY
New York : 1951

PN
2721
V32

Mr. Boris Brasol, the translator of this work, did not participate in the final editorial revision of the text of his translation and some of his annotations have been editorially omitted. Departures from his original translation cannot, therefore, be attributed to him.

American Council of Learned Societies

Foreword

The Russian Translation Project of the American Council of Learned Societies was organized in 1944 with the aid of a subsidy from the Humanities Division of the Rockefeller Foundation. The aim of the Project is the translation into English of significant Russian works in the fields of the humanities and the social sciences which provide an insight into Russian life and thought.

In the difficult problem of the selection of books for translation, the Administrative Committee has had the counsel and cooperation of Slavic scholars throughout the United States and Great Britain. It is thought that the books chosen will be useful to general readers interested in world affairs, and will also serve as collateral reading material for the large number of courses on Russia in our colleges and universities.

Since Russian history is a continuum, the volumes translated are of various dates and have been drawn from both the prerevolutionary and postrevolutionary periods, from writings published inside and outside of Russia, the choice depending solely on their value to the fundamental aim of the Project. Translations are presented in authentic and unabridged English versions of the original text. Only in this way, it is believed, can American readers be made aware of the traditions, concepts, and ideologies by which the thinking and attitudes of the people of Russia are molded.

It should, of course, be clearly understood that the views expressed in the words translated are not to be identified in any way with those of the Administrative Committee or of the Council.

THE ADMINISTRATIVE COMMITTEE
JOHN A. MORRISON, *Chairman*
HAROLD SPIVACKE
SERGIUS YAKOBSON
MORTIMER GRAVES
W. CHAPIN HUNTINGTON

Author's Preface to the Third Edition[*]

After the Great October Socialist Revolution many very valuable memoirs and other source materials pertaining to the history of the Russian theatre were published, and the study of the Soviet theatre began and established itself on a firm foundation.

A textbook of the history of the theatre in the U.S.S.R. is now indispensable. Such a work has, however, not as yet been produced. Therefore, the Central Administration of Educational Institutions of the Committee on Art of the Council of People's Commissars of the U.S.S.R., proposed to the author of these lines that he prepare the third edition of his textbook History of the Russian Theatre, the first edition of which was published in 1908 and the second in 1913. For obvious reasons much of the material in that book has become out-dated, and therefore is in need of substantial revision. Nevertheless the reader is offered the third edition of a previously written book, not a new work.

Changes in the textbook were made to accord with the suggestions made at a special conference convened for this purpose during the current year by the Central Administration of Educational Institutions of the Committee on Art of the Council of People's Commissars of the U.S.S.R., jointly with the "Art" publishing house. The program dealing with the history of the Russian theatre, compiled by G. I. Goyan, a candidate for a graduate degree in the arts, and approved by the Central Administration of Educational Institutions of the Committee, was taken into account. In the treatment of the history of the popular drama and the drama of the period before Peter the Great, the respective chapters in the latest textbooks of Professors Yu. M. Sokolov and N. K. Gudzy were used. Many periods of the later history of the drama have been reinterpreted in numerous books by Soviet students of literature. In this field I was greatly assisted by my colleague in the local institutions of

[*] The original Russian work appeared under the title, *Istoriia russkogo teatra XVII–XIX vekov*, Third Edition, "Iskusstvo" Publishing House, Moscow-Leningrad, 1939.

higher education, A. I. Boguslavsky, candidate for a degree in philosophy. He compiled *in toto* Chapters VIII, IX, XII, XIII, XIV, and XV, while in Chapter XXI he wrote the section devoted to the plays of L. N. Tolstoy.

The account encompasses the history of the Russian theatre from its origin up to the end of the nineteenth century. This conforms to the program of the first year's study of the subject, as set forth by the Central Administration of Educational Institutions.

In the arrangement of the material, the greatest emphasis was placed upon the origin and development of realism on the Russian stage, which constitutes the fundamental and the most productive tendency of our entire art.

B. V. VARNEKE

Odessa, 1939

Contents

THE THEATRE OF THE FIRST HALF OF
THE NINETEENTH CENTURY

THE THEATRE OF THE SECOND HALF OF
THE NINETEENTH CENTURY

HISTORY OF THE
RUSSIAN THEATRE

(Seventeenth Through Nineteenth Century)

INTRODUCTION

THE FOLK ROOTS OF THE RUSSIAN THEATRE

In his address at the convention of Soviet writers on August 17, 1934, A. M. Gorky emphasized the importance of labor in the growth of all culture. Even the earliest stages of culture reveal "quite definite indications of materialistic reasoning which were inevitably caused by the processes of labor and by the sum total of the phenomena of the social life of ancient peoples." This observation applies similarly to the primitive phases of theatrical art in Russia, where for a great many centuries agriculture, the principal pursuit of the population, served as the immediate basis of artistic amusements and entertainments. According to Gorky's observation, the toilers' vocal creativeness served to coordinate their experiences, to embody their ideas in images, and stimulate the labor energy of the group.

Traces of these games and entertainments have been preserved for a long time. Even after the October Revolution, in the village of Likharevo on the Nerlia, a tributary of the Oka, within the boundaries of the former Vladimir Province, peasant women before sowing continued to celebrate the "Nettle Fast Eve," in which the game that evolved from the routine of daily work was closely bound up with ritual. These rituals coincided in every detail with the ancient Greek sowing festivals out of which, at the dawn of European culture, the Hellenic theatre came into being. Aside from sowing, such games accompanied every phase of agricultural labor: harvesting, binding and gathering of sheaves, and the removal of the grain from the field to the granaries. At times these games culminated in brilliant and animated shows performed by most of the workers, particularly by the girls. Thus, to the accompaniment of the words "having harvested two fields and plowed the third one—return and lie down," the sheaf was tied around with a string of red wool, hands were washed so that the wheat would grow clean, and the sickles were bound with grass so that next year hands would not be cut. After that the harvest women turned three somersaults, or lay down on the earth, all the while repeating the words: "Little field, little field, give thou back my strength for another little field!" Occasionally, alongside the sheaves wreaths were also twined. Then a white veil and a wreath were put on a harvest woman chosen by drawing lots, while her girl friends, wearing wreaths, turned towards the east, bowed three times, and, lined up in a long row, they all returned home singing songs. Sometimes arms were affixed to the sheaf and it was dressed up in a sarafan and a headband, or trimmed as a straw scarecrow with a woman's garment, and decorated with beads, ribbons, and flowers. In other localities not a sheaf, but a loaf of bread, baked from the newly harvested wheat, was carried. In the village the procession was solemnly greeted by the village landowners, carrying bread and salt. The wreath was placed on a landowner's head, while the sheaf was placed underneath the ikons. Here every detail is derived from the most ancient magic ritual, which in the past was practiced all over the world.

Usually beginning with Annunciation Day (March 25), there came the conjuration of Spring, that is, the magic ritual invoking the speedy arrival of Spring. Girls, as if imitating the birds' spring twitter, sang songs in different parts of the village, one choir calling to another. As one choir stopped singing, another began in the distance, and thus it went on from village to village. Frequently, the girls at the same time, holding tree branches with figures of birds made of rags, sang: "Larks, larks, do come flying to us, and do bring Fair Spring with ye!" All over Russia it was customary to bake dough in the shape of larks. This ritual, too, was founded in magic. The arrival of birds was one of the convincing indications of approaching Spring; by molding the figures of birds it was sought to hasten their arrival and, hence, the coming of Spring. The confusion of cause-and-effect relations is quite characteristic of primitive ways of reasoning.

The following discourse, in the form of conjuring songs, is held with Spring:

> Spring, Fair Spring,
>   What hast thou brought me?
> I have brought ye Fair Summer.
> Spring, Fair Spring,
>   What hast thou come on?
> On a little rod, in a little furrow,
>   In a wee oat-ear corn,
>   On a little wheat-cake.
> Spring, O Spring,
>   What hast thou come on?
> On a harrow, on a plow,
>   On a filly, filly black.
>
> O ye lark-birds!
> O ye larks!
>   Fly straight to the field,
>   Bring good health to us all—
> First to cows,
> And second—to sheep,
> Third—and last—to mankind.

When greeting the Spring, peasant women went out from the village to the field, and there, on a meadow free of snow, they spread out white linen and put bread on it, exclaiming: "That's for thee, Mother Spring!"

Aside from agriculture, games like these had their origin in other pursuits, such as cattle breeding, hunting, and weaving.

Games also accompanied certain events in family life, particularly weddings, which in many localities developed into elaborate performances requiring from the participants both natural talent and considerable practice. Beginning with the matchmaking and continuing up to the "bread feast" or a large meal on the day after the wedding, a number of scenic acts were performed, each of which was an integral part of the wedding festival. And preserved in these traditions are many customs and symbols of such factual situations as, by themselves, had long ago ceased to exist but nevertheless continued to constitute the source of the songs accompanying the nuptials.

At the wedding the principal character was the bride herself, and the better she played her part the more she was praised by those attending the party, whereas for failure to perform well she was subjected to severe criticism. Here, no place was left for individual creative initiative; everything was conducted according to a pattern established since time immemorial. Once adopted, the pattern remained inviolable. Custom required that the bride, when leaving her parents' home, should lament and implore protection against the "cruel enemy" who was seeking to alienate her from her beloved mother and her dear girl friends. This tradition was observed even when the marriage was a love match, and when nothing but the realization of a cherished dream actually awaited the engaged girl. Thus, in fact, the wedding constituted a performance in which the bride appeared as an actress performing a role which was as though written by custom. All other acts, songs, and words were not the expression of a feeling experienced at the particular moment but the reenactment of a pattern established by popular custom. However, apart from weddings, according to folk custom there were many songs which were not only sung but also accompanied by the performance of whole scenes.

Such, for instance, was the song recorded in the Verey district: "I will leave for China to make merry and to buy Chinese goods." The song pictures the willfulness of the wife. She persists in her obstinacy until the husband brings her costly presents; but later it occurs to him to bring her, for training purposes, a "most wondrous whiplash." A boy and a girl step out of the dancing circle and, as the song progresses, illustrate by gestures the words of the husband and wife.

Even until recent times, in certain localities of Simbirsk Province, during the wedding feast two peasant jesters used to step into the center of the hut, and one of them would begin to tell the story of his trip to the market for the purchase of peas. It developed that when a neighbor's cat ate his lard he killed her and used her skin for a fur coat. But the neighbor took the coat away from him. In revenge he abducted the neighbor's daughter—who resembled to a hair the bride!—and the priest married the couple. This narrative was constantly interrupted by questions from the second jester, so that a dialogue ensued for which the actors had to prepare themselves by memorizing their parts in advance.

In addition to the role of the bride herself, a complicated role was performed by her married sister, who complained in loud lamentations about the sad lot of the young bride in the stranger's home. A choir of girl friends dramatized the bride's taking leave of her relatives and her treasured belongings of the "fair beauty"—the ribbon symbolizing her "carefree freedom," her maidenhood. The role of the groomsman was a very responsible one. He was at once the bodyguard of the newlyweds and the supervisor of the entire nuptial ritual. This role was therefore entrusted to qualified specialists. Thus, Michael Kirillych, the grandson of the famous story-teller T. G. Ryabinin, participated in almost one hundred wedding ceremonies.

Many plays were adapted to specific holidays in which, under the guise of Christian nomenclature, pagan customs continued to survive for centuries. Thus, during the Christmas holidays, or during "Butter-Week," [1] which, in substance was completely analogous to the ancient Greek Dionysian rites and the Western carnival, the people masqueraded as bears, goats, foxes, gypsies, and robbers.

When calling on acquaintances, especially wealthy ones who could be expected to serve refreshments, the mummers used to begin conversing among themselves, staging little scenes taken directly from life and at times skillfully interspersed with bold allusions to the spectators' interests.

The frolic of "burning" or "seeing out" the Butter-Week was more complicated. On "Absolution Sunday," while the elderly people were "absolving" in the cemetery, the young people stole—stealing was essential—a peasant's sledge or a wooden harrow. With its teeth turned upward, they piled wood upon it, stuck a straw fagot or a straw scarecrow into it, and poured kerosene over it. In the evening they drove this "Butter-Week" through the whole village into a rye field, loudly singing: "Enough, Winter Dear, time for thee to hibernate." Or else this song:

> Butter-Week, dear guest of ours,
> Avdotyushka Izotyevna,
> Dunya white-faced, Dunya ruddy,

[1] The week preceding Lent.—Ed.

> Long braid, braid as long as three arshins,[2]
> Ribbon blood-red, ribbon ruble worth,
> Made-up eyebrows, eyebrows black,
> White and modish handkerchief,
> Fur cloak blue, and red lapels,
> Bast shoes solid, closely plaited,
> Linen stockings, stockings bleached.

After that the young folks began to tease one of the villagers known to be particularly waspish, deliberately provoking a brawl by their swearing.

When parting with the "Butter-Week," songs such as this one were sung:

> Butter-Week deceiver, thou hast deluded us,
> Left us nothing for Lent but a radish tail,
> Butter-Week, dear guest of ours,
> Avdotya Izotyevna,
> Much goods hast thou vainly spent,
> And thou hast drunk much good wine.

Finally, the "Butter-Week" was set afire with bundles of burning straw; boys raced one another with firebrands which were then thrown up in the air and scattered all over the field. The magic significance of this ritual is readily apparent: fire and racing with firebrands pertain to the spring sun ritualistic magic.

In the face of the extraordinary persistence of such customs, which almost precluded the replacement of folk traditions by innovations, one should not suppose that all these amusements in the distant past were identical with those we observe now. For instance, mummers are represented on the most ancient of the frescoes of the Sophia Cathedral in Kiev; yet it would be an error to transplant all these frolics to the Russia of the pre-Peter period.

These performances, which had their origin in peasant customs, later made their way into the milieu of the urban population and of merchants, and Ostrovsky introduced them in his comedy *Poverty Is No Disgrace* (Act II, Scenes 5, 6). Alexander Veselovsky has determined the process by which the leading soloist gradually became segregated from the mimic performance of the choir. The soloist having taken a position in the center of the stage in

---

[2] An arshin was equivalent to 28 inches.—Tr.

order to conduct the performance and direct the other actors, his part gradually increased in importance, attracting to itself the sympathy and interest of the spectators. Thus, on "Nettle Fast Eve," in the village of Likhorevo, old Vlasych is chosen by the peasant girls and peasant women, who draw lots with grain, and jesting Grandmother Marfa Baranova enters into a dialogue with him.

'The next phase in the development of the popular drama is the transition to its performance by professionals rather than by people acting as an avocation. A. M. Gorky, in an article "On Plays" (1932) observes that, "prior to the beginning of the seventeenth century, we had our own buffoons—our own 'meistersinger'—the wandering legend-tellers who disseminated all over the country different plays and songs about events connected with 'the great time of troubles,' about 'Ivashka Bolotnikov,' about battles, victories, and the death of Stepan Razin." These vagrant buffoons, it would seem, appeared in Russia in rather remote times, coming from Byzantium, whence they brought their name *skomorokh*,[3] which up to now has not lent itself to a really precise definition. In later days people ceased to distinguish them from the "spielmen," who came to us from Germany and wore the "Latin" dresses with short lappets.

In the *Novgorod Chronicles* of 1571, the following is recorded: "In those days, in Novgorod as well as in other towns and village districts, 'merrymen' (that was the name for *skomorokhy*) were drafted for the Tsar." The Code of the Tsar Fyodor Ivanovich (1589) distinguishes the dangerous buffoons from the "harmless" ones, that is, the peasants. 'Buffoons, leading bears, played on domras[4] and pipes, sang songs, and enacted various types of scenes, sometimes of a seductive character. Among other things, they introduced into Russia puppet shows which became very popular. The Church, seeing in the representatives of the secular—and, therefore, heathen—merriments sinful temptations, incessantly warned the people against them and bitterly condemned buffoonery. According to Stoglav's testimony buffoons wandered "in bands of sixty, seventy, and even a hundred men, forcibly taking food and

---

[3] Perhaps best translated as "buffoon."—Ed.

[4] The domra was an Asiatic balalaika with wire strings; in olden times a wind instrument.—Ed.

drink from the Christians in villages, abducting animals out of their stables, and causing bodily injuries to people on the roads."

It is known that in the early part of the seventeenth century some of our prominent boyars, for instance, Prince Ivan Shuisky and Prince Dmitry Pozharsky, maintained their own buffoons who used also to visit villages and hamlets "on their own," collecting— for that time—considerable sums of money. Thus, the petition of three boyar buffoons sent to Tsar Michael Fyodorovich in the year 1633, reveals that the three had collected thirty-seven rubles. This had its counterpart in England, where the actors of the Lord Chamberlain's company and of other nobles rambled in towns and villages, supporting themselves at the expense of the generous spectators. In Russia these "court" jesters would not always live with their masters. Roaming around the countryside, they did not hesitate to make money on their own account, in this connection taking advantage of their masters' authority. Local, or *zemsky,* residents were afraid to touch them, and that is why the statutory and grant charters of many princes, including the Moscow Grand Princes, Vasily Ivanovich and Ivan Vasilyevich, contain promises to the inhabitants that in their villages buffoons shall not resort to violence.

The participation of buffoons in the ancient Russian wedding ritual is borne out by ecclesiastical and governmental interdictions. Even in recent times, in the province of Oryol, before the bride was taken to church the song was sung: "As Natalyushka hired cabmen, seven pair of horses, and a cart to make it eight, now who's to give a lift to the buffoon? Play, do play, thee little buffoon, in this village and in that, so as to gladden Natalyushka's heart."

Buffoons appear in many legends of the North. Not long ago a legend "Vavilo and the Buffoons" was recorded in the North (in the anthology *Legends,* edited by N. P. Andreyev, 1938, No. 55), in which buffoons urge Vavilo, the plowman, to go merrymaking with them. They proceed to "a certain tsardom in order to outwit that dirty dog the Tsar, and his son Pereguda," and Vavilo, having succeeded in this task, is given the throne as a reward. Students of the legends ascribe to the buffoons an important role in the composition of the legends, and attribute many droll and obscene details to their creative imagination.

The close relationship between buffoon frolics and the tale about the wealthy visiting merchant Terenty and his young wife Olyonushka Klementyevna is undeniable. One morning Terenty, on leaving his house, meets a band of buffoons.

Merry-Andrews—folks polite,
Folks polite and also honest:
In their glance one sees a smile,
When they turn they always giggle,
Thus Terenty spoke to them:

"O ye merrymakers, jesters,
Ye buffoons, ye folks polite,
Ye polite folks, ye folks honest.
Ye have traveled long and far,
Ye have learnt what sorrow means,
Ye have learnt to soothe afflictions
And to cure the people's ailments."

Terenty asks the buffoons to cure his young wife. They tell him to go to a cloth store and buy a piece of fur (this was a requisite in their performances, and they were therefore called "fur bearers"). Thereupon they teach him how to cure, or train, his wife (No. 53 of the same anthology). They help him to chase his wife's lover out of the house. The whole dialogue between husband and wife is full of genuine humor. "A merrymaker, isn't he a consolation?" remarks S. K. Shambinago.

"Daring buffoonery" in Russia represented the interests of the toiling and exploited masses. Their railleries were directed against the princes, the boyars, and the priests, not only because it was from their exalted ranks that persistent attacks on the buffoon's artistry emanated, but also because the buffoons, as well as the rest of the people, considered the boyars and priests their cruel exploiters.

Oleari, who visited Moscow in the 1630's, gives this description of the buffoons' performances. "Wandering violinists sing shameful songs on the streets, while in their puppet shows other comedians present such acts for money to the youth of the common people and even to children; bear tamers have with them comedians who are able at any moment to produce a jest or a prank, as the Dutch call it, by employing puppets. For this purpose they tie a bed sheet around their bodies, lifting the loose end of it and thus arranging above their heads a sort of stage, and in this manner, walking along the streets, they produce on it various puppet performances. There is appended to Oleari's account an illustration of one such act by puppet comedians, in which it is not difficult to recognize a puppet scene (later to become very popular) dealing with a gypsy selling a horse to Petrushka.

ECCLESIASTICAL DRAMA

In ancient Russia certain performances which by their character were akin to the theatre formed part of the church service, bearing a remote resemblance to that from which medieval mysteries developed in the West. Orthodox divine service avoided the dramatic element, following in this respect the example of the Byzantine Church, in which theatrical divine service was tolerated only as a rare exception.

The ancient Russian divine service made use only of the beginning of the ecclesiastical drama. This included the "fiery furnace show," which was borrowed from the ritual of the Greek Church. It is impossible to determine when it first appeared in our divine service, but in the early part of the sixteenth century, before 1548, we already find the "furnace show" in Novgorod, whence, probably, it migrated to the cities of Vologda, Smolensk, Vladimir, and Moscow. On the Saturday before Christmas a special furnace, in the form of a pulpit, was placed in the church. Above the furnace, on an iron hook to which a censer was hung, a parchment image of a "God's angel" was so suspended that it could be raised and lowered from the altar by means of a cord. During the matins three "children" and two "Chaldeans" were called to supplement by their acting the reading of the holy text from the book of the prophet Daniel on the casting of the three Israelite youths, Shadrach, Meshach, and Abednego, into the fiery furnace. For the performance of the part of Shadrach a so-called *demestvennik,* or alto, was selected; for that of Abednego, a *nizhnik* or basso; and for the part of Meshach, a *vershnik,* that is, a soprano. Biblical verses formed part of their roles, so that it was necessary to choose the voices with particular care. A much more responsible part was given to the "Chaldeans." Upon receiving benediction from the Archpriest, the youths occupied their places near the "furnace," while the Chaldeans engaged in the following dialogue:

The first calls: "Friend!"

"What is it?"

"Are these the King's children?"

"Yes; they are the King's children."

"They do not obey our King's command?"

"They do not."

"And they do not worship the golden calf?"

"They do not."

"So we shall cast them into the furnace?"

"And we shall start burning them."

Following which the "children" were seized and rudely pushed into the furnace, while the Chaldeans walked around menacingly, blowing on the fire and flinging club moss from iron pipes. But when the image of the angel saving the youths descended from above, they fell down upon their faces, awe-stricken, and after that they themselves had to lead the children out of the furnace.

As a kind of reward for the performance of their parts culminating in defeat, the Chaldeans were permitted to wear their costumes throughout the Christmas holidays and to singe the beards of the passers-by with their smoldering club moss. Like all other mummers, they were thereupon obliged to take a dip in a break in the ice, thereby absolving themselves of the sin of wearing the devil's attire.

In Novgorod the Chaldeans used to receive monetary remuneration from the bishop. Their costume consisted of a short red jacket and a *turik*, a sharp-pointed wooden or leather hat, trimmed with rabbit fur or ermine and painted or gilded on the top! Oleari says that they dressed up as "Butter-Week jesters," and, in fact, the red color of their jacket suggests their kinship with the Western buffoons, while the very nature of their performances reminds one of the secondary roles in the medieval mysteries.

The "children" wore albs of fine white linen, with shoulder pieces of colored velvet and glossed linen stripes. The superintendent of the whole show was the children's teacher, or the choirmaster.

It is not known exactly when the "furnace show" was written out of the church ritual, but as a mere surmise it may be traced back to the eighteenth century. It is conjectured that the "furnace show" * came to us via Novgorod from the West, this being suggested both by the character of the dialogue and by the part played by the Chaldeans, as well as by their attire. In all probability their roles were taken over by the buffoons in the same way that professional actors assumed a most active part in performances of this kind in the West.

* Ecclesiastical, or religious, theatrical shows in Russia were by no means confined to the "furnace" performances. For instance, under the influence of apocrypha and, to some extent, the Gospels, special Christmas "den" shows were staged. These dealt with Christ's nativity; with the manger in which the shepherds and wise men out of the East found the Child; with Herod, and so forth. The principal dramatis personae in these shows were: Herod, the devil, the soldier, the old peasant woman, and the Cossack. The latter, with his heavy staff, frightens the evil forces, including the devil himself, who flees to the infernal regions. The recitals of the "den's man" were intermingled with religious chants and comic interludes. In like manner, the plays of the first Russian dramatist, Simeon Polotsky (1629-1680), bear a distinctly religious character.—Tr.

THE THEATRE OF THE SEVENTEENTH CENTURY

Chapter I

CHURCH–SCHOOL PLAYS

WESTERN PEDAGOGUES, in order to teach their pupils to use the Latin language fluently (which in that epoch was a requisite of all serious education), began as early as the fifteenth century to introduce into the school program the performance of Latin plays by the students. In this connection, the ancient repertory offered no great choice for pedagogical purposes. Terence's plays were most appropriate both because their style was elegant and their plots were relatively modest. For this reason his comedies were major items in the repertoire of school plays. However, among the teachers there were some who considered it dangerous and unsuitable to use the plays of a pagan author to educate their pupils. This consideration forced the teachers themselves to resort to the pen and begin writing plays. In these the ancient form was used for the elaboration of church traditions and for the glorification of kings and other eminent patrons of the school. School plays, serving at once as a means of church propaganda and for the training of schoolboys for public performances, were especially widespread in Jesuit schools, where they were used for the purpose of counteracting Protestantism.

Via Poland school plays penetrated the Kiev Academy, where for a long time they were produced not only within its walls (and there is reason to suppose that they took place within the Church as well), but also outside the Academy during summer vacations. According to the testimony of Metropolitan Eugene, "During the three May holidays all the pupils and teachers, as well as other people of intellectual interests, proceeded for entertainments to the Mount of Skavyka,[1] amidst the ravines in the proximity of the locality called Glubochitsa. There everybody took part in most innocent games, while the students sang canticles. Every year the instructor in poetry was obliged to compose comedies or tragedies for such promenades, while the other teachers wrote dialogues."

The strictly bookish character of the schooling of that period was reflected in the selection of dramatis personae for such plays. The personification of state and church; the mythological images and the deities of ancient Olympus; the "geniuses" of the respective lands and peoples; Wisdom, Faith, Hope, Conscience, and so forth—such were the personages taken directly from the pages of the textbooks to the stage of the school theatre.

On quite reliable authority it is reported that "during summer vacations (the needy pupils of the Academy) formed companies and departed to different provinces and suburban encampments for the collection of alms . . . performing dialogues, comedies, tragedies, and so forth. These excursions were called rehearsals." Owing to the fact that some of the school performances were transferred from within the Academy walls to the spaciousness of the country, at times a current of genuine literary talent broke through the school routine. For the most part this took place when the authors, setting aside bookish tradition, endeavored—even though not very skillfully—to set down life as they saw it; proverbs, adages, and songs served them in such cases as ready and useful source material. The lively nature of the school children must have been particularly receptive to these elements of the performances, in addition to which the official requirements of the managers of such performances by no means precluded the possibility of developing the genuinely artistic phases of the drama.

Among the examples of school drama that inspired the Kiev playwrights were a number in which the serious tenor of a play was interrupted after each act by the insertion of a humorous scene. These little scenes, which in the West were known as interludes, were also retained by the Kiev dramatists, who used them to depict everyday life, selecting character types familiar in the South, such as a gypsy, a Jew, a Cossack, and a Polish gentleman. Before

[1] The popular name for Mount Shchekavitsa.—Au.

long these little scenes began to merge with the popular drama, in so far as the authors adopted the practice of setting down not merely the things they read about in books and were taught in school, but also their own observations.

The interludes, in almost no way connected with the content of the main theme of the drama, were written not by its author but by special persons, and could hardly have had any particular significance in the opinion of those who had organized the spectacles. This explains why the interludes of many pieces were lost, whereas the scripts of the plays themselves were preserved. It could hardly have taken place if the true meaning of the interludes, which from the standpoint of their historical and artistic value far exceeded the significance of the plays themselves, had been realized.

Chapter II

THE THEATRE UNDER
ALEKSEY MIKHAILOVICH

WE HAVE no accurate information as to when the first theatrical performance took place in Moscow. The opinion has been expressed that the stream of Poles who flooded Moscow with the advent of the first Pretender[1] filled the city with unrestrained and seductive gayety, and also brought the theatre with them. At least a contemporary speaks with horror about

the enactment of hell by the unfrocked monk on the Moscow River:

And in this transitory life he produced fun for himself, while for his future life he moulded the emblem of his eternal abode which, in the state of Russia, is to be found nowhere but in the cavernous depths that no one dwelling on earth hath seen—a three-headed hell of formidable expanse, and both his jaws are made of loud-sounding brass as in a tinkling cymbal.

According to the view expressed by several students, the horrible object was nothing but a customary part of the contemporary stage settings needed for the staging of various religious plays where the action was sometimes shifted to hell, as in the miracle play about *Aleksey, Man of God*. However, other scholars, on the basis of

[1] The False Dimitry—also referred to as the "Alleged or Pseudo Dimitry" (alleged son of Ivan the Terrible) or the "Unfrocked Monk,"—who ruled from 1605 to 1606, having overthrown Tsar Boris Godunov with the aid of Cossack and Polish units. He was mistrusted by Muscovites, who believed he particularly served Ukrainian and Polish interests, and was murdered on May 17, 1606, when 200 Moscow boyars made their way into his private apartment.—Ed.

more trustworthy accounts, maintain that this hell was painted on the gates of the fortress built by the Impostor for military maneuvers.

Oral and written accounts of the theatre must also have reached Moscow through travelers who visited Western countries as members of diplomatic missions.

Stage plays were usually included in the entertainment at embassy receptions, and it was through these that the Russians first became acquainted with the theatre. The earliest account of such a performance was given by Avraamy, the Bishop of Suzdal, who in 1437–1439 was in the retinue of Metropolitan Isidor. The latter went to Ferrara and Florence for the purpose of participating in the Church Congress which took place there. While in one of the churches in Florence, the retinue attended the performance of a mystery-play, *Annunciation,* by Fra Belkari. Even though the bishop was unable to grasp the full meaning of the spectacle which he had never seen before, the external details of the performance did not escape his attention. He gave a minute account of the dimensions of the church as well as the scaffold erected in it, on which the plays were staged. He also described the costumes of the actors and the design on the curtain, and observed the draperies and the stage machinery, the arrangement of which he tried to comprehend to the best of his ability. Further, he described in detail the course of the performance itself, accompanying his narrative with quotations from the script of the mystery, a process which has enabled researchers to determine the title of the play he saw. In addition, he outlined the content of the *Mystery of the Ascension,* the author of which is perhaps also Fra Belkari.

These accounts apparently appealed to the readers and aroused their interest. What else could explain the existence of so many copies of this work which survive until the present time?

Further travels that brought news of theatrical performances to Moscow occurred in a later period; namely, the eighteenth century.

In the year 1658 the Borovsky governor of noble descent, Vasily Bogdanovich Likhachyov, accompanied by a clerk, Ivan Fomin, went to Florence. The play which they saw was performed on the Court stage. Because Likhachyov, like most of our early travelers, did not know foreign languages, he was unable to grasp the substance of the play, and confined himself to a rather incoherent account of the performance. His description is so superficial that it is not clear to the reader what he actually saw—actors or marionettes:

The duke ordered that the performance begin, and a chamber was exhibited; then it went down, and there were six changes [in the stage settings]. In these chambers there appeared a sea agitated by waves and fishes in the sea, and people riding on them, while above the chamber there was the sky with men sitting on clouds. Then the clouds with the people on them began to descend, and after a man had been seized from the ground by his arms the clouds went up again, while those men who were sitting on the fishes were lifted to the sky, much as the former men. Then a gray-haired man in a coach descended from the skies; and opposite him in another coach, a beautiful maiden. Race horses yoked to the coaches were like live ones, and they stamped the ground with their feet. The duke commented that one represents the Sun, and the other one the Moon [that is, Luna, which for this reason was represented as "a beautiful maiden"].

In another stage setting there appeared in the chamber a field full of human bones, and crows flew around and picked at them; and then again, a sea and small ships gliding on it and people seated there. In still another scene there appeared some fifty men in armor, and they started to slash one another with sabers and swords and fired arquebuses; about three men were ostensibly killed. Then exceedingly handsome lads and beautiful maidens in gold dresses came forth from behind the curtain and began to dance, performing all sorts of wonder-tricks. After that a young fellow appeared, begging for alms, and many loaves of leavened wheat bread were given to him, but he could not be sated. Now this play was staged eight weeks before the ambassador's arrival, and it was said to have cost 8,000 *efimki* (silver thalers[2]). During our stay in Florence three different comedies were performed.

The difference between this account and the memoirs of Avraamy of Suzdal is obvious. Apparently Likhachyov understood nothing of what he had seen, so that it is simply out of the question precisely to determine which performance he attended.

We find a comprehensive description of the theatre in the *Travel Diary* of P. A. Tolstoy of the year 1698. The author recorded that "in Venice operas and comedies are being performed, and they are so wonderful that no one can describe them ade-

---

[2] The German coin, worth three marks, from which the English word "dollar" is derived.—Ed.

quately. Nowhere in the whole world are there such wonderful operas and comedies." He described in detail the interior arrangement of "the chambers in which these operas are given, and which the Italians call theatre." He explained the plan of the pit, or orchestra, of the stage and of the boxes, which he called "closets." "In those theatres many closets are built five tiers up, and in one theatre there are two hundred closets, and in some theatres three hundred and more." Having described the arrangement of the stage, he turned to the stage settings. "In that chamber there are temporary stage pictures of great beauty." He was impressed with the large number of actors, sometimes as many as one hundred and fifty persons. He dwelt upon the costumes of the actors in detail. "Their costumes are very fine, of gold and silver, with many stones on them—crystals and reddish amethysts, while on others there are even jewels and large pearls." Such luxury is not inexpensive. "One opera is staged for a year at the cost of 30 to 40,000 ducats in Venetian coin, each ducat being worth fifteen Moscow altins." [3]

Of comedies, the traveler observed that "in Venice they are worse than operas, yet they are an amusing affair." Tolstoy, too, was most impressed by the luxury of the mise en scène in the Venetian theatres. He quoted costs in order to emphasize the foreigners' wealth, much in the same way as he described masquerade customs in order to picture a freedom of life uncommon among the Russians. The theatre as such, in fact, was of little interest to him.

Thus, although these performances provided very little food for thought for our travelers, giving them only a most superficial acquaintance with the nature of theatrical art, nevertheless, in the final analysis, they must have made some impression. The conception grew stronger in the minds of the Russians that the theatre was a requisite element of foreign luxury; the brilliance of the mise en scène delighted their eyes, while the magnificence of the costumes and of the stage settings acted as an incentive to competition. Therefore, in later times, when our first Westerners wanted to reproduce at home, in Moscow, a certain semblance of Western atmosphere, designed to evoke the envy and amazement of their less sophisticated compatriots, the thought naturally oc-

[3] The old Russian altin was worth three kopecks.—Ed.

curred to them of treating them to a theatrical performance among
other things.

From time to time, such performances must have been arranged
also by wealthy foreigners. Earl Carlisle, describing his journeys
through Russia, stated that in the year 1664 a comedy was staged
in the embassy on Pokrovka. From the foreigners' homes these performances must have migrated to the homes of our early Westerners who sought to make their household customs resemble the
attractive habits of the West. Artamon Sergeyevich Matveyev,
who was married to a Scotchwoman named Hamilton and who
lived in France, was the most prominent of these Westerners. In
1672 the Danish ambassador gave the following account of him:
Matveyev was so enthusiastic about the theatre that he even made
appearances on the stage, maintaining order among the boys
acting in a comedy.

It is to be regretted that the information included in this official
report is so brief that it does not permit one to determine whether
Matveyev had a company of actors of his own.

Under the influence of such men as Matveyev (an intimate
of Aleksey Mikhailovich), the Tsar during the latter half of his
reign forgot the grim ascetic decrees by which in 1648 and later
in 1657 he had forbidden his subjects any secular diversions,
severely punishing buffoons and ordering that their "phizes," i.e.
masks, be broken to bits and burned. In those days songs were
banished even from the wedding ritual. This attempt to convert the
whole country into one enormous monastery with a monastic
mode of living and senile behavior was least of all in accord with
the natural inclinations of the Tsar himself. The Tsar's visits in
1656 to Western cities must have attracted him to pastimes developing there undisturbed, particularly when after his second marriage—to Naryshkina, who had been brought up in the home of
Matveyev—he fell under the influence of the Westerners.

So, on May 15, 1672, two weeks before the birth of Peter the
Great, Aleksey Mikhailovich ordered Colonel Nicholas von
Staden, a friend of Artamon Matveyev,

to proceed to the Courlandian Duke Jacobus, and while in Courland
to enlist in the service of the great tsar the most competent mining arti-
sans, thoroughly familiar with all ores and skilled in their smelting, as

well as experienced and learned hornblowers able to stage all sorts of comedies.

At the outset fate was favorable to Staden, and he succeeded in engaging "for the amusement of His Majesty, the Tsar," Felten, the most prominent actor of that period, as well as Anna Paulssen, the famous prima donna of the Copenhagen Theatre. However, the journey to Moscow seemed to foreigners too hazardous to undertake without preliminary inquiries from their compatriots who had already settled in mysterious Muscovy. The reports received from there were by no means promising, and the comedians declined Staden's offer. He succeeded in bringing with him to Moscow only one hornblower and four musicians.

The idea of the necessity of organizing a theatrical troupe in Moscow was conceived by the Tsar as early as 1660. It was then, when giving commissions to Hebdon, an Englishman, that Aleksey Mikhailovich by a decree in his own hand ordered the hiring abroad of men "skilled in carving on wood and stone, glassmakers, and men familiar with the staging of comedies." And this time failure did not stop Aleksey Mikhailovich. Even prior to Staden's return, an attempt was made to do without outside help by simply resorting to domestic facilities. Luckily the "German Village" was right there, in Moscow; and, long since, foreigners coming to Moscow had been accustomed to settling in that village, creating alongside the ancient customs of Moscow life the semblance of a miniature European town, with all its temptations. Torn away from their motherlands and having to face a people not readily responding to friendship, foreign residents in the German Village must have tried to dispel their homesickness with diversions which they had brought from home. Probably they staged amateur shows, and Muscovites who were on friendly terms with the foreigners must have attended these shows. And so, when the scheme of inviting comedians from abroad failed, somebody who had attended these shows might have suggested to Aleksey Mikhailovich the idea of applying to residents of the German Village for assistance. And there they found the very things which Staden had looked for in vain in Riga and Stockholm.

No professional actor was found in the German Village. Instead there appeared a man to whose advantage it was to enlist the good

will of the Tsar, even by organizing shows. He was a native of
Merseburg, a Master of Arts, Johann Gottfried Gregori, who, as
early as 1658, had come to Moscow as a teacher in a German
church school. Before that he had been in military service in
Sweden and Poland. Thereupon, in Moscow, he became a pastor
of the so-called German "Officers'" Church, which was owned by
the newly arrived Germans. But he could not come to terms with
the prior, and this probably made him all the more eager to agree
to undertake a journey to Germany for the collection of contribu-
tions to the Church. At the time of his sojourn in Stuttgart, on
October 26, 1667, Gregori inscribed in the album of an acquaintance a poem in which, as it were, he refuted the attacks which
in those days were directed against everything Russian. The poem
began with the words: "Even though the brave Russian is called a
barbarian, nevertheless he is not a barbarian, and I openly bear
testimony that in that barbarian land there is almost nothing
barbarous." Highly praising the scenery of Russia, Gregori thus
characterized its inhabitants: "The townsman is not impudent;
he is satisfied with his lot; he reveres God and the Tsar; he is
honest in business. But if anyone challenges him, he firmly believes
that he has an innate right sooner or later to avenge the offenses
brought upon him."

Whatever Gregori's motives in this connection may have been,
the fact should be noted that among foreigners there were not many
such well-wishers of Russia.

After having spent part of the years 1667 and 1668 abroad,
Gregori became pastor of the new church in Moscow, in conjunction with which he founded a free school where children
were admitted without discrimination. Rich and poor boys, servants' children, captives of Turks bought as slaves, Tartars, Poles,
serfs (both male and female)—all were eligible for admission.
Religion, the German and Latin languages, arithmetic, writing,
and music were taught. Despite the considerable number of
pupils, the financial situation of both the school and its master,
Gregori, was far from enviable.

At this juncture it was suggested to Matveyev that Gregori was
able to "stage comedies." His training was probably limited to
participation in school shows during his student years. Fate,
which had compelled this German, unable to make a living in his

native land, to enlist in a Polish cavalry regiment before he became a Moscow pastor, now forced him to take the job of pro-
moter of theatrical shows in Russia.

It is possible, of course, that in his school Gregori had the
children participate in the performance of those dramas which
were standard features in the school curricula of Germany. Such
a performance may have suggested to Matveyev the idea of applying specifically to Gregori.

So, on June 4, 1672, the sixth day after the birth of Peter the
Great, an order was issued to "the foreigner Master Johann Gottfried to stage a comedy, and to use in the comedy the book of
Esther from the Bible, erecting for this show a new building,
and for its erection and for the purchase of the necessary equipment therefor to obtain funds from the Vladimir office. And by
virtue of the Tsar's decree a theatre was erected in the village
Preobrazhenskoye and it was fitted out with everything needed
therein."

Before issuing this decree, Aleksey Mikhailovich consulted his
father-confessor as to the propriety of permitting Germans to perform a comedy in the palace. The father-confessor cited the example of other Christian rulers, particularly the Orthodox Byzantine emperors, who had permitted such shows in their palaces, and
on this ground he deemed it possible to grant permission for the
entertainment in question.

In accordance with the Tsar's decree, Gregori, together with a
foreigner by the name of Lorenz Ringuber, who had come to
Moscow from Leipzig in the capacity of assistant to the sovereign's
physician, began to gather together children of various government officials and foreign merchants, and to instruct them in the
art of the theatre. All together, sixty-nine persons took part. From
the records of Ringuber we know that Gregori, with his assistance,
wrote a play, and that Ringuber rehearsed it with the boys for three
months, in the German and Slavic languages. He was assisted in
this task by George Hubner, the interpreter of the Foreign Office.
The church organist, Simon Gutovsky, and the "music-player,"
Timofey Hasenkruch, together with the musicians of the boyar
Matveyev, formed the orchestra.

"The comedy chamber" was about ten sazhen square and six

sazhen high; [4] it was surrounded by a fence with folding gates. The floor and the ceiling were covered with felt padding and after that trimmed up sumptuously with red and green materials and rugs. The Tsar's seat, up front, was covered with red cloth, while for the Tsaritsa and her daughters special seats were provided. These were built in the form of loges with a dense grille through which the ladies beheld the stage, thus remaining invisible to the other spectators, who were seated on wooden benches.

The stage, raised above the floor, was separated from the spectators by a beam and a balustrade. On the stage was a curtain or "trellis," which was drawn apart from the center to reveal scenery changes. Nor were the stage scenes, or "frames of perspective design," overlooked. These were made by the Dutch artist Peter Inglis, upon whom the title of "master of the perspective craft" was conferred. By the year 1674, there were already thirty-six such sets in the property rooms of our theatres.

One can form an idea of the costumes our early actors wore from the expense accounts of the period. Thus, on October 6, 1673, when the comedy on Tobias was being rehearsed, "Artamon Sergeyevich Matveyev instructed Master Johann Gottfried to draw from the revenues of the Galitsky Office thirty rubles against a voucher for the costumes of the angels, of young Tobias, and his traveling companions, appearing in the comedy." Under the date of October 9 there is this entry: "For the beards of the Jews and for minor repairs paid five rubles; artisan Henrik was paid for the repair of the crown." The spectators consisted of the Tsar's entourage, who were invited to the shows by special falconers and grooms.

Aleksey Mikhailovich was very much pleased with the performance: he praised and made much of the author of the play, Gregori, and the actor in the leading part, the son of Dr. Blumentrost; and he ordered that the copy of the play's manuscript presented to him be bound in morocco and framed in gold—which, however, did not succeed in preserving it. Here is what Ringuber recorded about this performance in his diary: "The play was performed on October 17, 1672. The Tsar, amazed by it, continued to pay attention for ten solid hours, without leaving his seat. No doubt, this will be the beginning of our good fortune."

[4] Seventy feet square and forty feet high (1 sazhen = 7 feet).—Ed.

This, then, was the incentive that drove the Germans to the stage.

Participation in theatrical enterprises became profitable. Even in the latter part of the same year (1672), the foreigner Frederick Gossen, who by order of the Tsar took part in a "comic performance," petitioned that "the rank of lieutenant be conferred upon him and that salary be paid him"; and on December 5, 1672, the Tsar granted his request.

In January, 1673, Matveyev announced that the Tsar's decree ordered "40 sable skins at 100 rubles and a pair of sable skins at 8 rubles be turned over to the Polish Office whence these be given as the Tsar's salary to Master Johann Gottfried for the production of the comic play about the reign of Artaxerxes."

Taking part in the theatre also paved the way to other favors from the Tsar. Thus, during Easter Week "Master Johann Gottfried and teacher Yury Mikhailov, as well as the actors in the Artaxerxes [5] play, were allowed to kiss the Tsar's hand and behold the Tsar's most serene eyes." The following postscript by a contemporary to this comment is particularly significant: "But prior to this pastors and children of foreigners in the service of the Polish Office were not allowed to approach the Tsar's hand." These favors bear witness not only to the personal benevolent attitude of the Tsar toward the new entertainment and its producers; only by means of such favors was it possible to reconcile the parents of our early actors to so dubious an occupation for their children. Ostrovsky, when tracing the origin of the Russian theatre in his comedy *The Comedian of the Seventeenth Century*, did not lose sight of this fact. He gave a graphic picture, on the one hand, of the despair of the old man Kochetov when he had learned that his son had become a buffoon, and, on the other hand, of his reaction to the information about the favors which were to be bestowed upon participants in the comic performance. And the old subclerk, who was at first ready to curse his son, became so tempted by the stories of the honor awaiting him that he himself brought the boy to Matveyev, begging, "Let him be the Tsar's comedian."

In the Moscow of those days many such episodes must have taken place, and only liberal rewards could have calmed the hearts troubled by this terrible temptation and quieted the complaints

[5] Ahasuerus in the Book of Esther.—Ed.

which the amusement of the Tsar must have aroused. Only by this means did it become possible to enlist the voluntary services of the children of twenty-six commoners and subclerks who, beginning in the middle of the year 1673, were turned over to Gregori for special training in theatre art, and who thus made up the contingent of the first dramatic school in Russia.

Even so, the status of these first actors was not enviable, as may be seen from the following petition:

To Aleksey Mikhailovich, the Autocrat, Tsar and Grand Prince of all the Great, Little, and White Russias, humble subclerk Vaska Meshalkin and his colleagues submit this respectful petition.

On the 16th day of June of this 181st year, by thine order, Tsar, we, thy slaves, were sent to the German Village for training in the profession of comedy under Master Johann Gottfried, but no salary or subsistence from thee, Tsar, was allowed us, and now we, thy slaves, going every day to the said Master, have worn out our clothes and boots, and we have nothing either to eat or to drink, and we, thy slaves, are dying from starvation. Merciful Autocrat, Tsar, and Grand Prince Aleksey Mikhailovich, of all the Great, Little, and White Russias, do confer thy favor upon us, thy slaves; do order, Tsar, that thy Tsar's salary be granted us for our daily food, so that we, thy slaves, serving in the profession of comedy, be not left to die from starvation. Do, Tsar, have mercy and grant our request.

The Tsar was moved and granted to each one of his comedians four halfpennies a day. Receipts for this money have preserved several more names: Nikolay and Rodion Ivanov, Timofey Maksimov, and Luka Stepanov. Along with Vasily Meshalkin, the author of the above petition, they are the first Russian actors of the secular theatre.

Thus, the first document signed by Russian actors is a tearful request to spare and save them from starvation. This petition, as it were, marks the beginning of an endless line of subsequent oral and written requests from actors tormented by hunger and poverty.

By the standard of that period, Aleksey Mikhailovich became a frequent visitor to the theatre. Here are the official records on the subject: On November 2, 1672, in the village of Preobrazhenskoye, near Moscow, "in the evening the Tsar went to see a comedy played by the Germans." In November, 1674, "in the village of Preobrazhenskoye a play was performed for the Tsar. The foreigners entertained the great sovereign when the Queen of Holofernes beheaded the Tsar, while the German and Artamon Sergeyevich Matveyev's house servants played the organ." On the same day "another comedy was staged for the Tsar in the village Preobrazhenskoye. And with the Tsar came his Tsaritsa, as well as his heirs and his daughters. And the same Germans and the servants of boyar Artamon Sergeyevich Matveyev performed for the Tsar a play in which Artaxerxes, acceding to the request of the Queen and prompted by Mordecai, ordered that Haman be hanged, while organs, flutes, and other instruments played, and there was dancing." Again in the same year, on November 4, in the village Preobrazhenskoye "the Tsar attended a show which was performed by foreign Germans and the servants of Artamon Sergeyevich Matveyev. They played the organ, flutes, and other instruments, dancing and staging other entertainments." On Thursday February 11, 1675, during Butter-Week, "the great sovereign had a comedy staged at five o'clock at night, and foreigners and servants of boyar Artamon Sergeyevich Matveyev staged different plays. And the performance was finished three hours before daylight." [6]

Foreigners—for instance, Magnus Hey, the Danish Ambassador also noted Aleksey Mikhailovich's fondness for the theatre.

Thus, the new fancy became one of the most beloved forms of entertainment at the Moscow court. Taking into account the paucity of the repertoire, the difficulties of producing stage plays in the early days of the theatre and the uncommonness of a venture of this kind (which must have involved complications and obstacles at every turn), it is obvious that one could not have expected more frequent theatrical performances in that period.

In addition to dramatic plays, ballet performances were staged at the court of Aleksey Mikhailovich, and, generally speaking, theatrical activity was gradually developing. Thus, Stefan Czyzynski, the son of a Polish nobleman of Lvov Province, a teacher of Latin by profession, who spent some time in the Monastery of the Kiev Brothers, staged in Moscow a "comedy about David with Goliath, and other comedies instructing some eighty persons of all ranks in the art of comedy."

The death of the Tsar put an end to this enterprise. Matveyev,

[6] The hours mentioned correspond respectively to ten P.M. and four A.M. in present-day reckoning.—Au.

the chief sponsor of these Western customs, was exiled to Pus-
tozersk, and on December 15, 1676, a Tsar's decree was promulgated ordering that "the chambers above the Apothecary Office
which were occupied by the theatre be vacated, and everything
that was housed in those chambers—organs, stage settings and
other theatrical equipment—be removed to a yard which formerly
belonged to Nikita Ivanovich Romanov."

The first playwright in Moscow was Simeon Petrovsky-Sintiano-
vich (1629–1680), a graduate of the Kiev Academy, who became
a monk. In Polotsk he presented a poem to Aleksey Mikhailovich.
Having later settled in Moscow, where he was called "Polotsky,"
he began to record in verse the various events in the Tsar's family
life, mastered the Muscovite dialect, and assumed the honored
position of tutor to the Tsar's children. When the theatre was
founded, he was also required to write plays. One of these, *About
Nebuchadnezzar, the Golden Calf, and the Three Children Who
Did Not Burn in the Furnace,* was a new version of "the furnace
show"; another, *The Comedy of the Parable of the Prodigal Son,*
was an elaboration of the parable included in the Gospels. The selection of these particular themes was hardly accidental; apparently
it is to be explained by the desire of the crafty monk to shield his
work from the attacks of the clergy, and he thus made his plays
closely resemble the Holy Writ. In the comedy about the prodigal
son he cleverly balanced the defense of the aspirations of youth
for knowledge and their gravitation toward Western civilization
with the advice "not to rely upon the light of reason but to abide
by the counsel of the elders."

In circles close to the court in those days, these questions were
of burning importance, and Simeon managed to reconcile the
proclivities of youth with the support of the influence of the older
people.

Polotsky's plays are distinguished from the "school" pieces by
their simplicity, their comparative proximity to reality, and by a
total absence of allegorical figures.

It is possible that he, as almost the only representative of court
poetry, had to take part in the revision of Gregori's repertoire,
which included the plays *The Doleful Comedy About Adam and
Eve, Joseph, Judith,* and *Bayazette and Tamerlane.* The first two,
in fact, do not in any way differ from the ecclesiastical plays of the

school theatre or from the compositions of Simeon Polotsky. The latter two are comparable to the repertoire of the so-called "English Comedians," who in the sixteenth century emigrated from England to Holland. There they borrowed and introduced into their plays the character of the jester who was called, after the favorite Dutch dish marinated herrings, "Pickle-herring."

An anthology of the plays of "the English comedians" came out in 1620, and we find in it the prototypes of all the plays which Gregori composed for Aleksey Mikhailovich's pleasure, except the prologues eulogizing the Tsar, which were written in Moscow. The comedy about Esther, or the so-called "Artaxerxes show," which was the first play to be performed on the stage of the Russian theatre, is an elaboration of one of the most popular items in the repertoire of the Anglo-German comedians. Here the biblical narrative is interrupted by scenes which bear the unmistakable stamp of that repertoire. The author particularly emphasizes the death of Haman on the gallows, as though relishing its dreadful details.

A number of scenes were specially introduced for Pickle-herring; they depicted the quarrels of the jester Hans Knapkäse with his wife. The scuffles, the jester's pranks and rather coarse witticisms converted these scenes into interludes with all their special features. The interludes gave the play that comic touch which, according to contemporary statements, characterized the performance of this play. The biblical tradition about the Jewess Esther, who became the wife of the Persian king and who, through her intervention, freed the court of the influence of the evil favorite Haman, prepared the ground for insinuations concerning the status of the young Tsaritsa, Natalya Kirillovna. Even in those days she began to wage a struggle against the influential court officials who aided with the relatives of Miloslavskaya, the first wife of the Tsar. This gave the play the immediacy of a modern play, enabling one to recognize prominent personalities of the court under biblical names.

Judith was similarly replete with references to the policies of Aleksey Mikhailovich. This play was characterized by its great complexity and large number of characters. It was divided into seven acts which, in turn, were subdivided into twenty-nine scenes. An interlude was introduced between the third and fourth acts.

In all, there were sixty-five persons in the play. And that was the reason why Aleksey Mikhailovich had to spend ten hours in the theatre.

The play began with a prologue, full of praise for Aleksey Mikhailovich. The plot had its counterpart in local conditions, and just as Judith appears in the play as a protectress of the Jewish people and their religion, so the same mission is attributed to the Tsar; and as a reward therefor he is promised happiness and victory. By these devices an old play, taken over from foreign sources, became associated with local interests of that period; hence the educational value and timeliness, which must have justified its presentation.

THE THEATRE OF THE
EIGHTEENTH CENTURY

Chapter III

THE THEATRE OF THE PERIOD
OF PETER THE GREAT

PETER I vigorously implanting in Russia all the distinctive features of Western life, did not overlook the theatre, with which he had become personally acquainted during his travels abroad. In order to introduce theatrical performances in Moscow, it was necessary to start anew, because the company which had functioned at the time of Aleksey Mikhailovich had now disbanded.

In 1701 a certain Yan Splavski, who had enlisted in the Russian service only three years before, was ordered to proceed abroad and invite a company to Moscow. In Gdansk (i.e., Danzig) he succeeded, though with great difficulty, in entering into a contract with a producer, Johann Kunst (Kunsht), who undertook to organize a troupe and "to please his Tsar's Majesty with all kinds of devices and amusements, and to hold himself in readiness to render good services." For this he was to receive an annual remuneration of 5,000 thalers, in addition to special subsidies from the crown for the erection of a theatre and the preparation of costumes and stage settings.

In the latter part of 1702 Kunst's company arrived in Moscow. The producer suggested that the erection of the "theatrical court" be started at once; it was to be twenty sazhen long, fifteen sazhen wide, and seven sazhen high.[1] The company was composed of "chief comedian Johann Christopher Kunst and his wife, Johann Morton Beidlar, Johann Plantin, Anthony Rodaks, Michael Wirt,

[1] That is, 140 by 105 by 49 feet.—Au.

[35]

Jakob Ertman Starkey, Karl Ernst Nitz, and Michael Yezovsky."

As early as August 6, 1702, the boyar Golovin, who accompanied Peter, wrote to Moscow:

> By order of the great sovereignty, issue instructions that the House of Comedy be built according to the dimensions and desires of the comedians, in the Kremlin of the town, on the left-hand side, as one passes the Nikolsky Gate, on the place taken from the Trubetskys near the city wall behind the stone guard-house. The cottages should be provided with windows large and numerous enough for all purposes, so that two men could climb through them; skylights should not be built because in a comedy light is not needed. The windows should have double bolts (order that they be affixed on the inside): bolts should be provided with hooks that can be drawn out and shut when it is necessary to close and bolt the windows to keep the premises warm, and also to have them opened whenever convenient. And near that house three or four cottages with small vestibules should be built for those arriving and desiring to see the comedy performance.

This plan probably constituted an order for Kunst, and it is known that he hoped to have the entire job completed in three weeks, provided he were given the necessary number of workers. But the Moscow supervisors, apparently having little sympathy with the venture, proceeded to delay erection of the theatre, either by raising objections to the selection of the site, which, to them, appeared too desirable for such a trifling enterprise, or expressing misgivings about Kunst's suitability, arguing that he lacked experience.

Their apprehension was also aroused by the selection of the play. "According to the conversation of the interpreters," wrote the clerks, "there is little decency in it." But, of course, these were merely excuses. The task which was entrusted to them did not interest them in the least, and seemed not at all worth their while. These delays could not have taken place had the Tsar been present in Moscow at that time. Since he was not, however, he was able to speed up his indolent superintendents only by writing letters. Be that as it may, by the end of the year 1702 "the wooden structure and in it the theatre, the gallery, the benches, doors, windows, with the ceiling lined with a covering on the inside, the roof covered with thin planks outside," stood ready on the Red Square. While this structure was being built, plays were given in a temporary theatre in the German Village, at the house of Peter's favorite, General Lefort, where a "comedy theatre and galleries" were also erected.

Kunst's company underwent considerable difficulties because of the constant arguments with the director, who apparently was not endowed with an easy and congenial temper. The main drawback of the company, however, was that its actors were unable to perform in Russian, with the result that the performances were inaccessible and incomprehensible to the majority of the Moscow residents. If Peter had wished merely to follow the procedure adopted by his father and arrange the performances for himself and a limited circle of courtiers, the German language of the actors would have raised no difficulties. But Peter sought to convert his father's personal entertainment into a popular diversion. For this purpose plays in a foreign tongue were proving altogether inadequate and almost useless. In order to overcome the predicament, several subclerks from different government departments were selected as early as October, 1702, and sent to Kunst for training, with a view to "teaching them to perform all sorts of plays diligently and with full understanding."

Shortly these pupils followed the example of Vaska Meshalkin and sent a complaint to the effect that, "making daily trips to the German Village,[2] they wore out and ruined their clothes and footwear." As a result of the petition they were paid 100 rubles and full salaries "according to the individuals—those who did more work were to get more, and those who did less work less." But even the salaries did not encourage these "unwilling actors" to be diligent about their tasks; at least Kunst sent complaints about their arriving late and their neglect in handling theatrical costumes. The director treasured these costumes very highly, pointing out that "they cost more than 1,500 rubles, aside from the Turkish and Persian ones which had still to be made." Nevertheless, even these costumes did not satisfy the fastidious tastes of the Moscow spectators. This is apparent from Kunst's statement:

I am making costumes and arranging plays at prices higher than have ever been heard of at the courts of other rulers, but even so I am compelled to listen to abusive reproaches because I am merely making linen costumes trimmed with tinsel. They do not stop to think that if it

[2] It was there that our second dramatic school was located.—Au.

were real gold, it would not, with candle lights, produce bright glitter, and it would not give the necessary theatrical effect. Moreover if real gold were used, 100,000 rubles would amount to nothing.

Even if one assumes that the wardrobe was not as gorgeous and costly as its owner contended, still this document continues to be highly valuable, graphically demonstrating the ignorance of the theatregoers of those days and their utter unpreparedness for such performances. Incapable of appreciating the substance of the play, they quibbled about superficial matters, trying to justify their displeasure with the subject matter by complaining that they were shown artificial, and not real, gold.

In the latter part of 1703, Kunst died, and the direction of the theatre and of the school was entrusted to his widow Anna and the actor Bendler (Beidlar); but they asked to be permitted to go abroad. Probably their request was granted because in March, 1704, a new man, Artemy Firsht (Otto Fürst), appeared as producer and teacher at the dramatic school. But, he, too, failed to satisfy everybody. At least, one of the comedians, Peter Baskov, sent in a complaint against him, accusing him of insufficient diligence in teaching the actors. The result was, Baskov charged, that "even those comedies which the comedians succeed in learning are performed without assurance, because of his lack of civility and of the knowledge of the language and because he, as a German, does not understand their Russian ways."

Our first actors were not only accused of indolence; their behavior did not meet with approval either, as may be seen from the many complaints against them. The following, for example, is a report dating back to the year 1705:

Russian apprentice comedians, without permission, walk about with swords, some of them not wearing swordbelts but carrying swords in their hands; and constantly visiting around at night, they indulge in drinking. In stores they buy merchandise on credit, but they fail to pay for it. And they engage in all sorts of brawls with those merchants, as well as with other sorts of people, resorting to dishonesty for purposes of extortion. In order to succeed in these extortions, they sue for slander, dragging people into various courts, avoiding the State Foreign Office where they are known. Having extorted bribes from people, they make settlements without awaiting the judgment of the court; they also cut off merchants' beards for the purposes of extortion.

From the remainder of the text it appears that in those days the comedians came under the jurisdiction of the Foreign Office, where they "were reprimanded for these shameful acts, but they despise that Office and they are disobedient in every respect."

This insubordination was shown by the following: "Vasily Telenkov, alias Shmaga, the drunkard," with "Roman Ammosov took some cloth away from a merchantman Ivan, son of Polunin." [3] On another occasion the same Vasily Telenkov instituted a court action for slander against the town-hall clerk, Yakov Novikov. At the trial it developed that "the strife and cursing were started by him, the comedian, and not by that subclerk." The Foreign Office sent a police inspector to "bring him to his senses." But this measure failed to produce the desired result, after which Fyodor Buslayev, an actor and Telenkov's own colleague, was sent to him. "And he, the comedian Vasily Telenkov, shouting loudly, declared that he would obey no one and was afraid of no one, and that there was no one who could bring him to justice, and he then uttered many insolent words. On that day, by order of the Foreign Office, he was apprehended and was ordered to be kept under arrest until further notice." The report concludes with the remark: "The work of the comedy will not be handicapped by his absence, because he is not engaged in many plays and has little work to do; but, being so slanderous, he may well be relieved of even those duties." The boyar Golovin, to whom the case was submitted, rendered the following decision: "the comedian Shmaga, the drunkard, shall be brought to the Office and flogged with rods; henceforth he, as well as other actors, should they take part in any such trickery, shall be brought to the Office and punished, each one according to his guilt, and the matter need not be reported to me."

This case vividly illustrates both the manners of the actors of those days and their social standing, which one would hardly call enviable.

The state budgets of the period of Peter's reign contain, among other things, information of considerable value regarding the budget of our theatre. In 1701 an appropriation was made "to the schools for the enterprise of comedies and for the teachers' subsistence, as well as for the theatre buildings, 2,176 rubles." In the

---

[3] Ostrovsky subsequently used the nickname Shmaga for one of the actors in the play *Guilty Without Guilt.*—Au.

year 1703, "for the production of a comedy in the Angulous Palace (Granovitaya Palace) and for refreshments during the Tsar's visit, 130 rubles." Apparently a special performance was staged in the Angulous Palace itself that year, because of some gala event, and it had to be fitted out for the occasion. In the same year, an appropriation of 200 rubles was made to the Russian comedians, and in 1704, 500 rubles to the aid of the Polish ambassador, the comedian Ivan Ruchner," even though the latter was probably entrusted with some diplomatic mission which was also highly paid. Again, in the same year, there was allocated "409 rubles for the staging of a comedy in the Angulous Palace, and 100 rubles to the comedians of Arthur First [Fürst?] for their diligence in theatrical performances."

Information is also available concerning the profits of the theatre derived from admission money. Seats sold for four prices: 10, 6, 5, and 3 kopecks. In 1703, "the sum of 406 rubles was collected from the audience, while during the following year, from May 15 to November 10, 388 rubles, 9 altins, and 4 pennies were collected" and the total admission fluctuated from 25 to 5 rubles for one performance. Out of this sum, "222 rubles, 12 altins, and 4 pennies were paid to Russian actors as their semiannual salaries, as well as wages to the theatre ushers, and other expenses." In the year 1704 it was computed that "the Russian comedians' salaries will amount to 345 rubles."

Yet, the subclerks were baffled with the following problem: "During this winter the actors were presenting only three comedies, and many of them remained idle, since they are not engaged in rehearsals of any particular comedies. In the future should they be paid a special gratuity so that they may better learn their parts?" It may be observed that these comparatively large sums were collected only at daytime performances during the summer, whereas in the winter, when plays were performed in the evening, the audience decreased because a special admission fee had to be paid at the gate, which immediately was reflected in the receipts.

In order to make the theatre accessible to the largest possible audience, Peter decreed on January 5, 1705:

Comedies shall be performed in the Russian and German languages; musicians playing on various instruments shall perform during these comedies on the designated days of the week (Mondays and Thursdays), and Russian spectators of all ranks and foreigners shall walk about unimpeded and freely, without fearing anything; and on these days the city gates in the Kremlin, in China-Town, and in the White Town shall not be closed until nine o'clock at night, and no road tax shall be exacted from those in transit, so that the spectators shall willingly visit the comedy.

The decree is the best illustration of Peter's intention to popularize the theatre among all classes of the people. However, in this respect the actors themselves constituted a real obstacle: the majority of the audience did not understand the Germans, whereas their Russian pupils apparently did not satisfy even the unpretentious tastes of the period.

In 1706 the theatre was closed. Having suffered a reverse with the theatre in Moscow, and having more hope in the Petersburg public, Peter wrote in 1720 to Yaguzhinsky, who was then in Vienna: "Try to hire a company of actors in Prague who are able to speak Slavic and Czech." Apparently Peter was hoping that the Czechs would be more easily understood by the Russian audiences and would teach the Russians the art of the theatre more quickly. However, Yaguzhinsky answered that there were only a few talented Czech actors and he was therefore able to hire only nine persons. At that, they were only of a sort that "can be used in interludes and not in the play itself," and besides "their language is very difficult to understand. And it was rare that, even over a period of a year or two, they perfected themselves sufficiently to act in a manner clear and agreeable to the audience." In addition, the Czechs insisted on rather high salaries, and made all sorts of demands; the attempt to organize a Czech theatre in Russia therefore did not materialize.

If Peter the Great's desire to popularize the theatre met with almost insurmountable obstacles among the masses, it took root among the higher strata of society in a comparatively short time. In this case, the desire to court favor with the Tsar probably coincided with a sincere enthusiasm for pleasant entertainment. At least, there is undisputed evidence that amateur theatrical performances took place during Peter's reign.

Bergholtz, one of the foreigners who visited Russia at that time, recorded in his diary on November 15, 1722, an account of a private theatrical performance at the home of the Duchess of

Mecklenburg. He was surprised by the fact that a professional actor participated in the performance, along with the duchess and the daughters of the nobility—the very actor who that day had received two hundred lashes because, when carrying posters around town, he had solicited money for himself, thereby placing the duchess in an embarrassing position. Nevertheless one of the girls who appeared in the play with the flogged actor, cast as a general's daughter, was in real life of princely family, while the part of the actor's wife was given to the daughter of a marshal of the dowager Tsaritsa, Praskovya Fyodorovna. Here it may be noted in passing that our stage performances pleased neither Bergholtz nor his compatriots. They were annoyed, among other things, by the fact that the curtain fell incessantly and the spectators had to sit in complete darkness, which in those days was by no means safe. At least, Bergholtz himself wrote: "During the last performance somebody stole a snuffbox from my pocket, and this time silk handkerchiefs were stolen from Alfred and Captain von Ilgen."

Tsaritsa Praskovya Fyodorovna was deeply interested in the theatre, and several documents have been preserved in which drop curtains (perspective pictures) "from the theatre near the Nikolsky Gate" were bought for her theatre because there was insufficient time to make new curtains. Stage scenery was also delivered to the home of Stefan Yavorsky and to Peter's favorite youngest sister, Natalya Alekseyevna.

She was probably the first princess of the Tsar's family who had visited the German Village and had become imbued with its atmosphere, strengthening still more her brother's affection for her. Knowing what would please Peter best of all, she often entertained him by staging a comedy. Here is what a foreigner wrote about her theatrical activities:

Princess Natalya, even prior to the Tsar's departure (in 1716), staged a tragedy, to which everyone was allowed to come. She ordered a big vacant house to be fitted out for the purpose, dividing it into loges and the orchestra. There were ten actors and actresses, native Russians who had never been abroad, so that one can easily imagine what sort of artistic performance they produced. The princess herself composed tragedies and comedies in Russian, borrowing the plots therefor partly from the Bible and partly from secular events. The harlequin, chosen from among senior army officers, broke in intermittently with his jests. Eventually a narrator appeared who explained the plot of the play to the audience, and, in conclusion, depicted the viciousness of all revolts and their calamitous outcome. I was informed that this whole drama described, under disguised names, one of the latest uprisings in Russia.

Another foreigner, Bassevich, reports that "Natalya Alekseyevna wrote two or three plays, fairly well conceived and not without a certain beauty of detail."

By comparing these comments we see that Natalya Alekseyevna's work in drama was precisely what her brother hoped for in the theatre: she staged dramatic plays not for the private entertainment of a limited circle of courtiers, but made them accessible to everyone. Furthermore, the plays performed in her theatre were of a serious character and had a direct bearing on current events, which, as will be shown elsewhere, was something Peter himself required from the repertoire.

In the cathedral library at Veliky Ustyug the manuscript of a number of roles taken from thirteen plays, accompanied by instructions of the director, has been discovered. It is believed that these are transcripts of the parts performed at Princess Natalya's theatre by the dwarf, Georgy Kardovsky, to whom the manuscript belonged, as evidenced by a notation in his own handwriting.

All of these are roles of elderly persons and could therefore have been performed easily by "the nimble little dwarf."

The plays from which the parts were taken were either of a religious character, their plots having been borrowed from the Holy Writ, or secular comedies. The religious plays included the comedy *About St. Catherine*, the comedy *Eudoxia the Martyr*, *Judith* (even the music for the Song of Amarfal from this play has been preserved), the comedy *The Prophet Daniel*, the comedy *To Christmas*, the comedy *St. Andrew*, the comedy on the *Mother of God*, and the comedy *Varlaam and Josaphat*. The following comedies were of a secular character: *Khrisanf and Daria*, *Peter's Golden Keys*, *On the Italian Margrave and the Excessive Frivolity of His Margravine* (this is an adaptation of the novel about Griselda, which found its way into Russian literature), and *On the Beautiful Melusina*.

In essence, these plays differ in no way from the basic repertoire of the period. Johann Kunst brought with him to Moscow the

repertoire and special features of the drama which, in the history
of the German theatre, are associated with the name of Johann
Felten, the famous impresario of the second half of the seventeenth
century. This former student of the Wittenberg, and later of the
Leipzig University, which conferred upon him the Master of
Arts degree, lent a much more literary character to his native
theatre, since he presented purely literary works on the German
stage.

Having long been in the service of the Duke of Saxony, Felten
must necessarily have adopted certain of the practices of the court
theatres of those days. This was reflected in the zealous propaga-
tion of the so-called *Haupt und Staatsaktionen* (that is, plays in
which the characters were mostly kings and other potentates) and
ballet performances, which were always particularly popular in
court circles. Thus, the climax of the comedy on the biblical
character Jacob was a ballet in which the twelve tribes of Israel
took part.

Under the influence of the Italian *commedia dell' arte*, Felten's
repertoire included a number of improvised comedies for which
only a general plan of the script was outlined in advance. Guided
by the outline, the actors could fill it in with scenes of their own
invention, so that the play gradually took shape in the course of
the preliminary rehearsals.

The students in Felten's company injected Pickle-herring's jests
into their improvisations. This comic figure survived on the German stage for a long while. In deference to the nature of the
plot, Pickle-herring was called by a different name at times and
assumed some new characteristics, which, however, could not
destroy his original features.

The following plays from the repertoire of the period of Peter
the Great have come down to us: *Scipio the African, the Roman
Chieftain, and the Perdition of Sophonisba, the Numidian Queen;
Prince Pickle-herring, or Jodelet; The Honest Traitor, or Frederico
von Popley, and Heloise, His Wife;* the comedy *On Don Juan and
Don Pedro; Amphitryon; The Precious Dupes* ("Dragye Smeya-
niya"); *Daphnis Who by Apollo's Amorous Wrath Was Turned
into a Laurel Tree.*

The plays which are no longer available were of the same character, as their titles indicate: *On Alexander of Macedonia (On the*

Grubetone Fortress in Which Alexander of Macedonia Is the Principal Personage); On the Trier Countess Geneviève; On Frantalpeï, the King of Epirus, on Mirandon, Their Son and the Seduced Lover; Two Conquered Cities, in Which Julius Caesar Is the First Personage; The Constant Papinianus; The Doctor In Spite of Himself (Le Médecin malgré lui).

Almost every one of these plays was a variation of the currently popular drama in the West. Thus we know only the beginning of the play *The Honest Traitor*, but even that makes it possible to determine its foreign source. It is a play of Andrea Cicognini, a well known Florentine playwright who lived in the middle of the seventeenth century, and whose plays were somewhat similar to Calderon's "cloak-and-sword" comedies.

When we compare the Russian version of *The Honest Traitor* with the Italian original, we see that we have a free rather than a literal translation, and that the Russian translator considered it necessary to cut the number of characters in the play and make certain other changes. Thus, the part of Lentulo in the Russian version combined two roles—those of Finochio and Solfettio, Frederico's servants. We have been unable to determine whether the Russian translator made the change because he believed that these characters were superfluous, or because he had to reduce the number of characters to the specified number of actors at his disposal.

Examining the text of our play, we can guess at least partly the type of stage sets that were used. The action frequently shifts from one place to another, but all the scenes can be acted in two sets, of which one was of the garden, and the other of Héloïse's bedroom. These stage sets could not have been too cumbersome, or the author would not have been able to introduce a new scene for the express purpose of letting a new character say a few sentences in front of a newly arranged set (Act I, Scene 8; Act II, Scenes 6, 9). Such generosity in the introduction of scenes would have been possible only with a simplified method of shifting scenery. The rear scene, set up in front of the inner curtain, represented a garden, and when it was removed and the curtain drawn apart (which in other plays was denoted by the remark, "The trellis [*espalier*] shall be opened"), there appeared a chamber representing Héloïse's bedroom. On the stage there was a bed with a canopy, underneath which the Marquis hid when Arzug (the Duke) came in, and underneath which Arzug later hid the Marquis's corpse in order that its presence might further embarrass his frivolous spouse.

The position given to Molière's plays in the repertoire of Felten's company was retained in the Russian repertoire. At any rate, in the official "description of the comedies available in the State Foreign Office under the date of May 30 of the year 1709" two plays are listed which are undoubtedly versions of Molière's comedies. These are *The Herculean Stock, in Which Jupiter Is the Principal Personage,* and *The Doctor In Spite of Himself,* a burlesque. It is not difficult to recognize in the former play which has come down to us a translation of Molière's *Amphitryon,* and, in the latter, his *The Doctor in Spite of Himself.*

It should be noted that the old French fable about the village sorcerer (*du vilain mire*) used in Molière's play, came to us much earlier, and it was recounted to Oleari as an original Moscow folk anecdote of the time of Godunov.

Comparing the Russian translation—not a very good one—with the original *Amphitryon* indicates that it was made directly from the French. The desire to translate with the utmost accuracy resulted in the use of certain turns of phrases completely alien to the Russian language.

The choice of this play by the Russian translator is fully comprehensible: the gay comedy of Molière, full of comic situations, was unlike the rest of his repertoire, too, in that the action took place between the gods and the rulers. This enabled the actors to make much of the sumptuousness of the production and to give the performance the gala quality which they loved so much.

The reasons why the attention of the Russian translators was drawn to Molière's other comedy, *The Doctor in Spite of Himself,* are even more obvious. Here, both the plot and its treatment are on the level of the simple and rather coarse jokes which were to the liking of the Russian theatregoers of that period—a fact which has been recorded by foreign travelers time and again.

Regarding the third of Molière plays, *The Precious Dupes (Les Précieuses ridicules),* which appeared in Russian during the period of Peter, it has been observed in all fairness that it was not very well adapted to Russian life and to the ideas of the early part of the eighteenth century. The unfortunate choice resulted in an even unhappier translation, although it should be remembered that this play could hardly have been produced on the stage. It was intended for production in Novgorod around 1708 only, before "the king of the Samoyeds." [4] The Russian version of Molière's one-act comedy is divided into two acts, whereas the remarks prefacing each act require the type of *mise en scène* that was used only in the interludes in Molière's plays. For instance, in the first act

the scenery must be designed and decorated with purple flowers, crowns, bows, and triumphal structures of the city of Paris, with the boroughs and surrounding villages. The music must be pleasing, melodious and sweet; two maidens from that land are to dance, and the people shall stand around.

The translator, making what is by no means a literal translation, added quite a few catchwords of his own, partly changed the relationships between the characters of the play, and introduced several details of his own fancy.

"The description" of the Foreign Office also preserved the name of one of our first playwrights, Semyon Smirnov, who wrote two plays: *Burlesque About Tener Lizetten, the Father Wine Merchant, Abridged,* and *Burlesque About Tonvurtin, the Old Polish Nobleman, with His Daughter, Abridged.*

Semyon Smirnov was one of Kunst's pupils. The supplementary word "abridged" (*perechnevaya*) shows that only the scenario was composed, and improvisations were later added to it. We have one of those interludes which afforded relief in serious plays and gave particular pleasure to the unsophisticated spectators. It consists of a number of almost disconnected scenes, brought together in such an amateurish manner that it is difficult to tell where one ends and the next begins and to determine their relationship to one another. In the beginning of the first scene there is an old "mountebank"; he examines his appearance and exclaims:

Where is to be found such a bold fellow, such a handsome, corpulent chap, who knows how to wrestle and to box and to run amuck with the

---

[4] That is, "king of the self-eaters"—a humorous title given to one of the court jesters of Peter the Great.—Au. (The original Samoyeds were a Mongolian people, who still live in northern Siberia.—Ed.)

goats! Indeed, there's no one like myself! I have bony hips and a heavy hand! When I strike a dead cock—all his entrails fall out at once. And if I strike a fly, its spirit leaves the body. And even if I have to deal with a whole bunch of gnats, I shall disperse them all as so many thieves. I am surprised myself that I was born that strong and bold, and that I'm here midst young and old!

This typical burlesque boasting, in which bragging and self-ridicule go hand in hand, was a favorite trick of all the popular buffoons, adapted from folk humor and introduced into the booths of puppet comedians and the Punch-and-Judy shows.

An old woman appears next; she begins to quarrel with the mountebank; she brings a poker and strikes him with it; but he grabs the poker, catches the woman, and, in the words of the stage direction, he twists her into a poker. He releases her only when she gives him her daughter as a ransom, and he takes her behind a screen with the words: "Let's go, my little friend; if you be nice to me, I will surely be eager to see thy home and have a good time there!"

In the next scene we see a Polish nobleman who sings a song, "Sad is life without a friend." His sorrow is dispelled by the old woman, who offers him a damsel. The man makes her a present—a gold ring—and promises to give her a better one in the future: "Thou must only love me, dear, and thou mustn't keep company with some other fellow."

The third scene is a dialogue between the damsel and the mountebank, who tries to tempt her with a ring. But the damsel's drunken "boss" then appears, and the damsel urges the mountebank to flee as quickly as possible because her "boss is a stubborn peasant, and will stab us both to death." She gives the mountebank her gold ring in order to get rid of him.

When everyone has settled down to go to sleep, the mountebank appears once more and insists that the woman make room for him in the bed. But the master wakes up, and seeing that there are three of them in bed, begins to accuse his wife of infidelity. The mountebank counters that the husband himself, in a drunken state, dragged him home and put him to bed. The husband, of course, does not recall any such thing—and it did not actually happen—and the mountebank meanwhile goes "behind the trellis," and from there shouts: "Ha-ha-ha! Oh, thou fool, thus let thy whole life pass! Well, I have robbed thee, and I shall not give back the ring!"

In the next scene a gypsy comes to the mountebank, and then a merchant joins them. The gypsy passes off the mountebank as his peasant and sells him to the merchant for thirty ducats. The merchant brings his new acquisition to his wife; but she is displeased with the purchase, and the interlude comes to an end with her words: "Isn't he cursed like a shaggy devil! There's no profit in him; he will eat us poor!"

The interlude, written in rhymed prose and later adopted by Butter-Week jesters, differs in no way from the jests of the popular theatre. Some of its details are so frank that its performance must have shocked the foreign spectators. At the same time, of all the interesting plays in our early repertoire which we have examined, the interlude is perhaps most closely related to the life of the people. It is the natural flowering of those buffooneries which found their way into Russia and took root at a time when there was no theatre whatsoever. Moreover, of all the early repertoire the interlude proved the most viable, and over a long period we see it revived repeatedly at fairs as entertainment for the crowds.

Peter was by no means indifferent to his theatre's repertoire. According to Bassevich,

The Emperor's taste, always sure and sound, even in those arts with which he is not completely familiar, prompted him to offer a reward to the actors if they would produce a moving play without that love theme which is constantly in the foreground, and a gay farce without all the burlesque tomfoolery.

Another foreigner, Bergholtz, recorded in his diary on January 13, 1724, a story told by one of the pages: "The Emperor ordered the actors to perform a play limited to three acts which would have no love plot, and one that would not be too gay but at the same time not too sad." These comments, coming from foreigners, fully justify the following statement of N. S. Tikhonravov: "For Peter the theatre had to serve the same purpose as the fervent and sincere sermons of Feofan Prokopovich; it had to interpret to the multitude of the people the true meaning of the acts of the reformer." Such a requirement could be met only by the school plays, but still they proved the least enduring part of our repertoire. They survived only for a short while, with rare performances after Peter's time and then only on special occasions.

Besides the court playhouse, during the period of Peter the Great there were school theatres in Kiev, Rostov, Moscow and in other cities.

Feofan Prokopovich's tragedy *Vladimir, Duke and Ruler of the Slavic Russian Lands Led by the Holy Ghost from the Darkness of Unbelief to Evangelical Light, in the Year 988 After the Birth of Christ* was particularly outstanding among the Kiev school plays. This "tragi-comedy" was staged on July 3, 1705. The glorification of the conversion of Russia to Christianity linked it to local traditions and interests. The prologue praises the most illustrious lord, church warden, our benefactor and Tsar, to whom the building up of this fatherland of Vladimir was entrusted by God, and who, following the path of victories equal to those of Vladimir and manifesting equal concern about Russia, as a son, reflecteth the image of his father.

The passage refers to Hetman Mazeppa, one of the most zealous contributors to the Kiev Monastery, at whose expense a stone wall had been built around it. The final chorus also sings praises to him, as well as to Metropolitan Varlaam Yasinsky and the guardian of the Patriarch's throne, Stefan Yavorsky, although not by name.

There was an allusion to the preparations, then under way, for the offensive against the King of Sweden, and the conviction was expressed that "the great leader will annihilate the haughty Swedish lion."

The play ends with the words:

Do grant fortitude and strength; grant long years and felicitous success to every undertaking, and constant victories in war; do grant good health, might and prosperous peace; grant all these to Tsar Peter, crowned, O Lord, by Thee, and to his trusted deputy Ioann!

The deputy was Mazeppa, who, with an army of 35,000 men, had already started an offensive against the Swedes.

It is noteworthy that in later transcripts of the play the prologue in which Mazeppa was glorified is eliminated, while the name Ioann at the end is replaced by the obscure "Christ's serf." Feofan, who became Peter's faithful collaborator, did not retain in his play the glorification of the traitor Mazeppa.

The scenes depicting the pagans Zherivol, Kuroyad, and Peyar and their despair over the triumph of Christianity are best of all. Their ignorance, superstition, and gluttony are portrayed not as abstractions but as characteristic of the worst types of the clergy of that period.

Subsequently, in his famous Ecclesiastical Statute, Feofan described the shortcomings of the clergy in the same terms in which he pictures the pagan priests. In the second scene of the second act, for example, Peyar uses the word *popa* instead of *zhrets*.[5]

The ecclesiastical theme did not, therefore, prevent Feofan from manifesting his talent for satire, while these innuendoes about the contemporary clergy make the play even more realistic, far removed from pure rhetoric. And the very subject matter of the play was based on ideas with which the society contemporaneous with Peter could not fail to be concerned. Feofan made Vladimir—that is, the great reformer of ancient Russia—the hero of his drama. The entire interest of the piece is centered on the struggle of the new enlightenment against the old obscurantism, while the sympathies of the author are unmistakably on the side of Vladimir, the champion of "the new law," which considered lack of education as the source of evil and of religious delusions. "Our race is cruel and ignorant, and hatred of education is to be blamed for it."

From Kiev the school plays, through the alumni of the Academy, spread all over Russia. As heads of various institutions, the Academy graduates inaugurated methods similar to those learned in Kiev, and simultaneously introduced theatrical performances. Thus, as early as 1727, dramatic shows were staged in the archbishop's school at Kazan.

In Siberia theatrical performances were first introduced during Peter I's reign by Filofey Leshchinsky, the Metropolitan of Tobolsk. A handwritten Siberian chronicle, dated 1727, states:

Filofey was fond of theatrical shows; he staged fine and expensive comedies; as the time for the spectators to assemble drew near, his grace ordered the cathedral bells to be rung, and the performances took place in a space between the cathedral and the St. Sergius Church, and it was there that the people gathered.

[5] "Christian priest" instead of "heathen priest."—Ed.

This innovation introduced by the Metropolitan Filofey was continued by his successors, several of whom were also Kiev Academy alumni. Sometimes the money collected during the performances was allocated for the teachers' salaries. Information has reached us that before Epiphany, 1737, the teacher of singing and reading, Peter Kiryakov, received a salary of 4 rubles "out of the comedy."

"State infants," as the posters described the Academy students, staged plays in the Moscow Slavic, Greek, and Latin Academy. Several brief scripts of these school theatre plays have come down to us. A particularly interesting one is *The Liberation of Livonia and Ingria . . . in the Schools of His Serene Tsar's Majesty by the Noble Youths in the Ruling City of Moscow, Briefly Depicted in the Month of February of the Year of Our Lord 1705.*

The script is prefaced by the following most curious "synopsis of the play":

The source or foundation of the play is derived from the Holy Writ, where reference is made to the invincible Israelite chief Moses, who through divine help delivered the Israelites from the bondage of Pharaoh; who by imploring the Almighty conquered Amalek, about which we read in the thirteenth, fourteenth and seventeenth books of Moses, the scenes being briefly arranged in three parts.

Peter's campaigns of conquest are described within the framework of the biblical tradition, since it was necessary to explain to the people their usefulness to the state.

All these plays have a strictly religious character, which was to be expected from pieces composed by ecclesiastics and performed on the stage of an ecclesiastical school. Nevertheless, they are closely related to the events and interests of the period, constituting an obvious panegyric to "the most pious Tsar Peter Alekseyevich." They eulogize his patron—the Apostle Peter—and Joshua the son of Nun, with whom we know Stefan Yavorsky compared Peter, from the church pulpit.

The exploits of the biblical hero furnished a most convenient pretext for the glorification of Peter's triumphs. Thus, the ecclesiastical plays became an arena for eulogizing Peter's military exploits, to which, as we know, the great reformer was by no means indifferent. At the same time these plays stressed the fact at every

turn that orthodoxy found a mighty protection under Peter's scepter. And when one considers that Peter's work met with severe condemnation from those who pretended to be the defenders of true
piety, and who, in their attacks upon him, did not hesitate to
identify him with Antichrist, the significance of these plays becomes even greater. School entertainment thus became a strong
weapon in defense of the Tsar's campaign of enlightenment. At
the same time the authority of the Church, as it were, blessed and
vindicated the reforms in which the supporters of the status quo
saw the influence of evil forces.

Another play, *The Dreadful Treason of the Sensual Life with
the Afflicted and Poverty-Stricken*, is a revision of the gospel parable about the rich man and Lazarus—a parable which served as a
source for the "ecclesiastical verses" of the popular minstrels. In
substance, this play was borrowed from the West. On its margins
there are many stage director's notes giving the actor's name for
each role, the description of their costumes, and the movements
prescribed for them. We are even informed what scenery and properties the production required.

In this connection it appears that each role, even the smallest
one, was assigned to a special performer, while for some of the
parts understudies were provided. Only the prologue and epilogue,
in which the Orthodox Church was symbolized, were entrusted to
one person; namely, Prince Baryatinsky.

The following remarks enable one to imagine how the stage
scenery was arranged:

The guardian-angel, carrying the Soul, enters heaven; the angel with
the key descends from heaven, throws the abyss open, and from there
flames and lamentations come forth. Death, having taken the Soul,
carries it away into hell, whilst the body is left on the earth, which
opens up with thunder and devours the body; and the feast-lover, from
Gehenna, seeth Lazarus in the bosom of Abraham.

Such notations indicate that during the performance the pictures
of heaven, earth, and hell were brought together on the stage.

The actors' costumes represented figures from the religious paintings of the West. For instance, "Sensuality" appeared on a "Seven-
Headed Serpent." "The Grace of God" appeared with the attributes
of a flaming heart pierced with an arrow, a chalice, and a laurel

wreath placed on the head; "The Lord's Judgment," with a sword in the right hand, and in the left hand a date (i.e., a palm) and a scepter, with a sword over the head; "Reward," with a scepter and a sword, the former bearing the inscription "Life to the Just" and the latter "Death to the Wicked." And so forth.

The first portion of another play, composed in 1704 by the teachers of the ecclesiastical school in Rostov, has been preserved. It eulogizes the martyr Dimitry Solunsky, whose name was given to the local Metropolitan. Far from Moscow, it was unnecessary to write a panegyric to the Tsar; and at the same time it was possible to voice dissatisfaction with the church reforms of that period. In the play Dimitry "expresses doubt as to whether it is better to fear the earthly or the heavenly Tsar, the Holy Ghost commanding that the Soul be devoted to the heavenly Tsar" (the latter supposedly practiced by the Rostov Metropolitan). In this way the authors of the play, having renounced glorification of the distant Tsar, partly eulogize the work of their local ecclesiastical superior, the Rostov Metropolitan.

Pupils other than those in the ecclesiastical schools used to stage plays. Dr. Bidlow, superintendent of the Moscow Hospital, engaged for his surgical school principally students of the Slavic, Greek, and Latin Academy, and staged similar performances in the hospital. Bergholtz described (January 4, 1723) one of these shows:

When we arrived in the theatre at the hospital we were taken into a shed so narrow and unsightly that in Germany it would be used only for puppet shows. There we met several German ladies and very few people of importance. The actors were young men who were studying surgery and anatomy under Bidlow, and they had never seen a real theatre. The play, *The History of Alexander the Great and Darius,* consisted of eighteen acts, nine of which were performed during the evening, the remainder the next day. Between the intermissions there were comic interludes, which invariably ended in a brawl. The play was a serious one, but it was poorly performed—in brief, everything was bad. His Highness [6] gave the young men 20 rubles and the Emperor personally gave them 30 rubles.

Even if we assume that Bergholtz, as a foreigner, purposely made much of his displeasure with everything Russian, his criti-

[6] The Duke of Holstein, of whose retinue Bergholtz was a member.—Au.

cism of the medical-student actors was probably justified. It is difficult to imagine that amateur actors in those days could cope successfully with their task.

The performance at the hospital bore a distinctly eulogistic character similar to the Western "Caesarian plays." One of these shows was staged on May 18, 1724, on the occasion of the coronation of the Empress Catherine I. In the Journals of Peter the Great, of that date, the following notation was made: "His Imperial Majesty deigned to have blood let from his left leg, and in the evening to attend a comedy." It is known now that the play which Peter and his wife saw at Bidlow's that day was *The Russian Glory, the Work of the Sovereign Emperor of All Russias, Peter I, Who Bestowed Benefactions upon Russia, and Who Created Out of Ignominy Russian Glory, and the Solemn All-Russian Triumph of the Coronation of the Most Serene Empress Catherine Alekseyevna, Represented in Person, at the Moscow Hospital.*

This is a typical school drama. It consists of an introduction in verse, of a prologue in prose, of two acts in verse, and then again an epilogue in prose. There are many persons in the play: Virtue, Russian Virtue—symbolizing Catherine—Bravery, Wisdom, Supreme Wisdom, Truth, Reason, Piety, Foresight, Envy, Pride, Anger, Fury, Cupid, Neptune, Mars, Glory, Victory, Flora, Russia, Turkey, Persia, Poland, and Sweden. The recitation of verses alternates with the singing of cantos.

The academic character of the play is also reflected in the abundance of Latin throughout. The title of the play appears in Latin; the names of some of the dramatis personae and the notations, of which there are not very many, are also in Latin. Finally, the persons in the play recite several original verses from Latin poets, particularly from Virgil's *Aeneid*. The profusion of the Latin language is not surprising. We know that sometimes entire plays were performed in Latin at the Slavic, Greek, and Latin Academy, whose connection with Bidlow's hospital we have noted. Probably the author used some medieval Latin piece for certain portions of the play. Otherwise what would have prompted him to introduce Supreme Wisdom (Sapientia) along with Wisdom (Pallas)? The Russian language furnished no ground for so fine a distinction. On the other hand, those portions of the play which had an unmistakable bearing upon current events were, of course, written for the first time.

The first act shows how Russia, as a result of military valor and the introduction of education, compelled her enemies to change from their former arrogant and contemptuous attitude towards her to respect and submissiveness. Glory proclaims in the third act: "Formerly Russia was harassed with cruel calamities, but now all blessings are showered on her, and all those who in times past took a haughty attitude towards her have now been brought to submission."

And then the former enemies of Russia—Turkey, Persia, and Sweden—are compelled to yield to "The Russian Eagle," and Mars announces: "Persian, Polish, and Swedish necks bow, the Russian Mars proclaiming: long live Russia!"

The second act, "About the Coronation," is devoted to the glorification of the Empress, Peter's closest companion in his great deeds. After the appearance of Piety, Cupid also greets Catherine: "Be welcome, Goodness and Russian Bounty. I congratulate thee and I fashion a crown for thee."

After the humiliation of Anger, Pride, and Envy, and an additional eulogy of Russian Virtue, Russia makes her appearance, uttering these words:

I behold thee, Russian Virtue, beautifully adorned. . . . And forsooth thou deservest this, since many a time, in war, and in peace, thou hast given us great comfort, and having refused to rest thine eyes with sleep, and having overcome feminine infirmity and weakness, thou hast boldly, in a manly way, protected thyself with a shield and hast attacked our enemies.

When one remembers that not only the coronation of Catherine, a non-Russian woman with a past, but even Peter's marriage to her had caused grumbling, the political significance of this play will be clear.

Once more it is obvious that Peter conceived of the school theatre too as a political weapon, by means of which he propagated his cherished ideas, defending and vindicating his measures before public opinion.

Another play dating from Peter's period, *The Play About Esther*, bearing all the marks of school plays of the biblical type and written at about the same time, served the same purpose.

The theme of this play—the Tsar abandoning his wicked wife and choosing a foreign woman who, because of her merits, fully justifies the Tsar's choice and becomes the source of much good for the people—was exactly parallel to the existing situation in Russia. The comparison of the newly crowned Empress with the touching heroine of the biblical narrative served the Tsar's purpose, vindicating his own acts by the authority of the biblical tradition. It was not without reason that Feofan Prokopovich, in a sermon delivered on the day of Catherine's coronation, specially emphasized the similarities between Catherine and Esther, to whom this school drama was devoted.

Chapter IV

THE THEATRE DURING THE TIME
OF PETER'S SUCCESSORS

EVEN THOUGH after Peter's death the Russian theatre was deprived of government support for many years, nevertheless there were individuals who, to the best of their ability, supported that institution which, having been introduced into Russian life with such difficulty, was in danger of disappearing.

Government clerks, former students of the Slavic, Greek, and Latin Academy, became impresarios, and later were joined by a group of literate house servants.

Although their school days were over, they occasionally revived theatrical performances and endeavored to convert them into popular entertainment, despite the fact that solemn school plays were hardly appropriate for popular diversion.

New plays necessitated new playwrights, however, and these were not always available. The repertoire of the court theatre, an intrinsic part of the belles-lettres of the period, was much better adapted to the playwrights' techniques and purposes. In this way the two different currents which developed after Peter's death converged into one stream: school shows were a training ground for the art of acting, while the court theatre contributed much through its repertoire.

Christmas holidays, with their masquerades, became the regular season for such shows, and because of this coincidence, the masquerades were commonly associated with the former buffoon entertainments. Police archives have preserved certain data concerning these theatricals.

On December 11, 1749, Kondraty Baikulov, the servant of Peter Kanishchev, a sergeant of the St. Petersburg infantry regiment, submitted through the office of the chief of police a petition, addressed to the sovereign, in which he wrote: "On this 11th day of December, I rented under a lease, beyond the Prechistensky Gate, in the parish of Holy Trinity, at Zubovo, in the house of Prince Nicholas Aleksandrovich Zasekin, four chambers, for the purpose of staging plays during the forthcoming holidays." He asked to be allowed to stage plays, after having paid the usual tax, and requested that the local police be instructed to afford protection against scuffles and noise during the performances. The lease which he had concluded with Prince Zasekin, submitted with his petition, read as follows:

I, Prince Nicholas Aleksandrovich Zasekin, have leased four chambers to Kondraty Baikulov, servant of Sergeant Peter Gavrilov son of Kanishchev, for staging a comedy, from this day of December until the 6th day of January. And during the performance I, Prince Nicholas, undertake to cause him, Kondraty, no hindrance whatsoever, and to raise no objection to the people from whatever social stratum they may come. I have received from the said Kondraty four rubles, and after January 6 am to receive an equal additional sum. And if I, Prince Nicholas, should in any way breach this contract, he, Kondraty, shall be entitled to retrieve from me, Nicholas, the entire cost sustained by him, Kondraty, for the production of said comedy, in witness whereof I affix my signature. And I am to attend the show, in witness whereof I affix my signature:

Prince Nicholas Zasekin.

The last clause of the contract is quite significant, demonstrating that even princes did not shun stage shows. On the other hand, a number of complaints were recorded about scuffles between lackeys accompanying their masters to the theatre, indicating that the most heterogeneous strata of society attended stage performances.

In the same year, and for the same period, that is, from December 25 until January 6, a company of twenty rented two chambers for theatrical productions in the house of the Court Chamberlain, Prince Andrey Fyodorovich Vyazemsky. The interest of the Moscow public in the theatre apparently was sufficient to justify simultaneous performances by several companies.

Petitions similar to those cited above are still on record, dating from the years 1755, 1757, 1758, and 1767. Since there are no indications that these petitions were altogether novel, such enterprises probably go back to a much earlier period.

Among the lessees, mostly various chancery clerks, there was "a pupil of the Kazan Seminary, who was studying Slavic, Greek, and Latin, one Ivan, the son of Varfolomey Nordinsky" (1755), as well as Ivan Ivanov, son of Golubev, a master inkmaker of the Moscow Printing Office (1768). The latter, together with a companion, expressed the desire to "maintain a show staged from printed comedies and all sorts of interludes." This suggests that even in those days there was some kind of surveillance of theatrical shows, which often overstepped the bounds of decency. The promise to produce "from printed comedies" served as a guaranty in this respect. The police used to grant such requests, detailing "two sentry grenadiers" to each of the shows, and granting permission "on condition that during the performances there be no brawls, noise, scuffles, and other indecencies"—in other words, no violation of public order.

To one of these petitions there is appended, among other things, "a list of the plays to be performed." The following plays are recorded on the list: *About the Brave Duke Friedrich of the Neapolitan Land; About the Tsar of Persia and the Scythian Queen Tamira; About Leander and Louise;* and *About Hippolytus and Juliet.* If the contents and the character of these plays are to be judged by their titles, they must have belonged to the category of dramas introduced in Russia through Felten's repertoire. The latter two plays are similar to the novels, widely read in Russia in the eighteenth century, *The Story of the English Count Leander and of the Marshal's Daughter Louise, Who Were in Love with Each Other, and About Things That Happened to Them;* and *The Story of the English Count Hippolytus and the English Countess Juliet, a Pleasant Adventure, Most Appealing to the Whole World, Which Recently, in the Past Century, Took Place in the English Kingdom, That Story Having Been Discovered and Published with Much Labor.*

In the absence of the original texts of these plays, it is impossible to tell whether they are Russian adaptations of already popular novels or translations of foreign plays.

The Comedy About Count Farson, several transcripts of which have been preserved, one of which is dated "November 5, 1738, in Penza," belongs to the same period. It is difficult to believe that the notation indicates the place of origin and the date on which the play was first performed. Most probably it refers only to the date of that particular manuscript, a copy of an earlier original. But this does not matter a great deal. Our script contains many stage director's notes, so that it was prepared not only for somebody's library but for use as a director's working copy. Therefore it may be presumed that in 1738 the play was produced; and, although the performance was only a revival, it indicates the character of the contemporary repertoire. Certain Polonisms suggest that this was a revised version of some novel which has not come down to us but was known to the Russian author through a Polish translation.

The modified version has the same merits as many other plays of the same origin. Its plot apart from its romanticism, common to other plays, must also have appealed to the audience at the time of Anna Ioannovna. The fate of Count Farson—who through the good graces of the regent had quickly reached the highest ranks and otherwise prospered—must naturally have brought to mind the fate of our court favorites, thus transporting the audience from Portugal to Russia and furnishing much material for contemporary comparisons.

School plays did not go out of existence immediately after Peter the Great's death. Under the new government, too, the schools endeavored to react to the stream of political events, guided by the same considerations that prevailed in the preceding period. For example, the biblical narrative about Haman, Artaxerxes, and Esther is introduced into the play *Stephanotokos* merely as one of the secondary episodes. Much more attention is devoted to the various allegorical figures, among whom Fidelity, bitterly denouncing Anger and Envy, occupies the most prominent place. They deprive her of her honor and "cruelly slay her," as a villainess, attributing to themselves her merits and glorious deeds. Stephanotokos, much like David when persecuted by Saul and Absalom, "unjustly deprived of his father's throne—oh, how bitter is the recollection!—suffers in exile and is afflicted with grief and sorrow, because foreigners and slaves had rebelled against him." But Hope supports and encourages Stephanotokos, while Fatherland urges him to act in defense of the persecuted. In the end, Stephanotokos ascends his father's throne, and Glory, flying to the four corners of the earth, announces the coming of the Golden Age.

Early critics of the play saw in it a portrayal of the events connected with the activities of the regent Sophia and with one of the last Streltsy [1] uprisings. They also sensed allusions to the unlawful deprivation of young Peter of his monarchy, and to the insidious intrigues of Sophia which finally brought her to a convent cell. Yet N. S. Tikhonravov emphasizes the fact that in the play it is "foreigners and slaves" who appear as Stephanotokos' enemies; they usurp "wealth and honor" and, using wile, envy, and wrath, confer honors and give money to "the boundless flatterers." "Whereas foreigners come to us destitute, with no merits and even deprived of their daily bread, they now live surrounded by wealth and glory"; among them "he who yesterday came poorly clothed today abounds in many riches." For this reason the faithful sons of the fatherland "are afflicted in their hearts, constantly recalling the names and glory of the parents of Stephanotokos, which appear to the world in all their magnificence," since "each day and each year those faithful to the fatherland and to Stephanotokos were doomed to live in great sorrow, so deep that nocturnal darkness seemed to engulf daylight itself." At last the happy day came: "By wondrous fortune" Stephanotokos ascended his parents' throne. The play, in no way coinciding with the fate of Peter, represents the lot of Elizabeth Petrovna up to November 25, 1741, when, to use Lomonosov's phrase, "our wronged people were kept in the most sorrowful night gloom."

According to a statement in one of the transcripts of this play,

Stephanotokos means one born to the crown; this name cryptically alludes to the acts of the most august, autocratic Monarch of Russia, the most pious sovereign Empress Elizabeth Petrovna, who, by reason of her ancestral and parental blood, was born to the crown of the Russian Empire. But, through the intrigues of her ill-wishers, she was deprived by the wicked slanderers not only of her heritage but even of bare necessities. Yet God, in his mysterious and inscrutable ways,

---

[1] The Moscow Guard; who rose against Peter and hoped to restore Sophia to power. The name Streltsy is from *strela*, arrow.—Ed.

brought her to the ancestral and paternal throne, adorning her with
that crown to which she was born.

Evidence contained in several manuscripts warrants the supposition that this play was written in 1742 in the Novgorod Seminary, by the monk Innokenty Odrovono Migalevich for a gala
performance to celebrate Elizabeth Petrovna's visit to the school.
Another play of a similar character was staged in Moscow, in the
Pokrovskoye village, as well as in the Smolny Monastery in
Petersburg. A transcript of one of the parts was found in 1735
in possession of Elizabeth's choirmaster, Ivan Petrov, against
whom court proceedings were begun. The cherished aspirations
of the future Empress and her coterie, therefore, provided the
themes of theatrical plays which were probably performed within
their own circle.

Eulogizing the rulers was also part of the task of the Kiev
playwrights. For example, in 1744 Empress Elizabeth Petrovna
undertook a pilgrimage to Kiev. In connection with this event,
a play, *The Piety of Marcus Aurelius,* was staged "through the
care and under the supervision of the archmonk Michael, rector
of the Kiev Academy."

The prologue of this play begins with a dispute between Anger
and Piety, symbolizing the sad condition of Russia after the death
of Peter and the benevolent rule of Elizabeth. Anger is, of course,
defeated here. Then five of Elizabeth's virtues appear on the
stage: Mercy, Truth, Veracity, Peace, and Valor. The last, among
other things, exclaims: "What tongue, what words can adequately express the fact that thou, Elizabeth Petrovna, in deed
and word, and in everything else, *art comparable to Peter I?*"
This passage expressly emphasizes that characteristic of Elizabeth's reign to which she herself attached special significance,
and which she considered the highest vindication of her policies.

The prologue of the play acclaims the recent victory over the
Swedes—a victory that gave Finland to Russia—while the piece
itself dramatizes the events in the life of Marcus Aurelius that are
useful in a comparison with the achievements of the Empress. Thus
using Roman names in no way distracts the playwright from his
immediate task, the glorification of Elizabeth. There is practically

no artistic merit in this limp and pallid composition, all the less so as the interludes which enlivened it have been lost.

The people of Kiev must have particularly enjoyed the play *The Resurrection of the Dead, a Future Common to All Men, Which to Those Suffering Unjustly in This Life and to the Aggressors Shall Prove Fatal, in Five Acts, for the Benefit of Those Awaiting It,* Staged by Georgy Konetsky, in 1746. The interludes for this play were written either by Georgy Konetsky or by the poet Tansky, whom one of his contemporaries called "a born versifier in the vulgar manner, after the style of Plautus," apparently wishing to accentuate his interest and skill in depicting the life of the simple people. In passing, it may be noted that Tansky was one of Gogol's forebears.

The interludes are closely linked with the basic text of the play. The characters—the peasant woman, the Jew, the Muscovite rogue, the Polish noblemen Podstoli and Bandoli, the hungry gypsy with his wife, and others—present a vivid picture of local life.

We possess several interludes dating from the middle of the eighteenth century in which certain colorful characters of the period are shown. One is the dissenter complaining of persecution, now praising Avvakum and Nikita, now arguing with the Jew as to whose faith is older—the gypsy appearing in this peculiar dispute as arbiter. Next the deacon appears with his children. By paying a ransom he tries to prevent his children from being sent to the Seminary; but he falls a victim to an impudent fraud. After that we have the canteen keeper with his cakes; a Greek who comes from Nezhin and bargains with the gypsy for a horse; and a Lithuanian and others described characteristically in terms of contemporary attitudes and modes of living.

Typical of these interludes is the one in which the gypsy takes part: in his dream he gets hold of some lard, but later he falls into the hands of a German physician and loses a tooth. Ostrovsky has included this interlude in the fifth scene of the second act of his comedy *The Comedian of the Seventeenth Century,* where it has been changed only slightly from its original form.

We have recently discovered another interlude of this period, *The Hatter and the Peasant.* It is characterized by extreme simplicity. The hatter complains that he has stocked a lot of merchandise, but that there are no buyers for his hats. He stops a passing peasant and urges him to change his hat: "Did the devil ever see honest men wearing such a hat? Put it on a beggar, and even he will spit on it and throw it away!" But the peasant has no desire to part with his old hat: "Why, it keeps the ears warm, just as a new one; and if I pull it over my eyes, even in biting frost the wind won't blow through it, no matter how hard it tries!" Yet the hatter cleverly tempts the peasant, chiding him for his stinginess, and in the end succeeds in selling him a hat. The bargaining is described in great detail. As the hatter skillfully advertises his wares, the peasant feels more and more tempted to buy a new hat.

Just after he has purchased it, a second peasant appears on the scene and begins to make him unhappy by insisting that the price he paid was too high. Meanwhile, now convinced that the hat is a good one, the newcomer asks the first peasant to let him try the hat on, which he does. Whereupon the second peasant, pretending to take a short stroll, asks the owner of the hat to wait—which he naïvely consents to do—and walks away. Presently a third peasant comes along, tells the first peasant that he has been swindled, and reprimands him for his extreme gullibility. At this point the duped owner of the hat leaves the stage, with the words: "Now, I'm off, and if I find him, I'll bind him and break his ribs!"

It is difficult to imagine anything simpler and more artless than this scene; and yet it correctly portrayed the character of the shrewd townsman skillfully deceiving the peasant-simpleton—a favorite theme of popular comedy. With their sharply drawn characters, the interludes succeeded in preserving the typical peculiarities of the language, tending to sketch each person in a style individual to him. This freed them from the purely bookish style of the other plays of our early repertoire, which unfortunately removed them from the realities of life. Nevertheless, they were created in a society familiar with subjects taught in schools, which explains the presence of remarks in the Latin language of the type used in school plays or the simple kind that a doctor uses.

Subsequently these interludes, full of life and completely contemporary, broke out of the framework of the religious and school drama, within which they were artificially compressed, and became an intrinsic part of the popular theatre, where the people are not only audience but playwright.

The interludes are obviously a part of the same stream of development as "the burlesque comedy," dating from the 1730's, in which the old comic theme of ridiculing ignorant physicians is elaborated in detail, and which is also replete with attacks against foreigners, especially the Dutch. This justifies the contention that the plays, as well as the popular interludes, emanated from circles which were opposed to Peter's innovations and became particularly active during that period.

From time to time in the latter part of the eighteenth century, Tobolsk seminarians used to include plays of a nonreligious character, such as *Maximilian, King Herod,* and *The Caliph for One Hour.* Sometimes, for the diversion of the townspeople, they staged plays in private homes. These were similar to the "rehearsals" by Kiev Academy students, but were finally prohibited "in order to avert moral disorders resulting therefrom."

Under Peter II (1727-1730) the court theatre was marked by a period of stagnation, but, with the ascent to the throne of Anna Ioannovna (1730-1741), there was a marked revival of theatrical life at the court. In honor of the coronation, the Polish King sent Italian comedians, headed by the comic actor Tomaso Ristori, as well as Reinhardt Kaiser (1673-1739), a composer well known in Western Europe. At first, plays were performed on a movable stage in private chambers; later, in the newly decorated Winter Palace, a room was especially set aside for the theatre and equipped with a stage. This was completed in the year 1734.

Foreigners produced Italian *commedia dell' arte* as well as interludes, in which, to the accompaniment of an orchestra and a chorus, a fat old jester and a young actress, a clever buffoon, made their appearance, i.e., the interlude *The Opera Impresario on the Canary Islands,* with its allusions to the attitude of the Russian public towards Italian theatrical performances.

In 1735 an Italian opera company headed by the composer Araia came to Russia. Araia remained in Russia from 1735 until 1759, and exercised an enormous influence on the development of our opera. A ballet composed of five dancers, headed by Antonio Rinaldo Fossano (in Russia he was renamed Fuzano) and his wife, "a clever dancer," Gilia Portesi, accompanied the opera company.

Stage scenery was designed by the Bologna architect Giovanni Buon. Russian dancers competed with the Italians. Among the former were military cadets of the land forces trained by the ballet master Lande. Among his pupils, Timofey Bublikov, who proved particularly skillful, was given permission in 1764 to go abroad for a period of two years "for the improvement of his dancing training."

Contemporaries reported that "Bublikov dances so skillfully that his very appearance on the stage provokes loud acclamations."

In 1738 Lande was called into court service as ballet master with the duty of training young people for the ballet, for which purpose twelve pretty little girls and twelve boys were selected from children of simple people. Among these Aksinya Sergeyeva and Lizaveta and Avdotya Timofeyeva particularly distinguished themselves. "Her Majesty's dancing school" was housed in the former palace of Peter I, on the corner of "Millionnaya" (Million), Street and the "Zimnyaya" (Winter) Channel.

Biron, the influential court favorite at that time, increased the influence of the German theatre. To please him a company was brought from Germany, among whom was the actress Caroline Neuber (1697–1760), who had acquired fame in her own country through a series of theatrical reforms.

The death of Anna Ioannovna and the defeat of the German group at court interrupted the work of the German troupe. The leading place was now assumed by a French company under the direction of Cerigny, who had been invited to Russia by Lande. For 25,000 rubles per annum this excellent company of actors performed at the court twice a week. Their repertoire consisted of Racine's and Corneille's tragedies and the comedies of Molière.

Even prior to the arrival of the French actors, the Italians had staged Araia's new opera, *Bellerophon*, to Bonecci's libretto. The leading male role abounded in allusions to the virtues of the new Tsaritsa.

In 1745 the actor Ackermann came to Russia heading a German

company, and later the Viennese ballet master Hilferding came, enthusiastically producing pastorals "of rustic gayety."

These foreign companies, acquainting the Petersburg population with all the types of plays of the Western classic theatre, completely satisfied the tastes of the court. Their instruction made possible the production of the first separate ballet, *Yarb, or Dido and Aeneas*.

Elizabeth Petrovna tried to encourage an interest in the theatre among her courtiers. The court *Harbingers' Journal* records:

A French comedy was performed at the opera house in her Imperial Majesty's presence. On the same day, during the performance of the said comedy, her Imperial Majesty deigned to observe that there were very few spectators both in the orchestra seats and in the upper tiers, and she expressed most graciously the desire that prominent members of the merchants' class, of either sex, be freely admitted to the opera house during the performance of tragedies, comedies, and interludes, on condition that they be not hideously dressed.

On another occasion the Empress, having noticed that a lady in waiting failed to attend a theatrical performance, "ordered that an inquiry be sent from her Majesty's person to the ladies in waiting as to whether they forgot that on this specified day a comedy would be performed."

The amateur theatricals written and staged by the pupils of the Noblemen's Corps were more important. These shows were organized by Prince Yusupov, the director of the Corps of Cadets, for their own pleasure and the entertainment of high officials. The cadets were able to familiarize themselves with theatre technique by attending foreign court shows, to which they were freely admitted.

The Corps produced its first play in 1749—A. P. Sumarokov's tragedy *Horeb*. In time, these performances progressed so well that cadets were invited to act on the stage of the palace theatre, and shortly thereafter a Cadet circle was formed, headed by Sumarokov, which was ardently devoted to literature and the theatre.

Peter's daughter was aware of the necessity of creating a Russian national theatre, and tried to substitute Russian professionals for foreign actors and native amateurs. These were found in Yaroslavl, where, as early as January 7, 1750, a comedy had been staged at the house of the merchant Grigory Serov. Comedies were also performed in the leather storehouse of Polushkin's sulphur and vitriol factory in Yaroslavl, by his stepsons, the Volkov brothers, the children of a Kostroma merchant.

Fyodor Grigoryevich Volkov (1729–1763), who is considered the founder of the Russian professional theatre, was the director of this enterprise, which was widespread in other cities also, i.e., Penza, where the comedy about Count Farson was staged. Authentic information about him is confused by legends, for which reason it is difficult to determine what influenced him to become so intensely interested in the theatre. It is only known that in 1746 his stepfather sent him to Petersburg in connection with some commercial business. There he worked in a German office in order to learn bookkeeping. He happened to go to the theatre and to the Italian opera in his leisure and was greatly influenced by these performances as well as by those of the students of the Corps of Cadets. He succeeded in going backstage, and made sketches of the sets and drawings of the stage plans. Upon returning to Yaroslavl after his stepfather's death, he devoted himself not so much to commerce and manufacturing as to the theatre, where he acted with his brothers and companions. Among his companions were students at the seminary, who knew the theatre because the local bishop, Dimitry Tuptalo, himself wrote and directed plays in which they acted.

Elizabeth Petrovna's decree granting permission to perform comedies in private homes (December 21, 1750) gave more leeway to such entertainments. Rumors about the Yaroslavl company reached her, and she ordered that the whole group be brought to Petersburg.

In the journal of the Court Chancery, February 1, 1752, there is an unmistakable reference to the fact that the actors from Yaroslavl were housed "in the Smolny Yard." The court provided for their entire subsistence and for a special attendant, appointed to them.

On March 18 of the same year, the *Harbingers' Journal* recorded that "at the usual time, in the presence of her Imperial Majesty and several illustrious personages, in a private performance, the Yaroslavl actors put on the comedy *About the Penance of a Sinful Man*, written by Dimitry, Metropolitan of Rostov."

This trial performance by the Yaroslavl actors in the presence of the Empress provided a test for their talents. Apparently they lived up to her expectations, for they remained in Petersburg. During 1752, they began to stage public performances, as may be seen from the following Court Chancery decree:

When the Yaroslavl actors shall perform plays at the German theatre, on the Bolshaya Morskaya, whereas there shall be tallow candles and fire pots with tallow; whilst in her Imperial Majesty's presence, not only wax candles and fire pots with tallow, but also firewood for heating the theatre.

Fully realizing that talent alone was insufficient preparation for future actors, the Empress saw to it that their education was improved. In this connection, on September 10, 1752, she issued a decree by virtue of which the Yaroslavl comedians Ivan Dmitrevsky and Aleksey Popov were to matriculate in the Corps of Cadets for the study of literature, foreign languages, and gymnastics.

Fyodor Volkov and his brother Grigory joined them later. In the corps they lived with the cadets, and were instructed in the sciences, the Latin, French, and German languages, and so forth, by the same teachers as the cadets. They differed from the cadets only in that they did not wear swords, which were part of the cadets' customary uniform. Their curriculum differed, too, in that they were taught stage technique and declamation. Their teachers were the military officers Melissino, Osterwald, and Svistunov, the translator of Molière's *Amphitryon*. Court theatrical performances, in which the Yaroslavl actors participated with the cadets, served as practical training.

By order of the Empress, the Palace Chancery maintained the Yaroslavl actors, and the "Smolny Yard" was their place of residence. The following document deals with their subsistence:

Her Imperial Majesty has deigned to order that, when the inhabitants of Yaroslavl arrive in St. Petersburg for their employment in private shows, kitchen attendants and the necessary plates and dishes for their meals shall be provided by her Imperial Majesty's Court out of the patrimonial estate, upon advice of the chancery. As regards their housing, they shall be quartered by the said chancery, at the expense of her Imperial Majesty's own patrimony, at the Smolny house, whilst meals and provisions shall be furnished by the same chancery, pursuant to advice already sent to it.

Volkov went about the task of improving his education with real enthusiasm, not limiting himself to what was taught in the regular courses. This is evident from "the most humble report" which he and his brother sent to the corps chancery, in which he explained that he had ordered several theatrical and "stage-scenery" books and, having no money to pay for them, had pawned his fox cloak and a red cloth mantle. "The approaching winter season makes it necessary to retrieve them, wherefore he asks that he and his brother be paid the entire salary due for this year."

Thus, a company of Russian actors came into existence at the court of Elizabeth; now it remained only to consolidate it, assuring its status by some legislative act.

Such an act was promulgated on August 30, 1756. Here is its full text:

For the performance of tragedies and comedies, we have now ordered the inauguration of a Russian theatre for which the Golovin stone house, on the Vasilyevsky Island, near the Cadets building, shall be assigned. For the said theatre we have issued an order to engage actors and actresses: actors from among choir boys and the Yaroslavl residents studying at the Corps of Cadets, such as may be required, and, in addition to these, actors from among other private people, as well as an appropriate number of actresses. For the maintenance of the said theatre, as specified in our present decree, reckoning from this date, an annual sum of 5,000 rubles shall be allocated, and it shall be paid by the state chancery, always at the beginning of the year from the time of the signing of our decree. Aleksey Dyakonov, one of the copyists of the Life Guards [2] Company, shall be appointed superintendent of the house. We have promoted him to the rank of army sublieutenant with an annual salary of 250 rubles, payable out of the sum allocated for the theatre. Appropriate sentries shall be detailed to the building in which the theatre is to be established.

We entrust the directorship of the said Russian theatre to Brigadier Alexander Sumarokov, who shall receive out of the same sum, and in addition to the Brigadier's salary, 1,000 rubles for subsistence and the maintenance of an orderly, besides the salary earned by him as a colonel, and henceforth shall be paid a full annual brigadier's salary. And he, Brigadier Sumarokov, shall not be removed from the army list, while for salaries to be paid to the actors and actresses, as well as to other persons employed in the theatre, he, Brigadier Sumarokov, has

[2] Patterned after the German *Leibgarde*. A highly selected military unit serving at the Imperial court.—Ed.

received a register from the Court. This shall be put into effect by our Senate pursuant to this, our decree: August 30, of the year 1756.

This act assured the status of Russian actors and laid the foundation of the Imperial theatres as permanent establishments, the origin of which should be traced to August 30, 1756.

Much as in Western Europe, where comedians were often included among sovereigns' retinues, Elizabeth used actors to add to the brilliance of her court. Hence, for years thereafter the Russian actor was included in the permanent retinue of the court. Therein lies the key to many aspects of the actor's service: the upper classes were destined to consider him as their entertainer, and therefore to hold him in contempt, from which he was unable to free himself even after the ascetic view of the Church had lost its influence. The Church, which had severely condemned acting during the early age of Christianity, adhered stubbornly to this negative attitude towards everything connected with the theatre.

Simultaneously, there was to arise, too, a fawning attitude towards society on the part of the actor himself, who through inertia remained an obedient servant of the whims and moods of those in power instead of assuming, occasionally at least, the responsible and independent role of a leader of public opinion.

On October 24 of the same year, Sumarokov, the newly appointed director of the Russian theatre, requested the chancery of the Noblemen's Corps to send him "the choirboys and Yaroslavl residents studying in the Corps" for "enlistment as actors, since they are all needed for that purpose." As a result, the following persons were assigned to him: choirboys Grigory Yemelyanov, Pavel Ivanov, Kozma Lukyanov, Fyodor Maksimov, Yevstafy Grigoryev, Luka Ivanov, and Prokofy Prikaznoy, and the Yaroslavl citizens Fyodor and Grigory Volkov, Ivan Dmitrevsky, and Aleksey Popov. To these were later added Gavrilo Volkov, Yakov Shumsky, and Chulkov, who were not students in the Corps of Cadets, as well as actresses Zorina, Avdotya Mikhailova, Marya and Olga Ananina, and Agrafena Musina-Pushkina.

Fyodor Volkov was the leading figure in this first contingent of our theatrical company. Even at school he showed evidence of a serious character. He spent the major portion of his salary of 100 rubles for equipment necessary for adequate dramatic training. He bought "six printed tragedies, a harpsichord and strings, a mirror for the tragedy and for the study of gestures." Off-stage he wore rather simple clothes, in this respect differing sharply from his brother Grigory who, on half his salary, was fond of playing dandy and spent much on his wardrobe. After completing his school studies Fyodor, according to a contemporary, "spent much of his time reading books useful to his profession, drawing, studying music, and learning everything he had not mastered. During his leisure time, he also constructed a small theatre for puppets (puppets which he had skillfully made himself); but he was deprived of the pleasure of completing this enterprise. In a word, while attending the Corps of Cadets, he exerted all efforts to emerge therefrom with a maximum of enlightenment, in which he fully succeeded."

Fonvizin, who was personally acquainted with him, has described him "as a man of great learning and replete with virtues, who, possessing much knowledge, could have become a statesman." Another contemporary, Derzhavin, called him "famous for his mind," while Novikov said that "this man, endowed with a great, broad, and penetrating mind, with sound and healthy reasoning faculties, and with rare talents, was adorned wtih much learning and diligence. He knew theatrical art in a high degree."

We possess information to the effect that Volkov also took a prominent part in the political life of that epoch. In the memoirs of A. Turgenev we read:

Under Catherine, the first person to enjoy her confidence, known to but few, was the businesslike person, the actor Fyodor Volkov, perhaps the first person to lay the foundation for the Empress' greatness. At the time of the coup d'état and her ascent to the throne, he acted wisely. When Catherine became Empress, she offered Fyodor Grigoryevich Volkov the post of a cabinet minister, and she also meant to confer upon him the Order of St. Andrew. Volkov refused all of these. He always had access to the Empress' study without being announced.

In August, 1762, proceedings were started to have Fyodor Volkov and his brother and forty other persons promoted to the rank of nobility; and they,

guided by their zeal for public welfare, did everything possible to prompt her Majesty's merciful heart to accept without delay the Russian throne, thereby saving our fatherland from the calamities which threatened it.

Volkov also had a prominent part during the coronation of the Empress, when there took place in Moscow a series of magnificent performances and entertainments which included a grandiose street masquerade, "Minerva Triumphant." The program of this show, which is still available, demonstrates the fact that its production required considerable skill of Volkov as the director. According to one contemporary,

The object of the masquerade was to ridicule the most common vices, especially the corruption of judges, gamblers, dissipators, drunkards, and libertines, and to portray the triumph of science and virtue over these vices. The procession was very crowded and long: many different chariots and vehicles were displayed, some of which were placed on enormous sledges and others on wheels, with people in various costumes sitting in them, representing different things and singing satirical songs composed for each particular subject . . . First, enormous giants, then extraordinary dwarfs passed by. And all this was arranged so well and decorated so splendidly and so sumptuously, whilst all the songs and poems were sung with voices so charming, that no one could have beheld the spectacle without experiencing the greatest pleasure.

For this masquerade Volkov paid with his life; he contracted a cold and died on April 4 of the same year (1763).

It is difficult at present to judge what theatrical talent he took with him to his grave. From the accounts of contemporaries who pointed out the defects in his declamation, we learn that he "performed with equal power tragic and comic parts, but that his true character was frenzied." Yet, it is well known how difficult it is to form a true picture of an actor on the basis of such general and vague accounts, which are largely influenced by personal predilections and the inclination of this or that observer.

At any rate, if Volkov did succeed in establishing the Russian theatre on a firm foundation, it was because of his own perseverance and his exceptional devotion to the venture. He goes down in history as a great figure in the Russian theatre.

The earlier historians of the Russian theatre credit Volkov with the writing of a number of plays, as well as other works in verse. Not one of them has come down to us, however, and this fact gives some reason to doubt the truth of such accounts. Apparently, there is more ground to ascribe to him the following epigram:

The horseman is praised; the fellow is bright, he looks mighty well; and others will say: The stallion is swell. Oh, stop it, don't argue: both the horse and the lad may be handsome all right, but both are but beasts, and thoroughly bad.

The theatre suffered a great loss through the death of Volkov. A. P. Sumarokov, the director of the orphaned theatre, composed the following lament:

> With me drain, Melpomene, thy tearful well!
> Lament and weep, disheveling thy hair:
> My friend passed yon; dear friend of mine, farewell!
> And o'er are Volkov's days; and o'er his earthly share!
> My spirit is confused and deeply moved by anguish,
> 'Neath me Pegasus' spring begins to languish.

Grief, however, did not prevent the selfish dramatist from reminding the reader of his own merits:

> For ye, O Russia's sons, I made Racine's art shine!
> For thee, fair goddess, did I build a lofty shrine!
> And now that shrine is doomed to face annihilation,
> Already shaken to its mighty stone foundation.

Further, he addressed one of Volkov's companions and asks: "Dmitrevsky, what shall we do now with this fate?"

Sumarokov did not choose Dmitrevsky arbitrarily; he was Volkov's closest companion. He had been summoned from Yaroslavl to Petersburg with him and there, because of his outstanding ability in the theatre, was second only to Volkov. After Volkov's death it was quite natural that all friends of the theatre should begin to look with hope to Dmitrevsky.

Chapter V

THE ACTORS OF THE SECOND HALF
OF THE EIGHTEENTH CENTURY

THE FIRST PAGES of the biography of Ivan Afanasyevich Dmitrevsky (1733–1821) provide ample ground for all kinds of doubt. According to legend, the name "Dmitrevsky" was given, in accordance with Empress Elizabeth Petrovna's wishes, to Archpriest Dyakonov's son, who had changed his name to Narykov [1] when he was about to matriculate in the seminary. It is said that at the time when Narykov rehearsed the part of Osnelda, the Empress summoned him to her chambers, personally provided his costume, and pinned an expensive diadem on his head which she asked him to keep as a souvenir. Narykov's charming appearance delighted her just as much as the vulgar and strange name Narykov displeased her. She was struck by his extraordinary resemblance to the Polish Count Dmitrevsky. "No," she said, looking admiringly at young Osnelda, "thou must not bear such a name; be Dmitrevsky. He was a count in Poland, and thou shalt be tsar of the Russian stage."

Even if the Empress had the perspicacity to foresee Dmitrevsky's theatrical successes, the authenticity of the anecdote is somewhat doubtful, since there is no evidence of a Polish count named Dmitrevsky.

On September 10, 1752, Dmitrevsky entered the Corps of Cadets, where he stayed four years. His final development and

[1] This name probably refers to the wide boards in barracks on which Russian prisoners and soldiers sleep.—Ed.

artistic achievements were greatly helped by his journey abroad in 1765 "for the improvement of his theatrical training." In 1767 he went abroad again; but this time he had an official commission to engage actors for the French troupe in Petersburg. These two journeys, which enabled him to study personally the acting techniques of such famous artists as Lekain, Clairon, and Garrick, have given rise to accounts which are hardly credible.

The earlier historians of our theatre persist in the version that while he was abroad Dmitrevsky not only became personally acquainted with the leading personalities of the Western stage but even competed with them in performances, invariably scoring triumphs over them. Even if we were to admit the possible superiority of the Russian self-made actor over such virtuosos of theatrical art as Garrick and Clairon, it is rather doubtful that Dmitrevsky's mastery of foreign languages was sufficient for him to recite French and English verse equally well. We may, therefore, presume that all accounts of Dmitrevsky's foreign triumphs are exaggerations of the approval which he won from Western celebrities in the course of his frequent contacts with them.

It has been said, for example, that once at a dinner party given by Garrick, the conversation turned to the subject of actors' techniques for simulating emotions. Garrick himself could either blush or turn pale at will, and after gay laughter could immediately shed abundant tears. All of a sudden, uttering inarticulate words, Dmitrevsky began to tremble, turned deadly pale, and fell fainting into an armchair. Everyone leaped to his aid, but Dmitrevsky got up, bursting with laughter. This quite plausible incident might well have been expanded by well disposed Russian patriots into a story of Dmitrevsky's triumphs in public performances.

Upon returning home from his journey abroad, Dmitrevsky had to give a public demonstration of his progress. One of his contemporaries wrote:

In order to demonstrate the difference between Dmitrevsky's former and present tastes and skills, the Russian tragedy *Sineus and Truvor* was produced at court in November. The incomparable playing of Mr. Dmitrevsky proved that his journey had been by no means futile.

Here is how another contemporary described Dmitrevsky's acting:

In tragedy his most successful roles were those of the Impostor, Yarb, and Sineus. He had a complete grasp of the characters he played, making up for the author's deficiencies by his acting. For instance, in *Dimitry the Impostor* he appeared before the audience leaning on the throne, wearing a mantle; by this despondent posture he gave a clue, so to speak, to the sombre meaning of the first monologue. In *Sineus*, when his brother's ghost appeared, he recited a long monologue. Moving backward with the chair, as though pursued by the ghost, he reached the finale of his recitation on tiptoe. This simple device produced an extraordinary effect upon the audience; everyone trembled with terror. Many of Dmitrevsky's contemporaries believe that in dramas and comedies he was even better, and they recall with delight that in *Amphitryon* his appearance would change so much by the mere substitution of a white handkerchief for a red one that the audience failed to recognize him, and he was able to maintain his disguise throughout the performance.

This account, along with others, corroborates that Dmitrevsky's success was due primarily to his intelligent and subtle polishing of his roles, which made him a first-class comedian, especially in parts pointing up a moral and requiring no emotional appeal or inspiration. Intellect and technical perfection rather than inherent talent accounted for his success, raising him far above the general level of contemporary actors. The same qualifications made him an excellent stage director and teacher for the succeeding generation of actors.

Therefore, in 1783, Dmitrevsky was appointed "supervisor of plays in the Russian Theatre," and in March, 1784, he was appointed "to teach the pupils, both boys and girls of the dramatic school—declamation and acting." An annual sum of 300 rubles was added to his salary for the "extra work."

At this point it may be appropriate to mention Dmitrevsky's part in the organization of one of our first private companies. In 1779 the management of the Petersburg Foundling Home sent fifty of its boys and girls to the impresario Carl Knipper[2] for training in dramatic art. At the end of three years he began to pay them, "according to their talents," salaries ranging from 100 to 300 rubles per annum, at the same time continuing to provide them with

---

[2] Distant relative of Olga Leonardovna Knipper-Chekhova, great actress of the Moscow Art Theatre (born 1870).—Ed.

housing facilities, firewood, and candles, as well as with theatrical equipment. Dmitrevsky, engaged by Knipper as instructor, was most diligent. Under the terms of his contract, he was obliged to give twelve lessons a month; but he actually came twice a day, gaining the special affection of his pupils. Among these, Anton Krutitsky, Kuzma Bomburov, and Sergey Rakhmanov eventually became famous.

Dmitrevsky's zeal alone, however, was insufficient to put this venture on a sound basis. Knipper took care of his pupils poorly, and, in addition to everything, the pupils "as well as the master began to misbehave, much to the disrepute of the school." The board of trustees was forced to discharge Knipper, and Dmitrevsky became the head of the theatre. Shortly thereafter, however, it was taken over by the court administration (1783), putting an end to its independent existence.

Dmitrevsky's pupils included every one of the distinguished actresses and actors of the next generation: Troyepolskaya, Sandunova, A. M. Karatygina, Plavilshchikov, Shusherin, Yakovlev, Krutitsky, and others. Dmitrevsky himself summarized his services to the Russian stage in the following petition submitted in 1802 to one of the members of the Theatre Directorate:

I flatter myself with the firm hope that my request for an annual salary of 1,200 rubles and a benefit performance every year will not be deemed excessive: (1) I have been teacher and supervisor of the Russian company for thirty-eight years; (2) I have contributed to the theatre more than forty dramas, operas, and comedies of my own composition, which are still being performed and bring in considerable revenues to the Directorate; (3) at the time when Prince Yusupov was director (1791–1799), in addition to taking part in the benefit performance for the Directorate and acting sixty-two times in tragedies and comedies, I contributed considerable profits to the box office by my feeble talents; (4) three times I kept the tottering Russian theatre going by providing new men, whom I did not engage from the outside but personally found here, trained, and successfully presented to the public; (5) there is not, nor has there been, a single actor or actress who has not taken advantage of my training and instruction, and, during my administration, no play has ever been produced without my participation in it, in the form of advice or suggested corrections in the staging; (6) for all these services which I have rendered in excess of my duties (save for special presents from the Great Catherine for work at the

Hermitage Theatre), owing to some mischance, I have never received
from the Directorate anything but thanks, so that neither formerly nor
after my retirement from the stage and from the supervisorship, have I
been given a single benefit performance, whereas some of my pupils—
and this, I swear, I say without any envy—are receiving higher salaries
and an annual benefit performance.

It is impossible not to recognize that, in view of Dmitrevsky's
work record, his demands were both moderate and completely
justified.

Leaving aside Dmitrevsky's original plays, which had no significance save for a passing success, let us dwell upon his general
literary works, which indicate the cultural level and scope of interests of one of our earliest actors.

As early as 1767, en route from a journey abroad, he gave to the
editor of the Leipzig magazine *Neue Bibliothek der schönen
Wissenschaften und der freien Künste* two works in manuscript.
Only his *Data on Certain Russian Writers* was published. It is
said that, after that, he continued to work on his manuscript history of the Russian theatre, despite the fact that the available
material on this newly founded theatre could not have been very
extensive. His work, which would have been of incomparable
historical value, was never published. After a careful revision, he
submitted his manuscript to the Russian Academy, where it was
destroyed by fire.

Dmitrevsky maintained contact with literature and authors during his entire life. Pushkin's friend P. A. Pletnyov writes about his
relations with I. A. Krylov:

Dmitrevsky, who had not been blinded by his successes and his fame,
was accessible to every young man who sought his counsel. As a public
figure, he felt that his dignity and honor required that he contribute his
experience to the public welfare. Having become friends, they remained friends ever after. Krylov used to come to Dmitrevsky's house as
he would to a relative's home. Over abundant dinners, in dressing
gowns, they were completely at ease with each other.

The outstanding playwrights of the eighteenth century, such as
Sumarokov, Knyazhnin, and Fonvizin, sought advice from Dmitrevsky who judged each one of them critically but justly and
gave very helpful suggestions. We know, for example, that his

advice prompted Fonvizin to revise certain portions of *The Minor*.

Dmitrevsky's position in literature was also recognized by the Russian Academy, which elected him to membership on May 3, 1802. By his subsequent work he proved himself completely worthy of this honor, carrying out conscientiously the tasks entrusted to him by the Academy. He analyzed certain plays and assisted in the translation of *The Journey of Anakharsis the Younger through Greece*, upon the Academy's request. He also helped on the Academy's purely learned projects, reviewing such scholarly works as A. Pavlovsky's *The Survey of the Little Russian* [3] *Dialect, or the Grammatic Explanation of the Existing Features Which Differentiated That Dialect from the Purely Russian Language, Accompanied by Various Comments and Observations on This Subject* (1805).

Dmitrevsky was a member of the committee translating Tacitus, as well as the committee in charge of publishing the periodical records of the Russian Academy. In 1807 he was asked to compose a eulogy to Sumarokov, which the Academy pronounced "very satisfactory both with respect to purity of style and the subjects and ideas most skillfully treated therein." The Academy decided to pay him 300 rubles for this useful contribution to literature, and to have him read the speech at the special exercises on December 17, 1807.

In 1787 Dmitrevsky left the stage and retired with an annual pension of 2,000 rubles. In 1791 Prince Yusupov appointed him "principal supervisor of all Russian theatrical performances, instructor of those not yet sufficiently skilled, organizer of the second Russian company from among those persons already in the service, and director of the school to ensure its efficient operation."

After that he acted only on rare occasions, in court shows at the Hermitage or in connection with special gala performances. In 1812 he expressed the desire to participate in the performance of Viskovatov's patriotic play, *Universal Military Service*. He was so weak that he had to be supported continuously by the other actors, and hardly anyone could hear him; but, according to S. T. Aksakov, he was warmly received, thunderous applause greeting each of his entrances and exits from the stage. And, of course, at the end of the drama, the audience called him back, unanimously and en-

[3] Ukrainian.—Ed.

thusiastically. It is noteworthy that the audience called for "Mr. Dmitrevsky," not simply for "Dmitrevsky." This special token of respect has been conferred upon no other actor, prior to or since Dmitrevsky. This show was his swan song on the stage. Although once afterwards—for the benefit performance of the widow and children of the deceased actor Yakovlev (1817)—he expressed a desire to appear in Shakhovskoy's ghost play, *The Meeting of the Uninvited*, illness prevented his carrying out this generous gesture.

Dmitrevsky lived several more years, but he became blind and was too weak to leave his bed. He died on October 27, 1821, having lived a life that shed rays of light on the opening pages of the history of our theatre. Even if that light was not overbrilliant, it was invariably pure, abundant, and invigorating.

Volkov's company, during its first period, was destined to share the fate of all early actors' companies in Western Europe. There were no actresses among them, so that women's parts had to be taken by attractive young actors who were reasonably plausible in the roles.

We know that, in his early days, Dmitrevsky was forced to play some feminine roles, and met with marked success. At the school theatres, at the Corps of Noblemen, and later, in amateur performances by the students of the Moscow University, actors substituted in women's roles for a long time. In Volkov's company, too, actresses did not appear until later. Apparently in those days it was most difficult to find a woman with enough courage to dedicate herself to so hazardous a venture as a career in the theatre. In view of the prevailing attitude of society towards actors, only a woman who by ill luck was torn away from normal family life would risk appearing on the stage; but here theatrical managers had to be extremely cautious in selecting volunteers. A mistaken choice was liable to undermine public confidence in, and sympathy with, the young theatres. This actually happened in Moscow in the 1770's, when the talented actress Ivanova caused the theatre managers a great deal of embarrassment because she was too fond of liquor and too lavish with her affections.

Even when the first contingent of actresses had been recruited with great difficulty, only young feminine parts were performed by women, while "comic old women" continued to be played by men for a long time. Some actors specialized in such roles; for example,

Volkov's friend Yakov Shumsky, who performed a number of roles of this type with great skill, among them the part of Yeremeyevna in Fonvizin's *The Minor*.

Agrafena Mikhailovna Musina-Pushkina, possibly also a native of Yaroslavl, was one of the first actresses in Volkov's company of Yaroslavl actors. Appearing on the Petersburg stage, she promptly won a prominent position in the company which was then being formed, and also gained the favor of the Empress. On September 29, 1758, Musina-Pushkina married Dmitrevsky. Under her husband's guidance, she had ample opportunity to improve her natural talent. Dmitrevskaya—she used her married name professionally—specialized in Molière's soubrettes. She played the roles of Arsinoé (*The Misanthrope*), Lisette (*The School for Husbands*), Claudine (*George Dandin*), Toinette (*The Imaginary Invalid*), Akulina, that is, Jacqueline (*The Doctor In Spite of Himself*), and Dorine (*Tartuffe*) with equal success.

Dmitrevskaya, as well as other members of the Volkov company, was sent to Moscow several times. About 1769 she retired from the stage, renouncing all theatrical triumphs and making room for younger talent in order to dedicate herself fully to the maternal duties of her large family. It is said that she died in 1788, leaving six sons and four daughters.

Tatyana Mikhailovna Troyepolskaya achieved even greater fame. Her reputation, however, was not due to the fact that she was more gifted than Dmitrevskaya. Troyepolskaya's type of leading tragédienne parts—as well as the character of her roles—placed her in the limelight and attracted the audience's attention to her.

Sumarokov's tragedies provided the majority of her best roles. She also played such roles as Ophelia and Juliet in adaptations of foreign classical tragedies. Although she rarely appeared in character parts, she was excellent as Célimène in *The Misanthrope*. This was due to her majestically superb figure, her attractive face, and her captivating, melodious voice.

Audiences, eager to draw a complete analogy between our theatre and the Paris theatre, used to compare Troyepolskaya with famous French actresses. Sumarokov found her the best actress for his tragedies. She appeared in his last tragedy *Mstislav* (1774) when she was quite ill, and the role of Olga was her last one. Her benefit performance was scheduled for May 23, after which she planned to go away and receive medical attention, but she died in her theatre dressing room that very day.

The social position of actresses in the eighteenth century may be gleaned from the fate of one theatrical married couple of that period, the Sandunovs.

In the latter part of the 1780's, of all the girl pupils of the dramatic school a future actress, called simply Lizanka, according to the custom of the day, attracted everybody's attention because of her good looks and musical talent. On January 29, 1790, she made a very successful début, using her stage name Uranova, in the part of Amor in the opera *The Tree of Diana*. Everything seemed to favor her—her stage success, the Empress' approval, and the personal happiness for which she was hoping when she fell in love with Sila Nikolayevich Sandunov,[4] one of her fellow actors. A son of a wealthy Georgian emigrant and a brother of the future professor at the Moscow University, he was not satisfied with a clerk's position and went on the stage, working under the supervision of the famous Shusherin. Because of his native talent and intelligence, Sandunov immediately distinguished himself in comedy roles, playing sly, young servants. In love, however, he had a rival in the person of the highly influential Count Bezborodko, whose slightest whim was gratified by Lizanka's immediate superiors—the directors of the theatre, Soimonov and Khrapovitsky. Hence the Directorate decided to get rid of the Count's unwelcome rival.

During Sandunov's last performance, before his departure from Petersburg on January 10, 1791, he made up his mind to recite from the stage a poem in which he alluded in unmistakable language to the reasons for his sudden departure. The public understood these insinuations, which were cleverly interwoven with the play itself. There was agitation in the theatre. The Empress learned about the incident, and was displeased with Soimonov's and Khrapovitsky's participation in Bezborodko's intrigues. Nor did Khrapovitsky help his cause by the slander about Sandunov which he repeated to the Empress. According to his own admission, it was received "coldly." A month after Sandunov's appeal for public justice, his fiancée, probably at his suggestion, petitioned the Empress during a performance of Catherine's opera *Fedul and His*

[4] Born 1756, died 1820.—Au.

Children. Lizanka submitted a letter to the Empress, begging her "to make me happy by uniting me with my dear betrothed."

Three days later the request was granted, and Lizanka was married to Sandunov. Both Khrapovitsky and Soimonov were discharged from the theatre management and Prince Nicholas Borisovich Yusupov appointed to take their place. Immediately after the wedding, Sandunov turned over to the pawn office for the benefit of the poor all the presents which his wife had received from Bezborodko as the price for her dishonor and offense.

But this was not the end of the couple's misfortunes: they were subjected to new insults from the recently appointed director. This compelled Sandunov in 1794 to lodge an official complaint in which he left it "to the tenderness of her Majesty's heart to judge how outrageous to a husband adoring his wife" was a situation in which "his wife's only crime was that she was devoted to her husband and did not wish to become a depraved woman in order to oblige ambitious careerists."

It appears that, under the pretext of a petty quarrel between Mrs. Sandunov and the theatre treasurer, Prince Yusupov dispatched four armed soldiers commanded by a sergeant to her apartment and ordered them to keep watch all night. After that Yusupov summonded the Sandunovs to his office and said to Liza "with utmost cruelty": "Thou art a regular Russian wench; get out of here! Thou art discharged!" Turning to her husband, he told him: "Thou shalt remain here under arrest; I will starve thee to death on bread and water!" When Lizanka asked what she had done to be treated like this, the prince declared, "I want it this way, and I know what I am doing." Then the order was given to "drag her forcibly out of the office." Mrs. Sandunov refused to leave her husband, however, and for two days stayed under arrest with him.

Trying to separate Lizanka from her energetic protector, Yusupov let Sandunov go, but forced his wife to stay under the pretext that she was a pupil in the dramatic school. He of course wanted to get rid of Sandunov, and at the same time stopped at nothing to detain his wife in Petersburg. The Empress freed the couple from their persecutors. On May 8, 1794, she issued a decree discharging the actor Sila Sandunov and his wife Elizabeth Sandunova from service in the theatre, according to their request.

Thus, it was only because of her husband's energy that Elizabeth Semyonovna Sandunova succeeded in avoiding the advances of highly influential theatrical patrons.

This case demonstrates the utter helplessness of the actress in those days, and the extreme insolence with which theatre management was able to treat actors in general.

The first regular theatrical performances in Moscow took place in the same year that the Court Theatre was officially inaugurated in Petersburg (1756). In that year students of the Moscow University high school began to stage performances at the University, under their director, the poet Kheraskov. Members of Moscow's best society were invited to the performances; the Empress "ordered" a reward of swords for the most praiseworthy actors. The company badly needed actresses, and published advertisements such as the one which appeared in the July 27, 1757, issue of the *Moscow News*:

Gifted women and maidens desiring to act in theatrical performances, as well as to sing and instruct others, should apply to the office of the Moscow Imperial University.

The demand of Moscow's audiences was greater than these performances could supply. To begin with, the premises of the school theatre were too small. A public theatre was needed, and in 1758 one was founded:

The proprietor of the Italian comic opera Locatelli [5] attached to the Court of Her Imperial Majesty, is granted most gracious permission to maintain at his expense an opera house in Moscow for the production and public performance of comic operas of his composition.

The site selected for the theatre was near the Red Pond, where the October Railroad Station is now located. In January, 1759, theatrical performances of the Italian opera company were started there, and permission was granted "to sell in that house brandy and different grape wines, English beer, as well as coffee, tea, chocolate, and fruits and confections of all kinds."

On Thursday, during Butter-Week, Locatelli organized in his theatre a masquerade with a lottery and card games, "omber, quintig,[6] piquet, and so forth," and also "in special rooms, on dif-

[5] Born 1715, died 1785.
[6] Game using five cards of one suit.—Ed.

ferent tables Faro bank games were played." But even extraordinary measures like these did not save him from going bankrupt three years later.

In 1761 his theatre was placed "under the patronage of the Moscow University," whose students began to act in it. Performances were given twice a week, on Wednesdays and Sundays. The Moscow University students proved to be not very reliable actors, however, which prompted I. I. Shuvalov to address the following letter to their director, Kheraskov:

I hear that our comedians act when it pleases them, and when they do not choose to perform, they stop playing in the middle of a comedy or tragedy, quitting the performance without finishing it, using the cold as an excuse. Such disorderly practices are not apt to yield good results or profits, and those people interested in working in the theatre are being discouraged. This also explains why considerably fewer people come to the theatre than formerly, and consequently money received from the performances is wholly insufficient to meet the expenditures. For these reasons, please give orders to the comedians that their duties are to be performed more regularly.

The document shows what kind of company was taken over by Locatelli from the University and the conditions with which actors had to contend. Conditions must have been really bad if the cold compelled actors to stop the performance and leave the theatre. Owing to such disorganization, he had to retire from the stage, abandoning his work as entrepreneur.

His successor was Colonel Titov, who assumed the responsibility for the maintenance of the Russian theatre, assigning the arranging of masquerades to the Italians Belmonti and Chutti; and in 1769 he also charged them with the management of the Russian theatre, which had been moved to the Znamenka. In 1771 Belmonti died during an epidemic of the plague, and the first director of the Court Theatre, A. P. Sumarokov, then living in Moscow in retirement, began to conceive the idea of organizing a theatre. Dmitrevsky had the same idea.

In spite of all their endeavors, however, neither Sumarokov nor Dmitrevsky succeeded in becoming Moscow entrepreneurs. They were outbid by a foreigner, Groti, who was later joined by a partner, the Moscow provincial prosecutor, Prince P. V. Urusov, who, however, assigned his rights to M. E. Medox.[7] Having wisely evaluated the situation, Medox managed to keep the theatre from 1786 until 1796. The new stone theatre he built on Petrovka Street was later destroyed by fire, and is replaced today by the Bolshoy Theatre.

Before long, however, Medox met a very dangerous competitor in the form of the Moscow Foundling Home which, in conjunction with the company from the Petersburg Foundling Home had decided to organize a public theatre. The Petersburg company was then playing in Knipper's theatre in the Tsaritsin Meadow. Medox instituted court proceedings, as a result of which a settlement was made stipulating that he was to engage the pupils of the Petersburg Foundling Home at the salaries they had been receiving in Petersburg, and provide them with instructors in declamation, music, and so forth. The Board of Trustees turned over its theatre to Medox, at the same time assuming the obligation to build another theatre, and assigning to him the income from it on condition that one-tenth be paid to the Foundling Home. It agreed further not to organize a theatre of its own and not to permit anyone, except Medox, to maintain a public theatre in Moscow.

We know that the Moscow company at the end of the eighteenth century was comprised of fifteen actors and eight actresses. The salaries of the two leading actors were: Pomerantsev, 2,200 rubles a year; and Shusherin, 1,300 rubles in addition to an apartment. Mariya Sinyavskaya, the leading actress, received 1,000 rubles. The lowest actor's salary was 72 rubles a year, and 120 rubles was the minimum for actresses.

From 1780 to 1805, comedies made up 44 per cent of the repertoire, and operas 32 per cent. Ballets were performed between the second and third acts, conforming to the practice in the West. A character opera of merchants' life, *The Bazaar,* by Mikhail Matinsky, a peasant serf of Count Yaguzhinsky, produced in 1783, was particularly noteworthy among the operas in the repertoire.

Ballets were staged by the ballet master Morelli, and performed by a foreign woman, Theresia Colonna, and the Russian dancers Mavra Poliskova and Matryona Andreyeva.

The fiery and impetuous actor Pomerantsev, endowed with an unusually fresh and real talent, moved the audience to tears, while

[7] Or Maddox.—Au.

his young wife, in addition to playing dramas, had a particular flair for maidservant roles, in which she played opposite Sila Sandunov, the inimitable impersonator of sharp-witted lackeys. The following actors also had a great success: the experienced and intelligent I. I. Kaligraf(ov) and his wife, who were excellent as Medea and Mrs. Marwood (in Lessing's *Miss Sara Sampson*); the gifted Sinyavskaya in the roles of tragic heroines, and Ozhogin, whose endless buffoonery brought country ladies on special trips to Moscow just to see him play. Elizabeth Semyonovna Sandunova, who came to Moscow with her husband, delighted the audiences during the entire first quarter of the nineteenth century, according to contemporary accounts; she reportedly "never had a rival" in Russian and Italian operas, and some of the regular theatre-goers preferred her to foreign guest artists.

One of the most prominent actors to distinguish himself on the Moscow stage was Yakov Yemelyanovich Shusherin (1753-1813). A son of a poor Moscow clerk, he had received no education in his early life. As a result of his trips to the theatre, dramatic art began to appeal to him so strongly that he became possessed with an irresistible desire to devote himself to it completely. Having had no training whatsoever, Shusherin at first was able to fill only the most modest position in the theatre; he felt quite content when he was allowed to copy some theatrical part at the rate of three kopecks per page, or to substitute for the sick prompter or to appear now and then in a servant's role.

Shusherin's energy and native intelligence soon enabled him to improve this unenviable position. It has been said that his advancement was aided by his passionate love for one of the leading actresses of the Moscow theatre, Mariya Stepanovna Sinyavskaya, prominent both for her beauty and for her talent. Of course, there was not the slightest probability that the gifted beauty and outstanding celebrity of the stage would pay any attention to an insignificant actor of walk-on parts. There was only one way to have any success with her, and that was to attain an equally prominent position in the company and become her stage partner. And so, after three years of intense work, Shusherin had achieved a fair amount of success in Medox's company and began to play second and even first male leads both in comedy and in drama. In 1786 he left the Moscow stage, on which he had won recognition, and became a court actor in the Petersburg theatres. In Petersburg he appeared in one of his most successful parts, Count Appiani in Lessing's *Emilia Galotti,* and soon managed to win the favor not only of the public but also of Catherine II, who praised his clever acting in her comedy *The Disconcerted Family.* He also played the leading role in Knyazhnin's tragedy *Vadim,* and in the Empress' play *The Early Rule of Oleg.*

Shusherin's appearance was not particularly favorable; his voice was neither resonant nor strong, and in emotional scenes it would sometimes get choked up. With such handicaps it was difficult for him to achieve great success in a heroic repertoire, especially against such a well qualified competitor as Dmitrevsky. At that time, however, the "doleful comedy" was beginning to achieve popularity, and it required actors capable of sentimentality and of shedding abundant tears. These requirements conformed perfectly to Shusherin's natural qualifications, and because of his exceptional industry he attained a marked success in the field. S. T. Aksakov, who knew him personally, asserted that "his art is undeniably next only to Dmitrevsky's, which is all the more noteworthy because he did not have Dmitrevsky's opportunities to educate himself by study and by observing other performers."

Shusherin's views on certain aspects of the theatre are noteworthy. Here, for instance, is what he wrote about rehearsals:

The rehearsal is the soul of the play; the play acquires its full value only when it has been properly rehearsed. Outsiders should never be admitted to a rehearsal; they impede the work and tend to distract the actors, and, in addition, in their presence it is awkward to criticize or to be criticized. The dress rehearsal must be conducted with as much care as the performance itself. One must assume that the play is not yet smooth; and, no matter how often it has been performed, it is absolutely necessary that on the morning of the performance it be rehearsed *mezzo-voce,* yet with all vocal intonations. All my life I have seen evidence of the necessity of abiding by this rule. Frequently I had to act when I was not feeling quite well, or when I felt somewhat distracted, or simply not in a good mood; the morning rehearsal was fresh in my memory and helped me in places where otherwise I might have become confused or made a wrong move.

Shusherin, obviously, relied not so much on flashes of talent as on constant labor and training. Early in the nineteenth century he enjoyed particular success as King Lear in a translation of Shakespeare's tragedy, and as Oedipus in Ozerov's *Oedipus in Athens*. In connection with the latter role, a contemporary magazine published a poem addressed to Shusherin:

> The mournful stalls were wrapped in meditation;
> Thine Oedipus was like his living incarnation.

Despite his resourcefulness and his ability to please his superiors, he soon had to recognize the fact that new talents had appeared on the Petersburg stage, and that it would be beyond his capacity to compete with them. He contemplated returning to Moscow and, meanwhile, continued to resort to ill humor and other less innocent devices in order to humiliate his rivals.

In the later years of his service in Petersburg he reluctantly left the apartment where he had lived with his inseparable companion Nadezhda Fyodorovna Kaligraf(ova), a retired actress, who had long occupied that place in his heart which formerly was reserved for Sinyavskaya.

In 1810 Shusherin resigned and settled in Moscow, where he purchased a small house; however, he did not quit the stage altogether. He was entitled to a benefit performance from the Theatre Directorate, and he was permitted to have it in Moscow. He asked Aksakov to translate the tragedy *Philoctetes* for this occasion. He also appeared in his crowning role of Oedipus, as well as in the part of the Negro Ksuri from Kotzebue's comedy, whose translator, A. F. Malinovsky, dedicated the following poem to Shusherin:

> Beholding thee I quite forgot the fact
> That not a Negro but Shusherin did act,
> And Kotzebue * himself would watch with admiration

---

* August von Kotzebue (1761–1819), a prolific German playwright of the sentimental school. For a while, he was theatre manager in Vienna. Subsequently, he entered the German diplomatic service and was sent to Russia, where he spent several years. He was an avowed pro-Russian. For this reason, and because he was accused of anti-patriotism, he was hated by the partisans of Young Germany. He was assassinated at Mannheim by a German student Karl Sand. In the latter part of the eighteenth century and in the early days of the nineteenth century, Kotzebue's plays were very much in vogue.—Tr.

The way thy Ksuri caused a deep sensation,
And to himself he'd say, delighted in his heart,
Here is the wreath that fitly crowns my art.

He scored such a triumph in this part that, according to the
accounts of eyewitnesses, "Poor Shusherin's back got tired from
bowing in every direction." But those who had seen him in former
successes noted a decline in his strength. S. T. Aksakov, for
example, observed that in the part of Yarb he restrained himself,
saving his energy, and playing with less intensity than was
needed; he merely declaimed, and used excessive mimicry. But
when he gave full reign to his talent he was superb, terrifying,
and fascinating: only a great artist could have produced such an
impression as Yarb.

Shusherin himself knew his shortcomings better than any one
else, and was dissatisfied with his acting. The year 1812 was a
calamitous time for the people of Moscow, and shortly after the
retreat of the French he died. Kaligraf(ova) died a short time
after that.

Peter Alekseyevich Plavilshchikov (1760-1812) was also a
noted artist of that period. The son of a Moscow merchant, he
received an excellent education, graduating from the University
in 1779. One of his colleagues wrote, describing how he and his
closest friends spent their time at the University:

They used to get together with P. I. Strakhov, Plavilshchikov's best
friend and colleague, who later became a professor, and start intermi-
nable discussions of things they had read and seen. Plavilshchikov, who
even then was a gifted elocutionist, would recite from memory entire
long monologues from Sumarokov's tragedies in his young, sonorous
voice.

Upon his graduation from the University, Plavilshchikov began
to teach, and revealed an independent intellect in his original
method of teaching Russian history. Teaching did not fully
utilize his natural talents, however, and, remembering his amateur successes in the University theatre, he made up his mind to
become a professional actor.

Despite the fact that he realized this ambition, Plavilshchikov
continued his pedagogical career, teaching literature "according
to his own plan" at the Academy of Fine Arts and the first

Corps of Cadets, and rhetoric "of his own composition" at the Mining Corps. His theatrical career began in Medox's theatre in Moscow. In the early 1780's he went to Petersburg, where he promptly became one of the best actors in the local company. Dmitrevsky exercised a beneficial influence upon the development of his talent.

According to contemporaries Plavilshchikov was especially gifted in the impersonation of positive characters, majestic kings of the ancient tragedies, and types full of dignity and moral grandeur. Tall and broad-shouldered, possessing an expressive and noble countenance, he created a favorable impression by his athletic good looks alone. Contemporaries have pointed out that he "excelled in parts where there was more reasoning and argumentation than action," that is—to use the terminology of a later period—in the parts of moralizers. A notable versatility enabled him to play the roles of Taras Skotinin and of King Lear with equal success. Like the majority of the actors of those days, he must have played in Petersburg, Moscow, as well as on provincial stages. It is known, for example, that he performed in Kazan.

Plavilshchikov was in no sense a traditionalist. Just as he had devised a new method of teaching, he tried, to the best of his ability, to develop some original idea, in all other fields of his tireless activities. His attempt to modify the general character of our repertoire, in which he was aided by appointment in 1781 as supervisor of the Russian theatre in Petersburg, is an especially interesting example. Succeeding Dmitrevsky as supervisor, he became the moving spirit of the work, using his outstanding organizing ability to the best advantage, replacing sick actors and in this way saving shows threatened with cancellation.

After about two years, when the director of the theatre, Prince Yusupov, refused to increase his salary, Plavilshchikov left Petersburg and settled permanently in Moscow. There, as the best and most highly educated actor, he was entrusted with a class in declamation at the Noblemen's Boarding School in conjunction with the University. He also organized and trained entire serf companies belonging to the wealthy theatre lovers N. A. Durasov and Prince M. P. Volkonsky. The latter's company was subsequently acquired by the directorate of the Imperial theatres. On the stages of these private theatres Plavilshchikov tried to produce plays which had never been performed before, and if they proved successful he brought them to the public theatre. He experimented in this way with some of Schiller's, Kotzebue's, and Regnard's pieces. In Moscow he gradually shifted to the parts of noble fathers and old men. In these the excessive utilization of tricks, which were peculiar to his acting even in earlier days, became even more apparent. At times he would shriek in a passage that required a soft voice, and on other occasions the expression of his face would change at the very moment when it should have remained calm.

Here is how a spectator described his acting in the part of Oedipus in Ozerov's famous tragedy:

With the dreadful exclamation, "Temple of Eumenides!" Plavilshchikov leaped from his seat and for several seconds stood as though dumfounded, shivering all over. Then, gradually regaining control of himself, he began to stare fixedly at one spot, and, using his hands as if to push the Furies away from himself, he continued in a trembling voice, with pauses: "Alas, I do behold them . . . they rush upon me with wrath and vengeance . . . (*indistinctly and impetuously*) and drag with them (*in complete exhaustion*) all horrors of Gehenna," and with the verse finished, he threw himself down on a rock.

The same person, however, called Plavilshchikov the "leader of simplicity and naturalness," which indicates that the significance of such accounts is only relative, and that qualities formerly considered marks of simplicity in acting would today be declared the height of artificiality.

On September 29, 1811, Plavilshchikov was elected an active member of the Society of Lovers of Russian Literature. One year later, as he was fleeing from the French on his way to Kazan, he died in a remote province.

Anton Mikhailovich Krutitsky (1751–1803), a graduate of the Foundling Home and a pupil of Knipper, was successful in comedies. His best parts were those of Faddey in Ablesimov's *The Miller*, of Harpagon in *The Miser*, and of Jourdain in Molière's *Le Bourgeois gentilhomme*. Eyewitnesses have said that in *The Miller* his acting was

perfection in the true meaning of the term; his ways and manners were those characteristic of the common people, but at the same time they were ennobled; his voice and glances—everything in him—was inimitable. He caught everything: accent, jests, dancing to the refrain of simple folk songs, even the slightest nuances common to our Russian millers—in short, everything.

Contemporaries praised Andrey Gavrilovich Ozhogin, whose mimicry was so perfected that half of his face would weep, while the other half was laughing.

Avdotya Mikhailovna Mikhailova, who came to Moscow from Petersburg, is also worth noting. In her youth she played in tragedies and operas, in her mature years the roles of coquettes and maid servants. According to Sumarokov, she acted "unsurpassably well" in the latter roles. She also won fame as an inimitable singer of Russian songs.

Vasily Mikhailovich Chernikov, a very handsome man and an excellent singer, also won distinction. He was very successful in servants' parts, which in those days were considered important, and he also held the post of supervisor of the Russian opera.

Chapter VI

THE RISE OF THE
PROVINCIAL THEATRE

INSUFFICIENT DATA make it impossible to determine the precise times when theatres were organized in individual provincial towns. We have to be satisfied with incomplete and fragmentary information, and console ourselves with the supposition that the nature of theatrical development in all cities was essentially the same, while differing in details.

It has been firmly established that during the eighteenth century the theatre was by no means confined to the capitals. We know that there was a theatre in Kharkov, for example, whose early history was recorded by so trustworthy a witness as G. F. Kvitka.

Theatrical performances in Kharkov date from September 29, 1780, when a vice-regency was established there. At that time noblemen in state service and government officials, arriving from various parts of the country, formed a social set which began to stage theatrical performances, among other entertainments, with great enthusiasm. These became particularly popular in Kharkov when Brigadier F. I. Kishensky was appointed governor of the province; he made use of a building which had been erected as a ballroom on the occasion of the Empress' trip through Kharkov in 1787.

In 1791 a theatre was begun in the hall, a stage was built, and wings as well as two stage settings—an interior and a forest—were painted under the supervision of a local artisan, while the curtain was arranged so that it could be easily raised and lowered. He conceived the clever idea of hanging a board over the lamps which, when called for in the script, produced the effect of night.

M. I. Veryovkin, a playwright, gives the following description of the arrangement of the theatre in another provincial town: "Upon my word, the theatre couldn't be better: the orchestra, consisting of twelve rows of seats, accommodates four hundred persons, and is covered with red woolen cloth. In the gallery the crowd was so dense that they seemed like a picture."

The company was formed in this way: on the invitation of the governor, young men employed as office clerks or draftsmen, and those who had not yet finished school, agreed to act with no remuneration whatever, merely for the sake of entertaining the public. It proved to be much more difficult to find actresses, who only relatively recently had appeared in the metropolitan theatres. In the provinces this attractive innovation, apparently, had not yet been socially accepted. "God preserve me from becoming an actress," declared every lady who, because of her supposed talent, was offered a part on the stage. "If in want, I would rather earn my bread by manual labor than to indulge in infamy." It was finally necessary to give up the idea of seeing ladies on the stage, and to entrust the performance of feminine parts to young government employees.

When everything was ready for the opening, the most prominent government officials in town subscribed to the boxes at the rate of fifty rubles for the whole year. The boxes were so spacious that each one could easily accommodate twenty persons. Armchairs in the orchestra cost four rubles for each performance, or twenty-five rubles per annum, while regular orchestra seats sold at sixty kopecks, gallery seats at twenty-five kopecks, and so on. The prices of the theatre seats were rather high in comparison with the low cost of necessities then prevailing in Kharkov.

The school provided its own orchestra of musicians and a choir, which had been previously organized, and were now called on to perform at the shows free of charge.

The audiences were very small, and each performance entailed a great deal of preparation by those whose time was already taken up with government service. It proved impossible to stage performances daily; they were given only on Tuesdays and Fridays, and very characteristically, no shows took place if these days fell on holidays. Plays began at six o'clock. A director, chosen annually from the group of theatre officials, was in charge.

The theatre had no printing facilities at its disposal, and announced the coming program by handwritten posters, nailed on the lamp post at the palace gate.

Shortly after the opening of the theatre, which under the circumstances was an essentially amateur enterprise, a man calling himself a real actor came to see the director. He was of course welcomed; and, without further formalities, after learning only that his name was Dimitry Moskvichev the director engaged him immediately as a member of the company. He made his début in *The Prince-Chimney-Sweeper, the Chimney-Sweeper-Prince*, which, because of the lack of the musical score, was given as a comedy rather than the usual opera.

During the performance Moskvichev, who was actually a deserting soldier from Oryol, noticed—to his horror—the governor of Oryol in the audience. The governor, passing through Kharkov by chance, knew him personally. Panic stricken, and forgetting his part, the actor was about to flee from the stage; but the governor, not wishing to break up the show, shouted: "Don't be frightened, Dimitry, don't be frightened! Go on, fear nothing!" Dimitry recovered his wits and managed to finish the performance to the audience's satisfaction. The next day an order was issued transferring Sergeant Dimitry Moskvichev from the Oryol to the Kharkov military company.

Moskvichev felt quite encouraged, and began to rehearse Ablesimov's opera *The Miller*. The locally trained actors, owing to lack of musical training, sang by ear, and a choirboy was selected for the part of Anyuta. The stage mechanic built a mill with a revolving wheel and a horse with moving feet, so that there was really something worth seeing. When, in the midst of the performance, a large red ball was drawn out from behind a green hill and the actors announced that the moon had risen, the audience was completely delighted and applauded thunderously.

Moskvichev, at his best in the part of the miller, began to sing:

> Listen, boys, it isn't trash:
> Our Saburov has much cash.

It should be noted that Saburov, a government official, was renowned for his wealth. When his name was mentioned, applause broke out, and Saburov himself started to laugh; but that was all. The next time Moskvichev tried a new tack and sang:

> Listen, boys, it isn't trash:
> Karpov's also full of cash.

Karpov, a very wealthy merchant who was also among the audience, blushed, mopped his perspiring forehead; but again nothing happened. Then Moskvichev tried a third version:

> Listen, boys, it isn't trash:
> Good Marukhin has much cash.

Marukhin, not a very rich merchant but a rather generous man, flung a purseful of rubles on the stage, which was what Moskvichev needed.

Such an easy and peculiarly simple relationship between actors and audience was characteristic of our provincial theatre until the end of the nineteenth century.

Having engaged a professional actor, the Kharkov theatre continued to gain ground and develop, adding the comedies of Sumarokov, Veryovkin, and others to its repertoire. When Moskvichev married young and pretty Lizaveta Gavrilovna, the daughter of a gypsy who had settled in Kharkov, the company acquired an actress and improved even more. When it was announced a few days after the wedding that the part of Anyuta in *The Miller* was going to be performed by a real actress and not by a boy, the curiosity of the Kharkov theatregoers rose to the highest pitch. On the night of the performance the theatre was crowded, and as the first actress on the Kharkov stage made her appearance there were endless shouts of "Encore" and applause; purses containing ruble coins and even chervontsi [1] were flung on the stage from every side. In those days this was the commonest way of expressing appreciation of actors.

With an actress in the company, it was possible to expand the repertoire. *The Good Soldiers, The Sbeeten* [2] *Seller, Misfortune from the Coach, Rosana* and *Lyubim, A Lovers' Quarrel, Arkas and Irisa,* and other operas were staged. Lizaveta Gavrilovna enjoyed particular success in all these plays. Now performances began to be given on holidays as well.

[1] Ten-ruble pieces.—Ed.
[2] A Russian hot drink of water, honey, and spices.—Ed.

In those days the theatre's prosperity was greatly aided by low maintenance costs. The majority of the actors were amateurs who received no salaries at all: only two actors and three actresses were salaried members of the company. The leading actors were paid seventy-ruble notes a year, and the others from thirty to fifty rubles. Benefit performances were nonexistent. The orchestra and all theatre attendants worked without remuneration. The actors' wardrobes were kept up by minor repairs and by adding bits of nankeen, coarse woolen stuff, and tinsel.

Before long a retired court actor, Konstantinov, appeared in Kharkov with a small company of his own, and was allowed to take the theatre over, maintaining it at his own expense. He became the first Kharkov theatre entrepreneur about 1795, and distinguished himself by the quality of the company's performance and the lavishness of the production. During his managership new stage sets were painted; the stage was covered with cloth; actors appeared in French coats embroidered with gold, spangles, and colored stones. Trapdoors, movable stage sets, and other staging devices began to be used.

At the same time, the actors' salaries were raised: Liza was paid three hundred rubles a year, and she was given a benefit performance; others received from seventy-five to two hundred fifty rubles. The ticket prices increased accordingly: a box sold at one hundred to one hundred twenty rubles a year, and subscribers had to decorate the boxes at their own expense. In these circumstances Konstantinov managed to make the theatre pay, and he would probably have continued successfully in Kharkov had it not been that state mourning at the death of Catherine II put an end to all theatrical performances, which were resumed only in 1808.

In Tambov theatrical shows were inaugurated by the poet Derzhavin, who was then governor. He organized amateur performances at his home, where, under his wife's direction, young girls sewed and decorated stage costumes as well as learned and rehearsed their parts. The governor's example was followed by other noblemen; for example, Brigadier Nilov, a landowner, organized a theatre on his estate. The plays included translations of French comedies and operas—for instance, Marmontel's *Zémire and Azore*—Sumarokov's tragedies, and Fonvizin's *The Minor*, with Lampelius, Nilov's family physician, in the role of Vralman.

The private theatres of wealthy individuals—just then starting —should be considered along with public provincial theatres as an indication of theatrical progress by the end of the eighteenth century. Because of their social standing and wealth, these men were miniature tsars, and wished to follow the example of the Petersburg court in every respect: the Empress had her theatre, therefore they had to inaugurate theatres of their own.

The theatre of Count Sheremetev on his estate Kuskovo, in the suburbs of Moscow, was one of the most striking establishments of this kind. His was the oldest and the best of the private theatres, comparable to the Petersburg court theatres and far better than the Moscow theatre of those days. It was built of excellent lumber, hewed from whole trees, while its excellently built interior, acoustics, stage, three-tiered boxes, and the orchestra, all bore testimony to the skill of its architect, the famous Valli.

At Kuskovo all types of performances were given, but operas were in special favor. The opulence of the theatrical properties may be realized from an inventory which lists 8 curtains, 194 settings, 52 side-sets, 68 minor decorative accessories, 17 large chests containing brocade, velvet, silk, cloth and woolen wardrobe articles, and 76 chests, boxes, and cardboard cases for footwear, costumes, and other requisites, such as arms, standards, banners, animal skins, bandores, masks, and multi-colored curtains.

Singers, musicians, actors, actresses, and dancers of both sexes were almost all serfs of the Count. Among the senior musicians there were also foreigners; the violinist Feier and the cellist Fatius played particularly well. The Florentine Cianfanelli, who with his wife joined the Sheremetev company after retiring from the court stage, was the ballet master. A special scenic designer, a serf by the name of Ivan Argunov, as well as a translator, Vasily Vroblevsky, were also on the theatre staff.

As we know, Count Sheremetev even married an actress of his troupe, Praskovya Ivanovna, a former serf, whose biography merits some detail. Parasha, born on June 20, 1768, was the daughter of the Count's serf Ivan Kuznetsov-Gorbunov. Because of her wonderful voice and good looks, she was enrolled in the Count's company, continuing to work in the fields during those hours when she was free from the theatre.

At the age of seventeen, she was already listed as "one of our foremost actresses." She continued her career until the end of the summer season in 1789, when Count Nicholas Petrovich, a young bachelor who had received a good education in the West, began to pay attention to her. After the death of his father the theatre at Kuskovo fell into disuse; but the new owner began to take a lively interest in it for Parasha's sake, devoting himself to the theatre with all his natural enthusiasm. Love for an actress became the motivation for the improvement of the entire theatrical enterprise—a common occurrence in that period and not restricted to serf theatres.

Parasha began learning "Russian and other languages." In the company which she joined, Peter Petrov and Chukhnov were the leading actors, while Marya Cherkasova and Arina Kalmykova were the best of the six actresses—or "comédiennes," as they were called to distinguish them from female dancers. The Frenchwomen Duvry and Chevalier were the actresses' drama instructors.

From the time when the Count became attracted to Parasha, the status of all the actresses in the company improved greatly. Wanting to surround his beloved with luxury and at the same time conceal the reason for her privileged position, he found it necessary to better conditions for her sister actresses.

All performances were built around Parasha, and were designed to exhibit her talent as favorably as possible. The Count gave her the stage name of Zhemchugova, the pearl (*zhemchug*) of the company.

Parasha was not only beautiful, she also attracted the Count by her spiritual charm. His relationship with her enriched and ennobled his own character. Exercising a very great influence upon him, she tried to use it for the accomplishment of the greatest possible good. She lived in special, comparatively modest quarters; precious paintings were the only decoration in her simple bedroom.

In 1798 the Count spread the rumor that Parasha was descended from the Polish noble family of the Kowalewskis, freed her from serfdom, and gave her the name of Kovaleva. In order to remove her from the environment in which she had grown up, he transferred the theatre from Kuskovo to Ostankino, another village in the Moscow suburbs, where he himself moved, and where the theatre continued. On November 6, 1801, he married her. But their happiness was short-lived: on February 3, 1803, a son Dimitry was born to them, and twenty days later Parasha died. The memory of this outstanding Russian actress is kept alive by people who sing the song of her first meeting with her future husband.

The theatre of Prince N. B. Yusupov—who had 21,421 serfs in fifteen provinces—was altogether different. From 1791 to 1799 he occupied the post of Director of the Imperial theatres. In Kharitonyev Lane in Moscow, opposite his home, "the girls of the theatre choir"—or "the Yusupov seraglio," as I. A. Arsenyev calls it in his memoirs—were housed in his other residence, surrounded by a high stone wall. Later, when the state theatres were no longer giving performances, Yusupov used to invite his intimate friends to the performances of the serf corps de ballet. On Yusupov's signal, the girls slipped off their dresses and appeared naked before the audience.

According to available information, the corps in the 1820's consisted of twenty-five girls in charge of a special "inspectress." They were all children of the Prince's serfs. They received no salary, and only the favorites were paid five rubles a month and provided with sugar. They were instructed by the famous ballet master Iogel, and they were also sent to the illustrious ballerina Hullensor ("Madame Hulen"), who was then performing in Moscow as a visiting artist. For every group of eight lessons she was paid 129 rubles and 60 kopecks. The girls were taught Italian for operas, and for a while the Italian Zerotti was their singing master. Frequently they were sent to the Russian and Italian theatres, where one or two boxes were provided for them.

Besides those in Moscow, similar performances were staged in the suburban village of Arkhangelskoye, on the Prince's sumptuous estate. The ballets were of a mythological character, such as *Medea and Jason* and *Zephyrus*, and also *The Barber of Seville*. The music of Rossini, whose name resounded throughout Europe in those days, was probably used for the last. It is impossible to be certain which operas were staged, but we have the title of the only comedy in the theatre's 1820 repertoire, *Fedinka and Luka*. After Yusupov's death all adult women dancers were emancipated. Some of them married, and others scattered all over Russia. One of them joined the Kharkov company managed by Stein, while the ballerina Anna Robutovskaya was engaged by the landowner Khorvat to organize a ballet for his serf theatre.

These serf companies in no way resembled one another, since their size and composition varied with the wealth of their individual owners. But few of them could afford to maintain theatres such as the one at Kuskovo. It is also interesting that while some theatres had only serf actors, both serfs and amateurs of society families appeared in the performances at others—for instance, in Prince A. I. Gagarin's or N. P. Sheremetev's theatres.

The artistic level of the theatre of that period is illustrated by Prince I. M. Dolgorukov in his account of the famous Nizhny-Novgorod theatre of Prince Shakhovskoy:

"What ability can one expect from a useless serf who at one's whim may either be flogged or be seated at the table?" Accordingly, Shakhovskoy's rather large group of actors performs like an ox hauling a load, when driven by a Circassian with a switch. I do not go into the reasons why a serf cannot possess outstanding talent. I simply state that theatrical entertainments at Nizhny are very good for amateurs of this kind, but the moment one calls them actors, one cannot look at their gestures without disgust; they do not act, but—to use a vulgar expression—they grimace. I repeat, however, as far as serfs go, even this is better than might be expected.

The owners' personalities were directly reflected in their companies. If, for example, the company of the Penza landowner V. I. Gladkov staged exceedingly licentious performances for his gratification, the Ardatov landowner Prince N. I. Shakhovskoy scrupulously watched over his company's morality. The house in which his actors lived was divided into separate dormitories for men and women. The Prince strictly forbade all contact between the dormitories, with the penalty of severe corporal punishment. All offenses against the theatre's morality were punished with penalties such as the "spiked collar": the guilty actor was placed in the middle of a room, and his neck was propped up with three poles. A special disciplinary method was devised for musicians in the form of a chair to which a chain and a dog's collar were fastened. The Prince saw to it that the actor, even during a performance, should not touch an actress, and that he stand at a distance of not less than one arshine from her; when she was supposed to faint he was permitted to support her only in a sham fashion.

Peter Vasilyevich Yesipov, a Kazan landowner, certainly could not have boasted of such pure morals, since he was fond of entertaining the public not only with theatrical performances, but also with the charms of his serf actresses. In time his company developed from a purely personal diversion of its owner into a public institution, and began to stage public performances. It should be observed that such landowners' companies often developed into public theatres not only in the provinces but in Moscow, too, where until 1806 the Petrovsky theatre company was composed almost exclusively of the serf actors of A. E. Stolypin. In that year the Tsar purchased the entire company of seventy-four members for the sum of 32,000 rubles. Among them there were outstanding talents. As early as 1793, an actress by the name of Varenka came into the limelight; later, she married a writer, N. I. Strakhov, the editor of the *Satirical Messenger*.

When serf actors appeared on the stage side by side with "free" artists, the names of the latter were distinguished by placing the letter "M" (that is, "Mr." or "Mrs.") before the name.

According to the conceptions of those days, it was easy to make an artist out of a lackey.

What's needed in the theatre [Suvorov wrote to his manager] is training and innocent enjoyment. Vaska is a good comic actor, but Nikitka will be better in tragedy. Only Nikitka must learn expression, which is easy when one follows commas, periods, colons, and exclamation and question marks. In rhymes, it will prove easy. In verse, cadences should be observed much as beat is observed in music, without which speech will be deprived of clarity, sweetness, and pathos; all this has to be explained to him plainly. Instead of Maxim and Bochkin, young peasant choir singers may be trained for comic parts. In addition, Alexander, the barber, must be made to learn French grammar little by little; Nicholas can take care of him once he's able to read.

A Frenchman who had lived in Russia a long time wrote an interesting account of the landowner B.:

His cooks, lackeys, and grooms, as need arose, became musicians, carpenters, shoemakers, and so forth; his chambermaids and housemaids, actresses, embroiderers in gold, and so on! They served simultaneously as his concubines, wet nurses, and nursery maids for his children whom they had borne. I used to attend his theatrical performances quite frequently. The musicians of the orchestra came dressed in different costumes in accordance with the parts which they were to play. At a whistle signal the curtain rose, they threw away their bassoons, kettledrums, violins, and bass viols and substituted a scepter of Melpomene, the mask of Thalia, or the lyre of Orpheus. In the morning these same men worked with a plane, a shovel, and a broom. During the performance it was particularly amusing to watch B. in his dressing gown and nightcap, majestically walking around the stage among the sets, encouraging his serf actors by words and gestures. Once, during the performance of *Dido,* the master was displeased with the acting of the leading actress. Jumping upon the stage, he gave poor Dido a heavy blow over the face, with the words: "I told thee that I would catch thee. After the performance go to the stable and get there the reward awaiting thee!" Dido grimaced with pain, resumed her part and continued her aria as if nothing had happened. Subsequently this actress was banished to a remote village, perhaps because, as a result of venereal disease, she had lost her voice.

There is nothing surprising in the fact that theatres ruined the landowners. In an article printed in Volume III of the *Satirical Messenger,* published by Strakhov in the latter part of the eighteenth century, we read:

Some feebleminded noblemen, having heard about the triumphant glory of the theatre, after visiting the capital, accumulate debts, squander their fortunes, and in exchange for these return home with a large group of musicians and actors, as well as wagons stuffed with stage sets and musical instruments.

A report of the Moscow "precinct officers," submitted in May 1797 to the Moscow chief of police and Pavel Nikitich Kaverin, gives an idea of the extent and character of these theatres. By order of the Moscow military governor Arkharov, Kaverin sent inquiries as to the number of private theatres in Moscow. By that time there were several private theatres. The amount of properties and the number of actors engaged varied in proportion to the wealth of their owners and their enthusiasm for the theatre, which governed the number of domestics they were prepared to sacrifice for art.

The *Moscow News* in the year 1793 carried this advertisement:

A girl of sixteen is for sale, a chambermaid, possessing a good voice, singing very skillfully, and therefore theatre lovers are hereby given notice that the said girl can act cleverly in a theatrical part, and also keep house and cook good meals. The price is to be ascertained at the house of Zobin, near the Church of John the Baptist.

Many posters of the serf theatres have been preserved. In the village of Surianino in Volkhov County, for example, the brothers Yurasovsky performed a pantomime ballet of the Moscow ballet master Glushkovsky, *The Robbers of the Mediterranean Sea,* or *The Benevolent Algerian,* "with battles, marches, and splendid scenes." It was announced that "Vanka Antonov, Vasyutka Khromina, and Donka Zyurina will dance *(pas de trois)* and Anisya Kartavaya, solo."

All these actors were serfs of the theatre owner, whose prestige and pride were flattered in accordance with their talents. In the periods between performances, or when the master's entertainment was discontinued, the actors returned to their former status, on a par with the other servants. All burdens which fell to the lot of serfs generally extended to serf artists, whose situation was, perhaps, not only not better but even worse than that of the other domestics.

Dramatic art was fraught with many difficulties to people of the intellectual and artistic level of serfs. Acting furnished added pretexts for displeasure on the part of their exacting masters, the consequences of which were sad indeed. We know of many instances where an actor who had just been playing the part of a mighty king in some tragedy had to endure flogging by his "hangman" after the performance.

Contact with art elevated the actor's soul and enlightened his mind, thus making the stigma of his serfdom the more painful. The flagrant contrast between "the elevating delusion" of the stage and the misery of life must have caused the serf actor painful moments. The situation of actresses was still worse because in most instances they were the odalisques of the serf harems.

Pushkin's friend P. A. Vyazemsky, referring to their theatres in his *Second Note-Book* (Paragraph 104), observes that there was also a good side to them:

Once there exists legitimate serfdom, then the employment of domestics in choirs and orchestras and as actors is not the worst despotic abuse of the landowner's temper. These enterprises gave the servants some education, at least literacy; and also, if not a love of fine arts, at any rate some familiarity with them. This somehow tended to develop humane feelings, to soften the prevailing customs, and to give the servants a glimpse of God's light. They learned by heart the words and thoughts of Fonvizin and Kotzebue, coming into contact, even in passing, with persons from a different milieu. For a brief moment they impersonated characters of another world; and as a result of this play-acting healthy seeds must have been planted in their minds, and in some—rare as they may have been—these seeds yielded a fertile harvest.

Chapter VII

THEATRICAL CUSTOMS OF THE
EIGHTEENTH CENTURY

EVEN AFTER the establishment of state theatres, the Petersburg nobility continued to stage amateur performances in which the Vorontsovs, the Apraksins, Countess Bryusova, and others took part.

Under Elizabeth's sponsorship of the theatre, these performances received added impetus, both in Moscow and in Petersburg. It is known that, even before she ascended the throne, Elizabeth spent her leisure hours enjoying comedies which were usually performed by the court choristers and young girls. Very often cadets of the Land Corps repeated at the court those theatrical shows which they had been producing at the Corps, and sometimes Elizabeth herself approved their costumes.

In the files of the state archives the following document, dated 1759, has been preserved:

For the production of the Italian opera *Alexander in India* the following operatic, ballet, and cadets' apparel and other costumes were used: tinsel ones, received from your Imperial Majesty's office, for 577 rubles and 58 kopecks; others, purchased from merchants, for 1,071 rubles and 5 kopecks; those belonging to the crown, for 592 rubles and 11 kopecks; money earned by workers, 388 rubles and 30 kopecks; the total sum expended on this opera being 2,628 rubles and 4 kopecks.

This document is convincing proof that these performances were liberally financed and produced with considerable luxury.

Catherine rather frequently arranged amateur performances at the Hermitage, which often began with a performance in which the highest strata of Petersburg society took part. A contemporary gives a long list of the prominent amateurs, adding, however: "It would probably have been difficult to play the tragedy more disreputably." At times, even "members of the Imperial family" participated in these performances. The example of the Empress was followed by those prominent persons who were closest to the court.

From the aristocracy these entertainments passed on to other strata of society. Indeed, the passion for the theatre grew so common that it became a subject for satire on the stage. The comedy *A Queer Gathering,* for example, depicts a Moscow commoner Petukhov who dedicates his entire time to the staging of private performances. According to his chambermaid, he is "stupefied by comedy, even though it drains much of his money." His passion is shared by "Mr. Krivoustyev, an eminent Kolomna merchant; his cousin Durkin; and Pustozvyakin, a nephew of the brother-in-law of a parish priest. They have lived in Petersburg a long time, have seen many comedies in private theatres, and are great connoisseurs." Krivoustyev even plans to have a theatre built in Kolomna, to which he can come "for a month or two during the summer and have comedies performed for him three or four times a week." An equally enthusiastic theatre lover is the clerk Chernilin who neglects his duties because of the theatre, and is consequently discharged. This very spirited play depicts quarrels among the amateurs over the assignment of parts, and a rehearsal of several scenes taken from plays characteristic of the repertoire of the period. It is possible that this is an adaptation of a foreign play, rather than an original piece. Even so, it could meet with some degree of success only if the passion for the stage, which was satirized in it, was comprehensible to the public.

The archives of the former Imperial theatres furnish sufficient material to judge the modes of living of the actors of the state company. Some were recruited from the pupils of the dramatic school, and others from persons who had previously acted on other stages—for example, at the "Knipper" theatre in the Tsaritsin Meadow. A considerable number of actors came from private provincial theatres, like Vasily Rykalov, who was formerly an actor "in the Tula governorship," probably in some landowner's company. On April 16, 1800, actresses and actors "from among serfs of the Shklov earldom" were enlisted in the state ballet troupe. These actors had belonged to the later disbanded company of Zorich, Catherine's well known favorite.

Information as to how actresses were recruited is even more meager. Some were engaged from provincial companies, but the majority came from the dramatic school, which supplied actresses for both the dramatic and the ballet companies. Very often women began in the ballet company and became dramatic actresses later.

Marriages between Russian actresses and their fellow actors were quite common. Sometimes they married while still attending the dramatic school, and in that case they were enrolled in the company as of the date of their wedding. It is interesting to note that among the many documents concerning the private lives of the actors of the eighteenth century there is only one dealing with a wedding of an actress who was authorized by her superiors to marry a person not on the theatre staff. This shows that an actress was held in such disdain that her marriage to a man not belonging to the theatrical profession was most exceptional.

Actors were permitted to marry only with their superiors' authorization. Failure to obtain such permission entailed severe punishment. For example, Storozhev, an actor of the Russian company, was arrested in the theatre office because of an unauthorized marriage.

The actors' salaries were fixed by special budget appropriations effected, in each case, with Imperial sanction. We know of four such budget appropriations during the eighteenth century: in each instance remuneration increased proportionately to the increase in the cost of living. Compensation of the leading actor increased as follows: 800, 900, 1,000 and 2,000 rubles. Meanwhile, the lowest salary paid to men remained stable at 200 rubles. Only in 1786 was it raised to 280 rubles; and five years later, in 1791, it dropped again to 200 rubles a year.

In addition to salaries, actors and actresses were entitled to apartments provided by the state. They were also given firewood or special sums for heating. Furthermore, on the strength of a regulation issued in 1789, four benefit performances were granted to the company: one during Sexagesima Week, the second during Holy Week, the third in September, and the fourth on Christmas. Money derived from benefits, after deduction of expenditures, was divided among all the members of the company, though not equally, since the leading actor and actress received considerably more than minor colleagues. The contracts of certain artists fixed the minimum sum which they were to receive from the benefit; and in case the amount received was less than the minimum the crown was obliged to pay the difference. Actors were also given benefit performances as a special reward for services to the management. In 1784 an actor of Spengler's German company was granted a benefit in recognition of the fact that his "under-age children were always employed for theatrical shows."

In those days, benefit performances were also given for "composers of comedies, tragedies, and operas whose works gave pleasure and won public praise," as well as for "conductors or composers of music as a reward for the same achievements."

Just as the management held benefits for actors of special merit, it imposed fines upon actors guilty of misdemeanors. In May, 1793, for instance, the administration ordered that a supplementary sum of 500 rubles originally granted to the actor Gomburov be confiscated and paid to the actor Vorobyev, whom he had struck over the head. This punishment was to be enforced until the contending parties reached a peaceful understanding.

Instead of providing an apartment, the crown sometimes paid actors rental allowance; but this was rare. Thus, in 1791, of the twenty actors of the company only three were receiving rental allowance. The practice of compelling uncongenial persons to live together frequently led to misunderstandings which had to be settled by the management. Sometimes actors were deprived of their apartments for misbehavior. Among others, the actress Pelageya Ryabchikova lost her apartment in 1800 because, "while in a state of intoxication, she was guilty of certain improprieties, which annoyed the other tenants."

The management paid pensions to the artists retiring from the stage, but the amounts were negligible. According to the 1766 budget appropriations, the amount was 200 rubles; that is, it equaled the lowest salary paid to either actors or actresses. It appears from the Pension Law that a fixed annual sum was appropriated for such pensions, so that candidates entitled to receive them had to wait a long time for payment.

Russian subjects were given preference over foreigners, in the distribution of pensions. Pensions were paid not only to actors who had grown old but sometimes to their orphaned children. For example, in 1793 the widow of the deceased actor Andreyan Prokofyev, with two minor children, began to receive "five rubles a month for subsistence until the children became of age."

An important item of expenditure for actors, which consumed a major part of the budget, was the purchase and upkeep of costumes. The theatre management of the eighteenth century prescribed that "state-owned costumes shall be confined to persons playing character parts only, while those performing ordinary roles shall do so in their own clothes." Artists were provided by the crown with historical costumes and with others they could not wear in private, such as common people's garments and various uniforms. However, even apart from these, actors bore many expenses of their wardrobes, especially since a regulation provided: "Inasmuch as every actor is obliged to have his own clothes, it shall be required that these be decent and conforming to their parts." The regulation warned that a stage costume "shall not be soiled or spoiled through neglect, under the threat of penalty and of its repair at the expense of him who shall cause same."

All this gave full discretion to the management, which at any given moment could place the artists in a difficult or even utterly helpless situation.

All actors and actresses were divided into certain categories. According to the 1766 budget, they were classified as follows: 1) the leading tragic and comic lover; 2) the second tragic and comic lover; 3) the third tragic and comic lover; 4) the noble father; 5) the comic father; 6) the first domestic; 7) the second domestic; 8) the moralizer; 9) the clerk; and, 10) and 11), two confidants. The female parts of the company were divided into these categories: 1) the first tragic and comic lover; 2) the second tragic and comic lover; 3) the first chambermaid; 4) the second chambermaid; 5) the old woman; and, 6) and 7), two confidantes.

In accordance with these schedules, artists were engaged for a specific category only, which had to be stipulated in the contract. At the same time, the management reserved the right to assign, at its discretion, any part to any actor. Barbara Novikova's contract is quite characteristic in this respect. It states that pursuant to her duties she, Novikova, shall be obligated to teach acting and singing in court theatres, whersoever she be ordered to do so, to take all leading female parts, and sometimes also male parts, both in operas and in comedies and dramas, assuming the said parts either singly or with the participation of others, regardless of whom she shall impersonate, be it a chambermaid or an old woman, a peasant woman, or some other character; briefly, she shall be obligated to perform and sing in such parts as the management may assign to her.

Such a wide variety of talents was necessitated by the character of the repertoire, which often combined opera and drama in the same piece. Parts in them could not successfully be played either by singers insufficiently trained in acting, or by dramatic actors, who were even less capable of singing opera. The actors most often benefited from such a combination: practice in singing developed their vocal cords, giving the necessary force to declamation, which in that period was essentially musical or like singing, whereas acting taught the operatic singer more intelligent phrasing, giving his acting the necessary reality.

The artists had to submit to the management in the assignment of the parts, and refusal to play a designated role was punished by a fine. Of course, in such a state of affairs the artists' self-respect must have suffered very frequently; this was expressed in a long range of complaints and conflicts between the artists and the management, the latter invariably winning out. Artists were by no means always tongue-tied and submissive. The former theatre director, I. P. Yelagin, wrote, for example:

Everybody knows how arrogant, disrupted and disobedient this un-bridled crew [the actors] have grown. They are guided by nothing but greediness. Professionals in the theatre will obey and esteem not only the director but the entrepreneur as well only when they are sure that their lot is wholly dependent on him alone; that only through him their ambitions and greed may be satisfied; that he may discharge them or prolong the term of their employment and raise their salaries. Only in these circumstances will they exercise their talents diligently, obediently, and to the public's pleasure. Yet the moment they get the slightest hint that with less labor and more pay, through other avenues, they can reach the object of their craving, they promptly become disobedient and disrespectful; and then there is no limit to the calumnies and lies which, not being fools at all, they will bring forward against the director and the management—to their patrons, duped by their simulated air of meekness and poverty.

In 1779 a dramatic school for the training of actors was established. It was designed for fifteen male and fifteen female pupils, who were to be taught, in addition to "primary, all other subjects." It was located in the so-called "theatrical corps" not far from the Winter Palace, between Millionnaya Street and the Moika Canal. By 1784, these quarters became overcrowded, and it had to be transferred to private houses.

The pupils in the school were mostly children of theatrical parents. Some serfs were also admitted, however. On August 30, 1797, for example, Chamberlain Nicholas Nikitich Demidov entered into an agreement with the dramatic school for sending there for a period of five years "three of his serf girls to teach them dancing"; and it was further stipulated that, after the five years, he should have the right either to let them stay with the school administration or to take them back. So far as the available documents reveal, the dramatic pupils were treated more or less decently. The school administration assumed, "on paper" at least, the obligation to clothe and feed them well. Whether or not this provision was carried out is, of course, difficult to say.

A decree of 1783 provided that

under the supervision of a committee and a director, a school be maintained in which Russian pupils of both sexes be trained for the theatre and instructed in music, dancing, and other arts required in theatres; the purpose of the school shall be not only to provide our theatres with personnel, but so to train them in all theatre arts that eventually it may become possible to substitute natives for foreigners.

Pupils were taught Russian, French, and Italian, mathematics, declamation, and acting; they were also instructed in playing the piano and other instruments, and in dancing and painting. In 1794, under Prince Yusupov, certain subjects of general education—namely, mathematics, foreign languages, and painting—were eliminated from the curriculum. Recitals were organized with a view to "training the pupils for public performance." There was also a small stage on which ballets, as well as dramas, were produced.

As a result of the 1794 statute, all pupils, according to their ability and aptitudes, were to be

continuously trained: (1) some in music; (2) others in dancing; (3) all of them in the Russian language, so that they may be able to read and write; and (4) to perfect their Russian style and to occupy their leisure, they shall be obliged to perform comedies and ballets.

Attention should be called to the expression, "to occupy their leisure"—certainly a strange explanation for the necessity of giving recitals, of prime and utmost importance to future actors.

When not occupied by work in the theatre, at court balls and rehearsals, pupils were required "to study all the time in the aforesaid classes, as provided in the school curriculum." At the same time, "musical pupils" were permitted to get leaves "for playing in orchestras, in clubs, and at private, but not vulgar, balls; and pupils should be allowed to engage in writing music of all kinds for outsiders." The right to grant leaves for such extraneous occupations was within the discretion of the school supervisor, with the provision, however, that money earned in this way was not to be retained by him, but distributed among the pupils engaged in such work or used to purchase things they needed.

A teaching staff was provided as follows:

(1) a dancing master for both boys and girls, with a salary of 300 rubles; (2) musical instructors teaching boys to play on different instruments, with 350 rubles in salaries for all of them; (3) a teacher of the Russian language for both boys and girls, with a salary of 150 rubles; and (4) an instructor in acting for boys and girls, with a salary of 300 rubles.

I. A. Dmitrevsky was appointed supervisor, and of course the government could not have made a better choice. The number of pupils, both male and female, during various periods of the eighteenth century varied from twenty-seven to sixty-four. During certain years there were considerably more male than female pupils; in other years there were more female pupils. In 1800 the director of theatres Naryshkin issued a regulation that there should be "fifty persons of both sexes" in the school at all times.

The repertoire consisted of plays purchased by the management at a specific price, as may be seen from the letter of Registrar Zakhar Kryzhanovsky in which he asked the theatre committee "with a view to encouraging his translation work, to purchase from him several scores of comic operas which he had translated into the Russian dialect." He fixed prices for the individual pieces at 50 to 200 rubles, bringing the total which he asked up to 600 rubles.

In 1784 a benefit performance was granted to "Secretary [1] Yakov Knyazhnin for those pieces which he has composed for the theatre, and which have already ben produced on the stage." Sometimes, the authors received monetary rewards instead of benefits. Thus, Plavilshchikov, instead of a benefit, was paid 300 rubles for his comedy *A Kind Relative*.

In order to systematize the repertoire, Catherine decreed:

In the selection of performances staged at the Court, although the final decision will rest with us, the director shall seek to abide by the principle of diversification, lest one kind of performance, instead of providing entertainment, grow boring.

She herself often took a hand in the planning of the repertoire; in 1783 her favorite, Lanskoy, acting under instructions from her, wrote, "Her Majesty wishes that next Monday the comedy *The Journalist* be performed."

The general status of our theatre in the eighteenth century leads one to believe that it was subject to a special censorship as to the "political propriety" of the plays. This is apparent from the fate of Knyazhnin's tragedy *Vadim*.

Plays were examined by a special censor, and the office in the latter part of the eighteenth century was occupied by Klushin, known for his translations of dramatic works. From the censor the plays were sent to the supervisor of the Russian company, who was in charge of their stage production. Emperor Paul used to intervene in censorship, and on October 23, 1798, he issued a personal order that "the comedy entitled *The Tale-Bearer*, written by Mr. Kapnist, be not produced on the stage." This severe measure, however, did not prevent him a year later, on October 31, 1799, from appointing Kapnist to "examine all pieces and correct them, because of his complete familiarity with these matters."

---

[1] Government title denoting relatively low standing in the table of ranks for civil servants, usually a civil servant of the tenth or twelfth category.—Ed.

The attitude of eighteenth century society toward the theatre was contemptuous, and the mere acquaintance of society people with actors, even such as Dmitrevsky, was censured by the zealous guardians of etiquette. The public affected by Francomania favored the French theatre, and Plavilshchikov bitterly complained: "When a French performance was given, a passer-by beheld a square blocked up with teams of six horses. But where will one find such a team during a Russian performance?"

Count F. V. Rastopchin's witty remark in connection with the opening of the new Arbat Theatre in Moscow, before 1812, is well known. "It is all very good," said he, "but it is insufficient: 2,000 serfs should be bought and assigned to the theatre; turn by turn, every evening, they should be charged with the task of impersonating the audience in the theatre: it is impossible to rely upon the public alone."

In the theatre, the audience behaved in a manner no way suggesting respect for art. Sumarokov, in the preface to his *Dimitry the Impostor,* presents the following picture:

It is unbecoming to those going to see *Semira* to sit cracking nuts right next to the musicians, and to consider that, once admittance money is paid, it is permissible to engage in fisticuffs right in the stalls, and in the boxes to recount, bellowing aloud, their stories of the past week, and to crack nuts. Many men and women in the Moscow audiences attend performances with no desire to hear uninteresting news, while nut cracking gives no pleasure to either intelligent members of the audience or to the actors, still less to the author who has labored for the public's entertainment. His service deserves reward—not punishment. You who have traveled and visited Paris or London, tell me: Do people there crack nuts during the performance, or do they, in their anger, flog drunken, quarreling coachmen, thereby spreading alarm throughout the pit, the boxes, and all around the theatre?

In passing it may be noted that Fonvizin's letters from abroad show that in the West, too, the public in those days often behaved noisily and unbecomingly. The criticism of this period was antithetical to a true understanding of the nature of dramatic art; it adhered exclusively to the didactic viewpoint. This is revealed, for example, in the review of *Juliet, or the Consequences of Seduction:*

What pleasure is there in showing in glaring dishonor a young girl who, in days gone by, would have been locked up in a convent, and who, today, would be sent away to some remote village and the rumor spread that she had died? What is the sense of summoning us to behold one who should make us blush or turn away from her? Gentlemen! Perhaps it may seem harsh to you, but don't be angry: I have a betrothed daughter. What good will she derive from the spectacle of a seduced one whose romance ends with her father—that unfortunate simpleton—first bursting into an uproar and then, after shedding a few tears, consenting to her marriage to the seducer? It goes to prove that in one way or another, whether honestly or dishonestly, the daughter will have her own way. That is not good. We are accustomed to beholding those who can captivate us, who will attract us, and who serve as examples for our children. Besides, what intelligent actress will of her own choice impersonate a woman whom the audience regards with a scoffing smile, asking themselves whether her stature resembles that of the character she portrays? Can she stamp out innate modesty, which is an inherent trait of all women, a trait with which they are born and with which they die? German fellows have flooded our theatre with seduced heroines, or, one might better say, damsels, and our young writers crawl after them.

A special theatre magazine also came into existence in the eighteenth century. The venture did not prove very successful—only one issue was published—and it was not until 1808 that the Russian theatre had a permanent publication of its own. The periodical first appeared in 1789, when a book in the German language entitled *Russische Theatralien* also appeared. The editor of the magazine was Sauerweid, one of the actors of the Petersburg German theatre, who announced in the first issue of the magazine its purpose in these words:

Since the theatre first came into being in Russia, it has experienced and initiated many and various changes. It has exercised an influence upon the public, and, in turn, many men of prominence and private people have introduced new blood into it by their talents, prestige, and authority. But what do we know about these things? Nothing, or next to nothing! At present the theatre is under Imperial patronage; and while all Germany is eager to have information about our theatre, it is receiving only a few completely misleading facts.

That is the reason why the magazine was published in German. Considering how anxious Catherine was to disseminate abroad information regarding everything taking place in Russia, it may be supposed that Sauerweid's journal enjoyed at least a degree of patronage from the Empress herself.

The magazine included, in addition to two rather insignificant pieces, an article by Sauerweid himself, *"On the Terms 'Comedian' and 'Comedians,'"* objecting to the terms because they were given also to various dancers and acrobats. Instead he suggested "actor" (*Schauspieler*). Following his article was a particularly interesting and detailed schedule of theatres in both the metropolitan and provincial districts. An article by a Petersburg theatre lover complaining about the fact that actors were learning their parts poorly, so that the prompter was very much in evidence, is also noteworthy.

Although the magazine failed after its first issue, the very fact of the appearance of a theatre magazine in Russia at that time clearly shows that the theatre was beginning to establish itself firmly.

The numerous satirical magazines of the eighteenth century also contained references to the theatre. The account of the tragedians in the *Satirical Journal* is interesting:

In the opinion of the actors, the legs and arms are more expressive than the face. With this premise in mind, they stretch one arm up, pressing the other one so closely to the body that during the entire performance they seem to represent a statue of the ancient type, or an ancient wrestler about to face his rival. They likewise consider it very beautiful to protrude their eyes, stretching forth the fingers of the acting hand so tightly that no power can bend them down again. They are also quite versed in vocal matters. Certain actors shout at the top of their voices, while others pronounce words in a singsong manner, so that a comedy nearly always sounds like an opera.

Chapter VIII

THE EIGHTEENTH CENTURY
REPERTOIRE

SUMAROKOV AND HIS TRAGEDIES

THE FIRST TASK which must have confronted the leaders of the revival of the Russian theatre was the planning of the repertoire. In 1787 a most interesting volume was published, which still is a first-rate source book for the study of the history of the Russian theatre. This is *The Dramatic Lexicon*, which was issued anonymously. It contains a comprehensive list of the plays that had been given in the Russian language up to that year, supplemented, in some cases, by sketchy notations of the circumstances of production of this or that play, and its performers. Among others, the following pieces are listed in the *Lexicon: Voltaire's Alzire* and *Nanine* (1766), *Zaïre* (1779), *The Indiscreet*; Beaumarchais's *The Marriage of Figaro* (1787), *The Barber of Seville*; Goethe's *Clavigo* (1770); Holberg's *Pride and Poverty*, *Plutus* (1765), *The Transformed Peasant*, *Artax* (1778); Goldoni's *The Liar*; Kleist's *Seneca* (1765); Corneille's *Cinna*, *The Cid*, *The Death of Polyeucte*; Lessing's *Emilia Galotti*, *The Young Scholar*, *The Treasure*, and *Miss Sara Sampson*; Molière's *Tartuffe*, *The Misanthrope*, *The School for Wives*, *The School for Husbands* (1757), *George Dandin* (1758), *Le Bourgeois gentilhomme*, *Scapin's Deceits*, *The Miser*, *Amphitryon* (1761), *The Sicilian* (1766); Racine's *Athalie* (i.e. *Gapholia*, 1784), *Esther* (1783); Shakespeare's *The Tragedy of King Richard III* and *Julius Caesar*.

The number of classic plays of the Western repertoire which appeared in Russia during the first two decades of the Russian theatre is ample proof of its merit. These plays which enriched our then meager literature enabled the Russian theatre to make a great contribution to Russian culture, for, thanks to the theatre, comparatively soon after the original plays came out, their translations were made available to us.

Around the young theatre the work of translating was conducted very intensively; for example, most of Molière's plays appeared during one year (1757). From the very beginning, there was a group of translators who tended to specialize in the translation of individual authors; thus the majority of Molière's plays were translated into Russian by Ivan Kropotov, while Andrey Nartov concentrated on translations of Holberg's works.

Original Russian dramas, too, found an audience in the theatre revival. Alexander Petrovich Sumarokov (1717–1777) is undeniably the best Russian playwright of the period. He wrote his first tragedy, *Horeb,* in 1747, and it was published in the same year; it was not produced until 1749, however. *Horeb* was followed by *Hamlet* (1748), *Sineus and Truvor* (1751), *Artiston* (1751), and *Semira* (1751). The lack of a Russian company must have been a severe handicap to Sumarokov, since the performance of his plays, in the absence of better actors, had to be entrusted to cadets and officers of the Ground Forces' Training School. The emergence of Volkov and his company eliminated this difficulty, while Sumarokov's appointment as director of the first Russian theatre gave him still more leeway. After the establishment of the theatre, he wrote the tragedies *Yaropolk and Dimisa* (1758), *Vysheslav* (1768), *Dimitry the Impostor* (1771), and *Mstislav* (1774).

Sumarokov borrowed most of the plots for his tragedies from Russian history, both ancient and more recent. He considered that his prime object in the theatre was to bring to Russia the best works of the French classic theatre. His views on tragedy were derived from the famous manifesto of classic poetry, i.e., Boileau's *L'Art poétique,* in imitation of which he wrote his *Epistle on Versification.*

The style of Sumarokov's tragedies corresponds exactly to the characterization of the aristocratic classic tragedy which P. N. Sakulin gives in his book *Russian Literature:*

The construction was subject to rigid rules, of which the first was the famous rule on the three unities [1] and the division into five acts. The action is developed in a lofty heroic tone, completely eliminating the comic element. The heroes are men of high social standing and of strong passions (kings, princes, military commanders and so on). Their speeches are full of pathos and are expressed in the form of solemn declamation. Rhetoric, "the music of eloquence," is no less valued than the tragic element. The core of the tragic struggle is usually the conflict between reason and duty ("one's solemn duty," to use the eighteenth century expression) on the one hand, and emotions—particularly love—on the other. The psychology of the heroes is developed in accordance with the principles of rationalism and follows the pattern originally laid out by the author, who conceived his heroes as type patterns without variation. The contrast between positive and negative characters is sharply drawn. Schematic heroes correspond to schematic situations (*loci communes* of playwrights). Following the laws of literary didacticism, the tragic conflict must result in the triumph of virtue and the punishment of evil. This predetermines the outcome of the tragedy.

Sumarokov's obvious literary dependence on the French classics prompted Pushkin to make disparaging comments about him: "the most unfortunate of imitators"; "a weak child of other people's vices."

Is it fair, however, to accuse Sumarokov of excessive enthusiasm for the Western theatre? The development of other theatres forces us to conclude that national drama very often comes into being only as the result of long years of apprenticeship in foreign theatres which have been established earlier. Only after such a prolonged schooling can the theatre pass through its imitative period and begin to put forward its own creations alongside foreign or borrowed models.

[1] See Sumarokov's *Epistle on Versification:*
> The tragedy reveals the depths of lamentation.
> Diversion should not vainly tempt thine eyes and ear,
> Three hours cannot embrace the scope of three long years,
> So let brief hours be the measure of thy play;
> Then to myself, in ravings lost, I'd dare to say
> That even though thy skill be carefully concealed,
> Yet life, yea life itself, is brilliantly revealed.
> Nor should thy place become the source of great confusion,
> For if thou choosest Rome, it is a vain illusion.
> To shift to Moscow first, and next to try Peking:
> Beholding Rome, to Rome I wish to cling.   —Author

Belinsky was more condescending toward Sumarokov than Push-kin. Although he denied that the author of *Horeb* and *Dimitry the Impostor* possessed any talent, he emphasized the fact that "he did contribute much to literary taste in Russia as well as to the liking for the theatre." He called him "a bold and indefatigable worker" of the type that is "important, useful and indispensable to the success of literature."

Soviet students of literature have repudiated the charge that Sumarokov slavishly imitated French patterns. The latest research indicates that he tried, within the framework of the French classical system, to reveal a certain degree of independence in the form of fewer "arty" devices, in restraint, simplification, and even "naturalness."

Politically, Sumarokov belonged to the stratum of the aristocratic intelligentsia which was dissatisfied with the despotism of the tsarist regime, the unrestricted rule of the bureaucrats, and the unlimited arbitrariness of serfdom. One of his favorite writers was Voltaire.

Sumarokov often used the stage as a rostrum for the expression of his social opinions, which were bold and progressive for that period. "In highly emotional speeches Sumarokov's heroes preached the ideal of civic virtue as obligatory for monarchs as well, since they are crowned as rulers 'for the general good,' and should found their laws on truth. Thus, tragedy was a means of social education." (P. N. Sakulin.)

Sumarokov, like Racine, dealt at length with love, generally focusing the interest in the play on the heroine, as a result of which he became a kind of protagonist of a new attitude toward women. Following an era of obscurantist views he was the first to present the ideal of the moral and social significance of womanhood. He was the first to champion a woman's right to an independent emotional life, and the first to distinguish the moral aspect in love from the sensual one.

Despite his liberalism, however, Sumarokov remained faithful to the class interests of the nobility, whose rights and privileges he stanchly defended. He bitterly opposed the peasant movement— the Pugachyov uprising.

Sumarokov's contribution as the founder of Russian playwriting was rated highly by his contemporaries. I. A. Dmitrevsky, for example, submitted the following comprehensive characterization of him to the Russian Academy. In the oratorical style of the period, Dmitrévsky calls him the darling of Apollo, the friend and confidant of the muses, the expert observer of nature. "He was the first among those sweet-voiced singers who, by their enchanting melodies, have lured all the muses to Russia, who have raised Helicon in the Petropolis, and who have fused the sprightly waters of Hippocrene with the transparent streams of the Neva."

Dmitrevsky continues: "The fame of Sophocles, Euripides, and Corneille, and particularly that of Racine and Voltaire, inspired Sumarokov's soul: he deserved a place among them in the temple of immortality." But they had precursors, while "our Sumarokov had no one but himself, nothing but his heart, to guide him, and he was able, even as an adolescent, to compose an excellent tragedy, the most difficult and demanding task in all literary creation."

THE TRAGEDIES OF KNYAZHNIN AND NIKOLEV

Yakov Borisovich Knyazhnin (1742–1791), Sumarokov's son-in-law, was his immediate successor in the field of tragedy. The young poet's literary career began in 1769, with the production of the tragedy *Dido,* which promptly made him famous.

Knyazhnin continued with a series of successes, and very soon assumed a prominent place among the founders of the tragic repertoire. He wrote seven tragedies in all (*Dido, Vladimir and Yaropolk, Roslav, Vladisan, The Mercy of Titus, Sophonisbe,* and *Vadim*).

In 1783 Knyazhnin, in honor of his literary achievements, was elected one of the thirty charter members of the Russian Academy. In his playwrighting he followed the principles of classicism, imitating the tragedies of Racine, Voltaire, and others, frequently borrowing his subject matter from them. Krylov satirized his imitativeness in the stage character Rifmokradov (Rhyme Thief), while Pushkin in *Eugene Onegin* called him "mimicking."

In most of Knyazhnin's tragedies the action can hardly be attributed to any specific historical period, particularly since he himself gives no indications of chronology. His heroes are portrayed as all white or all black, incarnating sublime loftiness or unlimited in their perfidy; only the confidants of the respective leads provide some contrast. The confidants are introduced among the dramatis personae for the sole purpose of providing the heroes with foils for the expression of their thoughts and feelings. Otherwise the heroes' lengthy monologues would be excessive; even so, the resulting dialogues are, in essence, only thinly disguised monologues.

In order to acquaint the audience with the facts and circumstances of the play and to explain the relationship between the characters, the author has his hero narrate to his confidant facts with which his status should have made him familiar; yet without this preface the whole play would be incomprehensible to the audience. The device, which was originated by the early dramatists, is in no sense an invention of Knyazhnin's; but it is precisely for this reason that it is particularly characteristic of such tragedies. Here, the epic element encroaches, as it were, on the field of pure drama. Using a lavish brush for the portrayal of all his characters, the author delineates his hero's character with special force and thoroughness. Each of his individual traits, each nuance of his moods, is described in special monologues as well as throughout the dialogue. This method gives each characterization extraordinary preciseness, leaving the audience in no doubt as to the nature of the hero; but it also makes the hero's remarks boringly monotonous. The five acts of the tragedy could have been greatly shortened if the author had been able to strengthen his heroes' parts in some other way than excessively prolonging their speeches.

Compared with Sumarokov's tragedies, Knyazhnin's are characterized by more complicated plots and improved stage effects.

Influenced by the French educators, Knyazhnin, an admirer of Voltaire and a friend of Radishchev, used the stage far more than Sumarokov to propagate liberalism and civic virtue. In this respect the tragedy *Vadim* is particularly interesting; and the contrast he drew in it between the principles of republicanism and monarchism caused real alarm in government circles.

According to his son, he wrote *Vadim* and turned it over to the contemporary theatre director, G. F. Strekalov, even prior to the French Revolution. Strekalov found nothing prejudicial in it, and went so far as to distribute parts among the actors; but when the French Revolution broke out Catherine was terrified of even the slightest threats to her autocratic power. Realizing the situation, Knyazhnin withdrew his tragedy. After his death, by order of

Princess E. R. Dashkova, President of the Russian Academy, the manuscript was printed in Part 39 of the Academy's bulletin, *The Russian Theatre*. Hundreds of copies were sold within the first few days, and certain persons found it necessary to report the matter to the Empress. The Empress likened the printing of *Vadim* to the publication of Radishchev's famous *Voyage* and, on meeting Princess Dashkova at the palace, asked sharply: "What have I done to cause you to publish books opposed to my authority?"

The Senate, having examined the tragedy on Catherine's order, resolved: "To burn the said book as replete with arrogant expressions, injurious to the lawful autocratic rule, and therefore intolerable within the boundaries of the Russian Empire." The tragedy was destroyed, and only a few copies survived.

From a political standpoint, one of the most outspoken portions in *Vadim* is the monologue of Prenest (Act II, Scene 4). As late as 1871, the publishers of *Russkaya Starina* (Russian Antiquity), who reprinted the piece, were compelled to delete four lines from that monologue. Among others, it contains the following verses:

> Where is the hero crown'd who did not go astray?
> Ay, where the king, intoxicated by the bane
> Of his pretended grandeur that did not turn vain?
> Autocracy has caused much harm both far and wide,
> And even virtue's not immune to its malignant tide,
> Whilst setting passions free, invariably it brings
> A chance to make vile tyrants of anointed kings.
> Behold those potentates in ev'ry place and land.
> Divine their power, but corrupt, indeed, their hand.
> And just to show ye how their fury leaps and darts,
> And so as to enrage their foul and haughty hearts,
> I showed them all calamities, distress and woes
> Which ever on all men and lands their rule bestows.
> And 'round the throne the censors of dishonest guile
> Exalt those gods with flatt'ring words and cunning smile,
> Comparing culprits crown'd with all that is divine,
> And drown their slaves in blood to make their glory shine.

The banning of the play perhaps increased rather than decreased the number of its admirers. As late as 1817, A. F. Voyeikov wrote in his poem "Art and Science":

My most beloved tragedy's *Vadim*.
What fiery force Knyazhnin bestowed on him,
That Novgorod Brutus, that Caesar—whose renown,
Whose fame alone, shines in the glitt'ring crown.
Yes, liberty through bliss thou madest dear.
The other's tigerlike, and not benign,
Yet virtue makes him seem to men divine.
To both—alas—has fate grim fame provided,
And so their battles are ever undecided:
Here's civic pride, there—glory of a king—
No deeper note Corneille did ever ring.

Among second-rate writers of tragedy in the eighteenth century some notice should be taken of Nicholas Petrovich Nikolev (1758–1815). Having made his literary début with a satire, so popular in those days, he continued to write until his very death, and having grown blind at an early age, he sought comfort in poetic creation.

Nikolev was greatly devoted to the theatre, as well as to other forms of art, and his plays, to which he largely owes his reputation, may be considered as a token of his devotion. His best piece is *Sorena and Zamir*. Its plot is based upon the story of the Russian Tsar Mstislav's love for Sorena, the wife of the Polovetsian Prince Zamir, whose power Mstislav had usurped.

Produced in Moscow in 1785, the play met with immense success. The Moscow Commander-in-Chief, however, upon its denunciation by certain people, found the tragedy unfit for the stage and submitted the manuscript to the Empress, marking the particularly dangerous passages. Here is one:

Forever vanish thou, that fatal law
That is derived from the imperial frown.
Can bliss be sought where pride does wear the crown,
Where hearts are chained with just the whim of one?
Not aye do kings regard thee as their son.

Catherine's decision in the matter was a curious one, and may serve as a typical example of her hypocrisy. She wrote to Bryusov: "I am surprised, Count Yakov Aleksandrovich, at the fact that you suspended the performance of the tragedy which, I understand, was well received by the public. The meaning of the verses which you have noted has no bearing upon your Empress. The author challenges the despotism of the tyrants, whereas you call Catherine a mother."

The literary style of *Sorena* indicates the strong influence of Voltaire's tragedy *Alzire*. In certain respects his tragedies *Eriphile, Mahomet,* and *Semiramis* are also reflected in Nikolev's play.

THE COMEDIES OF SUMAROKOV AND KNYAZHNIN

Prior to the appearance of Sumarokov's comedies Russia had had only a series of translations. Therefore the history of the Russian comedy as a literary production also began with him. Although the exact dates of the appearance of his various pieces are not yet known, Sumarokov himself said that *Tresotinius* "was begun on the 12th of January, 1750, and was completed on the 13th," and that the comedy *The Monsters* (or *The Arbitration*) was written in the month of June, 1750, at the seaside court resort. There is no doubt, however, that he turned to comedies after writing several tragedies. He expressed his views on comedy in the following verses:

> The comedy is called to better life through laughter;
> It must make people laugh, and let them think thereafter.
> Think of a soulless clerk who sits in his *prikaz*,[2]
> Or of a judge who can't make sense of an *ukaz*.
> Or take that dandy with his silly haughty air,
> And lifelong dream about the beauty of his hair,
> Who thinks that he was born for naught but amours,
> And hopes to catch a wench who for the same thing clamors;
> Or take a Latinist who in his dissertation
> Must use that *ergo* word in ev'ry fool citation,
> Or next—a proudling ass inflated as a frog,
> Or else—a miser who will suffer as a dog
> To save his penny. Or—a gamester.

In this verse it is clear that, since comedy must "better life through laughter," it will inevitably be didactic in character.

Didacticism is generally characteristic of eighteenth century literature. Proceeding on the assumption that men's vices result

[2] *Prikaz* was normally an order; as used here it refers to a government office. —Ed.

from their ignorance of virtue, literature described the infamy of vice in order to point a moral.

Sumarokov turns his didactic derision on specific types. In his own comedies, for example, he ridicules "clerks"; he dedicates his *Narcissus* to the portrayal of a dandy; and he ridicules almost the same type of dandy in *A Petty Quarrel*. Minodora, in the comedy *The Mother-Rival*, serves as an example of those "fool wenches" whom the dandy tries to seduce; the learned pedant was satirized in *Tresotinius* and *The Grafter*; the miser, in *The Guardian*; and so forth. Sumarokov borrowed almost all of these types from the foreign plays that served as his models. His plays, too, are by no means original creations. Thus, *The Dowry by Fraud* is an adaptation of Molière's *Le Malade imaginaire*; *The Cuckold Through Imagination* is an imitation of the comedy *Le Cocu imaginaire*. In *A Petty Quarrel* and *The Querulous Woman* much has been borrowed from Molière's *Les Précieuses ridicules* and *Les Fâcheux*.

The plots of all these plays are limited to a strictly circumscribed set of episodes revolving around a rather simple love intrigue which invariably ends in a happy marriage. In the beginning of the piece, the path to the altar is blocked by some obstacle, usually either a wicked guardian trying to appropriate the fortune of his young foster daughter and at the same time to take advantage of her youth and beauty, or a foolish mother unable or unwilling to pick a worthy husband for her daughter. The obstacle is usually overcome by an adroit domestic, wholeheartedly devoted to his young master's interests, who is helped in the cause by a chambermaid, serving his master's fiancée. The chambermaid not only is well disposed towards her fellow domestic, but matches him in cunning and in devotion to her mistress. As a reward for this, when at the end of the play all obstacles have been overcome, and the leading characters are happily married, the lackey and the chambermaid find their own share of happiness. The routine, borrowed from the Western comedy, was sometimes modified, but its fundamental character remains the same.

The names that Sumarokov chose for his characters are interesting. The following persons appear in the comedy *The Guardian*, for example: Chuzhekhvat, Sostrata, Valery, Nisa, Paskvin, and Palemon. Most of these names are purely conventional, and often they cannot be associated with any specific social or national group.

Only one, Chuzhekhvat (Robber), the name of the leading character, though conventional, was selected in order to characterize the person. The majority of names of the characters in Sumarokov's plays are of this type. These descriptive names are used far more frequently than the conventional ones of foreign origin, which are, of course, more helpful in determining the source and history of each part. Sumarokov's successors realized the drawbacks of such names, which were alien to the Russian language and did not substantially clarify the characters. And so, gradually, they fell into disuse in our comedies. Yet the coining of equally descriptive names, but of a strictly Russian stamp, became all the more common, as we see in the best known comedy of the eighteenth century, *The Minor*, with its Prostakov (Simpleton), Skotinin (Beastlike), Starodum (Old-Fashioned Thinker), Kuteikin (Priest's Son), and so on.

Of all the aims which Sumarokov set forth for the author of comedies, the one in which he, as an author, succeeded least was making people laugh. In this respect, he was handicapped by excessive repetition and monotony which tired and bored the audience. In addition, the intention "to better life by laughter" resulted in an exaggerated emphasis upon moralizing, usually represented by the young heroines. The desire to give them as many virtues as possible, including good sense, removed any vestige of reality and turned them into walking caricatures.

We should also note the decided spottiness with which Sumarokov wrote some of his comedy roles, a defect that is much less noticeable in his tragedies. Along with fully delineated, and therefore completely successful, roles we find in practically each of his comedies some parts that are not at all rounded out. Minodora's role, in the comedy *The Mother-Rival*, is treated well; so is the part of Razmarin in the comedy *The Querulous Woman*, or that of Khabzey in *The Monsters*.

An excellent feature of Sumarokov's comedy is its rather animated and brisk speech, which is better than that in the translated comedies. He has the distinction of having introduced comic prose into Russia, thus paving the way for Fonvizin.

In spite of the fact that Sumarokov imitated foreign patterns in his comedies, they are also an integral part of Russian life of the period. He often used his comedies to express his reaction to con-

temporary events. He satirized many of the negative features of
the government, as well as the way of life, the customs, and culture
of the nobility. He criticized bureaucracy and injustice, ignorance
and pseudo learning, greediness and parsimony, dandyism and
modishness, the ill-treatment of domestics, the cruelty to serfs, and
so forth. Thus, despite their conventionalism and formality, Sumarokov's comedies do reveal true traits of Russian life.

Knyazhnin's plays mark a real step forward in the development
of Russian comedy. *The Braggart* and *The Queer Fellows,* for
instance, are in many respects better than his tragedies. He has
drawn his characters skillfully, and, as a result, they are specific
enough to provide rich material for a gifted actor.

The structure of Knyazhnin's comedies is far better balanced
and much more finished than those of his predecessors. They have
fewer superfluous scenes and characters; their language is more
animated, imaginative, and powerful.

They are also more realistic; the characters' manners and conversation echo the author's faculty for observing the life about him.
Criticism of the empty and corrupt nobility and of the abuses of
serfdom resound more distinctly.

N. P. Nikolev's comedies, *Tested Constancy, An Attempt Brings
No Harm, or The Successful Experiment,* and *The Ambitious
Versifier,* are typical "intrigue" plays. The action is developed primarily through adroit lackeys and soubrettes who have nothing in
common with Russian life. The comedy *The Ambitious Versifier*
(1775), which was produced in Petersburg in 1781, is the most
interesting of Nikolev's plays.

Empress Catherine II's comedies should also be noted. They are
didactic pieces conforming to the contemporary taste in literature,
and to that attitude towards the theatre which found characteristic
expression in the inscription on the curtain of the Hermitage
Theatre: *Ridendo castigat mores* (Laughter improves customs).

The action of Catherine's first comedy *O Times!* (1772) takes
place in Moscow at the house of Mrs. Khanzhakhina, and portrays
three types of women, Khanzhakhina, Vestnikova, and Chudi-
khina (Hypocrite, Gossip, and Queer Behavior), whose very names
indicate their characters. This play, as well as the subsequent
comedies *The Saint's Day of Mrs. Vorchalkina* and *Mrs. Vestni-*

kova and Her Family, condescendingly scoff at certain defects of the middle stratum of nobility.

Vanity, lack of culture, prejudice, gossip, blind imitation of French fashions, and so forth, of which society women were guilty, are subjected to particular censure. In the comedy *The Antechamber of a Prominent Boyar* the audience beholds a number of persons who come to an eminent nobleman's reception expecting great and expensive favors. Foreigners, Frenchmen and Germans in a motley group, take turns with pure Russians—all united by one desire—to live off the treasury.

The comedies *The Deceiver, The Duped,* and *The Siberian Sorcerer* were written with the special aim of exposing the "charlatanism" of the masonic societies, in which Catherine II vaguely sensed political tendencies hostile to her.

All the other rather numerous comedies of Catherine, much like those we have mentioned, are no better artistically than the mediocre plays of other dramatists of the period. Their significance is lessened also by the fact that they are not original, but foreign plays adapted to Russian customs.

In addition to comedies, Catherine wrote historical plays and comic operas.

She concealed her authorship. There were rumors in society that the Empress wrote plays; many people tried to discover who the author was, but the Empress' name was never officially mentioned. Even in her correspondence with foreign friends, Catherine rarely mentioned the fact that she wrote plays; this enabled them to pretend that they did not guess who the author of these plays actually was, and to flatter her excessively. The Empress' secretaries (Kositsky and Khrapovitsky) helped her considerably in the composition of her plays.

LUKIN AND PLAVILSHCHIKOV
THE TEARFUL COMEDY AND THE BOURGEOIS DRAMA

Along with the still prevailing classicism of the nobility during the second half of the eighteenth century a new tendency arose in Russian playwrighting, which reflected the tastes and aspirations of the merchants' class and the bourgeoisie.

The bourgeois drama began to compete successfully with the

classical tragedy, and the tearful comedy with the classical comedy. The rise of these new genres is perhaps due to the desire to democratize the theatre, to make it possible to portray on the stage the life of ordinary mortals and not only that of royalty, and to bring the drama closer to truth and simplicity.

"Comedy is opposed to sighs and sorrow," was Boileau's motto in poetry. This purely artificial separation of gayety and sorrow was abolished by the exponents of the new school, who also protested against other inflexible rules of classicism.

Plays in this new style certainly were a big step forward from the standpoint of realism and truth; yet they retained excessive sentimentality and inordinate didacticism, and the heroes' virtues were still exaggerated.

The idea and examples of bourgeois drama and of the tearful comedy came to Russia from the West, principally from France. The originators of these dramas are the French writers Destouches, La Chaussée, Diderot, Beaumarchais, and Mercier, who had been influenced by the English theatre. In their works one sees the beginnings of the ideas which paved the way to the bourgeois revolution of 1789.

Russian translations of pieces such as Lillo's *The London Merchant, or The History of George Barnwell* (1764) and Diderot's *The Affectionate Father* and *The Illegitimate Son* (1766) began to appear in the 1760's. Yelagin translated practically all of Destouches's plays. During the last decades of the eighteenth century, the following plays were translated: *Waverly* by Soren; Mercier's *Jenneval, or The French Barnwell* (1778), *The False Friend* (1779), *The Deserter* (1784), *The Destitute* (1784); and Lessing's *Miss Sara Sampson* and *Emilia Galotti* (1788–1789).

As was to be expected, the classicists were very hostile toward the new drama and attacked it vigorously. Sumarokov was particularly bitter in his criticism. In connection with the production of the Russian version of Beaumarchais's comedy *Eugénie,* published in Moscow in 1770 by Nicholas Pushnikov, the angry playwright wrote:

A new and filthy kind of tearful comedy has come into being; it has come into being but . . . the seeds of Racine's and Molière's style will not be lost. Inasmuch as our theatre has scarcely started, such wretched taste, particularly in the age of the Great Catherine, is out of place.

And in order to prevent its advent, I have written Mr. Voltaire concerning these dramas, but in a very short time they have already succeeded in insinuating themselves into Moscow, not daring, however, to appear in Petersburg. They have won general praise and applause despite the fact that *Eugénie* is disreputably translated, and that the actress performing the part of a "bacchante" under the guise of *Eugénie* played impudently. The translator, a clerk of some sort, praises this applause to the skies, which flatters the audience and encourages their tastes. A clerk has become the judge of Parnassus and the arbiter of the tastes of the Moscow public! Of course, we have to expect the day of doom in the early future. But is it possible that Moscow will give more credence to a clerk than to Mr. Voltaire and myself, and that the tastes of the people of Moscow are identical with those of that clerk?

Lukin (1737–1794) and Plavilshchikov (1760–1812) both advanced the cause of the bourgeois drama and the doleful comedy in the Russian theatre and wrote original plays of this type.

Defending the new, democratic tendency in drama and criticizing the noblemen's classicism, Lukin and Plavilshchikov also fought for the national independence of the Russian theatre; they strove, both by their plays and by drawing the theatre closer to real life, to permeate it with folk origins and to attract more representative audiences. In his endeavor to create a national theatre in which Russian life would be reflected, Lukin considered it necessary to "subordinate to our customs" even translations or adaptations of foreign plays. He categorically opposed everything in drama that did not conform to the Russian way of life, whether it was a particular kind of manners or using foreign names for the cast.

In the preface to his play *Rewarded Constancy* Lukin wrote:

It has always seemed inappropriate to me to listen to a foreigner describing and calling for the improvement of a peculiarly Russian defect—even when that defect in our customs calls for improvement. Time and again I have heard members of the audience say that not only their intelligence but also their ear is offended when characters in the play, though behaving somewhat in the Russian way, are named Klitander, Dorant, Citalida, Claudine, and deliver speeches in a way completely alien to us.

In advocating the elimination of foreignisms from Russian comedies, he advanced arguments which indicate clearly that he intended to make plays as natural as possible.

Lukin's attitude toward the actors' problem is also worth mentioning. He was a strong exponent of the theory that playwrights should write keeping in mind the types of actors at their disposal. He wrote in the preface to *The Spendthrift Reformed by Love*:

Being closely acquainted with the actors, I tried to correlate my work on the comedy with their aptitudes. For this reason, instead of making Zloradov a more sedate character so that he could exercise more authority over Dobrosedov, I turned him into a giddy goose in the first acts; and this enabled Mr. Popov, familiar with characters of this kind, to act in my comedy all the more successfully.

Unlike Sumarokov, who particularly valued the approval of the higher strata of society and bitterly complained that the theatre attracted mediocre audiences, Lukin was interested in attracting a broader public. Here is what he wrote to a friend in the provinces concerning the opening of "An All-Peoples' Theatre":

Living as you are in the country only slightly interested in the theatre, you may not have heard this gossip, and I would have felt guilty had I failed to tell you about something that every person devoted to the public weal is entitled to know. The theatre was opened on the second day of Easter; it was built on a vacant plot beyond Malaya Morskaya. Our common people manifested such an extraordinary interest in it that they ignored all the other entertainments—some of which are not entertaining at all—and attended these performances day after day. The actors are amateurs from different localities; among them two or three are fairly gifted, while all of them are excessively enthusiastic. This popular entertainment may produce not only audiences but also writers, who at first will be unskilled but eventually will improve. Briefly, I earnestly assure you that these performances are very good for the people and, therefore, deserve great praise.

Lukin also wrote in detail about his interesting conversations with his neighbors in the audience and with the actors. Among other things, he mentioned the fact that the hero's part was performed by a typesetter. And he wrote this with not even a shadow of raillery or contempt; on the contrary, he was quite sympathetic with the fact that people coming from the toiling masses were trying to raise themselves to a level of serious and wholesome entertainment. Indeed, he must be included among the first men in Russia who were ardent advocates of a people's theatre.

N. S. Tikhonravov pointed out with complete impartiality:

In the history of the theory of our comedy Lukin took a step forward, but still rather a feeble one. His own statements indicate that he was primarily concerned with the outward aspects of comedy (clothes, speech) which were out of harmony with Russian life, and, therefore, the reform itself was then limited to external aspects. Lukin, although advocating bringing comedy closer to the social life of the people, imitated the French in virtually all his comedies, with the exception of *The Spendthrift*. He failed to grasp the fact that the contents of a comedy should come directly from the life of society, while the adaptation of foreign comedies to Russian customs is a fallacy.

Among Lukin's plays the one-act comedy *The Peddler*, adapted from a French comedy, deserves special mention. The action of this play takes place in an open masquerade, where the peddler—that is, a tradesman in knickknacks—puts up his shop and sells his wares to those attending the masquerade. This strictly artificial device enabled Lukin to introduce into the loose-jointed play a whole gallery of typical members of society of that period. As each one buys an article according to his tastes and predilections, the peddler utters a few pointed and rather spiteful remarks concerning his customers. The characters include: the two fashionable women Nimfodora and Maremyana, accompanied by their escort Polidor; a retired court official Pritvorov; Vzdorolyubov (Lover of Humbug); Legkomyslov (Superficial One); Obiralov (Swindler); Verkhoglyadov (Ninny), whose names reveal their characteristics; and further, the old wooer Starosvetov (Old-Fashioned) as well as the poet Samokhvalov (Self-Praiser), who was perhaps patterned on Sumarokov.

The cast also includes the peddler's workers Miron and Vasily, who have just come from Galich. They are not necessary for the development of the action, but Lukin's attempt to bring out the idiom of their peasant speech is a substantial step forward. Here is one of Miron's retorts:

"Thanks, brother Vasyuk, for having unlocked the counter, since I have been chatting away my time with a boyar. You see he's the fellow who cares little for overseas junk, and who is eager to scold those who pay Christian money for it."

In the preface to the comedy Lukin admitted that he was incapable of capturing the full vividness of peasant speech: "The reason is that, not being a landowner, I have lived little with peasants and rarely conversed with them." Farther along he wrote, in an angry outburst against the serf owners which graphically expresses his social credo:

Verily, not all those who happen to own lands understand peasant speech, and not many landowners can be found who, out of Christian duty, take the trouble to look into these poor creatures' lot. There are those also who, because of their excessive wealth, look upon peasants not otherwise than as animals created for their lust. These haughty persons, living in luxury, often mercilessly ruin these good-hearted country folks who labor for our subsistence. Sometimes one sees innocent peasants' blood dripping from their gilded carriages, unnecessarily harnessed with six-horse teams. Thus, one may say that only those know peasants' life who, by nature, are humane, and who, considering them as equals, take good care of them.

From the standpoint of content *The Peddler* is certainly a didactic play. Both the virtuous peddler and the moralizer Chistoserdov (Pure-Hearted) point the morals. Following the custom of plays of this type, Lukin's comedy combines didacticism and satire.

Another of his plays, *The Spendthrift Reformed by Love* (1765), is typical of the bourgeois drama which he tried to promote. The didactic and sentimental nature of this play did not prevent him from creating several more or less vivid roles, so that from the standpoint of character delineation it is among the best in the eighteenth century repertoire. Lukin, the careful stylist, took a great deal of care to coordinate the characters' language with their inherent traits. The satire in the play is directed against the abuses of the contemporary judiciary.

Lukin's ideas on the Russian national theatre and on the portrayal of truth on the stage are discussed in a most curious article of P. A. Plavilshchikov, which deserves particular attention because Plavilshchikov was an actor, and therefore completely familiar with the requirements of the stage. The article, "On the Theatre," is noteworthy, too, as an indication of the contemporary interest in the theatre, and of the prevailing cultural level. However, he was a well educated person, and, therefore, more cultivated than the average actor.

Among other things, Plavilshchikov in this article raised the question:

Of what use is it to a Russian that a certain Tartar Genghis Khan conquered China, and accomplished much good there? Of what import is it to us that a certain Dido is in love with Aeneas, and that Yarb rages in his jealousy? What do we care about the irreconcilable strife portrayed in the *Sarcophagi of Verona*? First, we have to learn about the things that have occurred in our native land. Kozma Minin, the merchant, is a character most worthy of being glorified on the stage.

Believing that on the Russian stage priority should be given to everything Russian, and, above all, demanding that the theatre be truthful and realistic, he strongly protested against the prevalence of translations and adaptations:

We have filled our theatre with either imitations or translations which not only do not elevate it, but keep it enslaved and make it crawl before the originals of these translations; moreover, we borrow not from the root but from the branches. French tragedy flourished on the Greek root. Every translation is far inferior to its original, while the translation from a translation is still more inferior.

In the heat of polemic ardor he went to extremes, denying practically all merit to plays of the foreign repertoire.

Plavilshchikov also sharply criticized the theoretical rules of French classicism. The unity of place, in his opinion, compels the author "to resort to stories which, however beautiful, are never capable of moving one as strongly as the action itself."

The unity of time is nonsense, since "if dramas encompassing many years, months, and weeks fail to deceive the spectator spending but several hours in the theatre, how can twenty-four hours be compressed into two hours?"

According to Plavilshchikov, the most suitable themes for tragedy were those relating to Russian history; for comedy, plots borrowed from the life of the lower strata of society. He asked the playwrights: "Where have you hidden merchants, clerks, workers, and the entire middle class? Aren't they worthy of being represented on the stage?"

The four-act comedy *The Store Clerk* (1804) is Plavilshchikov's most characteristic play. It was produced for the first time in Moscow on the stage of the Petrovsky Theatre. Its action develops around the merchant class, which is portrayed rather satirically. This is particularly true of the treatment of the two principal characters: Khariton, a rich merchant who tries to appropriate his foster son's house in a series of speculative deals, and Khariton's wife, Mavra Trifonovna, who has many traits in common with Mrs. Prostakova.

Literary critics have expressed the idea that Plavilshchikov's *The Store Clerk* was the prototype for Ostrovsky's play *Poverty Is No Disgrace*. It is true that the plays are somewhat similar in plot; in both, the merchant's virtuous clerk, overcoming many obstacles, marries the boss's daughter who, for a while, has been threatened with a marriage to a repulsive rich man. At this point the similarity ends. However, the attempt to establish a connecting link between Ostrovsky's and Plavilshchikov's plays is quite justified: Plavilshchikov must be considered one of Ostrovsky's earliest predecessors. He wrote about the same milieu as our great playwright and succeeded in portraying it graphically. Therein lies his undeniable merit.

Plavilshchikov did not confine himself to the representation of the merchant class, however. His *Wretched and Solitary One*, which was produced for the first time in Petersburg on April 7, 1790, deals with the life of the peasants. The principal character is a homeless farmhand, Matvey. Plavilshchikov succeeded in compressing into the straightforward plot a number of successful characterizations. We have the village elder, substantially a very kind-hearted but vain peasant, and his downtrodden wife Isavna; the kulak—Paramon in embryo; and the nobleman's butler, Khvatov, a rogue with a certain amount of good nature, who has become a stranger in the village.

In spite of the fact that one finds in Plavilshchikov's comedies many artificialities and a good deal of the "commonplace," taken over from the French and at times far removed from Russian life, the subject matter, the handling of the characters, the language— all are proof that the playwright endeavored to approach the realities of life as closely as possible. The significance of these comedies in the struggle for the establishment of a Russian national theatre is undeniable.

Veryovkin (*Thus It Should Be*, 1773) and Kheraskov (*The Persecuted*, 1775, and *The Friend of the Unfortunate*) must also be included as writers of tearful comedies and bourgeois dramas. The latter, however, from the standpoint of his work in general, came closer to being a disciple of Sumarokov's. In the year 1790, the anonymous author of the comedy *A Queer Gathering*, ridiculed the sentimental dramas of the new type. The theatre lover Petukhov, satirized in the play, announces that he has written a "drama" entitled *Prison's Interior*: "All this produces in me something I even now cannot describe; I am a regular peasant woman when it comes to this sort of thing."

FONVIZIN AND KAPNIST

An outstanding place among Russian playwrights of the eighteenth century certainly belongs to Denis Ivanovich Fonvizin (1744–1792), whose comedies, according to Belinsky's apt comment, "slaughtered the savage ignorance of the older generation and the crude gloss of the superficial half-education of the younger generations."

Fonvizin's literary work began in 1761, and *Coryon: A Comedy in Three Acts Adapted from the French into Russian* was the first of his plays to be produced. *Coryon*, as Academician N. S. Tikhonravov noted, was written in a style more like Lukin's than anyone else's. There is nothing in it that would promise a future great playwright. The only way in which *Coryon* differs from Lukin's comedies is that it is in verse, and is even more didactic, a characteristic of all of Fonvizin's works. Just as Lukin's comedies constitute a transition from mere imitation to original comedy, *Coryon* is a kind of turning point in Fonvizin's work from translations to *The Brigadier* and *The Minor*.

On June 29, 1766, Fonvizin read the manuscript of *The Brigadier* to Empress Catherine. The dates of its first performance and its publication are not accurately known. Yet there are many facts indicating that the play was frequently performed even after its author's death.

Fonvizin's contemporaries were well aware of the typicalness of the characters in *The Brigadier*. Count N. I. Panin, having listened to the play at one of the readings, said to the author:

I see that you are well acquainted with our ways of life; every one of us has a close relative like Brigadier's wife: no one could say that he has no such grandmother or aunt or distant relative as Akulina Timofeyevna. This is an outstanding comedy of our mores.

Some of the characters in *The Brigadier* are very typical of the nobility during Catherine's reign; for this reason the play, apart from its purely literary merits, constitutes a rather valuable record of the history of our society. One of the most representative parts in the play is that of the Brigadier's son Ivanushka, a first-class dandy, inordinately enthusiastic for France and French ways. He is completely of the opinion, then prevalent among certain strata of society, that only "intercourse with the French and a journey to Paris can civilize at least some Russians," and that "Russia could be called civilized only when Petersburg becomes Paris; when the Russian tongue is spoken in foreign lands as much as French, or when our peasants understand French."

Even prior to Fonvizin, the character of the fop was well known to the Russian public from Sumarokov's comedies *The Monsters* (1750) and *A Petty Quarrel* (1750), and Holberg's comedy *Jean de France,* which Yelagin translated into Russian under the title *French-Russian* (first produced in 1764). The latter play exercised a marked influence on Fonvizin, as we see from the treatment of the character of Ivanushka and the general handling of the play's subject matter.

Ivanushka differs in many respects from his prototype, however, and Fonvizin has given him many original and witty, typically Russian traits.

The characters of the Councilor's wife and the Councilor himself are also easily recognizable; she is a fashionable woman preoccupied with dresses and "sweet romances"; he is an opinionated bigot, an example of the most repulsive traits of former bureaucrats, in whom greed was combined with hypocritical humility and carefully concealed lewdness.

The Brigadier's wife, an extremely ignorant woman who became insane from stinginess, partly anticipated Mrs. Prostakova.

The majority of the characters in *The Brigadier* closely resemble those in the satirical magazines of the period. The language in *The Brigadier* far excels that of Fonvizin's earlier plays; free from bookishness, it is vivid, flexible, and expressive. One need only compare the language of the Councilor's wife with that of the Brigadier's wife.

Even prior to Fonvizin, many attempts were made to create the role of a foppish woman; yet Fonvizin in his somewhat simple and unsophisticated Brigadier's wife was the first to succeed. He found the proper style for her, a real contribution.

A. M. Gorky calls *The Minor* the first "of the splendid and, perhaps, the most constructive form of Russian literature—the socially critical-realistic school," and Alexander Veselovsky observes:

The powerful moral indignation of the satirist; traits taken from life itself; a galaxy of well drawn characters; the wealth of laughter ranging from the hilarious to the tragic; the social and literary merits; the idiomatic speech never before used in Russian comedies—all make Fonvizin's comedy far better than any of our other contemporary plays. At the same time, the elements of eternal truth in the play have placed it in the Pantheon of the Russian comedy, side by side with a few immortal creations.

In this play Fonvizin bitterly attacked the abuses of serfdom, the coarseness and ignorance of the landowners, the corruption of the courts, and the mutilation of education. These were precisely the subjects that were dealt with by the journalism, comedy, and satire of his period, beginning with Sumarokov and continuing until the end of the eighteenth century. Fonvizin was far from the first to satirize these aspects of our national life, but he was the first to satirize sufficiently well to assure a lasting life for his plays.

The playwright's best character is Mrs. Prostakova. The spiteful, self-centered, and ignorant wife had been done on the Russian stage before him; but he drew Mrs. Prostakova with such completeness and expressiveness that she has overshadowed all her predecessors. Mr. Prostakov, Mitrofanushka, and Skotinin are also rather vivid characters, and Fonvizin revealed enormous talent in the portrayal of minor roles. Trishka, Vralman, Tsifirkin, and Kuteikin, for example, appear on the stage only a few moments, yet each one of them is a well rounded character. The names of all these Fonvizin heroes, from Mrs. Prostakova and Mitrofanushka all the way down to Vralman, became bywords long ago.

The characters in Fonvizin's plays are so graphic that rumors spread—as with every great satirical work—that they were patterned on contemporary people.

The language of *The Minor* is most brilliant. It is rich, pointed, and spirited. Each character in the play possesses his or her individual and highly characteristic manner of speech.

Fonvizin achieved the vitality of his characters and their language primarily by observing life itself. It has been said that when Fonvizin was writing the scene between Skotinin, Mitrofan, and Yeremeyevna he took a stroll in order to think it over carefully, and happened to come across a scuffle between two peasant women. He stopped "to watch nature," and when he wrote the scene upon his return home, he used the word "grapple," which he had just overheard.

Fonvizin borrowed certain ideas from books, however. The material on Mitrofanushka's education and his tutors' personalities was suggested by Rabelais's famous novel.

Fonvizin often followed I. A. Dmitrevsky's suggestions for the drama. F. A. Kony, one of the first biographers of the actor, contends that Fonvizin wrote the piece especially for Dmitrevsky, who, appearing in the part of Starodum, produced it at his benefit performance. No doubt the suggestions and advice of so apt a student of the theatre as Dmitrevsky must have contributed much to the perfection of Fonvizin's play.

The strikingly realistic descriptions of the landowners' way of life, the profoundly typical characters, the broadly social subject matter of the play, all combined to destroy the framework of the classical comedy into which the tradition-bound playwright had tried to compress his ideas.

The classical influence, however, is evident in the choice of romantic interest (Milon-Sophia), in the compliance with the rules of the three unities, in the "symbolic" names of the cast (Skotinin for beast, Pravdin for truth, Kuteikin for ecclesiastic), and particularly in the characters of the moralizers (Starodum, Pravdin). Fonvizin revealed no originality in creating these parts, but appropriated them *in toto* from his predecessors. P. N. Sakulin has observed with justice: "From an artistic standpoint, these proved to be abstract and formalized figures, although it in no way offended contemporary audiences, who especially enjoyed the moralizers' speeches."

The censors prevented the production of *The Minor* for a long time. According to official information, its first performance took place on September 24, 1782, with the following cast: Starodum—Dmitrevsky; Pravdin—Gomburov; Milon—Markov; Mitrofanushka—Chernikov; Skotinin—Sokolov; Tsifirkin—Krutitsky; Vralman—

Mikhail Volkov; Kuteikin—Petrov; Prostakov—Zolin; Trishka—
Rakhmanov; Mrs. Prostakova—Avdotya Mikhailovna Mikhailova;
Sophia—Milyevskaya; Yeremeyevna—Shumsky. Shumsky's playing
a woman's role is not surprising. Even for a long time after the
appearance of actresses on the Russian stage, the parts of the so-
called comic old women were successfully taken by men. Shumsky played the role of Yeremeyevna with real mastery, and it was
considered to be among the best in his repertoire.

The first performance of this play was crowned with complete
and well deserved success. *The Dramatic Lexicon* commented:

Performed for the first time in St. Petersburg, on September 14,
1782, for the benefit of the leading court actor Mr. Dmitrevsky, to an
overcrowded theatre and an audience which showed its approval by
flinging purses. The part of the nurse, to the great delight of the
audience, was played by the former leading court actor Mr. Shumsky.
. . . This comedy is replete with witty passages; it has a large cast, and
each sharply drawn character attracted the public's attention.

Shortly thereafter *The Minor* reached the provincial theatres.
We know that it was performed in Kharkov and in Tambov,
during the very first years of the theatres in those cities.

In all the eighteenth century repertoire, perhaps only *The
Slanderer* may be considered to be on an artistic level with *The
Minor*. V. V. Kapnist (1757–1824) wrote it in 1796, after com-
posing several solemn odes and satires *On Customs*.

The Slanderer was produced on August 22, 1798. The actor
Krutitsky performed the part of Krivosudov very successfully, and
his acting contributed to the success of the play. In gratitude Kapnist turned over to him the title to his comedy and allowed him to
retain the proceeds from its sale. It was enormously successful;
it was performed four times in succession, arousing much comment
in society. The success of the piece offended and incited persons
who had reason to believe that the author was attacking them.
They were seconded by others who saw in the play a temptation
to magnify the faults of the servants of justice, thus inciting hatred
of the courts.

The malcontents won out. In less than a month the play was removed from the repertoire, the printed copies were seized from

Krutitsky, and it was withdrawn from circulation. Kapnist himself narrowly escaped exile.

The Slanderer was probably not produced again befor. 1805. In the first part of the nineteenth century it was given more or less frequently. It was last performed in 1853 at the Aleksandrinsky Theatre, several times with marked success.

In the dedication of the comedy Kapnist sets forth its moral in these words:

> With Thalia's brush I pictured for my nation
> Vice, calumnies, and graft, in their abomination,
> And let the world now laugh at its ugly face.

Kapnist's theme was by no means new. Corrupt and bribed judges, under the influence of graft, and violating the principles of justice, were subjects of ridicule both in satirical magazines and in the theatre. Sokolov's comedy *The Judge's Saint's Day,* which depicted the corruption, ignorance, and greediness of judges, is one of the best of *The Slanderer*'s predecessors.

Kapnist attacked all these faults of Russian justice with increased vigor. The principal characters in *The Slanderer* are: the president of the Civil Court, Krivosudov; its members, Bulbulkin, Atuyev, Radbin, and Parolkin; the public prosecutor, Khvataiko; and the secretary of the Civil Court, Kokhtin.

Krivosudov, the chief exponent of justice, is graphically described in these verses:

> The civil president, the Court's supreme curator,
> Is Judas in disguise and truth's most flagrant traitor;
> He never acted straight—not even by mistake—
> His pockets bulge with graft, graft is his only stake.
> He feels that by no law he ever will be bound—
> Thus cases are adjudged with neither truth nor ground.

The members of the Civil Court are worthy "colleagues" of Krivosudov:

> They all are in accord, they have a common way.
> One member of the Court is almost daily drunk,
> And so his head is full of nonsense and of junk.
> His colleague's fond of naught but lively hunting-grounds
> Where hares are chased around by packs of eager hounds
> Which even God-sent truth will readily attain.

The public prosecutor is a "patent thief":

> The thing beyond his reach alone he will not steal,
> And graft for truth or lie—is what he calls square deal.

The entire play is devoted to the description of the activities of the members of the Court. Kapnist showed his heroes both in their official duties and in their private lives. He had the courage to produce a court session on the stage which left the audience awe-stricken. His third act, which represents a drinking bout staged by the judges at the expense of Pravolov, the rich man who gets them all drunk, is particularly successful. The intoxicated judges sing this little song:

> Grab, fellows, grab, it's not a tricky task.
> Grab all you can—this is our only aim.
> What is the use of hands, emphatic'ly we ask,
> If not to grab whatever be the game?
> Grab, fellows, grab—it is our only aim!

This song reveals best of all the ideology of the class which Kapnist chose to satirize. His success in describing the criminal activities of judges such as Krivosudov and his colleagues was achieved not by means of abstract discourse, but by embodying his ideas in living dramatic characters. The images of Krivosudov, his wife, and Pravolov are among Kapnist's most successful parts. The world of judges and government officials portrayed in *The Slanderer* most nearly approximates that in Gogol's *The Inspector-General*. Kapnist's comedy may justifiably be considered along with the greatest Russian comedies, if one is to consider *The Slanderer* as a decisive advance towards that excellence which *The Inspector-General* was to achieve.

Chapter IX

SUMMARY OF THE EIGHTEENTH CENTURY

PETER'S CUSTOM of using the theatre to record events important for the state or for the Imperial family continued in full force during the reigns of his successors.

Such shows were staged at the court both in Russian and in foreign languages, and a special person was engaged to write them. In the 1740's this office was held by the Italian Bonecci, who came to Russia from Florence about 1742. Having later obtained permission to return to Italy, Bonecci entered into an agreement

to prepare every year, during his sojourn in Italy, and dispatch in good time to the chancery of His Imperial Majesty's Court, two dramatic pieces of his own composition in connection with the following most solemn dates: the first for the Coronation Day of His Imperial Majesty —that is, April 25th; and the second for Her Imperial Majesty's Saint's Day—that is, September 25th. For this service, according to the contract, he was entitled to a remuneration of 200 rubles per annum.

In 1744, during Elizabeth's journey to Kiev, the students of the local Academy staged a performance in her honor, in which the Kiev Prince Vladimir, appearing in the midst of the Greek gods, called the Empress his heiress.

Prince M. M. Shcherbatov, referring to Catherine II, in his well known essay "On the Corruption of Customs in Russia," stated:

Praises to her thundered everywhere, in orations, literary compositions, and even in ballets staged in the theatre, so that I myself heard her say at one of the performances of the ballet portraying the Chesma Battle at the Corps of Cadets: "Il me loue tant qu'enfin il me *gâtera.* (He praises me so much that, in the end, he will spoil me.) I should be happy if impulses of the soul would conform to these words, but alas!" When she uttered this remark, her soul was intoxicated with pomp and flattery. Nor did Ivan Perfilyevich Yelagin make any effort to flatter her less either privately or publicly. While he was director of the theatre, many works were composed in her honor; ballets glorified her deeds; the great arrival of the Russian fleet in Morea would be announced with great fanfare; the Chesma Battle would be glorified; or Spring would be dancing with Russia.

N. Emin used the Swedish victory in 1790 as the subject for a one-act prologue, in which, among other ancient deities, Minerva appeared, and, addressing herself to her father Zeus, praised Catherine for the fact that "no one among the crowned heads has ever abided so piously by the code enacted by me."

Felicia (Catherine), whom Minerva's discourse praised, was the patron of arts and education. "She cleared the way for maidens and youths to learn straightforward truth and wisdom, and to direct their aspirations to the good of their countrymen." Catherine is also eulogized for establishing a Foundling Home, which will save from death "the unhappy fruit of unmarried love." The whole population is to see in Felicia the source of its welfare.

The specific ideas and even the characters of this prologue are so similar to Derzhavin's pompous odes that Emin's dependence on his famous contemporary is obvious.

These spectacles offered little opportunity for acting; luxurious stage sets and elaborate scenic effects were their main adornment. The public attended these performances not for entertainment but to express their feelings of loyalty; and the authors wrote such plays in the hope of a liberal reward for their ardent eulogies of the Empress and her favorites.

Performances of this kind were also staged in the provinces, for instance at Tver, when the Empress' grandsons, Alexander and Constantine, were passing through that town. A play written by Michael Prokudin, an officer of the Guards, was staged at Vladimir to celebrate the establishment of the province's governorship.

In connection with the opening of a school at Tambov, G. R. Derzhavin, the governor of Tambov, produced at his home a prologue of his own composition in which the Hermit appeared in a forest amid Greek muses, offered praise to "him who in the woods paved the way for them to light, magnificence, and splendor."

There are even exceptional cases of the prologues being staged as late as the early part of the nineteenth century, especially in the provinces. Their artistic value is negligible. They deserve mention only because they strikingly reveal the theatre's dependence, during the first decades of its existence, upon the court. For the court, the theatre served to display its splendor and spread the glory of the Imperial family, as well as to express their views on individuals and events advantageous to the court and the social strata which supported it.

With the growth of public consciousness, however, the theatre began to rid itself more and more of the influence of the court, and grew from a mere court appurtenance into a powerful weapon of art and enlightenment.

The Russian theatre of the eighteenth century inscribed a brilliant page in the history of Russian art, and brought many illustrious artists to the foreground. The shackles of ecclesiastical interdict, which for centuries had chained the creative power of the people, were shaken off. Our theatre was established in a sound, though imperfect, way, and began to catch up with the Western theatre then producing Shakespeare, Molière, and Lope de Vega, playwrights whom no one in Russia, except a few travelers, had ever seen on the stage. The Russian translations of their works, though not completely satisfactory, made their charm accessible to people who could not have read them in the original.

Our leading playwright, Sumarokov, was quite proud of Voltaire's approval of his adaptation of Racine's *For the Russians*. Sumarokov's successors brought the progressive comedies of Diderot and other "enlighteners" to our stage. Along with artificial and spurious pieces, whose only use was the gratification and amusement of the court and landowner circles, the comedies of Knyazhnin, Fonvizin, and Kapnist came into existence. *The Minor* was an excellent mirror in which the author came face to face with Russian reality, and looked directly at it, without distortion, and reproduced it with a wonderful artistic understanding" (V. O.

Klyuchevsky). And that mirror could not help reflecting all the vileness and deceit of a rotten regime where idlers and ignoramuses were sovereign rulers of "serf souls."

In the course of several decades our opera managed not only to master the achievements of Western music but to provide ample scope for the creative efforts of the former serfs who, even in Italy, had by that time made a great contribution to music.

All in all, our eighteenth century theatre was not a place for the "interpretation of foreign whims" but for developing native talent. Our actors—Russian Lekains[1] learned not only the complicated methods of classical acting, but also the art of giving real enjoyment by simple and sincere acting wherever the germ of realism in plays permitted it; and they were particularly moved by the beauty and truth of folk songs. Thus, the early amusements of our native buffoons were gradually interwoven with the well learned techniques of Western masters in drama, opera, and ballet.

Sir George Macartney,[2] the British Ambassador to the Russian Court (1764–1766), wrote about our theatre, "I attended the performance of *Hamlet* and of *Mérope* with pleasure. Even though these pieces are mere adaptations, they are excellently suited to the Russian stage. . . . Sumarokov reformed the Russian theatre from the standpoint of decorum, practices, and sumptuousness of production."[3] Such is the comment of an observer not at all disposed to judge overindulgently.

Our young theatre gradually grew from an object of noblemen's entertainment into a theatre for the people and for their creative expression. Many talents developed to full artistry despite the adverse conditions which were prevalent in the serf theatre. And the broad support of the people, who quickly adopted one of the most complex of cultural expressions, strengthened the theatre and taught it to mirror their joy and their sorrow.

[1] Referring to Henri-Louis Cain, celebrated contemporary French actor.—Ed.
[2] Macartney (1737–1806) was sent to the Court of St. Petersburg in August, 1764, to conclude a commercial treaty with Russia.—Ed.
[3] *Russkaya Starina*, 1887, No. 9, p. 522.

THE THEATRE OF THE
FIRST HALF OF THE
NINETEENTH CENTURY

DURING the first half of the nineteenth century the repertoire and the directorship of our theatre expressed the tastes of the upper strata of the nobility and the court aristocracy. Hence, we have the encouragement of plays permeated with loyalty to the crown, and produced with a great lavishness that was particularly obvious in the ballet. But soon a people's movement called forth by Napoleon's invasion, the contacts of the nobility—who had not forgotten the 1789 Revolution—with Europeans, and the spread of education brought the progressive elements of society into conflict with despotism. Conventional classicism in art was followed by romanticism, and later, by realism. The plays of Pushkin, Griboyedov, Lermontov, and Gogol were full of condemnation for government policies. Shchepkin came up from the serf class. In addition to actors favored by the court (Karatygin, Sosnitsky), there developed the stormy talent of Mochalov, who was ardently supported by Belinsky's young radicals. In opera, folk melodies were brilliantly used by Glinka—music unappreciated by the court, which in those very years began to expend fabulous sums on imported Italian musicians.

Chapter X

THE ACTORS AND THE REPERTOIRE
OF THE EARLY PART OF THE
NINETEENTH CENTURY

THE SHORT REIGN of Emperor Paul left practically no mark on the work of the Imperial theatres. Any changes in the theatre that were made during his reign were without great significance. Once, noticing two ballet dancers among the spectators at a regimental parade, he asked how they happened to be there and, learning that they enjoyed this spectacle, promptly issued a decree that in the future the ballet company be obliged to attend every military parade held in front of the palace.

Alexander I was not fond of the theatre, and besides, the complicated political situation compelled him to spend much time away from the capital. The government officials in charge of the theatre management, therefore, had a free hand. Director of the Theatres, Naryshkin, and later, Tyufyakin, with their appointees, were autocratic masters of the theatre's fate.

Along with the official administration, in the early part of the century, a group of persons though not officially connected with the theatre, exercised a strong influence upon the whole course of theatrical life. With their financial independence and education, they formed the élite of the capital's enlightened and wealthy elements. Many of them had formerly lived in the West, especially in Paris, where they had pursued Napoleon's retreating armies. In the West they had become acquainted with the theatres and with the acting of the great Talma and the beginning career of the famous actress Mademoiselle George. Upon their return to Russia, they tried to realize on our stage those things which had so delighted them in Paris.

With leisure time at their disposal, these theatre lovers attended performances almost daily. Because they had their favorite seats in the first rows on the left side, they became known as "the left flank." In the memoirs of theatre enthusiasts of the period, the influence of "the left flank" upon the plays and the actors is frequently mentioned. Some of them became theatre habitués in order to spend time with actors and actresses. The correspondence between P. A. Katenin and A. M. Kolosova indicates how well our theatre lovers of those days knew the French theatre. An exile on his Kostroma estate, Katenin inquired from Kolosova, who was then visiting Paris, about the actors whom he once had seen there; and he went into the most minute description of their acting, so that nothing was left to Kolosova but to confirm the correctness of Katenin's observations. Having learned about the forthcoming production of a new play in Paris, Katenin speculated as to the possible distribution of the parts; and in most cases his guesses proved to be correct.

Knowing for whom each part in a French piece had been written, and intimately familiar with the actors' special talents, these theatre lovers were in a position to make suggestions to the actors when adaptations of French plays were produced on the Russian stage.

Eighteenth century satire frequently ridiculed contemporary acting as well as the prevailing customs in the theatre. For instance, N. I. Strakhov in *The Correspondence About the Mode* (1791) had one of his characters (an actress referring to her fellow actors) entreat Mode: "Do make the screaming of the actors and the whispers of the actresses bearable, and do see to it that people find it pleasant when we speak in singsong and when, performing their parts, they squeal." These somewhat exaggerated defects, of course, persisted in the nineteenth century, and for a long time it was necessary to wage a stubborn battle against them.

Among the theatre lovers were such men as Katenin and Gnedich, whose interest in the theatre proved most beneficial. Attending practically all performances, they could not help noting the growth of every actor's talent. No matter how good an actor was, if he came to a standstill in his development and stopped working to improve his technique, he could no longer satisfy these habitués who, in this way, constantly made for the actor's progress. Theatre lovers frequently helped the actor by pointing out to him the part from the Western repertoire that would suit him best. In this way our stage benefited from excellent examples of the foreign repertoire about which neither our actors nor the theatre directorship would otherwise have known. The assistance included suggestions as to the translation of the play, and the translation would often be timed for the leading actor's benefit performance.

In those days translators had the silly habit, inherited from the preceding century, of not confining themselves to exact translation but adapting a piece "to our customs." The "customs" of the play were by no means made "ours," and the play was completely un-Russian, even though the translator substituted Russian words and names for the foreign ones. During Alexander's reign, not even Molière's plays escaped this barbaric remodeling: Célimène became Prelestina (Delightful) in the Russian theatre. Because of this, it is now virtually impossible to determine which comedy of the period's repertoire was original, and which was a translation, unless the original is well known.

The theatre lovers' criticisms constituted a kind of extension of the actors' school training. In case disagreements arose among theatre lovers as to the progress of their favorites, however, the actor was the one to suffer, because each habitué, supporting his artist, tried in every way to undermine the rival artist's success. The gifted actress A. M. Kolosova (1802–1880), who later married the famous tragedian Karatygin, is a striking example of this. The daughter of the well known ballerina Kolosova, she made up her mind, after graduating from a boarding school, to go on the stage.

At first she chose as her instructor the exceedingly influential Prince A. A. Shakhovskoy. Here is how she describes his system of instruction in her memoirs:

As a teacher of declamation, Prince Shakhovskoy trained several good actors for comedy. In tragedy, however, his instruction was faulty. Shakhovskoy's pedagogic method consisted in listening to the recitation of his pupil, whether male or female, and thereupon reciting himself, insisting upon a slavish imitation of his manner: this was something like playing or whistling over all sorts of tunes to a trained bullfinch or a canary. He indicated, moreover, at which particular verse one would have to step on the right foot, drawing the left one aside, and at which point one was to swing over to the left foot, stretching out the right foot. This pose, in his judgment, gave the elocutionist a majestic air. One verse was to be uttered in a whisper, and, after a pause, he would indicate, with both hands, the actor standing near by, and have him recite the concluding monologue quickly. It was not difficult to memorize his technical expressions, yet it was hard not to be led astray and not to be swayed by one's own feeling.

Kolosova tried to vindicate Shakhovskoy's system on the ground that for the most part he had to instruct completely illiterate people who would, for instance, stubbornly insist on calling England not "Albion" but "Albino."

Not satisfied with his teaching, Kolosova turned to P. A. Katenin for instruction. Shakhovskoy and his very influential friend, Governor General Miloradovich, began to attack her bitterly and to deprive her of her roles. She then decided to withdraw temporarily from the stage and go to Paris with her mother. There she took lessons from the famous Talma, who originated the realistic form of declamation, and from the actress Mars. While in Paris, she corresponded with her teacher Katenin, who was dying of boredom in exile on his Kostroma estate. The correspondence would do honor to our best educated contemporary actress. In addition to acting, the letters discussed all the literary news, with which the young actress was apparently completely familiar. After she became a prominent actress, sharing successes with her husband until 1844, she translated the play *Esmeralda*, adapted from Hugo's novel. Her training in Paris proved of great value to her. Célimène in *The Misanthrope* was later the best part in her extensive repertoire.

On her return from Paris, Kolosova had to put up with the dissatisfaction of Shakhovskoy and his friends for a long time. When she was invited to Moscow as a guest-artist and, by order of the Governor General, detained for one day beyond her leave, she was put under arrest at the office of the theatrical management.

P. A. Karatygin, in the preface to the excerpts from his father's diary, drew a vivid picture of the status of actors during Alexander's reign:

Sixty years ago the attitude of Russian society toward actors was by no means similar to that in ancient Rome, where the calling of an actor was considered honorable. Our Roscii [1] were looked down on by the nobles from the heights of their supremacy and were treated as buffoons, as persons belonging, if not to a reprobate caste, then at least to a useless and perhaps even harmful one. Actresses, female singers, and dancers, in contrast, enjoyed gentlemen's favors. But, speaking of these, they could have cited Liza's words in *Woe from Wit*:

> Let us beware more than of any sorrows
> Of masters' wrath as well as of their love!

There were but few honest priestesses of art. The nobility's outward patronage of talented actresses merely masked flirtation and immoral designs. In order to please the patrons, the theatre management gave every encouragement to their female favorites, and played down the actress' rivals. . . . The slightest disrespect on the part of women or men colleagues towards the ballerina odalisque, led to cruel punishment by their superiors. In that golden age becoming an actor deprived every nobleman who dared to put his foot on the theatrical stage of all personal rights and privileges; for a nobleman, having become an actor, was at the mercy of the theatrical management, which had at its disposal very convincing punitive measures in the form of jails and reform schools. Female singers and ballerinas, as we have mentioned, were usually "kept" by noble patrons. The majority of the actors were noted for their inability to behave with dignity. Bachelors, moving in a set of rich merchants, drank heavily and combined the humiliating role of parasites with the despicable role of jesters and entertainers.

Married men, good husbands and fathers, humbled themselves before the venerable public, especially in anticipation of the benefit performance. Until 1833, in all the capital's theatres it was customary to announce to the audience from the stage the plays which were to be performed the next day. When benefit performances were announced, the beneficiaries themselves, both men and women, would sometimes lead out their minor children on the stage in order to soften the hearts of the audience. When a benefit performance was granted to the widow or orphans of an actor, this practice was always followed; and the younger the children the greater the assurance of substantial returns.

Having planned the benefit performance, the actor or actress, assisted by the author or translator, began to compose the text of a poster—not less than eighteen inches in length—full of the most alluring descriptions. Adjectives such as "mysterious," "dreadful," and "bloody" were

[1] Quintus Roscius Gallus (c. 126–62 B.C.), born a slave. Roman actor famous for his grace and elegance on the stage, especially excelling in comedy; a friend of Cicero.—Ed.

inevitable. The list of new sets, effects, costumes, down to the number of gunshots to be fired and of Bengal lights to be used—all these added spice to the benefit performance poster. Beneficiaries with families added to the play divertissements in which their minor children would recite fables, sing, or dance. Five days or so prior to the benefit perform- ance some of the theatre personnel would begin their round of calls at the homes of the patrons and benefactors.

The cashier Solntsev, who was well acquainted with the Petersburg theatre lovers of the Alexander period, led the theatrical Argonauts on their expeditions. Splendidly dressed, beneficiaries made visits first to His Highness Count Michael Andreyevich Miloradovich, after that to the nobles, then to the eminent merchants, and after them the second- guild "persons," and finally to rich plebeians. . . . Where the actors were not received, at least tickets were usually bought. In some homes, the actor or actress would be shown to the door, not very politely. Those who bought tickets received programs printed on colored paper (some- times they were even printed in gold on satin). Patrons, of course, paid more than the fixed price of the ticket. (Otherwise what would have been the use of these solicitations?) Many respectable family men, members of our dramatic, operatic, and ballet companies, would start out on these humiliating ventures in jesters' costumes, wigs, and stage make-up. . . . Moreover, they would take their little children along with them, dressed in Russian or gypsy costumes, and force them to dance to the accompaniment of a guitar or a *torban*.[2] The artists of the Imperial theatres competed on a level with organ grinders and street jesters! Not one of them would have considered this kind of practice either odd or humiliating.

In the beginning of the nineteenth century there were two brilliant actors in the Russian theatre: Aleksey Semyonovich Yakovlev and Catherine Semyonovna Semyonova. The artist to whom Shusherin eventually had to cede his place, Aleksey Sem- yonovich Yakovlev (1773–1817), was the son of a Kostroma mer- chant. At an early age he became an orphan and was cared for by his guardian, also a merchant. Having received his early educa- tion from a kind-hearted neighbor, a woman engaged in baking Eucharistic wafers, and later in a parish school, he became his guardian's clerk. Yakovlev's passion for reading prevented him from concentrating sufficiently on trade, and a salesman in a neighbor- ing shop excited his imagination through his stories about the

[2] Ukrainian stringed instrument similiar to a guitar, but without metal frets on finger board.—Ed.

theatre. He and his friend went to see the tragedy *Dimitry, the Impostor* with Shusherin in the lead, and this produced such an impression on them that they decided to organize their own performances at home.

Later, when Yakovlev was no longer dependent on his guardian and had gone into business for himself, he was still absorbed in reading and in the theatre. He even tried his hand at writing plays. The suicide of an army officer, for example, furnished him with the material for *The Desperate Lover*. He was particularly fond of reading Plutarch, and wrote in one of his poems, "Without Plutarch my life seems weary." Subsequently, his subjective state prompted him to read the literature of the Masonic order. This brought the gifted merchant to the attention of an influential theatre lover who introduced him to Dmitrevsky; and Dmitrevsky directed his talent throughout his entire career.

Yakovlev's manly beauty, his sonorous, moving voice, and his expressive, sincere declamation immediately appealed to Dmitrevsky, who forthwith expressed the desire to work with him seriously and coached him in the part of Askold in Sumarokov's *Semira*. He then unhesitatingly arranged a public début for his pupil as Askold, which took place on July 1, 1799. On September 1, Yakovlev was engaged in the Petersburg Company. He was particularly successful in the translated plays of Kotzebue—as Meinau in *Misanthropy and Repentance* and as the patriot Wolf in *The Hussites Before Naumburg*. According to contemporary accounts, the power of Yakovlev's talent lay in the depth of his feelings and the passion of his acting. Impulsive inspiration, rather than careful and well thought out preparation of a part, was responsible for his success, completely unlike Shusherin.

Zhikharev, one of the most ardent theatre lovers of those days, described Yakovlev's acting in his memoirs:

The more I see Yakovlev, the more he astonishes me. Today he amazed me in the part of Meinau in the drama *Misanthropy and Repentance*. What a talent! How masterfully he acted in certain scenes, especially in the one where Meinau weeps real tears at the thought of his wife's treachery and of the loss, with her going, of his whole life's happiness. With incomparable and genuine feeling he uttered the words, "Be welcome, you long absent guests"—words which made the audience burst into tears; and the pantomime of the unexpected meeting with his wife when, just as he enters his host's study, he sees her unexpectedly, and, all shaken, he turns back abruptly. This scene is the height of perfection! I never imagined that an actor without any the-atrical tricks, without wearing an elaborate costume, by the mere power of his talent, could move the audience so profoundly.

Yakovlev himself wrote of his acting as well as of the tastes and requirements of the audiences of those days:

During my first years in the theatre I tried to play this way and that way, but to no avail. Then I made up my mind to utter modestly but firmly, as the occasion warranted, the words: "Rosslav, I'm crowned with laurels, but still I am in shackles!" Then what happened? The audience was dead-silent, not the slightest applause! Well, I said to myself, never mind, next time I will treat you to your heart's content! And, in fact, at the next performance of Rosslav, at this place, I cried out the words as loudly as I could, so that I grew ashamed of myself, and lo! the audience got terribly excited, and almost all of them jumped off their seats. . . . Later, when the public began to like me, I began to act more boldly and more intelligently; however, I had to work assiduously to rid myself of the desire to give the public a treat in well known passages. Ambition is the devil's gift.

Faulty education was often manifest in Yakovlev's acting, for instance in thoughtless and unwarranted gestures. Like all other actors of his type, he played unevenly: within one part, along with excellent passages, there were completely unpolished scenes; and, just as he could act superbly when in high spirits, his playing when uninspired was very bad. Intoxicated by success, he stopped working to improve his acting; his only aim was to adapt himself to the tastes of the audience—and the audience in those days for Russian shows was not overdiscriminating or well informed. According to contemporaries, persons who knew French even slightly considered it unbecoming to attend Russian performances; and the actors were justified in their complaint that, on the days of French performances six-horse teams stood in long rows outside the theatre, while on Russian nights one hardly saw a single team. The Russian performances appealed only to rather dull people, the middle class, and the simple people. Yakovlev became overconfident, because of exaggerated praise from that type of audience.

With the appearance of Ozerov's tragedies *Oedipus in Athens* (performed for the first time on November 23, 1804) and *Fingal*

(December 8, 1805), Yakovlev's triumphs increased. According to contemporaries, after certain of his speeches in these roles "the theatre groaned with applause." But the climax of his career occurred on the night of the first performance of Ozerov's third tragedy, *Dmitry Donskoy,* on January 14, 1807. That was during our second war against Napoleon; the feeling of vengeance over the disgrace of Austerlitz was steadily rising. When Yakovlev opened the play by uttering with unusual dignity the famous verse, "The time has come to wreak vengeance on our foes," the theatre was shaken by applause, and the reception increased until it reached an extraordinary pitch, according to an eyewitness:

When Dmitry Donskoy, offering thanks for the victory, knelt down and, extending his arms toward heaven, said,

"To thee, O Lord, who rul'st all kingdoms and all things,
To thee hearts' praise is due, to thee, O King of kings!
Great God, bestow on Russia bliss and august fame,
Make all her haughty foes obedient and tame,
So that they might exclaim, all trembling 'fore her sword.
Ye nations, learn and know that great is Russia's Lord!"

everybody was seized with such enthusiasm that no words can adequately describe it. . . . Many spectators embraced each other with rapture. People even started shouting "Encore"—unheard of in a tragedy! Actors did not know what to do. Finally, the audience in the front rows began to shout, "Repeat the prayer!" and Yakovlev came out to the footlights, knelt down and repeated the prayer. Even then the ecstasy did not subside.

These great stage successes were darkened, however, by Yakovlev's most unhappy private life. He had the misfortune to fall in love with a married woman, an actress. The love which he bestowed with all the ardor of his passionate nature was not returned, and it became the disaster of his life. Neither liquor, nor love of other women—not even marriage to a young actress, the daughter of a court musician, Shiryayev (August 16, 1815)—could cure his spells of melancholy. He used to express his gloomy moods in verse.

Beginning in 1813, these spells became increasingly frequent. With his alcoholic excesses his once beautiful voice grew hoarse; he was inspired less and less often, and, aware of his decline, turned almost all of his parts over to a young actor, Bryansky. Only in the roles of Agamemnon in Racine's *Iphigénie* and Karl Moor in Schiller's *The Robbers* did he have fleeting moments of brilliance, reminding one of his faded talent.

On October 24, 1813, Yakovlev made an unsuccessful attempt at suicide, after which his return to the stage was greeted with general rejoicing. Four years later, however, illness undermined his health, and he died at the age of forty-four.

A contemporary poet wrote the following epitaph:

No more is Yakovlev, that Russia's great Lekain!
He plunged our hearts in grief, with dread he smote them down,
In Dmitry and Rosslav he set our souls aflame,
And now he rests in peace, proud of his laurel crown.
Fair Art and he were one, to Fame he gave his name.

While Yakovlev was living, Catherine Semyonovna Semyonova shared his fame. After his death she assumed uncontested first place among nineteenth century actors. Catherine Semyonova (1786–1849) was the daughter of a landowner and one of his women serfs. She was sent to the dramatic school, where Dmitrevsky, always quick to discern stage talent, took notice of her immediately. He permitted her to perform responsible parts on the stage even before her graduation. At that time she played Nanine in Voltaire's comedy of the same title (1803), and she participated in the performance of Plavilshchikov's *Yermak* and in Ozerov's *Oedipus* (1804). After graduation she was at once engaged in the company on unusually favorable terms as the female romantic lead both in comedy and in tragedy, with an annual salary of 1,200 rubles plus 200 rubles for her personal wardrobe.

Prince Shakhovskoy took over the direction of her career, coaching her in many parts. Semyonova helped win admirers for the classical repertoire by performing many classical roles. Men of letters translated, or rather adapted, such plays especially for her, convinced that, by participating in them, Semyonova would assure their lasting success. N. I. Gnedich, for example, translated *King Lear* for her in the French adaptation of Ducis.

However, her stage career was very closely linked to the name of Ozerov. Pushkin remarked about him:

There, Ozerov was once applauded
With young Semyonova, and lauded
By all the folk, whose tears he wrung.

How true! Most of Ozerov's plays were written in the obvious
hope that Semyonova would act in them. Both *Fingal* and, particularly, *Dmitry Donskoy* owe their extraordinary success to Semyonova. But she, in turn, found Ozerov's tragedies an excellent
vehicle for her talent. Their gifts developed simultaneously, each
complementing the other, and making for mutual success.

After Shakhovskoy, N. I. Gnedich became Semyonova's adviser;
and he transmitted to her his own style of reciting verses. It was
said that she learned her parts from copybooks in which every word
was either underscored or overlined by Gnedich, depending upon
whether the voice was to be raised or lowered, while between the
lines, notations were made in brackets, such as: "with rapture,"
"with contempt," "gently," "in delirium," "beating the chest,"
"raising the hand," and "lowering the eyes." He was enamored
of the famous actress, which was a further reason to foster her
talent. When presenting her with a copy of his translation of *King
Lear*, he wrote:

Accept, Cordelia, *King Lear* of mine.
He's thine, adorned by that fine gift of thine.

The performances of the famous guest-actress George (1808)
also influenced Semyonova's acting. All theatrical Petersburg was
interested in her performances, particularly since society's curiosity
was greatly aroused because of her friendship with Napoleon.
George's original manner of declamation also evoked interest: she
declaimed verses not in the usual way but drawlingly and in a
singsong fashion. She also impressed the audience when, after
speaking forcefully and loudly, she lowered her voice suddenly to
a whisper, still audible in the farthest corner of the theatre. Words
uttered in a whisper were enunciated so clearly that each stood out
particularly sharply. George was fond of trying to impress the
audience by going from extraordinarily quick speech to separate
words and whole sentences spoken with slow deliberateness.

Semyonova did not miss a single play in which George took
part. Both she and her friend Gnedich felt that George was be-

coming the leading light in the Petersburg theatrical world, and that, even after her departure, she would spoil Semyonova's success. In order not to cede her supremacy to the Frenchwoman, Semyonova was forced to enter into an open contest with her rival. For this purpose, Gnedich translated *Tancred*, in which George had appeared. On January 9, 1809, Semyonova performed the role of Amenaide in *Tancred*, with George in the audience. The French actress was the first to pay tribute to Semyonova's talent, and the public acclaimed her "the Russian George."

In this part Semyonova demonstrated that she had fully mastered the principal features of George's dramatic style. The public, seeing that *our* Semyonova played almost as brilliantly as the illustrious foreign actress, admired her all the more. True, some connoisseurs asserted that in imitating George's style she destroyed her inherent gift, and that her acting deteriorated from that time. In 1811 the rivalry between George and Semyonova again shifted to Moscow, where they appeared in the same roles. This competition increased the interest in the theatre and divided the public into two camps: "the Georgists" and "the Semyonovists." The latter won at least the battle of generosity by presenting Semyonova with a diamond diadem costing 100,000 rubles, after her benefit performance in *Tancred*. During 1811 the box-office receipts in Moscow totaled 400,000 rubles, thanks partly to these actresses.

On October 7, 1818, A. Ya. Bulgakov wrote to Prince Vyazemsky about Semyonova's Moscow appearances:

The Russian Georgine came to visit us. Everybody is rushing to the theatre, so that Maikov, the theatre director, has become more important than Tormasov, the Governor General. Semyonova played Antigone, Mérope, Iphigenia, and she is expected to appear as Amenaide, Xenia, and Mary Stuart, and will go away after her benefit performance. The theatre is crowded.

Several days later a certain Sushkov appeared in the theatre, and when the curtain fell, he began calling for Semyonova, who had not played on that particular day. People told him: "For goodness' sake, Semyonova did not act today!" But Sushkov, who was drunk, cursed and continued to shout: "Give us Semyonova!" The Chief of Police tried to stop him, but he retorted: "Bring on Semyonova! I have 1,000 rubles for her in my pocket! I will fling this money to her on the stage!" He was thrown out and made to sign a pledge never to revisit the theatre. This episode is indicative both of Semyonova's great popularity and of the contemporary manners of the audience.

Contemporaries have written that, in playing Catherine, Semyonova's appearance, from facial expression to her manner of walking, had a sublime and exceptionally noble quality. An excellent tragédienne, she was unable to play in ordinary dramas, which seemed to diminish her talent, and which, by their prosaic nature, did not do her justice.

Pushkin, in his *Notes on the Russian Theatre*, wrote of Semyonova:

Graced with talent, beauty, and a live, genuine feeling, she developed her own style. Semyonova never did have a prototype. The soulless French actress George and the everlastingly enraptured poet Gnedich were merely able to give her a glimpse into those secrets of art which she divined through the revelation of her own soul. Her free, invariably lucid acting, the grandeur of her animated gestures, her pure, even, and pleasing voice, and the frequent bursts of genuine inspiration—all these were part of herself and were borrowed from no one.

She adorned the works of the unfortunate Ozerov, and it was she who created the roles of Antigone and Moine; she brought life to the measured lines of Lobanov; it was through her lips that we came to like Katenin's Slavonic verses, which, though full of force and fire, are devoid of music and taste. In the hybrid translations, concocted by combined efforts and unfortunately all too banal, we heard only Semyonova, and it was her genius that kept on the stage all these lamentable compositions of the fraternity of poets, who, one by one, disclaimed fatherhood. Semyonova has no rival. Prejudiced talk, momentary offerings, and transitory novelties, have long ceased, and she remains the sovereign queen of the tragic stage.

Pushkin admits: "Speaking of Russian tragedy, one mentions Semyonova—and, perhaps, her alone."

There were many who were not enraptured by Semyonova, however. She also had enemies among the public. The "supervisor of the repertoire," Khrapovitsky, recorded in his diary the following account of the public's disapproval of her acting:

Because of ill health Semyonova sang not so well. When she was called back to the stage, a civil servant from the Department of Mines,

Ilman, whistled, hissed, and loudly called her a "shabby old cat," in which matter the police took action.

Semyonova's position was seriously shaken when classical tragedy gave way to romantic drama. In this connection she made a mistake common to actresses. She began to play roles that did not conform to her gifts, performing ingénue parts for which her magnificent beauty was unsuitable, or "vaudeville" parts, which suited her particular talent still less.

Cantankerous and quarrelsome in her relations with her colleagues, she had few friends in the company. She always quarreled with Yakovlev, and she did everything possible to persecute every young actress whose popularity began to threaten her position.

She learned how to distinguish the theatre habituées with whom she could express her power. When young Zhikharev, who was madly in love with the theatre but occupied no prominent position, tried to express to her his delight with her acting as sincerely and simply as he would have when congratulating less prominent artists, she received him so coldly that he never spoke with her again. Had it been a more influential man instead of Zhikharev, she would undoubtedly have treated him as affably as she did most influential persons. One of these, Prince Gagarin, who almost openly enjoyed her favors, later married her, bestowing wealth and the title of Princess upon her. In those days this was the height of an actress's worldly ambition. Semyonova was able to eliminate everyone who stood in her way only because of this support by the aristocracy. When Kolosova's teacher Katenin, a brilliant Guard's officer and a translator, openly criticized the acting of Semyonova's pupil Azarevicheva, Semyonova, backed by Count Miloradovich, the Governor General, had him sign an absurd pledge not to attend the theatre on days when Semyonova was scheduled to play. Shortly thereafter he was exiled for many years to his Kostromá estate. Wits used to say that Katenin was smashed against the "Gagarin" quay. Thus Semyonova avenged herself on Katenin because he introduced her rival Kolosova into the theatre.

The management inaugurated a hitherto unheard-of practice of paying Semyonova extra remuneration in excess of her regular salary for every performance. But even this did not satisfy her, and she resigned from the theatre several times.

During the reign of Alexander I, actors were divided into four categories: (1) *emplois*, (2) their *doublés*, (3) *utilité* actors, and (4) *accessoires*. The same categories obtained in the budget for the Imperial theatres under Nicholas I. In 1803 a special committee classified the artists of drama, tragedy, and comedy, according to the following types:

actors—lead, young lover, second lover, honorable father, semi-character role of comic *raisonneur*, vulgar comic, first and second domestics, comic peasant, simpleton, confidant, and minor actors;

actresses—lead, young mistress and first coquette, second mistress and young duenna, innocent parts, honorable mother and semi-character part, comic old woman and character part, first chambermaid and vivacious part, second chambermaid.

This classification according to *emplois* was obviously borrowed directly from the French, without even an attempt to find Russian expressions for the respective terms. It continued in government-sponsored theatres until 1882. In tragedy there were the additional *emplois* of: (1) kings; (2) queens and honorable mothers; and (3) young queens, usually played by the same actresses as the romantic leads.

On December 29, 1805, an Imperial decree stipulated that Imperial theatres were to be opened in Moscow, where hitherto only private performances had been given. After the decree was issued, private theatres continued to retain a degree of independence, although within the framework of the Imperial theatres, and subject to supervision from Petersburg. The extent of this dependence varied wtih individual theatres.

On December 28, 1809, the establishment of the Moscow "State" dramatic school was approved, and the training school for many generations of artists established. It was natural that the government should take better care of the theatre in the capital than of the new theatre in Moscow. In 1803, for example, the budget for the Petersburg Russian company was 54,000 rubles, and that for the Moscow company only 35,000 rubles. For wardrobe Petersburg received 36,402 rubles and 33 kopecks; Moscow, 26,292 rubles. For stage sets Petersburg received 45,706 rubles and 87 kopecks; Moscow, 26,292 rubles. The school in Petersburg received 49,956 rubles; the school in Moscow, 16,660 rubles. And in the following years the ratio of the appropriations remained practically unchanged.

In 1815, Prince D. V. Golitsyn as the Military Governor General was supervisor of theatre performances in Moscow. He actively meddled in the work of the government-sponsored theatres, and succeeded in overriding the more competent but less influential theatrical management.

The Moscow company was composed largely of former serf companies of different owners. For example, the Imperial theatre purchased Prince Volkonsky's company, crediting the actors with all their previous service in the private theatre.

The nucleus of the Moscow company was former serf-actors of the landowner Stolypin. His entire theatre having been purchased by the crown, actors transferred from the serf to the Imperial company continued to be subjected to corporal punishments. For instance, the singer Butenbroch was flogged with rods before her wedding. In the magazine *The Northern Messenger* in the year 1804, the following question was raised about the acting of the remarkable Moscow serf-actress Barancheyeva: "Can Barancheyeva, in favorable circumstances, be a good actress? Let others answer the question—not me. Had Rubens, Garrick, and Dietz been serfs, they would not have brought fame to their native countries."

The low educational level, both professional and general, of our actors was artificially maintained by a series of measures which could hardly be called just. As late as October 11, 1827, a decree by the Tsar stated that government officials, subject to the authorization of the Minister, might be engaged as actors only after being deprived of their ranks, and after their rank certificates had been taken away from them. This measure naturally discouraged them from becoming actors, and resulted in a situation whereby the theatre management, according to its own admission, "was compelled to look for players among social strata almost devoid of education, and who acquire some knowledge of dramatic art only by actual practice."

As a result of Napoleon's 1812 invasion, the Moscow theatre was badly disorganized. Part of the company evacuated to Kostroma with the management, and part of it dispersed. After Moscow had been liberated from the enemy, the young theatre was by no means restored overnight. Many actors who joined the Moscow troupe came either from the private stage or from the Petersburg crown theatre.

Among the actors in the Moscow theatre during the first quarter of the nineteenth century who particularly distinguished themselves were the Sandunovs, Plavilshchikov, the Pomerantsev couple, and M. Vorobyova, the latter especially well suited for the performance of roles in Kotzebue's dramas. The importance of the Pomerantsevs was described by Makarov, the well known theatre lover of the period, in these words: "In a period dominated by classicism, the Pomerantsevs were remarkable for their lack of affectation and their understanding of human nature—all that our stage requires—so that even our classicists were compelled to respect them."

Among the Petersburg actors, Shusherin, Krutitsky, and especially Yakovlev continued to enjoy enormous success. According to Raphael Zotov, Yakovlev's favorite part was that of Dmitry Donskoy:

Yakovlev was in love with that role, and he played it excellently. His challenge of the rival in the second act, the gloomy home-coming and his return from the battlefield in the fifth act, were invariably played with especially great skill. No one since Yakovlev has ever been so profoundly steeped in the role of Dmitry. Audiences of that period did not dwell upon all the historical inconsistencies of this play, merely admiring Ozerov's beautiful verses warmed with a flaming love for the fatherland.

Krutitsky always performed brilliantly the parts of the first domestic ("the high livery," according to contemporary stage terminology), so important in comedy. Knyazhnin's comedies *The Eccentric People* and *The Braggart,* which provide such a rich field for actors of this type, were retained in the repertoire especially for Krutitsky.

During Alexander's reign Rykalov was a remarkable actor in Molière's plays in the Petersburg theatre. Here is an account by a contemporary theatre admirer of his performance of the part of Geronte in *Scapin's Deceits:*

What a splendid comic figure! The face, the stature, the manner of walking, the movements—all these in him are so clumsy, so naturally stupid, that his mere appearance makes one burst into laughter; and the voice, the diction—these are nature itself: no strained effects, no exaggeration, no vulgarism; briefly, one beholds not an actor but a real Geronte. But in the scene where Scapin declares to him that the Turk has kidnaped his son and demands ransom, Rykalov surpassed all my expectations. All that I had previously heard about his excellent acting in this scene was nothing compared with what I saw. How droll, how funny his despair was! With what an amusingly pitiful air he untied his purse, repeating all the while those well known exclamations!

Rykalov was equally skillful in comedy and tragedy. His prestige as a frank and unbiased instructor of young playwrights was almost equal to that of Dmitrevsky in the preceding century.

In strongly caricatured parts—for example, Skotinin—Rakhmanov was very successful, while his wife was an inimitable comic old woman. "And all this without screaming, without affectation; everything is so natural and fine," R. M. Zotov wrote.

The leading comédienne was M. I. Valberkhova (1788–1867). According to D. M. Sverbeyev, both she and other comic actresses in Petersburg

were distinguished by a most proper bearing on the stage; they did not indulge in singsong, nor in screaming, as was the custom among Russian ladies of the middle class. This was all the more remarkable as our actresses had no one to imitate. Next to Valberkhova the most talented was Vorobyova the First, a very young and pretty actress who had just married Sosnitsky.

In addition to these Petersburg actors who had established themselves in the eighteenth century, contemporaries have noted the stage achievements of Ponomarev, Vorobyov, and Nimfodora Semyonova, the sister of the famous actress.

Bulgarin made the comment:

Nimfodora Semyonovna Semyonova in her youth was an incarnation of animated, spirited grace. The lovely features of her face, her eyes full of fire and tenderness, her size and stature, and her manners and gestures—all these combined made her perfect. Her voice, although not strong, was very agreeable, and she sang quite pleasantly in short operas and vaudevilles. Besides, she was an admirable actress in two contrasting types of role: ingénues and young matrons. In the latter she was distinguished by the nobility of her performance and an exquisite fashionable tone, which is a very rare phenomenon on our stage.

Bulgarin says of Ponomarev:

His acting was altogether inimitable. This sort of thing is completely forgotten! His voice had a certain comic expression. He created the role of an old-fashioned office clerk on the Russian stage, a type which no longer exists either in real life or in the theatre. This type has gone forever as has the country lackey! When Ponomarev appeared on the stage in a light green uniform, in a red jacket and red vest, wearing a flat three-cornered hat, and began singing office-clerk couplets in his goatlike voice—it was just too funny! One would almost die of laughter when Ponomarev—I forget in what particular entertainment—sang in a tearful voice a doleful song about the abolition of an inn on the Strelka [3] which used to be a favorite meeting place of inveterate chancery clerks. In parts of comic lackeys, even when they were not particularly witty, Ponomarev by his manner alone used to make people laugh until they shed tears. In *The Minor* he was unique: there he copied nature itself.

The actor Vorobyov was short and rather stocky; nevertheless, even off the stage, his movements were quick and agile. His acting was natural, always true to the character he was impersonating.

Among the other actors of the same period the tragedian Lápin, who was particularly popular with the Petersburg public, deserves mention. Contemporaries claimed that he acted nobly and with a sense of "utmost discretion." He lacked animation, however, and was at his best in plays requiring no enthusiasm.

In those days the Samoilov couple were prominent on the Petersburg stage. Samoilov, a rather clever man, possessed a resonant and moving tenor voice. His wife, who was forced to play in operas, might have been unrivaled in soubrette roles, which particularly suited her because of her naturally vivacious speech, uninhibited gestures, expressive and naïvely mischievous face, and extraordinary naturalness.

During the first half of the nineteenth century, our dramatic actors continued to appear also in opera. The company was divided only in 1836, when, with the production of *The Inspector-General,* the opera was combined with the ballet, and the drama became the exclusive prerogative of the Aleksandrinsky Theatre.

Yakov Grigoryevich Bryansky (1791–1853)—his real name was

[3] The "Point"—that is, the end of Yelagin Island, from which an excellent view of the Gulf of Finland may be had.—Ed.

Grigoryev—may be considered as Yakovlev's successor. During the time when he still held a more or less important official position, he was passionately devoted to the theatre and spent his last pennies to attend performances on every free evening. Shakhovskoy, upon his ardent request, took him as a pupil. At that time Shakhovskoy headed a young company composed largely of his own pupils. They played at the so-called Kushelev theatre on the Malaya Millionnaya, a moderate-priced theatre with broadly representative audiences. It was at the Kushelev that Bryansky began his theatrical career. He made every effort to perform tragic parts, but his instructors limited him to romantic roles in comedy and in vaudeville. He appeared in this type of part in almost all of Shakhovskoy's pieces. He also took the male lead in Griboyedov's play *The Newlyweds*. His acting was successful even though classicists were displeased with him because he recited verses in too simple a fashion.

In 1811 Bryansky joined the Bolshoy Theatre. There he succeeded in playing the tragic role of Iodai in *Gapholia*, which Yakovlev had performed so well. After Yakovlev's death all his parts were gradually assigned to Bryansky. There was a marked difference in the acting of these two artists, however: Yakovlev achieved his inspiration and genius through capricious transports of emotion. The somewhat cold Bryansky, on the other hand, was distinguished by the detailed preparation of his parts. This was, as it were, the substance of the difference which obtained later between Mochalov's and Karatygin's acting.

Bryansky continued to play tragic roles until Karatygin began his brilliant career, then voluntarily gave them up and turned to "more mature roles." He played Philip in *Don Carlos,* Christiern in *John, the Earl of Finland,* Iago in *Othello,* Franz Moor in *The Robbers,* Miller in *Wile and Love,* Stern in *Fingal,* Oedipus in *Oedipus in Athens,* Minin in *The Hand of God Saved Our Fatherland,* and Shuisky in *Skopin Shuisky,* and *Yelena Glinskaya.* He also played the parts of Shylock, Ugolino, Quasimodo (in *Esmeralda*), and so forth. He was at his best in the roles of the musician Miller and Quasimodo.

Belinsky, on his arrival in Petersburg in 1839, wrote of Bryansky's acting:

By the noble, unaffected, and stately manner which he displayed in the part of Justinian, Bryansky gave one the feeling of a king; his somewhat drawling diction, however, sounded so strange to a barbarian Muscovite that I was not at all satisfied. I am impatiently looking forward to seeing Mr. Bryansky in so-called romantic parts, such as Miller and Quasimodo, which he reportedly plays excellently. Bryansky is preeminently a Petersburg actor, and for this reason he will hardly please the Moscow public. The Petersburg theatre is one of tradition in which art has been passed on from one talent to another, in which the names of Dmitrevsky, Yakovlev, and Semyonova are still alive. Bryansky is one of the bright stars of that classical constellation.

Bryansky's leaning toward plays of the standard repertoire should be noted. He was particularly fond of Shakespeare; this led him to translate *Richard III*, which he accomplished with outside assistance. For his benefit performances he preferred Shakespearean plays. He spent much energy on the production of Griboyedov's great comedy, which was given in full for the first time at his benefit performance.

His devotion to literature made his house a meeting place for men of letters, which proved very useful to him in his work as instructor of dramatic art.

He was known for his independent character, particularly apparent in his relations with his superiors, who invariably maintained a respectful attitude toward him.

Realizing the fact that his health was declining, Bryansky retired on a pension and went to Samara for a rest. He returned to the stage, however, not long before his death.

This is what Pushkin wrote about him:

Yakovlev is dead! Bryansky took his place but did not replace him: perhaps Bryansky has more decorum and, generally, has more dignity on the stage, is more respected by the public, knows his parts more thoroughly, and does not become suddenly ill in the middle of a performance; but, even so, what coldness, and what a heavy monotonous tone.

> To me, he'd better drink
> If he can only act and think.

Yakovlev used to have wonderful flashes of genius—at times impulses of the vulgar Talma. Bryansky is the same in every role. The ever smiling Fingal, Theseus, Orosman, Jason, Dmitry—all are equally inanimate, strained, and boring. In vain one tells him: Get stirred up, dear fellow, let yourself go, grow angry, now, now! Awkward, measured, inhibited in all his gestures, he knows not how to use either his voice or his body. In tragedy, Bryansky has never moved anyone, and in comedy he has never made anyone laugh. In spite of this, as a comic actor, he has his advantages and even genuine virtue.

One of the first most noteworthy men in the theatrical profession during the first half of the nineteenth century was Prince A. A. Shakhovskoy (1777–1846). Having graduated from the Boarding School for Young Men of Noble Birth at the Moscow University, where he developed a liking for theatrical performances, he went to Petersburg and entered the military service. There he lived with the family of a well known Russian ballet master, Lesogorov Walberch, who introduced him to the theatrical world and provided him with an entrée backstage. He also became friendly with a set of young men who, to use his words, "indulged in writing, aimed at becoming poets, and were passionately devoted to the theatre." Presently he came into contact with Dmitrevsky, who suggested that he try his hand at the fashionable art of playwrighting. Shakhovskoy himself wrote about his first experiments as a playwright:

At the age of eighteen, having learned nothing thoroughly and having a dilettante interest in writing articles, I rushed into the theatrical profession. The popularity of comedies in verse delighted me, and I made up my mind to gratify my ambition for the applause with which the orchestra and gallery greeted such witticisms as that same audience would be ashamed to repeat before their sisters and daughters. And so I —truly still a humble youth—tempted by evil examples and by this easy method of gaining reputation as an author, wrote a one-act comedy (*A Woman's Jest*): it pleased the men, and made some prominent members of the audience laugh. I was called for by name, which in those days was a rare thing. Fortunately my comedy was produced in 1796, however, and official duties put an end to my authorship. The pen was replaced by the gun.

On April 22, 1801, Shakhovskoy was appointed chief of the repertoire section of the theatre management. His official work in the theatre dates from that time; it was more than a mere conscientious discharge of duties, however. He was indebted to the Director of the Theatres, Naryshkin, for the appointment.

Shakhovskoy was commissioned to go to Paris in order to engage a French company. In France, as well as in the countries en route to Paris, he diligently studied the theatre and styles of acting which were unfamiliar to him. He was particularly interested in Monvel, who was known for the simplicity of his acting, and in Talma, whose innovations later proved so useful to him. He took home the methods of training young actors which he learned through conversations with the best actors in those countries.

Shakhovskoy was an active member of "The Forum of the Friends of the Russian Language," and was close to its leader, A. S. Shishkov. He was drawn to Shishkov by dislike of the contemporary language, "perverted by piled up ignorance and ugly words of Tartar or unknown origin, which replaced the euphony of Slavic words." These ideas were rather ineffectively reflected in his plays, however.

In 1808 Shakhovskoy took an active part in the publication *The Dramatic Courier,* and later, upon his own request, he became a member of the Russian Academy, where he frequently read his plays. The peaceful course of his artistic life was interrupted in 1812, when he joined the ranks of the Tver militia.

Subsequent disagreements with the director, Prince Tyufyakin, compelled Shakhovskoy temporarily to resign his official position in the theatres, even though unofficially he continued his work. When A. A. Marikov was appointed director, he again entered the service, setting down the "rules and regulations on the internal management of the Imperial Theatrical Administration." These received Imperial sanction on May 3, 1825, and remained substantially intact for almost a century.

On January 23, 1826, Shakhovskoy was permanently discharged from service in the Imperial theatres. The remaining twenty years of his life he devoted to translating and writing original plays for the theatre, as well as a number of articles on the history of the theatre. In addition, he taught dramatic art to beginners.

His contact with the theatre was also maintained in his private life through his friendship with the actress Yezhova, for whom he solicitously wrote various roles in his plays. He proposed marriage to her many times, but she invariably answered: "I would rather be the beloved Yezhova than a ludicrous princess."

Shakhovskoy lisped, hissed, could not pronounce the *r*'s, the

s's, and the *sh*'s, and distorted other letters. When excited, he used
to mutter, swallowing whole words, which made it difficult to understand his speech. Nevertheless, his outstanding knowledge of
dramatic literature and enormous personal experience made him a
very valuable dramatic teacher. Best of all, he was able to explain
the nature of a given part, the fundamental moods of the particular character, and the changes brought about in him by the progress of the play.

Pimen Arapov stated that

his first stipulation with actors was that they learn their parts thoroughly. He could not stand their resorting to a prompter; when he came
to a rehearsal, he used to take a seat at the proscenium, near the
prompter, leaning on his cane. He watched the progress of the play and
explained to the actors the meaning of each scene, the situations
involved in them, and the various transitions. He became angry and
considered it a personal insult if an actor failed to strike the right
intonation in his part; and then and there he would issue orders to
the director concerning costumes and properties. There was nothing
for the director to do except to look after the actors' exits and the place-
ment of the supers. Shakhovskoy insisted that rehearsals be conducted
properly, and did not tolerate over confident actors who read their
parts in an undertone or from copybooks, or those who made additions
to or deletions from their parts.

Shakhovskoy's opinion of the duties of the director quoted by
P. A. Smirnov in his reminiscences about the famous theatre lover,
is noteworthy:

In my judgment the director must be a well educated person,
fully conversant with everything pertaining to the stage. He must also
be one who has made a profound study of the public's tastes and of
those secret ways which he should employ—and this is a national necessity in order to improve its taste and make it capable of distinguishing
quality from buffoonery. He must achieve all this by means of the
classification and the distribution of the parts. Inasmuch as every author
is living in the midst of artists, the director should see to it that
the actors, first, read without the prompter's assistance, secondly, know
their respective places, and, lastly, try to discover the finesses and the
so-called effects during the rehearsals without depending upon inspiration, which is the gift only of the chosen few who are blessed with
genius. It is insufficient for the stage manager to know all the actors
by their names and to be able to deprive them of benefits to which they

are entitled. No, he must know their souls, their leanings, and, finally, their inherent abilities, so as to distribute the parts without error and justly to insist on their correct diction and appropriate gestures. The director, in his capacity of supervisor and instructor, must be respected by everybody, and he should be obeyed, not because he is feared, but because he is known to be right. Finally, the director must not be a member of the company proper, but a person whose wholehearted zeal and flaming devotion to art, rather than petty careerism should absorb his interest exclusively.

Shakhovskoy's enthusiastic nature, his exaggerated feelings, and his very comic appearance furnished ample material for all sorts of anecdotes. Here, for instance, is what S. T. Aksakov tells about the rehearsal of the play *A Love Letter*, in which Shakhovskoy considered Yezhova's part particularly effective:

The time came for the scene in which Yezhova had to sing a long aria. The actress made several mistakes. Shakhovskoy, seated in an armchair, merely kept bowing to her at every mistake; but although he remained silent his face expressed such a comic sorrow that it was actually both funny and pitiful. Yezhova was apparently embarrassed by Shakhovskoy's outward composure, and when her turn came to sing again she began singing verses from another opera. The prince crawled unobserved from his armchair, knelt down, and fell at her feet. The rehearsal was halted. For a long time, without changing his position, Shakhovskoy continued to mutter in a most doleful and screaming voice: "O Lord, why dost Thou chastise me! Do have mercy on me, the sinner! I humbly thank thee, Mother Katerina Ivanovna!" And suddenly, leaping up with the frenzy of an enraged tiger, he screamed in a mad, inhuman, Calibanlike voice: "So this is our acting. From the beginning, tomorrow—we'll take it from the beginning!"

Shakhovskoy's own plays are quite uneven, both in content and in quality. Apparently he succeeded best in comedies. Pushkin mentioned them when referring to the contemporary theatre:

> There, mordant Shakhovskoy unrolled
> A swarm of comedies, all bold.

He was particularly caustic in the comedy *A Lesson for Coquettes,* or *The Lipetsk Spa,* in which, in the name of the poet Fialkin, he attacked the character Zhukovsky, on the ground of his being sympathetic to romantics and romanticism.

In a letter to E. P. Meshchersky, Shakhovskoy called romanticism "a veritable progeny of the revolution":

Aside from the spirit of debauchery, which is an intrinsic part of the
Parisian revolution, present-day French romanticism, long, long ago
made its appearance beyond the Alps and in the vicinity of the Pyrenees
Mountains, penetrated Spain and later England, where it swam over—
not without getting wet—to Germany, and there, already mutilated, was
further perverted by contemporary Frenchmen.

He portrayed a typical romantic, under the name of Count Pron-
sky, in an amusing vaudeville *The New Stern.* Of his comedies, *A
Love Letter* and *Negligent Housekeepers* were given more frequently than others. He also wrote historical plays, for example,
*Lomonosov, or The Recruit Poet, The Falcon of Prince Tverskoy,
or The Betrothed on the White Steed.* The events of 1812 provided him with the material for his vaudeville *The Cossack Poet,*
in which Ukrainians were so inaccurately represented that
Ukrainian critics have spoken of Shakhovskoy's ignorance of both
their language and their ways of life.

His play *Aristophanes,* as well as the comedy *The Horseman,*
in which Bryansky played the leading part in Petersburg and
P. S. Mochalov in Moscow, were more successful. The characters in
the former, on which very little research had been done, were not
very successful except for Xanthippe, the wife of Socrates, which
Shakhovskoy wrote for Yezhova. The entire play is composed of
verses from Aristophanes and Euripides. (Shakhovskoy always
acknowledges these borrowed parts.) Sometimes he merely re-
hashed—rather imperfectly—other authors' plays, for instance, Voltaire's *Chinese Orphans* and Gresset's *The Wily,* which gave
P. A. Vyazemsky a pretext to attack him in caustic verses.

The Bigamous Wife, which was given in the capitals until 1870,
survived on the stage longer than any other of his plays. In it he
tells the story of a merchant's daughter who is kidnaped by a robber chieftain; she later marries a merchant, but the robber abducts
her from her husband and children, and it takes a detachment of
soldiers to restore her to her family. Attractive stage sets; boats
sailing on the Volga; the siege of the robbers' camp; the appearance
of mummers in the first act; songs, dances, and girls' games; the
scene of the fire—all these must have appealed to the audience.

Shakhovskoy succeeded in picturing fairly correctly the character of merchants' entertainments and in composing several songs closely resembling the style of popular songs. In this respect *The Bigamous Wife* is interesting as an attempt to portray the merchant class. Its merits are obvious, compared with Plavilshchikov's plays. Shakhovskoy's attempt in the second act to represent several typical beggars and their benefactors is quite clever. His figure of the blind man Savvati is decidedly successful. All this is valuable as a departure from the traditional patterns.

The principal defect of the play lies in the author's utter inability to motivate his characters' conduct. Why Grusha falls in love with the robber and likes him better than Roman, how she later feels about going from one husband to another, whether she yearns for her husband and son after returning to her first husband—all these things are not clarified in the play. For this very reason the role of Grusha, whose part was first performed by the beautiful actress, Teleshova, is essentially passive. Shakhovskoy also failed utterly in the part of Roman. He did not, apparently, have any first-hand knowledge about an infatuated merchant, gently cooing with his wife, and the character emerged as artificial and abstract.

In his articles on the history of the Russian theatre which appeared in special theatrical magazines in the 1840's, Shakhovskoy revealed such an inordinate partiality for the tragedians of the eighteenth century that editors often felt compelled to print notices to the effect that they did not share his views.

R. M. Zotov, one of Shakhovskoy's closest collaborators, considers the following to be his best plays: *The Half-Gentlemanly Ventures; Quarrels, or Two Neighbors; The Cossack-Poet; The Lipetsk Spa; The Meeting of the Uninvited; Lomonosov; One's Own Family; Don't Listen If You Dislike It; Negligent House-keepers; Ivanoy; The Tempest; Aristophanes; The Falcon of Prince Yaroslav; Finn; Thou and You; Fyodor Grigoryevich Volkov;* and *The Bigamous Wife.* "These plays," he adds, "form such a constellation on our dramatic horizon that they demand a posthumous laurel wreath for their author."

In Moscow, where Shakhovskoy moved after his resignation, there were also theatre lovers among the nobility, headed by F. F. Kokoshkin.

With regard to the training of actors in the past, I. A. Goncharov, in a letter to P. D. Boborykin (October, 1876), draws this conclusion:

They used to be saved not only by their individual natural talent, but by a whole school—one might say a dramatic academy—headed by Kokoshkin and including such men as Shakhovskoy, Zagoskin, Pisarev, and a wide circle of Moscow amateurs and stage connoisseurs (which in those days was quite large indeed) where writers and actors worked hard in the drama. There, large groups of professionals and nonprofessionals used to study, act, and receive their training. From early morning until late at night Kokoshkin spent his time in the theatre, of which he was director and in which he virtually lived. He had a stage of his own, and at home he also worked with the artists. Here literature and theatre joined hands.

Chapter XI

TRAGEDY IN THE EARLY PART
OF THE NINETEENTH CENTURY

LONG BEFORE the Patriotic War of 1812, with the increasing power of Napoleon, national self-consciousness began to develop noticeably. The more direct the threat to the greatness and security of Russia, the more strongly this feeling manifested itself. The year 1812, and Russia's successes in the West which followed, strengthened and consolidated this tendency. These feelings also permeated literature, which acquired a patriotic tone, and were reflected in the contemporary theatrical repertoire. A series of patriotic plays appeared, the chief virtue of which lay in the fact that the audience found in them the reflection of their own attitudes. For this reason, their success, which was occasionally tremendous, in no way depended upon their artistic merits, which they sometimes did not possess. Nevertheless, certain pieces remained in the repertoire for a long time.

The public's patriotism may be appreciated from the following incidents. During the performance of Viskovatov's drama *Universal Military Training*, one member of the audience, observing that everybody on the stage was donating his possessions, flung his pocketbook on the stage and said: "Here, take my last seventy-five rubles as well!"

On the day when the news of the Klyastitsky and Kobransky battle was announced, the Russian opera *Ancient Christmas Holidays* was being given. Sandunova started singing "Praised be God in Heaven," as called for in her part; then suddenly she stopped, stepped forward to the footlights, and began to sing:

> Praised be our brave Count Wittgenstein
> Who crushed our enemies. Glory!
> Praised be our valiant General Tormasov
> Who defeated our foes. Glory!

Applause and hurrahs thundered throughout the theatre. Then in a low voice she continued:

> Praised be our brave General Kulnev
> Who gave his life for his Fatherland. Glory!

The audience and the singer herself burst into tears.

One of the best known plays of the patriotic repertoire of the first quarter of the nineteenth century was the three-act tragedy *Pozharsky* by M. V. Kryukovsky (1781–1811), which was produced for the first time on May 22, 1807. The invasion of the Polish aggressors and their expulsion from Russia were used as a basis for comparing the subject of the play, its individual scenes, and especially certain expressions, with contemporary events, thus assuring a success which it could not have attained on artistic merit. The part of Prince Pozharsky was performed with enormous enthusiasm by Yakovlev, who found it well suited to his majestic talent. Later, this tragedy was produced as the opening performance in the newly erected Aleksandrinsky Theatre (1832).

From an artistic standpoint, the tragedy *Dmitry Donskoy* by Vladislav Aleksandrovich Ozerov (1770–1816) was much more significant. According to contemporaries, he "wrote better in French, and began studying Russian at a rather late age; his mind encompassed the whole repertoire of Corneille, Racine, and Voltaire."

Ozerov's first tragedy, *Yaropolk and Oleg,* presented in 1798 and written closely after the style of Sumarokov and Knyazhnin, met with no success. But even the first performance of *Dmitry Donskoy* in Petersburg on January 14, 1807, proved an overwhelming triumph. The public called endlessly for the author, and director Naryshkin himself escorted Ozerov to his box. Such an obvious triumph had never before been achieved by any playwright. Of course, the principal cause of the success of *Dmitry*

Donskoy lay in the patriotic pathos of the tragedy, in the analogy between Russia's liberation from the Tartar yoke and the contemporary struggle with Napoleon. "In 1807," P. A. Vyazemsky wrote, "when Russia's eyes were fixed on the struggle of her valiant sons with the power of a formidable enemy who was forging the chains of slavery for Europe, Ozerov, in his tragedy *Dmitry Donskoy*, reminded his compatriots of the great period of Russia's ancient glory." By the end of the war with Napoleon the play had grown still more popular. According to a further statement by Vyazemsky, "After the events of 1812, which had been partly anticipated, *Dmitry* became an even more popular tragedy in our theatre."

In its dramatic structure, *Dmitry Donskoy* substantially adhered to the rules of classicism: the three unities, confidants, messengers, a great number of highly emotional monologues, "elevated" style. It is distinguished from the tragedies of Sumarokov and Knyazhnin by the more complex psychology of its characters, and a touch of sentimentality and subjectivity. Here we find evidence of the new literary taste (sentimentality). For the sake of "tender susceptibilities" Ozerov introduced into his tragedy the love theme (*Dmitry's* love of Xenia, daughter of the Nizhny-Novgorod prince); but he failed to integrate it into the plot of the play.

Ozerov's mastery of the drama reached its highest point in *Oedipus in Athens*. The plot of this play was borrowed, not from the original source, the famous tragedy of Sophocles, but from the French piece by Ducis. Produced for the first time on November 23, 1804, it met with enormous success. The audience was particularly delighted with the ringing and musical verses of the tragedy, of a kind which had never before been heard on the stage. Ozerov also wrote the tragedies *Fingal* (1805) and *Polyxena* (1809).

In *Oedipus*, *Fingal*, and *Polyxena* the sentimental style is even more noticeable than in *Dmitry Donskoy*, notwithstanding the fact that those plays too adhere to the classical form. This stylistic dualism is the most characteristic feature of Ozerov's writing, and represents the last phase of Russian classical tragedy—soon destined to cede its place to romantic and realistic tragedy.

The subject matter of Ozerov's tragedies reveals a number of progressive elements: protest against religious superstition and against the oppressed status of women; attacks against "the great lords"; and defense of "the common people" and of man's right to self-expression.

Very soon Ozerov found himself among the forgotten writers, along with Knyazhnin and Sumarokov, so that romantic playwrights did not have much competition to overcome. Even while he was still alive, Shakhovskoy succeeded in relegating him to the background, and Belinsky had good reason to write in 1834: "In our day no one is going to deny the poetic talent of Ozerov; yet, at the same time, hardly anyone is going to read him, or still less be enraptured by him." Only ten years later Belinsky stated: "At present Ozerov is completely forgotten by the theatre; he is neither played nor read." Pushkin was much more critical in his attitude: "I dislike Ozerov not because I envy him but because I love art. Ozerov's fame is already withering, and in about a decade, when genuine criticism comes into existence, it will disappear altogether." He found Ozerov's shortcomings due to the fact that "he did not attempt to give us a popular tragedy, believing that for this purpose it was sufficient to select a plot from national history. He forgot that the French poets took the plots for their tragedies from Greek, Roman, and European history, and that the most popular tragedies of Shakespeare were based on Italian *novellas*."

Among foreign writers whose works were included in our early nineteenth century repertoire, August von Kotzebue (1761–1819) is the most prominent, if one is to judge by number of plays produced. There was some justice in the remark that "Kotzebuism" reigned on the Russian stage. This playwright was amazingly prolific, writing about a hundred plays published in eighteen volumes, which were diligently translated into Russian.

Kotzebue was a typical dramatic craftsman. With his practical stage experience and knowledge of its requirements (at one time he was in charge of the Vienna theatre) he easily managed to write any type of play that pleased public taste. In his literary manner and composition he most nearly approximated the authors of the "bourgeois" drama. Despite the colossal success which his plays enjoyed in the early part of the nineteenth century, his biographer wrote in 1840 that they were then completely forgotten.

One of Kotzebue's most popular plays in Russia was his five-act drama *The Hussites Before Naumburg.* At present it is difficult to surmise what in this play appealed to our public. To begin with, there is nothing historical in it, and the play itself, with no changes, might be attributed to a totally different place and period. It is a picture of the sufferings of "a whole city" besieged by the enemy. The play had a number of highly emotional scenes: the spectacle of the virtues of its hero Wolf, the sight of defenseless children doomed to cruel death, and the despair of a mother leading her children to their imminent death.

The popularity of Kotzebue's plays prompted Russian playwrights to compose works in obvious imitation. Among these, N. Ilin's *Liza, or The Triumph of Gratitude and Magnanimity* and *Conscription of Recruits,* as well as N. Fyodorov's *Liza, or The Consequence of Pride and Seduction,* met with great success. Fyodorov borrowed the plot for his play from Karamzin's novel which was then in vogue. During the same period, along with Kotzebue's plays, the compositions of such great playwrights as Schiller were produced on our stage, although not everybody admitted the superiority of Schiller the artist over Kotzebue the artisan.

The success of Kotzebue's plays, of the doleful comedy, and of the translations of Schiller's tragedies unified the advocates of the French classical drama, who were still unable to reconcile themselves to the violation of the traditional rules of classicism. The magazine, *The Dramatic Courier,* founded in 1808 with the close participation of A. A. Shakhovskoy, I. A. Krylov, and A. I. Pisarev, was the sounding board for these views. But the efforts of the classicists failed to stem the tide of the romantic drama.

Chapter XII

VAUDEVILLE

EARLY IN the nineteenth century our comedy repertoire consisted principally of revivals of comedies of eighteenth century playwrights. Fonvizin's plays were especially popular, and were presented several times each year both in Petersburg and in Moscow. Certain comedies not often given in the eighteenth century acquired a delayed popularity in the nineteenth—for example, those of Ivan Andreyevich Krylov (1768–1844). Krylov's plays thus served as a connecting link between the eighteenth and nineteenth century theatre.

At the age of sixteen he composed a comic opera, *The Coffee Box* (1784), which depicts, according to L. N. Maikov, "rathei simply and without caricature, the provincial life which Krylov had known in his childhood and youth." The play describes the life of the peasants under serfdom. From an artistic standpoint it is very weak; the verse is so imperfect that it is difficult to believe that Krylov wrote it. The only virtue is its language—natural, simple, and close to the people's speech.

In Petersburg, Krylov became very friendly with the famous I. A. Dmitrevsky, who was fond of patronizing and advising young writers. Although Krylov faithfully submitted his plays, even the advice of so great a theatre expert failed to assure their success. His comedy *The Wags* (1787 or 1788) caused him a great deal of trouble, because he had used the eminent playwright Knyazhnin and his wife as prototypes for the leading characters, an inept versifier Rifmokradov [1] and his wife Taratora.

[1] That is, Rhyme Thief.—Ed.

Krylov's first successful play was the one-act comedy *The Pastry*, ridiculing the supporters of sentimentality. In it he gives a vivid image of an elderly lady Uzhima, who goes mad in a delirium of sentiment. It was first produced in Petersburg on July 26, 1802, and thereafter in Moscow (January 25, 1804) for the benefit performance of Sandunov, who probably played the part of Vanka. We know, too, that it was staged in a "nobleman's theatre"—at the home of one of Krylov's supporters, Olenin.

Krylov's comedies *The Millinery Shop* and *A Lesson to the Daughters*, picturing the nobility's passion for the French language and French fashions, were particularly popular. F. F. Vigel gave the following account of them:

What can be gayer, cleverer, and more entertaining than his two comedies *A Lesson to the Daughters* and *The Millinery Shop*, which were performed in 1805 and 1806? Could one possibly ridicule more caustically the Gallomania prevailing both in the Capital and in the provinces, than these pieces do? The orchestra was always packed for frequent performances of these plays, and the audience laughed heartily.

Both of these comedies reflect the patriotism which then pervaded society.

In addition Krylov wrote a comedy *The Author in the Antechamber*, the comic operas *The Crazy Family* and *Sleeping Powders* or *The Kidnaping of a Peasant Woman*, a magic opera *Ilya the Valiant Knight*, and a tragedy *Philomena*. His tragicomedy *Trumf* (1801—a satire on Paul I and his court) was banned by the censorship, and was not published in Russia until 1871, when it appeared in *Russkaya Starina* as a reprint from a foreign publication.

Along with revivals of old comedies, the repertoire of the early part of the nineteenth century included something new; namely, the vaudeville borrowed from the West.

The word "vaudeville" is derived from the provincial French *vau de Vire*—valley of Vire—a name given to the songs of the French poet Olivier Basselin (1350–1408), *Chansons de Val de Vire*. These simple and gay songs, often in a bantering tone, were particularly popular in the seventeenth century. Subsequently the term "vaudeville" came to be applied to plays which included such songs. A number of writers of the second half of the eighteenth century specialized in composing vaudevilles which were played either before or after the main piece. In 1792 a special *Théâtre de Vaudeville* was established in Paris.

In 1844 the well informed French critic Théophile Gautier wrote:

If the flame of genuine comedy is still glimmering anywhere, certainly it is not in the big theatres, but on twenty small stages where it is broken up into short scenes fashioned by different hands. This comedy, called vaudeville, is a diversified form, animated and witty, sowing Attic salt in handfuls, and showing customs with a casual yet pointed veracity. Its only shortcomings are its uncivilized tongue and intolerable music. And even though, more than anything else, we treasure perfection of style, we must admit that in this inexhaustible creative pattern there is a certain vigor and originality. This is a purely French genre. The Greeks had their tragedy; the Romans, their comedy; the English and the Germans, their drama; but vaudeville is completely ours. It is really to be regretted that the rules of classicism have prevented many noted men of letters from mastering this form, so pliable and so suited to flights of the imagination, and adaptable to all styles, even poetry.

The principal aim of vaudeville is to amuse and delight the public. It has no serious intent; and it does not strive for theatrical immortality. This is well expressed in the following verses of one of our vaudeville authors:

> When did a vaudeville strive for any long duration?
> How can it reach old age without evading blight?
> And if it does not lisp, and if it isn't bright
> As happy babes so full of animation,
> It surely will be doomed and lose all its delight.

Plots in vaudeville almost always revolve around the struggle of the enamored couple with obstacles impeding their happiness, which, in the end, they successfully overcome. Interwoven in the plot are current motifs dealing with customs, literature, and, occasionally, social topics. Despite the characteristics common to every vaudeville, it is possible to trace several distinct varieties: some vaudevilles are simply dramatized anecdotes; others, primarily portrayals of amusing and unusual characters; and still others rely heavily on effects and an elaborate production.

It was not accidental that vaudeville was enthusiastically promoted in Russia in the early part of the nineteenth century, at a time when the influence of prominent patrons upon the theatre had so markedly increased. Because of the firmly established custom of benefit performances, actors began to feel a need for new plays, and welcomed anyone who introduced them. Composing even a short play for a benefit performance helped one to claim a connection with the theatre, which was quite the fashionable thing at the time. Authorship assured one at least some sort of position in theatrical circles. Naturally, under these conditions, really good writing was rare, and crudely constructed pieces were the rule. The vaudeville form was particularly well suited to this looser type of composition. Such couplets as these were composed with good reason:

> Without the vaudeville trash
> There is no benefit night,
> Yet naught but ben'fit cash
> Saves actors from their plight.

Repetilov in *Woe from Wit* gives a very accurate account of the way a vaudeville was written:

> I set myself to work, and less than in an hour
> A calembour was born—sort of fancy's flower.
> And others would stand ready, my pun from me to snatch—
> A vaudeville then six fellows would promptly start to patch;
> Then music is composed by half a dozen boys,
> While others will applaud it with merriment and noise.

Often vaudevilles were "patched" in an even simpler way: just find something from the abundant literature of French vaudevilles that has not yet been used, change the French names to make them sound Russian, and translate it more or less accurately into Russian. In extreme cases even the names of the characters in the play were left intact, and among our vaudevilles there are a considerable number of Fanchettes, Lisettes, Jeans, Simons, and the like.

In spite of the presence of couplets in vaudevilles, it was not at all necessary for the vaudeville author to know how to write poetry. When P. A. Katenin's friend N. I. Bakhtin decided to write a vaudeville for a benefit performance, he requested Pushkin (through Katenin) to compose couplets to replace the poor French ones. It is not known whether Pushkin consented; but such a division of labor appears to have been admissible. It should be remembered, too, that the vaudeville author was assisted by the composer, so that the success of many vaudevilles was enhanced by the fact that their music was composed by such talented men as Kavos and Verstovsky.

Thus, it is difficult to conceive of any other type of plays better suited to the abilities of society dilettantes. They managed to acquire the reputation of playwrights with the least effort.

Vaudeville was not less useful to actors. Those who had a voice and could cope with a not too difficult score, as well as act with a certain animation, were assured success in vaudeville.

In V. N. Davydov's opinion, the vaudeville furnished particularly suitable material to "short-charge" actors, who found it difficult to sustain creative effort during a long theatrical performance, but were able to express themselves fully and brilliantly in a short one-act play.

Khmelnitsky and Pisarev were the first writers to develop the Russian vaudeville in strict accordance with French patterns, and including all the variations of the French counterpart.

Nicholas Ivanovich Khmelnitsky (1789–1846) was one of the most talented authors of comedy prior to Griboyedov. It does not matter that the majority of his plays are either translations or adaptations of foreign plays, because he succeeded in bringing to the verse of the comedy a new simplicity, pliancy, and smoothness. His masterly dialogue was also a major improvement in the technique of our comedy. His translations of Molière (*Tartuffe* and *The School for Wives*) are very good, and he revealed a great deal of taste by renouncing the idea of adapting the plays to Russian customs and of substituting Russian names for the original ones. These translations are far superior to the adaptations of his predecessors. Khmelnitsky wrote a great number of vaudevilles, including, *The Prattler, The Pranks of the Enamored, The Irresolute, Chief Cook Felten, The New Paris* (opera vaudeville), *Greek Ravings, The Russian Faust, Grandmother's Parrots, Actors in Their Own Circle, A Fashionable Incident, Mutual Trials, Castles in the Air, Quarantine,* and *Marriages Are Made in Heaven.*

Perhaps his best play is *The Prattler* (adapted from the French comedy of Boissy), in which the leading character is Count Zvonov, an incredible chatterbox, a braggart and gossip, somewhat reminiscent of Zagoretsky.

The parody-vaudeville *Greek Ravings, or Iphigenia in Tauris* is a precursor of the later operettas dealing with mythological subjects. Not only is the myth of Iphigenia itself caricatured, but the religious institutions of the Greeks, the friendships of Orestes and Pylades, and all other elements of the tragedy are parodied.

The vaudeville *Castles in the Air*, owing to its entertaining plot and lively action, remained in the repertoire longer than any other of Khmelnitsky's pieces. It was played even in the latter part of the nineteenth century.

Aside from vaudeville pieces, Khmelnitsky is known as the author of two historical plays: a tragedy based upon the life of his ancestor Bogdan Khmelnitsky,[2] and a comedy *The Tsar's Word*, dealing with Peter's reign.

Alexander Ivanovich Pisarev (1803–1828), notwithstanding his early death, is generally considered to be the best Russian vaudeville playwright, and the critics think several of his pieces are the best vaudeville produced anywhere. Having begun to write while still in the University Boarding School, Pisarev soon joined the literary circle of Shakhovskoy, Kokoshkin, and Zagoskin. This involved him in polemics with representatives of other literary camps. His attacks on Polevoy, editor of the *Moscow Telegraph*, were particularly bitter.

Pisarev wrote twenty-three plays, the majority of which were translations or adaptations of foreign plays. His comedy *Lukavin* deserves special mention. It depicts the adventures of a young man deceiving his guardian with whose wife he is flirting, and planning to marry his pupil for the sake of her dowry.

The chief interest of the vaudeville *A Trip to Kronstadt*, adapted from the French, lies in the character of the Voronezh landowner Kleshnin, filled with a passion for the sea. The role provided rich material for an actor, and it is said that Shchepkin played it superbly. According to Pisarev's own admission, "the acting of the incomparable Shchepkin also assured the success" of another of his vaudevilles, *The Tutor and the Pupil*. There Shchepkin per-

[2] Ukrainian Hetman Bogdan (Bohdan) Khmelnitsky, who led the Cossack rebellion against Polish rule in 1648.—Ed.

formed the part of the tutor Schelling, who is devoted exclusively
to learning and is convinced that his pupil Hippolytus is still nothing but a child, although the "child" has been married for over
three years to a poor noblewoman, Ludmila, by whom he has a
baby. It is interesting that Pisarev gave the stupid pedantic tutor,
who in this vaudeville is duped by everybody, the name of the
philosopher Schelling, who was then highly regarded by certain
circles of our society.

Pisarev had a great success with the vaudeville *Busybody*, in
which the character of Repeikin is excellently drawn. He pokes
his nose into everything and undertakes all sorts of things, considering himself as a first-class expert, whereas, in fact, he spoils
everything he touches. The itch to meddle in every venture without examining it carefully, even leads him to arrange the wedding
of his rival with a girl whom he himself intends to marry. This
part, which was also played by Shchepkin, is among the finest in
the vaudeville repertoire.

Two vaudeville-operas by Pisarev dealing with Oriental life,
The Caliph's Amusements and *The Magic Nose, or the Talismans
and Dates,* based on changes of costumes, transformations and
dances, belong to the category of vaudevilles emphasizing elaborate production.

His *Fifteen Years in Paris, or Not All Friends Are Alike* is unlike any of his other plays and should, in fact, be classed as a melodrama.

Here and there in Pisarev's vaudevilles we hear a note of social
criticism, which is hardly characteristic of vaudevilles of that period. For example, in *The Caliph's Amusements* the injustice of
laws and the corruption of judges are revealed:

> Men, we'll find, on serious thought,
> Throughout the world are quite the same:
> Though of judges there're a lot
> Justice ev'rywhere is lame—
> Laws are ev'rywhere forgotten,
> Weak men serve the mighty peer,
> Judges ev'rywhere are rotten,
> Truth's remote and all too dear.

Contemporary topics and critical tendencies are more apparent
in vaudeville during the 1840's. During Nicholas I's reactionary

reign, when freedom of speech and of the press was completely suppressed, vaudeville unexpectedly became one of the few outlets for public dissatisfaction. The criticism in the vaudevilles themselves was mostly of an innocent and superficial character, but the public itself would provide what the author, held in the iron clutches of censorship, was unable to say. P. A. Karatygin's vaudeville *The Bakery*, for example, was very popular because of this couplet of Karl Ivanovich Kleister:

> Police constable himself
> Buys our cakes and loaves of bread.

The actors made such an expressive gesture at the word "buy" that the public readily drew the appropriate inference about the constable. F. A. Kony (1809–1879) began to introduce into vaudeville seeds of genuine political and social satire. In his pieces *The Prince with a Toupee and a Cataract* and *Petersburg Lodgings* he endeavored to circumvent the censorship and criticize those aspects of the autocratic police system which people most abhorred.

In *The Prince with a Toupee* there are bitterly satirical verses on the policy of Nicholas Palkin:

> Nothing critics know but cursing!
> Lock them up with the insane!
> Let them there keep on rehearsing—
> This is wisdom true and plain.
> To maintain both peace and order
> All the students should be placed
> In the care of a strict warder—
> This is wisdom pure and chaste!
> No oppression or vexation!
> Revenues are to be raised
> Through additional taxation
> Of the sot by liquor crazed.
> Vengeance now will freely flutter,
> But my spies will put a curb
> On whoever dares to utter
> Words that public peace disturb.
> And all folks, with great elation,
> Will exclaim: Here's freedom's age!
> Let them dream of liberation:
> We shall keep in store our rage.

Still, the majority of vaudevilles in the 1840's, too, were pure entertainment—a tendency which was fostered by the government's theatrical policy.

Most of Kony's other vaudevilles are not much more than character anecdotes, which is clear from their very titles: *The Bridegroom by Proxy, Devils Dwell in a Calm Pool, The Deceased Husband, The Husband in a Chimney, Titular Councilors at Home, Don't Fall in Love Insanely, The Husband of All Wives,* and *The Hussar Girl.*

The vaudeville themes of P. A. Karatygin (1805–1879) are equally insignificant and anecdotal. A brother of the famous tragedian, and himself a fairly skillful comic actor and an experienced epigrammatist and extemporizer, he wrote forty-six vaudevilles, twenty of which are originals, and the others adaptations from the French. The more popular among these were the following: *Young Housekeepers of Old Bachelors; Borrowed Wives; Two Wives vs. One Husband; A Wife and the Umbrella; An Adventure at a Spa; The Officer for Special Missions; Civil Servants' Uniform;* and *A House in the Petersburg Suburb.* The distinguishing mark of Karatygin's vaudevilles, as compared with the work of other writers, is their closeness to the life of the people.

P. S. Fyodorov (subsequently the director of the Petersburg theatres) and the Moscow director S. P. Solovyov should be listed among the second-rate vaudeville authors.

Among Fyodorov's innumerable plays the vaudeville *The Duck, or A Glass of Water* was particularly well adapted for the stage. Easy dialogue, action, and a great many showy scenes—especially when Martynov played the leading role of the irascible old father —made the audience forget the absurdity of the plot.

During the early period of his literary career, N. A. Nekrasov also wrote vaudeville under the pen name Perepelsky (*Fedya and Volodya, An Awl Cannot Be Hidden in a Sack, Grandfather's Parrots, That's the Meaning of Being in Love with an Actress,* and so forth).

The vaudeville of the 1840's differs from that of earlier days in its heroes and its social setting. The merchant, government clerk, plebeian, and commoner have taken the place of the nobleman-aristocrat; instead of a stage set of a landowner's mansion or a drawing room in a nobleman's house in the capital, we have a commoner's apartment in the Petersburg Suburb or a merchant's store.

Vorobyov (1805–1860), under the nom de plume Nicholas Timofeyevich Lensky, was the most talented among the vaude-villists of the 1840's. In 1824 he began his career on the Moscow stage, where he played young men's roles and bridegrooms in comedy. As an actor he met with no success until he began translating comedies and vaudevilles; his writing enhanced his popularity as an actor. In all he wrote about seventy-two plays, published together in the six-volume *Theatre of D. T. Lensky* (St. Petersburg, 1874). His only original piece is a libretto to Verstovsky's opera *Gromoboy*. He also contributed much to Russian literature as a translator of Béranger.

His work was correctly evaluated by one of his friends:

Lensky's whole life was dedicated to art; he worked hard and always honestly. Even at an early age, beginning with his first experiments in translation, he met with brilliant success. Pushkin himself prophesied great popularity for him. For twenty years his plays attracted a large public to the Bolshoy Theatre, who came to enjoy one of his one-act vaudevilles such as *Both Good and Bad*. Lensky wrote for Shchepkin, Repina, and Saburova, and these actors owe much of their success to his literary gifts, so marked that his adaptations were better than the originals. To mention only one: *Leo Gurich Sinichkin* is an adaptation that will long outlive its author. Most of his plays were successes—some were triumphs.

Lensky's five-act vaudeville *Leo Gurich Sinichkin, or The Provinical Débutante* (produced first in Petersburg in 1840) enjoyed a particularly prolonged success. It is an adaptation of a French play, *The Débutante's Father*, with added allusions to the Russian provincial theatre. It therefore may be considered as a precursor of Ostrovsky's plays portraying theatrical customs, and most closely resembles *Talents and Their Admirers*. It tells the story of a provincial manager Pustoslavtsev (patterned on the manager Vysheslavtsev) completely dependent upon aristocratic patrons who regard the female members of his company as their harem. Unashamed, they make overtures to a young actress making her début, who does not even dare to take offense. Without a patron's support it is impossible for her to secure a role, since the manager is indifferent to a talented actress not graced with a rich patron, or

not "the favorite godchild of the local governor." Customs of the
provincial theatre are vividly described in the following verses of a
theatre lover:

> Your theatrical career,
> How's it to be built up here!
> Stage success, who can here claim,
> If the stage is naught but shame?
> What a building, what a hall!
> What spectators, above all!
> Lenten butter, tallow grease
> Smut one's face as with some fleece!
> Back scenes, drops, stage sets, screens,
> Costumes—all are wonder scenes!
> Actors, actresses embrace
> All that's beauty, charm and grace.
>
> . . . .
>
> Tragedies are full of fun
> Just as soon as they're begun!
> Merry laughter loudly rings
> At the sight of queens and kings!
> Verses are in singsong read,
> And with nonsense one is fed.
> Hands are stretched now up, now down
> As would act a foolish clown.
>
> . . . .
>
> Actors here, though very bad,
> Will indulge in any fad.
> Impresarios will cast
> Any job on their poor cast.
> Operatic parts they'll take
> If cash profit is at stake.
> Even "Askold's Tomb" will do
> When naught better is in view.
>
> . . . .
>
> In the provinces we see
> Ballets staged for people's glee.
> Costumes are so rich and smart
> That with laugh they fill one's heart.
> No offense will now be stressed—
> Briefly, here's how they are dressed:
> Sylphs appear in scarlet tights,
> Zephyrs make in boots their flights.

> Your thearical career,
> How's it to be built up here!
> Stage success, who can here claim,
> If the stage is naught but shame!

Despite the fact that Russian vaudeville had such gifted representatives as Khmelnitsky and Pisarev in the 1820's and Lensky, Kony, and Karatygin in the 1840's, critics regarded its popularity as a symptom of decadent taste and degradation of dramatic art.

Belinsky wrote of our vaudevilles:

To begin with, they are mostly adaptations from French vaudeville; consequently, couplets, witticisms, amusing situations, intrigue, and denouement—all these are ready-made; one has only to learn how to make use of them. And what is the result? Lightness, naturalness, and animation which, despite one's self, gratified one's imagination in a French vaudeville—that wit, those charming follies, that talent for coquetry, that play of the intellect, those grimaces of fantasy—all those vanish in the Russian version. There remain merely ponderousness, clumsiness, artificiality, two or three puns, two or three equivocations—and nothing more.

On another occasion he wrote:

Vaudevilles translated from the French, or adapted from the French, as announced in theatre programs, are, as a matter of fact, neither translated nor adapted: they are forcibly dragged from the French stage to the Russian. What wonder, then, that they appear before the Russian audience disheveled and distorted, with dull witticisms, flat jests, and poor verses. Dress a Frenchman in a dark gray tunic, gird him with a belt, put leggings and bast shoes on his legs, tie somebody's bushy beard on his face, and make him even curse in Russian: still he will not be a Russian muzhik, but to his own and your regret will continue to be a Frenchman in the guise of a Russian peasant. Consequently he will be neither a Russian nor a Frenchman, but a caricature of both, with no face of his own.

Gogol judged vaudevilles even more severely. He considered that their popularity was one of the principal causes of that decadence in the theatre which completely prevented actors from realizing their artistic talents.

Chapter XIII

GRIBOYEDOV

ALEXANDER SERGYEVICH GRIBOYEDOV (1795–1829), the author of the immortal comedy *Woe from Wit,* began to write for the theatre in his early youth. As a fourteen-year-old student he wrote a parody *(Dmitry Dryanskoy* [1]*)* on Ozerov's popular tragedy *Dmitry Donskoy.* In 1812 he left the university and enlisted in a hussar regiment; and, while stationed in the western provinces he became very friendly with Prince A. A. Shakhovskoy, who was also in the army. The friendship was very helpful to Griboyedov at the beginning of his theatre career. Under Shakhovskoy's influence, he adapted the French comedy of Cruezé de Lesser *Le Secret du ménage,* under the title *The Young Couple,* produced in Petersburg on September 29, 1815. It resembles very closely the one-act comedies which at that time fashionable theatre lovers used to compose for their actress friends. In Petersburg, Griboyedov, along with N. I. Khmelnitsky and A. A. Zhandr and his other companions of the front rows of the orchestra, composed or, rather, translated comedies either for Valberkhova, or Semyonova.

On February 11, 1818, *Feigned Infidelity* was produced. In a letter to Katenin, Griboyedov wrote that this play was based on *Les Fausses Infidélités* by Barthe, and that he intended to present it to his good friend Semyonova for her benefit performance. The play was produced in Moscow, where it was so poorly performed, according to Griboyedov's account, that the theatre director Kokoshkin "humbly apologized to me, because my delightful verses were

[1] That is, Dmitry, the Trashy One.—Ed.

being so horribly distorted by the actors who refused to follow instructions."

In the same year, 1818, the comedy *One's Own Family, or The Married Fiancée,* which Griboyedov wrote with Shakhovskoy and Zhandr, was produced. It is far superior to the preceding plays. The verse—free, flowing, and expressive—is not so unlike that in *Woe from Wit.* The description of the life of the people is graphic; real characters are shown on the stage, and their psychology is true both as to time and as to place. The best proof of the play's merit lies in the fact that it continued to be produced during the entire nineteenth century. In the 1890's it was given in the Aleksandrinsky Theatre, with Savina in the leading role. After the revolution it was successfully revived by one of the studios of the Moscow Art Theatre.

The Student, a three-act comedy in prose, written with Katenin's direct assistance in 1817, is still more interesting. The authors particularly succeeded in the characters of Benevolsky, an enthusiastic, provincial youth naïvely dreaming about a career in government service and the fame of a poet, and his patron Zvezdov, a giddy and vain Petersburg gentleman who, strictly speaking, is completely idle but dashes here and there, busying himself with thousands of things, and makes it a rule to act contrary to any advice, however sensible and wise. The satire, the natural dialogue, and the departure from the conventions of French dramatists distinguish *The Student* from those "fashionable bagatelles" which constitute the bulk of the repertoire of the period. Several roles in it foreshadow characters in *Woe from Wit*—Zvezdov somewhat resembling Repetilov, and the hussar spendthrift Sablin reminding one of Skalozub.

On November 10, 1819, Griboyedov's *The Rehearsal of an Interlude* was staged, having been written especially for Bryansky's benefit performance. In those days such interludes were written by Shakhovskoy, Khmelnitsky, Zagoskin, Kokoshkin, and others. They were staged to enable many actors to take part in the benefit performance and to make it as interesting as possible by performing their most successful scenes.

In 1823, for the opening of the theatre season at the Bolshoy Theatre which had been erected on the site of the one destroyed by fire, Griboyedov wrote a prologue entitled *The Prophet's Dream,* dedicated to Lomonosov.

On September 11, 1824, the vaudeville opera *Who's the Brother, Who's the Sister? or One Deceit After Another* was staged in Moscow. The music for it was composed by Verstovsky, while Griboyedov and Prince Vyazemsky wrote the text. They wrote the piece at the request of F. F. Kokoshkin for the benefit performance of his favorite, Lvova-Sinetskaya.

All these dramatic pieces of Griboyedov—even the best ones, such as *One's Own Family* and *The Student*—have little originality; their artistic significance is not great, and they were not destined to make the author famous.

Although the great comedy which made Griboyedov's name one of the most cherished in the Russian theatre was conceived while he was still at the university, it absorbed his creative imagination for many years, and until the end of his life he did not cease to improve and perfect it. Indeed, it became his "poetical diary," with which he never parted. He used this piece, which he had originally conceived in the form of a "dramatic poem," to express his loftiest ideas, his most cherished aspirations, all his emotional warmth, and his whole creative genius.

The original title of the comedy, *Woe to Wit,* more graphically than the final one conveyed its fundamental idea: the struggle of a solitary, clever, and noble man against a "crowd of torturers," against the stupid and vile rule of the Famusovs, the Skalozubs, and the Molchalins, and the tragic outcome of that conflict. Griboyedov's letter to Katenin (January, 1825) furnishes valuable material for an understanding of his philosophy:

In my comedy there are twenty-five fools to one reasonable man, and that man, of course, stands in conflict with the society surrounding him. He is understood by no one. Nobody forgives the fact that he is somewhat better than the rest, and that in the beginning he is gay—this is a vice! "To jest and ay to jest—how can you stand for that!" He holds the eccentricities of his former acquaintances up for some scrutiny; but what is to be done if there is no trace of nobility in them! His banter is not caustic until he is driven mad; even so—"a serpent, not a man." And later, when personalities become involved, when "our kind are provoked," he is declared anathema. "He delights in humbling one, in little pricks; he's spiteful, haughty, foul." He cannot tolerate vileness:

"O mighty God! He's a Carbonari!" Somebody, out of mere wickedness, spreads the rumor that he is insane; no one believes it, yet everyone repeats the tale, and, finally, the voice of evil reaches him. In addition to this the girl for whose sake alone he has journeyed to Moscow has an aversion for him. Everything becomes clear to him; he spits in the girl's face and everybody else's, and that's the end.

Griboyedov's hatred of the autocratic serf regime, "the quagmire state" where "merit is measured in direct proportion to the number of slaves and decorations," and his championing of the rights and liberty of man, permeate *Woe from Wit*. The play, written on the eve of the December 14, 1825, uprising, is full of stirring progressive political and social thought, which makes it one of the best literary expressions of the Decembrists' ideology.

The piercing satire, directed against the "eminent scoundrels," the indolent and ignorant nobility, the stupid serf owners, the "bootlicking and scheming" officials, the dull and reactionary militarists, the ignoramuses, cringers, denouncers, "ominous old women, old men growing decrepit o'er fiddlesticks and nonsense," sounded like a gunshot in the black and silent night of the Russia of Arakcheyev.[2]

Chatsky, the hero of the comedy, the passionate opponent of the political system and the social customs of that world of violence and oppression, was considered by many contemporaries and by later generations as a direct portrait of a Decembrist. "The melancholy figure of Chatsky," wrote A. I. Hertzen, "which withdrew into irony, appeared at the very end of Alexander I's reign, on the eve of the rebellion at the Isaac Square: he is a Decembrist."

Griboyedov must have anticipated that Imperial censorship would bar his comedy from the stage; and to disarm his enemies he bitterly renounced certain of the boldest passages in the original version. He wrote:

The first draft of this dramatic poem, as I conceived it, was much better and more significant than the present one, clad in a frivolous

[2] Aleksey Aleksandrovich Arakcheyev (1769–1834), Minister of War and head of the secret police under Paul I and Alexander I—"Alexander's conservative watchdog" and "Paul's drill sergeant," according to Sir Bernard Pares. Known for his ruthless suppression of revolts arising from the unpopularity of the "military colonies."—Ed.

dress which I was compelled to put on it. The childish ambition to hear my verses in the theatre, the ambition that it meet with success there, prompted me to spoil my creation as much as possible.

Nevertheless, the piece was categorically banned, not only for stage presentation, but even for publication. This interdict did not succeed, however, in stopping handwritten copies from being very broadly circulated, and in a short time it was as well known as the clandestine verses of Pushkin and Ryleyev. Decembrists made many copies of *Woe from Wit*, and distributed them throughout Russia as a means of political propaganda.

The following comment of A. A. Bestuzhev is characteristic of the Decembrists' attitude toward the piece:

The handwritten copy of Griboyedov's comedy *Woe from Wit* presents a phenomenon such as we have not beheld since *The Minor*. A great many characters portrayed boldly and graphically, a vivid picture of Moscow customs, real emotion, intellect and wit in discourse, hitherto unknown fluency, and the conversational quality of the Russian language in the verses—all these lure, attract, and stagger one. A man with a heart will not read it without laughing, nor without being moved to tears. . . . Posterity will properly evaluate this comedy and rank it among the best of folk creations.

Belinsky, who at first (during his brief "reconciliation with reality") adopted a negative attitude toward *Woe from Wit*, wrote of it in 1840:

It is the noblest humane creation, an energetic (and also the earliest) protest against abominable reality, against government officials, grafters, debauching noblemen, against the fashionable society, against voluntary servility, etc., etc., etc.

From the point of view of style and dramatic form, *Woe from Wit* is also an extraordinary and peculiar phenomenon in the theatrical literature of the period. At first glance, it is a classical comedy with many of the traditional characteristics as developed by the best of the French classicists, particularly by Molière. The obligatory rule of classicism—the three "unities"—is complied with, and the traditional love intrigue is also retained. Among the characters are some set types as required by a classical comedy; the names of some of the characters are symbolic, and so forth.

Attempts were even made to draw a parallel between *Woe from Wit* and a specific classical comedy, Molière's *Misanthrope*. Such comparison, however, merely tends to accentuate Griboyedov's independence. He managed to put into a traditional frame a completely new and original content, brilliantly overcoming the schematism and convention of classicism.

"I write as freely as I live," he said; and actually one is astonished at the genuinely inventive boldness which he reveals at every step in his creativeness.

In the style of his comedy [P. N. Sakulin justly remarks] we observe various peculiarities which deviate from the classical pattern. Having confined himself to four acts instead of the traditional five, Griboyedov also renounces a confused plot construction. Within the frame of the classical unity of three he develops the action of his comedy with extraordinary, Pushkin-like ease. It seems as if a solid steel spring has been inserted into the structure of the comedy, and this spring, without shocks and jolts, expands from act to act, driving its action with strict precision. Griboyedov does not hesitate to introduce into the structure of high comedy some features of light comedy, and even of vaudeville (for instance, Repetilov's exaggerations). He replaces the annoying and dry didacticism of the moralizers with the ardent orations of Chatsky, full of living ideas. The characters are all full-blooded, and some of the heroes have become living symbols. The author quite frequently makes use of definite prototypes, without fearing "portraiture." On the stage we see live, real people with lines from everyday life and extraordinarily colorful speech. Even contemporaries are astounded by the language and verse of the comedy. Much of it, in the form of pithy proverbs, has become part of popular speech and is immortalized. . . . A first-class poet, Griboyedov easily overcame the restraints of classical dogma. Making use of the foundations of the classical pattern, he created an architectural edifice of a new and genuinely artistic style of high comedy.

In *Woe from Wit* the victory of realism over "classical dogma" is particularly apparent in the creation of a remarkable gallery of generalized portraits of the Famusov Moscow. Griboyedov considered that the playwright should blend the individual traits of his character with the traits typical of other people like him. "Portraits, and only portraits," he wrote to Katenin, "form the substance of both comedy and tragedy; however, they comprise certain traits that are common to many other persons, while some traits are common to the human race at large, in so far as every man resembles all his two-legged brethren." In his view, portraits must be realistic without degenerating into caricature or artificial schemes invented by the author. "I hate caricatures; in my picture you will find none," he said. Molière's miser seemed to him "unbearable," and he wittily called him "anthropos of his own [Molière's] fabrication."

These artistic principles are brilliantly realized in *Woe from Wit*, where each character is both an individual and a type, and where generalization is so well handled that the Famusovs, the Molchalins, and the Skalozubs became definitive names which still live in our everyday language. We know how often V. I. Lenin used to resort to Griboyedov's images, applying them to the enemies of the toilers. "If around us, or within ourselves," wrote Lunacharsky,[3] "there are fragments of the Famusovs, the Molchalins, the Repetilovs, and so forth, we must smite them with an iron hammer, burning this abomination out of ourselves and out of others."

The boldness and originality of *Woe from Wit* provoked a hail of criticism from the jealous supporters of classicism. Their infuriation with Griboyedov is well illustrated by this epigram:

> Do not contend that two by two is four:
> Read *Woe from Wit*—you'll see that it is not.
> Four acts in it, yet not as heretofore
> Will two by two make four, but merely naught.

Pushkin, having himself experienced the oppressiveness of literary prejudice and stagnation, made this excellent rebuttal to the critics of *Woe from Wit*: "A dramatic author should be judged by the laws which he himself considers binding upon him; therefore, I do not condemn either the plan or the denouement or the propriety of Griboyedov's comedy."

Only the character of Chatsky provoked Pushkin's rejoinder. Chatsky (as "ardent a dreamer in the land of eternal snow" as Griboyedov himself) realistically portrayed the best and most progressive group of the young noblemen intelligentsia, and at

[3] Anatoly Vasilyevich Lunacharsky (1875–1933), Director of the People's Commissariat of Education 1917–1929; long-time revolutionist, member of the Central Committee of the Communist Party of the U.S.S.R., and author of many works on drama and the theatre.—Ed.

the same time was a sounding board for the author's ideas. This provided the scenes in which Chatsky recites his lashing monologues with an inevitable element of artificiality, which, at first, even such connoisseurs of drama as Pushkin refused to excuse. He wrote of Chatsky: "Everything he says is very clever. But to whom does he say it? To Famusov? To Skalozub? To Moscow grandmothers at a ball? To Molchalin? This is unpardonable. The first characteristic of a clever man is his ability to discern at the first glance with whom he is dealing, and not to cast pearls before the Repetilovs, etc." *

Griboyedov himself ardently defended the artist's right to originality and to noncomformance to tradition: "He who is more apt to abide by school precepts, by rules of habit, by grandmothers' traditions, than by his own creative powers, if he be an artist, let him break his palette and his brush, his chisel and his pen, and let him throw them out of the window." He was not to see his work of genius on the stage. The pupils of the Petersburg dramatic school rehearsed it for their school play. Griboyedov was much interested in the production, and on several occasions he visited the school either alone or with friends. Yet even this performance failed to take place. Count Miloradovich, having learned about it, ordered that it be cancelled.

Woe from Wit was played for the first time in Petersburg in 1830, without the third act, and with other substantial deletions. It was not produced in full until 1869. Of the first performance of Woe from Wit on Bryansky's benefit night, Khrapovitsky recorded in his diary: "Contrary to expectations, the play was received without enthusiasm."

The first performance was given with the following cast: Karatygin, Chatsky; Ryazantsev, Famusov; Semyonova, Sophia; Bryansky, Gorichev; A. M. Karatygina, Natalie Dmitriyevna; Grigoryev, Zagoretsky; Dyur, Molchalin; Mongotier, Liza; Kunin, Skalozub; Yezhova, Khlestova; and P. A. Karatygin, Repetilov. This assignment of parts is extremely curious. It was based on the division of the characters in the play according to the traditional categories. Chatsky recites noble monologues, and therefore his part was assigned to the hero. The role of Sophia was given to the tragic actress Semyonova, whose acting possibly conveyed a

* Varneke's quotation from Pushkin's remarks is incomplete.—Tr.

traditional character to her part, emphasizing its seriousness and dramatic effect.

It is noteworthy that Griboyedov himself had planned Sophia's part for A. M. Kolosova; but when it did not appeal to her he made her promise to play the role of Natalie Dmitriyevna, which apparently was the part he considered psychologically closest to Sophia.

Subsequently, I. V. Samarin, an artist of the Moscow Maly Theatre, was reputed to have been the best Chatsky. The actor P. M. Medvedev wrote in his memoirs about Samarin's acting in this "crowning" role of his repertoire:

I saw him in this part in my childhood, and also when I was fifteen, so that I am in a position to judge his acting soundly. It was great. His first act and his entrance were perfect. The audience actually did believe that he "hastened," "rushed," and "was revived by the meeting." Within my recollection no one was ever able so to feel and master the verse as Samarin did. What flexibility in the intonations of the voice! What speed in the transitions from one subject to another—wonderful! What merriment and humor in the recollections of childhood. How he managed to draw with Griboyedov's verse—indeed, draw—the portraits of Moscow society! Youth, sarcasm, bitterness in places, pity for Russia and a desire to stir her up—all this combined, and with his flaming love for Sophia, poured forth like a fountain.

The great Shchepkin probably gave the most perfect impersonation of Famusov's role.

Time failed to lessen the value of Griboyedov's drama. In 1872, Goncharov wrote:

The comedy *Woe from Wit* stands apart in literature, distinguished by youthfulness, freshness and greater viability than other literary works. It reminds one of a centenarian around whom everybody, having outlived his day, dies and falls, while he, healthy and fresh, strolls amidst the graves of the old and the cradles of the young, so that it occurs to no one that his turn will also come some day.

More than half a century has elapsed. Griboyedov's comedy has become an integral part of the cultural heritage of the free peoples of our socialist country, side by side with Pushkin, Lermontov, and Gogol, as one of the earliest "people's creations" which is the pride of Russian national art.

There is much interest in the surviving fragments of the plays which Griboyedov wrote subsequent to *Woe from Wit;* namely, the plan of *Rodamist and Zenobia,* the plan and sketch of a scene from *The Year 1812,* and excerpts from *The Georgian Night.*

The tragedy *Rodamist and Zenobia* deals with the conspiracy of lords against the tyrant tsar, and its failure due to the fact that the conspirators have no contact with the people. ("The people do not participate in their venture—it is as if they do not even exist.") This theme reflects, perhaps, Griboyedov's thoughts on the causes of the failure of the Decembrist uprising.

In the tragedy *The Year 1812* he had in mind an epic of Russia's recent struggle against the French aggressors. The tragedy was to be based upon the bold antithesis between the heroism and self-denial of the people, and the cowardice and treachery of the nobility and "the servants of the government." In violation of all "literary decorum," Griboyedov selected a serf-peasant "M." for his hero. The antiserfdom theme of the tragedy is fully apparent in the final episode: The war is over, "old abominations— M. is again subjected to his master's rod," and in despair, he commits suicide.

When Griboyedov was last passing through Moscow on his way to Persia, he told his friends: "I will write no more comedies; my gayety has gone, and without it there can be no good comedy. But I have a completed tragedy." These sad words apparently refer to his last work, the tragedy *The Georgian Night.* Bulgarin thus describes the plot of the play:

A certain Georgian prince, as a ransom for his favorite steed, gave to another prince his youthful slave. This was an ordinary occurrence, and therefore the prince gave no thought as to its consequences. Presently, the slave's mother, the prince's former wet nurse as well as his daughter's nurse, appears, reproaching him for his inhuman deed; she reminds him of her service, demanding that either her son be allowed to come back to her or she be permitted to go with her son and become the slave of the same master as he, and she threatens the prince with Heaven's wrath. At first, the prince becomes angry; then he promises to return her son; and then, in the princely fashion, forgets his promise. The mother, however, remembers that her child has been torn away from her heart, and, being an Asiatic, she plots cruel revenge. She goes to a forest, invokes the Delhis—the evil spirits of Georgia—and enters into a compact with Hell in order to destroy her master's family. A Russian officer appears at the house—a strange creature, judged by his sentiments and ways of reasoning. The wet nurse prompts the Delhis to make her charge, the prince's daughter, fall in love with the officer. The girl elopes with her lover from her parents' home. The prince seeks revenge. He searches for the pair, and sees them on the summit of St. David's mountain. He takes a rifle, aims at the officer, but the Delhis fling the bullet into the girl's heart. But the angry nurse's retribution is not yet complete. She insists that the rifle be given her in order that she may kill the prince; but instead she kills her son. The inhuman prince is punished by Heaven for his indifference to parental feelings, and he learns the price of his child's loss. The wicked nurse is punished for having desecrated by vengeance a noble impulse. They perish in despair.

This tragedy, like *The Year 1812,* must have sounded a strong protest against a serfdom which doomed people to the horrors of slavery.

If Griboyedov had succeeded in completing all these dramas, they would have marked the beginning of an entirely new phase in his literary development. At any rate, they are eloquent proof of the fact that even after *Woe from Wit* his creativeness continued to be intense, blazing new paths for the Russian theatre. Like Pushkin, he obviously felt the mighty influence of Shakespearean drama and sought to create a popular historical drama which would reflect in dramatic characters the progressive ideas of his age.

Chapter XIV

PUSHKIN

PUSHKIN, THE FOUNDER of the Russian literary language and the father of the new Russian literature, was also our greatest reformer in the field of playwrighting, completely breaking away from its previous line of development and leading it onto a new path.

Pushkin had been captivated by the theatre from childhood. According to the reminiscences of his sister, O. S. Pavlishcheva, he loved as a child "to improvise little comedies, used to organize performances like a real theatre, where the brother was both author and actor and the sister represented the audience." On one occasion "the audience" hissed at the comedy *The Kidnaper*—kidnaped by the youthful author from his favorite, Molière. At the lyceum Pushkin, collaborating with his schoolmate M. L. Yakovlev, wrote a comedy *Thus It Goes in the World*; and he also began a five-act comedy in verse, *The Philosopher*. At Tsarskoye Selo, he enthusiastically attended the plays which were staged in Count V. V. Tolstoy's private theatre.

In the stormy years of his Petersburg life following graduation from the lyceum, Pushkin became a full-fledged theatre habitué, "an honorary citizen of the backstage, a severe theatre critic, and an inconstant admirer of lovely actresses."

Membership in the Green Lamp club, at the meetings of which heated discussions about the theatre took place; visits to the famous Shakhovskoy's "garret," where prominent theatre people like Griboyedov, Khmelnitsky, Zhandr, and Katenin used to assemble; personal acquaintance with the outstanding artists of the drama and the ballet (Semyonova, Kolosova, Sosnitsky, V. Karatygin, Istomina)—all these drew the young poet into the very midst of the theatrical life of the capital, involving him in the controversies between the theatre factions.

Later, when in exile "in deserted Moldavia," Pushkin continued to take an interest in all the news of the theatrical world, filling his letters to Petersburg friends with questions about actors, playwrights, and theatre lovers: "How are the Vsevolozhskis? How's Mansurov? How's Barkov? How are the Sosnitskys? How's Khmelnitsky? How's Katenin? How's Shakhovskoy? How's Yezhova? How's Count Pushkin? How's Semyonova? How's Zavadovsky? How's the whole theatre?" "I crave the theatre," he confesses with anguish.

In this period Pushkin wrote two plays with completely dissimilar conceptions of playwrighting: a "high" historical tragedy *Vadim* on the subject that had been popular in radical literature ever since the time of Knyazhnin, the uprising of the people of Novgorod against the first Varangian princess; and a comedy about a gambler in the spirit of the "fashionable" comedies of Shakhovskoy and Khmelnitsky (which, in turn, sprang from the French comedy repertoire of the early part of the nineteenth century).

During a brief stay in Odessa, he was enthusiastic about the Italian opera—which, according to contemporaries, ranked with that of Petersburg—and about its master, the "delightful Rossini." As in the past, the poet was enchanted by all the allure of the theatre:

> What of those dreams midst brilliant pieces?
> The lorgnette, its glances keen?
> Those rendezvous behind coulisses,
> The prima donna? Ballet's sheen?

In his solitude at Mikhailovskoye, again cut off from direct contact with the theatre, Pushkin studied Shakespeare intently and, as a result, was inspired to write a "romantic tragedy" of the history of the Russian people. The poet by this time felt prepared for such a "literary feat." ("I feel that my soul has fully developed. I am able to create," he wrote in a letter to a friend.) In 1825 he wrote his greatest work, *Boris Godunov,* which constitutes an epoch in the history of Russian drama.

Upon his return from exile, Pushkin again became a devoted habitué of the capital's theatres, and once more turned to the idea of a "fashionable" comedy. He made a rough draft of a play, *At Length Decided They to Quit Moscow,* and tried a translation from the French of Casimir Bonjour, *Le Mari à bonnes fortunes.*

The following list of plays which Pushkin had in preparation in the late 1820's is most interesting: *The Avaricious Knight, Romulus and Remus, Mozart and Salieri, Don Juan, Jesus, Berald of Savoia, Paul I, The Enamored Devil, Dimitry and Marina,* and *Kurbsky.* The plots of these works, covering a broad historical period from ancient times to the eighteenth century, and concerned with the most divergent lands and peoples (Judaea, Rome, Italy, Spain, Russia), indicate the extraordinary range and diversity of the new dramatic conceptions which excited the poet's creative imagination.

Only three of these plans were destined to materialize: during the "fertile" 1830 autumn at Boldino, Pushkin finished *The Avaricious Knight, Mozart and Salieri,* and *The Stone Guest.* With *The Feast During the Plague,* which was written at the same time these pieces form a cycle of "dramatic scenes," or "short tragedies," which mark a new and remarkable phase in the evolution of the poet's career as playwright.

The Water-Nymph (1832) marked Pushkin's departure from the pattern of "miniature tragedies" and his new researches in the drama.

During the last years of his life, he became rather indifferent to the theatre, or, more correctly, to what was then happening in the Russian theatre, probably because his standards of dramatic art were much higher than those prevailing in the theatre of that period. Nashchokin, obviously referring to this time, stated, "Pushkin did not like either our university or our theatre; he held neither Karatygin nor even Mochalov in high esteem." We do know, however, of Pushkin's interest in the production of Gogol's *Inspector-General* at the Moscow Maly Theatre, his friendship with M. S. Shchepkin, and his insistence that the famous actor write his memoirs.

Pushkin's last work as a dramatist was the unfinished *Scenes from the Age of Knighthood* (1834–1835), and plans for plays on the executioner's son and on St. Joan, upon which he was working at the same time. These opened up to our drama entirely new vistas.

Not only was he a great playwright, he was also a remarkable dramatic theoretician. His reflections on theatrical and playwrighting problems still have a great deal of meaning. Among his numerous articles and memoranda on the theory of drama, the following should be mentioned: "My Observation on the Russian Theatre," 1820; "On Dramatic Works," 1825; "On National Quality in Literature," 1826; "On Byron and His Imitators," 1827; sketches for the preface to *Boris Godunov*, 1827–1831; "Notations on the popular drama and on Pogodin's *Martha the Mayor*, 1830, and on Shakespeare," 1834. Further expressions of the poet's ideas about the theatre and comments on plays and playwrights are scattered through his correspondence, especially in his letters to Vyazemsky, Katenin, Gnedich, N. N. Rayevsky, and his brother.

August Schlegel's book *A Course on Dramaturgy* and Guizot's articles on the *Life of Shakespeare* exercised a certain influence on Pushkin's views of the theatre.

Realism and the folk quality were the two fundamental and immutable principles of the whole playwrighting philosophy of the mature Pushkin. It is precisely from the standpoint of these tenets that he condemned French classicism, with its conventionality, its historical falsehood, its schematism in character delineation, its aristocratic exclusiveness and aloofness from the life of the people.

Giving full credit to Racine's *Phèdre* for its "verses full of meaning, precision, and harmony," he considered its plan and characters as "the height of stupidity and a complete zero from the standpoint of inventiveness." His sense of realism was unable to reconcile itself with the fact that the stern "half-Scythian Hippolytus" had been converted by Racine into "a well brought-up, urbane and respectful boy"; that Theseus resembled "Molière's first horn bearer," and so forth. Despite his appreciation for Corneille's *Cid*, he said of this tragedy: "Corneille's Romans are Gascon barons, if not Spanish knights." He sharply criticized the dramatic poetry of the French classics: "the arbitrary rules of the 'unities,' the artificiality of the confidants' roles, the unnaturalness of the asides." "Unity of action should be maintained," he wrote, "but time and place are too capricious, which results in many restraints so that conspiracies, weddings, declarations of love, state conferences, feasts, all take place in the same room! The excessive speed or the constraints upon the development of action—confidants . . . asides are equally incompatible with common sense."

The "court etiquette" of the classic tragedy went counter to Pushkin's democratic leanings. He ridiculed "its timid affectation, foolish arrogance, and its habit of looking at people of higher position with some sort of servility, which gives to them a strange, inhuman quality." He wrote about Corneille, "His rigid muse was powdered and rouged," and called Racine, ironically, "Marquis Racine."

Pushkin compared the artificial and aristocratic theatre of French classicism, which so restrained the poet's creative freedom, with the Shakespearean theatre, in which "popular passions" had free rein, inhibiting laws and limitations were unknown, and the somewhat coarse, plain language of the "city squares" was used. "I am firmly convinced," he said, "that the folk laws of the Shakespearean drama, and not the court etiquette of Racine's tragedy, befit our theatre."

It was precisely in the Shakespearean theatre that Pushkin found the genuine artistic realism which he had always been seeking (even though he called it by another term—"genuine romanticism"). This realism, in his opinion, lay not in outward "verisimilitude" in the "strict correctness of the color of the costume for the time and place," but in profound psychological veracity. "Truth of passions, genuineness of feelings in given circumstances —that is what our reason requires from the playwright." Side by side with "verisimilitude of feelings" he placed the "verisimilitude of characters." Shakespeare's images fascinated him by their extraordinary depth, vitality, many-sidedness, dynamism—by everything that was absent in the French classical tragedy. "The types created by Shakespeare are not, as in Molière, types of a given passion, or of a specific vice; they are living beings, replete with many passions and many vices; circumstances reveal to the audience the varied and complex characters. Molière's Miser is covetous—and that's all; Shakespeare's Shylock is avaricious, shrewd, spiteful, fond of children, witty."

In Pushkin's opinion, Shakespeare's theatre was the fullest and most striking realization of his cherished idea of a people's theatre. "Drama was born in a city square," he wrote convincingly, "and was a form of recreation for the people." He regretted that in its subsequent historical development drama "left the square and, on the insistence of educated and aristocratic society, moved to palaces." He considered that its decadence and degeneration had resulted directly from its isolation from the people, and from the "squares." "In palaces drama changed its aspect, its voice grew lower"; "drama relinquished the universally understood language, assuming a fashionable, select, and refined dialect." Pushkin dreamed that drama would get back to the "coarse plainness of popular passions, to the spontaneous reaction of the squares," to "a language understandable to the people." And, to him, the Shakespearean drama was the pattern and ideal of the people's drama.

For depth and truth, Pushkin's ideas about the theatre and the drama had no equal either in Russia or in the West. In general, his views on the theatre were tied in with the demands which he made upon actors. Even as a youth the poet criticized those actors who failed to act with sincerity and remained indifferent to events taking place on the stage.

In a poem "To a Young Actress" (1815) he described Claire's (Clairon's) acting in the following words:

> . . . to Milon young
> Thy love thou seek'st to prove sans passion;
> Or when thou art in bitter tears,
> A frigid "Ah!" is all one hears,
> And in a chair thou sink'st in placid fashion.

In his view this frigidity, this formalism of acting, was undeniably connected with the general character of French classicism. To the mature Pushkin realism was the ideal of dramatic creation: the actor's profound understanding and truthful impersonation of his role; the actor's genuine sincerity and feeling in its performance. Probably Laura's acting in *The Stone Guest* will serve as a model for these requirements:

FIRST GUEST

I swear to thee, Laura, at no time
Didst thou perform and act with such perfection:
How deeply didst thou understand thy part!

SECOND GUEST

How didst develop it! With what power!

THIRD GUEST

With what art!

LAURA

It's true that I succeeded
Today in ev'ry word and ev'ry gesture:
I freely gave myself to inspiration,
Words flowed as if 'twas I that gave them birth,
Yea, not slave memory, but heart. . . .

Pushkin made the laws of the Shakespearean theatre the basis of the reform which he sought to accomplish in Russian playwrighting through his tragedy *Boris Godunov*. In the sketch prepared as a preface to that work he wrote: "Being firmly convinced that the antiquated patterns of our theatre need to be reformed, I constructed my tragedy in accordance with the system of our father Shakespeare." "Following Shakespeare's example," we read further, "I confined myself to the portrayal of the period and of the historical characters without striving for theatrical effects, romantic pathos, and the like. The style of the tragedy is a composite one. It was necessary to show common and coarse people." In another sketch, he added: "I imitated Shakespeare in his free and broad delineation of the characters—in his casual and simple treatment of the types."

Following Shakespeare's practice, he introduced popular scenes into his tragedy. Much like Shakespeare, he renounced the classical unities and the division into acts, freely shifting the action from Moscow to Cracow, from the Tsar's palace to an inn, and encompassing within the framework of his play a whole historical period, from 1598 to 1604. The "much esteemed Alexandrine verse" which was used by the French classics is, in *Boris Godunov*, replaced by the blank five-foot iamb of the Shakespearean dramas.

Shakespeare's influence is also apparent in the creative method of *Boris Godunov*, in the principles of its dramatic structure, and even in the similarities between its individual situations and scenes and the historical chronicles of Shakespeare (the precepts of the dying Boris to his son and the monologue of the King in *King Henry IV*, Part II, Act IV, Scene 5, the election of Boris to the Tsardom and the election of Richard III to the throne, etc.). This did not deprive Pushkin, however, of his artistic independence and individual peculiarities of style. With a freedom inherent in poetic genius, he not only applied Shakespearean methods, which were dominant in his playwrighting, but also made discriminating use of certain classical devices. For instance, it has become axiomatic that the classical tragedy influenced him in creating the character of Boris Godunov. Boris, as distinguished from the other characters (the Impostor for one), is portrayed as complete, fashioned so as to permit of no development in the course of the dramatic action, and thus closely resembling the characters of Racine's heroes (specifically Athalie).

Pushkin's freedom and independence are most fully revealed, however, in the ideological content of his tragedy, in his approach to the solution of historical problems, and in his understanding of the laws and compelling forces of history.

In *Boris Godunov* he set as his aim "to resurrect one of the past epochs in all its truth" and to depict "one of the most dramatic periods in modern history." For his tragedy he made full use of Karamzin's *History of the Russian State,* data derived from the Nikon Chronicle, and Shcherbatov's *Russian History,* as well as the Pushkin family records which he found at Mikhailovskoye. But, quite apart from a number of deviations from Karamzin which he made in specific instances and in details, it would be futile to look in *The History of the Russian State* for the idea which is the driving force of the Pushkin tragedy, and which constitutes its pathos; namely, the idea of the irreconcilable conflict between the people and the tsar's authority—of the mighty, even though still not fully developed, power of the people.

Pushkin's well known words to the effect that the "object" of tragedy is "man and the people, man's fate and the people's destinies" are fully applicable to *Boris Godunov*. The people whom Karamzin mentions only in passing, Pushkin introduces as characters in the play, who assume their appropriate places in the events unfolding in the drama. Whole scenes are dedicated to the people ("The Red Square," "The Maiden's Field," "The

Moscow Cathedral Square," "Place of Execution," "The Kremlin," "Boris's Mansion"). With extraordinary vividness he reveals in these scenes the utter indifference of the people to the fate of the tsars and to the interests of the ruling classes; their rebellious spirit ("The people are always clandestinely leaning towards sedition"); and their terrible watchfulness in the face of the approaching events ("The people remain silent").

In the opinion of Professor Zhdanov:

Pushkin, in the portrayal of the fate of Tsar Boris, also chose his own path, one along which Karamzin was not, and could not have been, a guiding light. Karamzin's Boris ascends the throne as a beloved Tsar of Russia with whom the boyars and the people are unanimously in sympathy. Even the first scenes of Pushkin's drama show Boris as the alleged choice of the people. Karamzin attributes Boris's misfortunes to his pathological suspiciousness. The misfortunes of Pushkin's Boris are explained by the historical circumstances in which he found himself, by the moods of the boyars and of the people: the boyars remembered their lordly ancestors, the people remember St. Yury's Day.

Karamzin, faithful to religious and academic views of history, saw in the Impostor a chastisement imposed by Heaven upon the tsar-murderer. Pushkin explained the rise of the Impostor on social and historical grounds—not at all as an instrument of "Heavenly Providence," but as a puppet of Polish noblemen, the traditional enemies of the Russian state, who used him in their impudent aggressors' adventures.

> What do they care if I am really Dmitry?
> I am a mere excuse for wars and strife,
> And this is all they care about.

Pushkin's remarkable character of the chronicler Pimen is certainly a wholly independent creation; he could not have derived either from the dramatic works of Shakespeare or from the historical works of Karamzin. Beneath the lofty calmness of Pushkin's words are concealed aroused feelings and strong passions. He does not merely "depict" all that he has experienced in his life, but pronounces his judgment on events and men, delivering his stern and burning verdict. This type of tragedy is touched with the author's rich lyrical gift.

Notwithstanding Pushkin's insistence that a playwright be ab-

solutely objective ("impassiveness, no prejudice, no favorite notion"), *Boris Godunov* was not only a lucid picture of history,
but also a live reaction to current political events. Time and again
the poet impressed upon his friends the closeness of his tragedy
to those ideas and attitudes which aroused progressive Russians
on the eve of the Decembrist uprising. In a letter to N. N. Rayevsky (1829) he wrote: "It is replete with charming jokes and
subtle insinuations pertaining to the history of that period, just
like our Kiev and Kamenka private jokes. . . . One has to understand them—this is a requisite condition."

There are many contemporary allusions in *Boris Godunov*: the
selection of the period itself (a time "of many rebellions"), the
character of the usurper-tsar, who ascended the throne by means
of murder (analogy with Alexander I, connected with his father's
assassination), and the picture of repressive government measures
closely resembling those of the Arakcheyev régime—

> Can we be sure of our humble lives?
> Each day we all are threaten'd with disgrace,
> With prison, cowl, Siberia, or fetters—

and in the characterization of the moods of the peasants, among
whom, by the end of Alexander's reign, unrest had become widespread:

> Let the Impostor try
> To promise them the ancient Yury's day—
> At once there will be fun.

The principal reason for the political timeliness of Pushkin's
tragedy in the 1820's was the description of the complete social
isolation of the autocracy, which was supported neither by the
nobility nor by the people, and which was incapable of assuming
leadership in the struggle against the foreign invasion of Russia.

Pushkin felt a high measure of artistic satisfaction with *Boris
Godunov* because in it he fully realized the artistic aims he had
set himself. In September, 1825, the poet wrote to his friend
Vyazemsky:

I congratulate you, my joy, upon a romantic tragedy in which Boris
Godunov is the leading character! My tragedy is finished. I read it over
to myself and started clapping my hands and exclaiming: Look at Pushkin! Look at the son of a bitch!

Pushkin's friends, who beforehand had been expecting much from his tragedy (one of them wrote, "You are destined to follow along the path leading to the development of the national theatre"), greeted it enthusiastically. Vyazemsky called it "a mature and noble creation." Baratynsky commented on it as "a wonderful work that will mark an epoch in our literature."

Pushkin's readings of *Boris Godunov* in Moscow literary circles created an extraordinary sensation. Here is how M. N. Pogodin described one such reading:

Even up to the present—and this took place almost forty years ago—blood begins to quicken at the very recollection. . . . The first scenes were received silently and calmly, or, to speak more precisely, in a state of perplexity. But as the reading progressed feelings grew stronger. The scene of the chronicler with Grigory astounded everybody. It seemed to me that my dear, beloved Nestor rose from his grave to speak the words of Pimen. And when Pushkin reached the point where Pimen gave the account of Ivan the Terrible's visit to the Kirilov monastery, and of the monk's prayer,

> Let our Lord grant mercy, love, and peace
> To him whose soul is suffering and stormy,

it was as if we all lost our minds. Some of us were in a burning fever; others were shivering. Hair stood upright. One person was unable to restrain himself. The silence would suddenly be broken by an outburst of exclamations. . . . The reading came to an end. For a long while we stared at one another, and then we all leaped towards Pushkin. Embraces, shouts and laughter mingled with tears and congratulations. Hear! Hear! Let's drink a toast!

The enormous success of the author's readings of *Boris Godunov* aroused the government's anxiety. Pushkin was severely reprimanded by Benkendorf for having dared to read his tragedy without the permission of the Imperial censor, and was compelled immediately to submit the tragedy "for the personal approval of the Emperor." The following letter to Vyazemsky, written in October, 1825, while he was still at Mikhailovskoye, indicates how little hope Pushkin entertained that it would be kindly received at the court. "Even though it is conceived with good will, yet I couldn't completely hide my ears under the fool's cap—they stick out!" Nicholas, not wishing to bother to read the manuscript, ordered that it be turned over for comment to "some loyal person." As a result, there appeared *Notations on the Comedy About Tsar Boris and Grishka Otrepyev,* the author of which, we now believe, was Bulgarin, an agent of the Third Department.[1] In accordance with the *Notations,* the Tsar wrote the following resolution: "I believe that Mr. Pushkin's aim would be achieved if, after the necessary purification, he should transform his comedy into an historical tale or novel, similar to Walter Scott."

Pushkin indignantly rejected this attempt on the part of the Third Department to interfere with his work, and, in his answer to Benkendorf, wrote with much dignity: "I regret my inability to change what I have once written." As a result of Bulgarin's denunciation, *Boris Godunov* was banned by the censors for four years. During that period only a few excerpts were published.

The continuing struggle which, beginning in 1829, Pushkin, assisted by Vyazemsky and Pletnyov, waged to get *Boris Godunov* approved, finally brought results. In April, 1830, the tragedy received Imperial sanction, and late in December it was published in a separate edition (of course, with a number of censorship deletions and "corrections"). The government's concession in the matter of *Boris Godunov* is, of course, primarily explained by the fact that, as years went by, the political edge was taken off passages in the tragedy which, when it first appeared, might have been interpreted as referring to contemporary conditions.

The publication of *Boris Godunov* caused much newspaper and magazine comment. In the reactionary press there was an outburst of rude attacks and abuse. In the New Year's issue of the *Northern Mercury* the following verses appeared:

> And Pushkin has grown weary,
> And Pushkin makes us tired,
> His verse is dull and dreary,
> His genius—not inspired.
> He published for the nation
> His *Boris,* weak and crass,
> Indeed, a poor donation—
> On New Year's Eve—alas!

Liberal and democratic critics also failed correctly to evaluate *Boris Godunov.* Polevoy in the *Moscow Telegraph* accused the

---

[1] Government department of political police.—Ed.

poet of "slavish" dependence on Karamzin, of neglect of any rules, "of a disconnected medley of scenes, skipping from one subject to another." Nadezhdin (Nadaumko), polemizing in the *Telescope* with Polevoy, likewise saw a wide variety of "defects" in *Boris Godunov*, and tried to mitigate his criticism by totally ambiguous approval of individual parts of the drama.

There were very few reviews which can be considered on the level of the Pushkin tragedy (such as the unfinished article by Delvig and an article by I. Kireyevsky). Belinsky wrote favorably of it: "As a giant among pygmies *Boris Godunov* still towers over a multitude of quasi-Russian tragedies in proud and stern solitude, in the inaccessible majesty of a strictly artistic style and noble classical simplicity."

The stage presentation of *Boris Godunov* was not permitted for a long time. The attempt of the Maly Theatre in 1833 to obtain permission for the production of the Fountain scene proved unsuccessful. Hence, Pushkin was destined not to see a performance of the tragedy for which he had bold plans "to reform our stage." Not until September 17, 1870, was *Boris Godunov* finally produced in Petersburg at the Marinsky Theatre. The part of Boris was played by Leonidov, and that of the Impostor by Samoilov. Notwithstanding the pomp and beauty of the stage sets, which were painted by the Academy members Shishkov and Bocharov, the play had no success, apparently because of the poor acting and the crude distortions of the text of the tragedy.

The myth that persisted throughout a whole century that *Boris Godunov* was unsuited for the stage was refuted only during the Soviet regime. Pushkin's play, which in A. M. Gorky's judgment is "our best historical drama," had a brilliant interpretation at the Leningrad Academic Theatre of the Drama and the Moscow State Academic Maly Theatre, and later on many other stages. It was played not only in Russian but in the languages of the many other nationalities of our country.

The cycle of "miniature tragedies" is an intrinsic part of Pushkin's struggle for the adoption of Shakespearean principles in our playwrighting. These plays are perhaps the best illustration of Shakespeare's influence on the portraying of "diverse and many-sided characters," shown in the entirety of their inner lives, with all their "passions and vices." However, the "miniature tragedies" differ considerably in style from *Boris Godunov*. In contrast to the popular historical drama, with its vast canvas, large number of characters, and swift changes in dramatic situation, the "miniature tragedies" contain a series of short self-contained "dramatic scenes" dealing with specific moments in the lives of small groups of people. "Drama," Pushkin used to say, "has become master over passions and men's souls." All four plays of the Boldino cycle were devoted to an analysis of personal tragedies and the portrayal of dramas taking place in "the human soul."

It is said that the "miniature tragedy" was suggested to Pushkin by *Dramatic Scenes* of the English dramatists Barry Cornwall and Wilson, whom he had closely studied during his exile at Boldino.

Perhaps nowhere are the universality of Pushkin's genius, his wonderful creative appreciation of any period and any nation so brilliantly apparent as in these "miniature tragedies," transporting the reader from eighteenth century Germany to ancient England, from Renaissance Spain to medieval France. With extraordinary boldness and depth he revaluated the characters of world literature, characters that poets throughout the centuries had developed (the Miser and Don Juan), and, by injecting new life into them, made them appear in a new light.

Belinsky considered *The Stone Guest* as the best of the "miniature tragedies": "pearl among Pushkin's creations, the richest and most gorgeous gem in his poetic crown." Pushkin rid the traditional conception of Don Juan of vulgarity, cynicism, artifice, and boasting, and gave it intelligence and courage, youthfulness and *joie de vivre*, and genuine enthusiasm. The Don Juan theme served him not for moralizing purposes but for the glorification of the transforming and potent force of love. In answer to the question whether anything new could be added to that theme after Tirso de Molina, Molière, and Mozart, one European critic said: "Pushkin proved that it could."

In *The Avaricious Knight* Pushkin not only produced a remarkably concrete picture of medieval customs, and an almost sculptural likeness in the figure of the Baron of the terrible power of avarice over the human soul,[2] but achieved a significant sociophilo-

---

[2] The precursors of Pushkin's miser in world literature were Shakespeare's Shylock, Molière's Harpagon, Walter Scott's Dwining and Isaac.

sophical generalization of the idea that the all-pervading power of money constitutes a threat to the moral life of society:

> A whim, and stately mansions will arise,
> And lovely nymphs, in gayly smiling crowds,
> My gorgeous parks will suddenly invade,
> And muses, too, will come and pay their tribute,
> And genius free, to me, will humbly bow.

It is here that our poet revealed the insight of a genius which, at the dawn of capitalism, enabled him to expose capitalism's pernicious influence on people in Russia, and to forecast its destructive influence upon men.

"From an ideological standpoint," wrote Dostoyevsky, "Pushkin created nothing more sublime than the monologues in *The Avaricious Knight*." It should be added that the Baron's monologue is an excellent example of triumph over the conventional monologue form.

"In its sustained characters (the miser, his son, the duke, and the Jew), its masterful arrangement, moving pathos, wonderful verse, its completeness and elaboration—in every way this drama is a major great work worthy of the genius of Shakespeare himself" (Belinsky).

In *Mozart and Salieri* [3] Pushkin with extraordinary psychological understanding portrayed another passion which rules men—envy. Pushkin shows envy in its most subtle manifestations, tracing its course from the hidden beginnings to its full development, when it completely absorbs men's souls and is even capable of driving them to crime. At the same time, this short but extremely pithy and profound drama raises one of the most vexing problems of art: the question of toil and creativeness, inspiration and craftsmanship, genius and talent. The carefree Mozart, "the insensate," "the idle gadder," who attains the heights of art effortlessly, is contrasted with Salieri, the indefatigible toiler, ascetically renouncing all earthly joys for the sake of his creation, a craftsman who has "dissected music as a corpse" and "tested harmony by algebra."

The characters of Baron Philip and Salieri [Professor Blagoy wrote] are perhaps the most convincing proofs of the breadth and extraordinary

[3] The preface and dedication of Beaumarchais to Salieri's opera *Tarar* and Wackenroder and Tieck's book on art and artists (*Phantasies About Art for Friends of Art*) are considered to have been sources of this drama.

power of Pushkin as a realistic artist. From all we know about Pushkin, we can be certain that the sunny, bright, and infinitely generous nature of Mozart is much closer to his psychological make-up than those grim monomaniacs the Miser and Salieri. And yet, Pushkin writes of them with such expressive power and such tragic greatness that they are among the most glorious artistic achievements in world literature.

Finally, in *The Feast During the Plague* (for which Wilson's *The City of the Plague* served as a source), the poet sets forth the problem of life and death with great depth and boldness. The atheist Walsingham, presiding over the feast, exclaims in his drinking song:

> There is delight and thrill in war,
> In ocean's mighty splash and war—
> 'Midst nightly gloom—'long tempests' lane,
> O'er grisly gulfs that threaten death,
> In the Arabian hurricane,
> And in the plague's pernicious breath.
> All things that to the mortal heart
> Grim peril potently impart
> Are full of boundless fascination
> As immortality's true pledge:
> Blest he, who shaken with agitation,
> Knows how to grasp it and to fledge.

Here the path is clearly mapped out along which proud thought and man's indomitable will may score a victory over the fear of death.

During Pushkin's life, only one of his "miniature tragedies," *Mozart and Salieri,* was produced on the stage—on January 7, 1832, at the Bolshoy Theatre in Petersburg, for Bryansky's benefit performance. It is not known whether or not the author was present, but an anonymous critic reported the reaction of the theatre management and the audience towards the play:

It is surprising, even incomprehensible, that Bryansky, a man understanding the value of true poetry, had the nerve to produce these scenes at the beginning of the show. Some of those present did not hear them because, having just entered the theatre, they were either looking for their seats or getting settled in them; others, although already seated, were unable to hear anything owing to noise made by the door and the scraping of feet by the public which was then arriving. Surprising!

Incomprehensible! True, the scenes in *Mozart and Salieri* are created for the few, but even they were unable fully to enjoy them.

Following the performance of January 27, the tragedy *Mozart and Salieri* was repeated on February 1, after which it was not given again.

The Avaricious Knight was announced at the Aleksandrinsky Theatre for the performance of February 1, 1837, along with the drama *Maria*, by Anselo, and a short play, *The Ladies' Doctor*. Because of Pushkin's death, however, the performance was postponed to February 2, while *The Avaricious Knight* was withdrawn and replaced by the vaudeville *The Sequence of Horrors*. In a letter to his brother, A. I. Turgenev offered this explanation for the withdrawal of the Pushkin drama: "They probably fear excessive enthusiasm."

The Water Nymph, which Pushkin wrote shortly after the "miniature tragedies," while resembling them in its general character, differs in its Russian national coloration and the liberal utilization of folk forms. Having tried his hand in the field of "folk song" and "folk tale" in the 1830's, he now sought to create a "folk drama."

I. N. Zhdanov observed long ago that the source of *The Water Nymph* was the comic opera of the Viennese playwright Hensler, *The Danube Fairy*, adapted for the Russian stage by Krasnopolsky (1803) and for many years performed with great success both in Petersburg and in Moscow. Having incorporated in his drama the basic plot of Hensler's opera, a number of its characters, and even certain factual and textual details, Pushkin still succeeded in creating an altogether new play, differing radically both in style and in genre. He converted the sentimental fairy tale, with its colorless and conventional characters and operatic effects, into a drama of the people with realistic characters and action that was both understandably developed and fully vindicated psychologically. Pushkin's creative independence is especially apparent in the remarkable image of the Miller (who does not appear in Hensler's opera); in the humane, passionate, and valiant character of Natasha (which has nothing in common with the "incorporeal" heroine of the opera); in scenes, conceived on a Shakespearean scale, such as the one where the Prince meets the insane Miller; in the vivid, folk quality of the wedding scene; and so on. Pushkin also introduced the seduction of the peasant girl by the libertine Prince, who, intent upon nothing but his own pleasure, was willing to crush a human life for the sake of a passing gratification. This episode gave to *The Water Nymph* a social note that was, of course, entirely missing from *The Danube Fairy*.

Pushkin's last dramatic work, *Scenes from the Age of Knighthood,* marked the poet's return from "miniature tragedies" to broad social-historical drama. This piece was inspired by his interest in Western European history, which he had had for twenty years—especially in its stormy and transitional periods. Its theme of the *Scenes* is the decadence and decline of knighthood, which was the result of its conflict with the bourgeoisie and the peasantry.

Pushkin's close attention to the problem of peasant uprisings, which became increasingly significant during the reign of Nicholas, and his reflections upon the fate of impoverished nobility, formed the basis of a number of creative themes during the last years of his life (*Dubrovsky, The Captain's Daughter*). *Scenes from the Age of Knighthood* is just one link in this chain.

Having begun to write his *Scenes* in the familiar four-foot iamb, Pushkin soon abandoned the metrical form and turned to prose drama, which had become popular in French literature in the 1820's. He was strongly influenced by Mérimée's tragedy *La Jacquérie,* and students have discovered marked similarities between these works in theme and dramatic structure. In his *Scenes* he succeeded as usual, however, in preserving his masterly originality, boldly utilizing his predecessors' experience for novel and independent creative purposes.

It is fitting to conclude the sketch of Pushkin's dramatic work with the well known words of Lunacharsky regarding the sum total of his work:

Pushkin was the Russian spring, Pushkin was the Russian morn. What was achieved by Dante and Petrarch in Italy, by the giants of the eighteenth century in France, by Lessing, Schiller, and Goethe in Germany, Pushkin achieved in Russia. It is good to love Pushkin—perhaps it is particularly good to love Pushkin in our day when a new spring has arrived.

Chapter XV

LERMONTOV

SCHILLER'S AND HUGO'S romantic dramas, which in the 1820's and 1830's had begun to capture the theatres in the West, signified the struggle of the progressive forces of European society against the world of feudal reaction. Romantics abruptly severed relations with court classicism.

While, in classical tragedy, the men of high social position are chosen for the heroes, romantic drama not only refused to glorify them but, on the contrary, considered the tyrants' depravity and arrogance as a disgrace. The romantic drama glorified people whom public opinion passed by with disdain or, at best, with indifference. The robber, the courtesan, the humpbacked court jester, the nobleman who had sunk to the level of a lackey—such were the persons who furnished the new heroes. Romantics were attracted by the task of contrasting outward brilliance and the inward sublimity of an unappreciated but genuinely noble soul.

Particularly interested in the unusual, the romantics were fond of historical drama since contemporary reality afforded less leeway for their imagination and furnished no material for those vivid and richly colored scenes of which they were so fond. While classicists chose for their themes mostly sagas from the ancient world, romantics were much more attracted to the Middle Ages and the Renaissance.

Romantics also departed sharply from the literary rules of classicism. The protest against established norms was, indeed, the distinguishing feature of the program of the romantics. They no longer patterned themselves on Racine, Corneille, and Voltaire, but on Shakespeare and the Spaniards.

In the preface to *Cromwell* (1827), which is regarded as the manifesto of romantic dramatists, Hugo provokingly proclaimed: "To couple unity of time with unity of place in order to make bars of them for the cage, into which are admitted, with much pedantry, those facts, peoples, and characters which by their sheer bulk crowd out reality—means to distort subjects and human beings and to make a mockery of history itself." He urged his supporters: "Let us abolish all systems, theories, and doctrines on the art of poetry; let us cast off this antiquated mass now concealing the face of art. Let us have no rules, no patterns—or, more correctly, let the general laws of nature constitute our only rules." He resolutely protested against the strict classification of dramatic pieces according to a specific type, as was advocated by classical dramatists, believing that the new drama must "compel the audience to pass continually from the serious to the humorous, from jocular episodes to heart-rendering scenes, from the stern to the tender." According to his view, in the new drama "the ugly stands side by side with the beautiful, and the monstrous with the graceful," "the ludicrous is the reverse side of the majestic," and "evil and virtue, shadow and light, blend together."

The most typical representative of progressive romanticism in Russian drama was Lermontov (1814–1841). His interest in the theatre dated from 1827, when as a thirteen-year-old boy, he came to Moscow from his grandmother's estate, Tarkhany, in order to enter the Noblemen's University Boarding School. At that time he wrote in a letter to his aunt, M. A. Shan-Girey: "As yet I have visited no gardens; but I was at the theatre where I saw an opera, *The Invisible,* the same one I saw in Moscow eight years ago. We ourselves conduct a theatre—and fairly successfully—in which wax figurines will play (do, please, send me my waxes)."

Two years later he had become an enthusiastic admirer of the Moscow actors, upholding their prestige in arguments with the residents of Petersburg. "Do you recall, dear Auntie," he wrote, "telling me that our Moscow actors are inferior to those of Petersburg? What a pity you were not here to see *The Gambler,* and the tragedy *The Robbers;* then you would have judged differently. Many Petersburg *gentlemen* agree that these pieces are performed better here than there, and that in many scenes Mochalov excels Karatygin."

In a letter to his aunt in 1831, Lermontov indicated his increasing interest in the theatre and the drama by an ardent defense of Shakespeare and *Hamlet:* "If he is great, it is in *Hamlet;* when he is really Shakespeare, the boundless genius, penetrating man's heart and the laws of fate, the original, that is the inimitable Shakespeare—it is in *Hamlet.*"

He conceived his first dramatic ideas in 1829. These were plans of tragedies patterned after Schiller, obviously inspired by the impressions of Mochalov's brilliant acting in *The Robbers* and *Wile and Love.* In the same year he also tried to write an opera libretto for Pushkin's *The Gypsies.*

A tragedy on the subject of Chateaubriand's *Atala;* a dramatic poem from the period of the Tartar invasion (on Mstislav the Black); a tragedy dealing with contemporary Russian reality "about a young man, not of noble descent, who is repudiated by society and by love, and humiliated by his superiors"—these were young Lermontov's plans in the field of drama for the year 1830. In 1831 he contemplated the tragedies *Marius* and *Nero,* dealing with the life of ancient Rome. None of these plans ever materialized, however.

The first play which Lermontov completed was a tragedy in verse, *The Spaniards* (1830). This youthful experiment reflects the main influences in the sixteen-year-old poet's reading: Schiller, Lessing, Walter Scott, Shakespeare, Hugo, and Byron, especially Schiller's *The Robbers, Wile and Love,* and *Don Carlos,* and Hugo's *Hernani.* In choosing Spain as the scene of the play, Lermontov partly followed a literary tradition dating from Shakespeare, which was particularly popular among the Western romantics in the early nineteenth century; in part, however, he chose Spain because of his own affection for what family legends had led him to believe was his ancestors' native land.

This piece is constructed along the lines of romantic tragedies, from beginning to end: it has a showy and involved plot; stormy action; the inevitable dramatic attributes, such as poison, dagger, abduction, and murder; strong passion; unusual characters; sharp contrast; and a tone of pathos.

Fernando is the typical romantic hero of *The Spaniards*—pos-

sessed of nobility, daring, a flaming soul, and an immovably muti-
nous will. Lonely, outcast and persecuted, he stands in irreconcilable conflict with his whole environment—with the vain, heartless,
vicious aristocracy, with the corrupt and depraved servants of the
Church. So he curses that world:

> Both paradise and hell are weighed on scales;
> And money of this world owns heaven's bliss,
> And wicked men make even demons blush
> By their insid'ous wile and love for evil . . . .
> And fathers traffic in their daughters young;
> Wives, selling husbands, are themselves for sale;
> Kings barter peoples; and the people, freedom;
> For the grandee's gratification, or
> To please a monk, a guiltless man is dragged
> Through countless horrors of a bloody rack.

Fernando's impassioned monologues are filled with the ideological
pathos of the tragedy: indignation against class and national oppression, the appeal for humaneness and justice, the longing for
equality and freedom cry out in them. Obviously, here are incar-
nated Lermontov's own cherished thoughts and feelings. This gives
the role of Fernando an especial fascination and convincing power,
despite all the rhetorical affectation of his speech and the frenzy of
his acting. Lermontov's exposé of the medieval Spanish aristocracy,
with which *The Spaniards* is filled, is very similar to the indignant
verdict which he later pronounced upon the Russian nobility of
Nicholas's reign.

The full text of *The Spaniards* did not appear in print until
1880, fifty years after it was written, and it was first produced on
the stage only after the October Revolution (in 1924, at the Studio
of the Russian theatre).

Lermontov's two other early pieces, *Men and Passions* (*Men-
schen und Leidenschaften*, 1830) and *The Strange Man* (1831)
marked his conversion to contemporary Russian realism. According
to N. Kotlyarevsky: "The poet began to draw material from life
and personal observations, while the characters began to speak in
prose instead of verse; dramatic effects were replaced by the
natural flow of everyday life; daggers, nocturnal attacks, and mysterious apparitions completely disappeared from the stage." Both
plays are autobiographical, particularly *Men and Passions*. In it the

main dramatic conflict arises out of the quarrel between the grand-mother and the father over the son. *The Strange Man* also de-scribes a family quarrel, but this struggle over the son takes place between father and mother. In both cases a love story involving the rivalry of two friends is woven into the family drama. The father's curses and the faithlessness of the beloved girl (imagined in the first play and actual in the second) caused the hero's tragic death.

The autobiographical character of the plays is most obvious, however, in the psychological similarity between the heroes (Ury Volin and Vladimir Arbenin) and the young Lermontov. What we know about the poet from reminiscences of his close friends and self-revealing passages in his lyrical poems coincides fully with what the third guest says about Vladimir Arbenin in Scene 13 of *The Strange Man:* "He possessed a fiery character and a restless soul; some deep sorrow had tormented him from childhood. God knows what its cause was. His heart matured before his mind; he learned the dark side of the world at a time when he was still unable to shield himself against its attacks or to endure them with indifference. His banter had no gayety; his spite against mankind as a whole was bitter." Arbenin's precursor, Volin, was equally ardent, impulsive, morbidly sensitive, embittered, and gloomy. Other characters in both plays are equally autobiographical: the grandmother, the father, the mother, Zarutsky, and so on.

From a literary standpoint the plays represent a peculiar combi-nation of the "romantic drama" and the folk comedy (in the spirit of Russian comedies of the eighteenth century.) Schiller's influence is strongly apparent in them, as in *The Spaniards.* The heroes' monologues are permeated with Schiller's humanistic pathos. The very uniqueness of their position, their loneliness amid the society surrounding them, and the loftiness of their ideas and aspirations are very reminiscent of the tragic heroes of the famous German romanticist. A series of separate episodes and motifs are directly traceable to a reading of *The Robbers* and *Wile and Love.*

The elements of Russian comedy are contained in the portrayal of the everyday existence of landowners, in their dialogues on everyday matters, and so forth. Opposition to serfdom is a remark-able characteristic of both plays. In *Men and Passions* the brutal willfulness of the landowners is personified by the obstinate, and foolish serf owner Marfa Ivanovna, who "keeps thrashing her housemaids" and goes straight from reading the Gospels to flogging a serf kitchenboy who broke a fifteen-ruble cup.

In *The Strange Man* a muzhik serves as the narrator of the dreadful tortures inflicted by a woman serf owner upon her peasants. Vladimir, the hero of the play, exclaims with anger: "To break the arms, to prick, to flog, to pull one hair after another out of one's beard. . . . O God! Each of my veins aches at the very thought of these things! . . . I would crush every joint of that crocodile, that woman! . . . Just to hear about it makes me enraged!"

In the opinion of scholars, such scenes in Lermontov's early dramas are "obviously based upon personal observations and represent his own childhood and youthful experiences." Belinsky's early play, *Dimitry Kalinin,* in addition to *The Minor* and *Woe from Wit,* probably served to accentuate Lermontov's opposition to serfdom. Copies of *Dimitry Kalinin* were circulated in manuscript form among the students of Moscow University.

Like Lermontov's first tragedy, *Men and Passions* and *The Strange Man* had to wait half a century for publication. The former piece has not yet been produced on the stage, while the latter was not produced until 1916, at morning performances in the Moscow Dramatic Theatre.

Lermontov's outstanding play, *The Masquerade,* a drama in verse, was written in 1835–1836, during that period of the poet's life when, having just been commissioned as an officer in the Hussar Regiment of the Guards he entered Petersburg society and was utterly shocked by its leaders, "the haughty offspring of fathers famed for their utter vileness."

From the standpoint of depth of thought and artistic power, *The Masquerade* should be included among his most mature creations, despite the fact that at the time of its completion he was only twenty-two years old. Like his other plays, it is essentially in the romantic school. In it, however, much more than in *Men and Passions* and *The Strange Man,* the romantic element is relieved by realism. Eugene Arbenin, the hero, says of himself:

> I was born
> With soul as lava boiling-hot:
> As long as lava stays unmelt
> Stone-hard it is; but grim his lot
> Who meets that flaming current.

This haughty and lonely character, concealing passions under the pretense of disdainful indifference for everything in the world, and touched with demonism, apostasy, and martyrdom, is most typical of Lermontov's heroes. Both Demon and Pechorin could have repeated Arbenin's bitter confession word for word:

> All did I see; it was my bitter fate
> To live through ev'rything and ev'rything to master:
> I often loved, more often did I hate,
> But grief was that which bound me all the faster.
> First, all seemed dear to me, then came contempt,
> To comprehend myself proved but a vain attempt.
> Nor did the world in me sense any worth,
> My life, I felt, was stamped with imprecation,
> And so—farewell, with neither sigh nor lamentation
> To happy dreams and blessings of the earth.

He further resembles the Demon in that he hopes for the healing of his spiritual illness—"the resurrection of life and goodness"—through ardent and strong love, which he experiences for the first time in his life through his love for a young and innocent girl. His tragedy, leading him to crime and ruin, is that he, like the forsaken spirit in Lermontov's poem, carries his death sentence within himself: his distrustfulness, egoism, and vindictiveness, which have developed in him as a result of his whole depraved life, poison his short-lived happiness.

Arbenin's whole personality, his spiritual make-up, his actions, and his words, confirm his romantic origin. Through the dense romantic veil, and despite the halo of mystery and demonism, however, he is portrayed with sufficient realism to establish his social milieu and his contemporariness. Cynicism, spiritual emptiness, the contention that life is "a well known charade for children's exercise," faith in the almightiness of destiny, and utter disbelief in the possibility of sensible reality—all these are "signs of the time," the result of that dark reaction and social disintegration which characterized the period during which Lermontov and his heroes lived.

Lermontov paints in boldly realistic colors the social and cultural background of Arbenin's tragedy. Unlike the episodic sketches of the landlord's modes of living in his early uncertain dramas, *The Masquerade* achieves a synthetized satirical picture which portrays the life of the capital's court society. The poet mercilessly reveals the miry passions and repulsive vices of that decadent world. The entire *beau monde* is represented as a group of cheats, intriguers, and murderers, opportunistic, greedy, and debauched. Card games and gossip have taken the place of cultural interests. The outward glamour of fashionable society is only a veil for its cruelty, hypocrisy, and emptiness. Every face wears a mask, everything in that world is a deceitful and trivial masquerade.

Lermontov used this idea again in his well known poem "January 1, 1840":

> 'Midst music and amusements' tension,
> 'Midst empty phrases learn'd by heart,
> Men's heartless faces gleam and dart—
> Those masks contorted by convention.

The literary sources of *The Masquerade* are manifold. The dramatic plot and the development of the intrigue (the lost bracelet, suspicion, jealousy, the poisoning of the innocent wife, insanity) in many respects remind one of Shakespeare's tragedy *Othello*, which Lermontov must have remembered vividly from his Moscow theatrical experiences. His literary devices and manner of character portrayal suggest the influence of the French romantic drama and melodrama. The satirical treatment of the nobility was inspired by *Woe from Wit*. The verse and language in *The Masquerade* are flexible and aphoristic; in their simplicity and naturalness they resemble conversational speech—which reminds one of Griboyedov's famous comedy.

Lermontov hoped to see his drama on the stage, and in October, 1835, he submitted it to the censorship office of the Third Department for authorization of its production at "The Imperial St. Petersburg Theatre." Benkendorf, Chief of the Third Department, considered it as a "eulogy of vice," and ordered that it be returned to the author "for the necessary alterations." Specifically, he insisted that its ending be changed "to make it conclude with a reconciliation between Mr. and Mrs. Arbenin." Lermontov changed nothing in the play, but he added a new, fourth act in which the Unknown tells Arbenin of the innocence of his wife whom he has murdered.

The new version of *The Masquerade* in no way satisfied the theatrical gendarmerie. Censor Oldenkop wrote:

In the new version we find the same indecent criticism of costume balls at the Engelhardts' house . . . the same impertinences against ladies belonging to the fashionable social sets. . . . The author was very anxious to add a new finale, but not the one which was suggested to him.

The following words are particularly characteristic of the reactions of the Third Department:

Dramatic horrors have ceased in France. Is it necessary to introduce them here? Is it necessary to inoculate our families with the poison? Ladies' fashions prevalent in Paris are being imitated in Russia, and that is an innocent matter. But imitation of dramatic deformities which were renounced even by Paris is more than horrible: there is no name for it.

Unwilling to give up the hope of producing *The Masquerade*, Lermontov made certain concessions. This time he subjected his drama to radical alterations which considerably weakened and emasculated it. Oldenkop was assuaged and approvingly commented on the third version: "The piece is now completely changed; only the first act is left in its original form. There is no more poisoning, and all indecencies have been eliminated." Despite the favorable report, production of *The Masquerade* was not authorized. Explaining "the inadmissible verses on the death of Pushkin," Lermontov gave the following account of the official reasons for the interdiction of his piece: "My drama in verse, *The Masquerade*, could not be produced on the stage because (as I was told) of its too sharp passions and characters, and also because in it virtue is insufficiently rewarded." Of course, the real reason why Nicholas's gendarmes did not pass the play was different. They feared its powerful exposé, and felt that no alteration would change the contempt for the fashionable rabble which permeated it.

The censorship of *The Masquerade* was not lifted until 1852. The first performance (at the Aleksandrinsky Theatre in Petersburg) might well have created a false impression of Lermontov's drama, however, inasmuch as it was seriously distorted by the deletion of entire scenes—and even acts, by the elimination of a number of characters, and so forth. In these performances V. A. Karatygin played the part of Arbenin, and Chitau that of Nina.

The Masquerade was first authorized for stage production in

1862 in the unabridged form of its second version. From that time on, it became part of the repertoire of capital and provincial theatres, which for a long time, however, regarded it exclusively as ostentatious material for guest and leading actors, and made no attempt to give a profound and correct interpretation of the play as a study of the period, and the like.

Pisarev, Roshchin-Insarov, Strelsky, and P. Samoilov were the most successful of the many actors who played the part of Arbenin.

The first production designed, not to display actors' virtuosity, but to give a broad interpretation of the drama, took place at the Aleksandrinsky Theatre on February 25, 1917. "Revolution had already started in the streets; shouts were heard; crowds with flags began to gather; tramways had ceased to run. Everything seemed deserted, and people were afraid. In spite of this, the theatre was packed." [1] This production (which subsequently was twice revised, in 1933 and 1938) has survived two decades and is still being given.

Arbenin's part is now usually performed by the People's Artist of the U.S.S.R., Y. M. Yuryev, who was the very first actor to interpret the character completely and profoundly, lifting it to the level of genuine tragedy.

In its general character and plot, Lermontov's last piece, *The Two Brothers* (1836), resembles his early dramas, *Men and Passions* and *The Strange Man*. He wrote in a letter to his friend S. A. Rayevsky on January 16, 1836: "I am writing the fourth act of a new drama based upon an event which I experienced in Moscow." In fact, *The Two Brothers* is based on episodes in his personal life. Students believe that the characters Yury and Alexander Radin reflect different aspects of Lermontov's own personality; Vera is based on Lopukhina, his early love; Prince Ligovsky, on her husband Bakhmetyev. The influence upon Lermontov of the German romantic tragedies, especially Schiller's, is still apparent in *The Two Brothers*, particularly in the motif of the play, the conflict between the brothers.

Dissatisfied with the completed play, Lermontov decided to use its characters and plot in a novel, which he began to write immediately (*Princess Ligovskaya*).

The Two Brothers was produced on the stage in 1915, as a

[1] *Theatre and Art*, 1917, Nos. 10–11.

jubilee performance of the Literary Fund at the Marinsky Theatre in Petrograd. The actors included: V. N. Davydov (Radin, the father), Y. M. Yuryev (Yury Radin), and Gorin-Goryaninov (Prince Ligovsky).

Lermontov's playwrighting, brought to an abrupt end by his premature tragic death, established the ideas and aesthetic principles of progressive romanticism in the Russian theatre. Like Schiller and Hugo, his principal models, he created plays of high romantic pathos, great passions, and strong characters. Their entire ideological content was directed against the feudal serf regime—against despotism and reaction. They beat with a warm love for man, who suffocated and perished "in the land of serfs, the land of masters," the country of the "blue uniforms" of the gendarmes.

Lermontov was influenced not only by the romanticists, however. His interest in Shakespeare, as well as his love of Pushkin and Griboyedov, opened up to him the vistas of realism which were apparent even in his early plays and were glaringly apparent in his remarkable *Masquerade*.

The tragic fate of Lermontov's plays eloquently demonstrates what an enemy the realism of Nicholas's reign was to the development of a progressive-romantic tendency in the Russian theatre. At the same time, the government strongly supported the reactionary romantic drama and tearful melodrama with which well-meaning and loyalty-conscious authors flooded the theatre.

THE MELODRAMA OF KUKOLNIK AND POLEVOY

The bureaucratic romanticists eulogized not those who boldly defied the sources of power in the world, but those who had emerged from bitter experience with meek and pure souls. Cautiously ignoring the rebel protests, the bureaucrats would bestow full favor on their humiliated victim. And the master of the earth would be transformed from a tyrant into a source of mercy, who, as the piece drew to a close, nobly rewarded innocently wronged virtue.

In the works of the reactionary romanticists, sympathy with the common people uncorrupted by urban culture, was transformed into sugary eulogy of "the good old times." Genuine patriotism gave way to the glorification of autocracy, orthodoxy, and nationalism. Amidst the enthusiastic cries of the poet "madly adoring" his motherland and his monarch, could be heard the harsh commands of military parades. The playwright constantly saluted, as it were, some omnipresent superior, and by the whole course of his play prepared and roused the public for the presentation of solemn demonstrations. Even romanticists of the bureaucratic stamp preserved to a remarkable degree the quality for which Hugo was considered as "a literary talent." This epithet is even more applicable to them.

They piled up in their dramas highly complex theatrical horrors, believing that that would make them direct descendants of Byron, and their contemporaries did not wish to—and perhaps could not—distinguish real talent from stage tricks.

In order to reconcile the audience to the indescribable villainies and implausible passions in their plays, they invented mystical motives. "Pour a whole sea of blood over the stage," wrote S. P. Shevyrev, "but show the finger of God in the spectacle, and, without turning away from it, a man will kiss the smiting hand, strengthening his own soul by the sight of the suffering victims."

In the technique by which they portrayed their characters, these playwrights remind one of the artistically vulgar engraved pictures of the Last Judgment, where all men are divided into two sharply contrasting groups: the godly and the sinners. In their works there are either staggering villains or men of extraordinary supernatural virtue. Alexander Veselovsky has aptly observed: "The whole of life, all the cosmic conceptions of medievalism, were classified according to symbols: a man belonged either to heaven, to hell, or to purgatory, but hardly ever did he belong to the earth which he trod." The same may be said of the heroes of this type of drama. Their language was marked by extraordinary affectation and pathos.

Melodrama was even more popular during the period of Nicholas I. In Russia it was closely related to the romantic drama proper, but designed to cater to the less fastidious spectator. Its methods reached the ultimate in vulgarization.

In the West, melodrama, as its name indicates, originated from the combination of drama and music, the latter accompanying certain passages of the action. The first outstanding piece of this kind was Pixérécourt's melodrama *Coelina, ou L'Enfant du Mystère*.

Produced in Paris in 1800, it was given wtih tremendous success 387 times in succession.

The scenic effects in melodrama were achieved by crude devices and very gaudy colors. The plots were based on the glorification of virtue and the chastisement of vice. In them we find constantly recurring types: persecuted innocence, the out-and-out swindler, and the well intended go-between.

Originally, the melodrama consisted of three acts, but it subsequently developed into a great many scenes full of romantic details, and playing on the audience's emotions by its sharp contrasts in swift succession. Music strengthened the effect by heightening the most striking scenes in the piece: trumpets sounded when the tyrant made his appearance, and flutes wailed dolefully when persecuted innocence made her exit.

Melodrama began on our stage in the season of 1818-1819, when Victor Ducange's drama *Thirty Years, or A Gambler's Life*, translated by a theatre official Volkov, was produced in Petersburg. Because of the play's outstanding success (due largely to Bryansky's acting), the translator made up his mind to bring more plays of this type to Russian soil. Later, more and more original melodramas were produced, in addition to the translated versions.

Nestor Vasilyevich Kukolnik (1809–1868) was perhaps the most prominent of the reactionary romanticist playwrights. His first work, *Torquato Tasso*, is a typical Russian romantic drama with the usual attributes: the characters' utter lack of motivation, and the heroes' extraordinary verbosity (there are speeches which are three printed pages long, while the length of Tasso's part exceeds the normal capacity of an actor). It was first produced in Petersburg, September 27, 1833, with indifferent success.

Kukolnik's next attempt, *Almighty's Hand the Fatherland Has Saved*, brought him much more renown. Performed on Karatygin's benefit night, January 15, 1834, the tragedy portrayed the "Period of Strife" and Michael Fyodorovich Romanov's election to the throne. It is difficult to imagine a more monotonous play: all the characters remain completely unchanged from the beginning to the very end, making the play nothing but a series of declamations.

Artistically it is in no way superior to *Torquato Tasso*, its only advantage being that it is shorter. From a political standpoint this drama, conceived in a burst of patriotism and monarchical spirit, conformed precisely to the tendencies and aims of the government; and it was, therefore, given a very elaborate production. To attend the play and express delight over its merits was a kind of testimonial of loyalty. Magazines declared that in this play Kukolnik "was the first to show us a genuinely popular, vigorous, broadshouldered Russian drama." Only Polevoy's *Moscow Telegraph* took a critical attitude, and it was consequently banned by the government. Kukolnik's success and Polevoy's failure were recorded in the following witty epigram of a contemporary:

> *Almighty's Hand* three miracles has wrought:
> The fatherland was saved and liberated;
> Its author with a cross was decorated,
> And Polevoy—reduced to naught.

Even during the succeeding reign, *Almighty's Hand* was used by the government to incite feelings of loyalty. Thus, in the spring of 1866, after an unsuccessful attempt on the life of Emperor Alexander II, the fifth act of this tragedy was performed in Moscow, with the participation of Shumsky, Samarin, and Sadovsky, and served according to *Intermission,* as a pretext for "enthusiastic demonstrations." In the same year the tragedy was presented in Petersburg with the same result.

The tragedy *Prince Michael Skopin-Shuisky* also dealt with the "Period of Strife." It was produced on January 14, 1835, also for Karatygin's benefit-performance. Michael Skopin-Shuisky is highly idealized in the play, while Catherine, who poisons him, is an unsuccessful attempt to create a Russian Lady Macbeth. The principal hero, however, is Prokopy Lyapunov, who repents having served the thief of Tushin and becomes Skopin's most devoted friend. Upon learning of Catherine's crime, he compels her to drink the poison with which she had murdered Michael, and at this point he thunders the exclamation which has become a favorite trick of our provincial tragedians: "Drink under the knife of Prokopy Lyapunov!"

In addition to those already named, Kukolnik wrote *Giulio Mosti* (continuation of *Torquato Tasso*), *Jacobo Sannasar, Domenicino* (in two parts), *Christopher's Statue, Prince Kholmsky, Ivan Ryabov, Boyar F. V. Basenok, Lieutenant-General Patkul, The Orderly, Ermil Ivanovich Kostrov, Ioann Anton Leisewitz,* and other pieces.

F. A. Kony, in a review, accurately pointed out: "Kukolnik's talent for dramatic creation is very much like that of Alexandre Dumas père. Both are equally inclined to resort to overinvolved plots, affectation, historical coloration, interpolated scenes, and horrible theatrical effects."

Nicholas Alekseyevich Polevoy (1796–1846) was an equally typical playwright of the Nicholas period. Even as a child he was attracted to the theatre after reading Sumarokov, Kheraskov, and Knyazhnin. He began at once to compose plays the heroes of which were Napoleon and Bennigsen, or Tsar Aleksey Mikhailovich. At the age of fourteen, he attended theatrical performances at the Markaryevsky Fair for the first time. There Kotzebue's plays produced a lasting impression on him. Ever after that he wrote about the theatre, and the magazines he edited devoted much space to the stage. It was only toward the end of his literary career, however, that he turned to playwrighting. During the last eight years of his life he wrote thirty-eight plays of the most diverse types. He was extraordinarily prolific, but most of his pieces were written hastily and without finish, so that their quantity far exceeds their quality.

In the midst of his journalistic career, Polevoy conceived the idea of translating something from Shakespeare. He hoped that this would revive enthusiasm both in the audience and in the actors, who, although wholly dissatisfied with the contemporary repertoire, were convinced that Shakespeare's plays were not suited for our stage and, for that reason, could not be successfully produced. In spite of this prejudice, Polevoy translated *Hamlet,* the most philosophical of Shakespeare's dramas.

Of all the pieces he had written for the stage, this translation had the greatest appeal. Through it Russia became acquainted with *Hamlet,* and for a long time his translation was considered to be the best. In the opinion of P. P. Gnedich, however, Polevoy did not understand Hamlet's character. Failing to grasp both Hamlet's spirit and style, Polevoy converted the Wittenberg University student into a fop of the thirties. He bestowed upon the Danish prince languishing sentimentality, which Shakespeare had of course not intended. He had him express himself in well rounded, trivial phrases typifying the effete man of the translator's period, rather than a powerful Renaissance character. Without feeling bound by the original, he made up whole sentences which shocked Shakespeare's admirers but delighted his contemporaries.

Polevoy wanted P. S. Mochalov to play his *Hamlet,* and offered his translation gratis for the actor's benefit performance. Mochalov did not at once accept the offer, however, convinced that Shakespeare was not suited to the Russian stage. If the report of Polevoy's brother Xenophont is true, Nicholas Alekseyevich, by his advice and suggestions, greatly helped Mochalov to master the extraordinarily difficult part of Hamlet.

On January 22, 1837, the Shakespearean tragedy was produced on the Moscow stage. Mochalov played the part of Hamlet; Shchepkin, Polonius; and Orlova, Ophelia. The success was astounding. In the same year it was given in Petersburg, with V. A. Karatygin in the leading role. His interpretation was altogether different from that of Mochalov, but the success was equally great. Belinsky's famous articles on the translation of *Hamlet* were instrumental in bringing about its production in our theatres.

Polevoy wrote an original "dramatic play," *Ugolino,* which was performed for the first time in Petersburg on Karatygin's benefit night, January 17, 1838, and again on January 21 of the same year in Moscow, on Mochalov's benefit night. It became a favorite piece in the tragedians' repertoire; it was produced in the provinces, and as late as the end of the nineteenth century it was given at M. V. Lentovsky's theatre, the Buffoon, in Moscow.

Ugolino is based on an episode in Dante's poem, the action taking place in medieval Italy. Its artistic merits are negligible: it is replete with all sorts of horrors, and its characters are either incredible villains or meek angels. Everything occurs suddenly, by the whim of the playwright, who deems it unnecessary to provide any motivation either for character or for action. Referring to *Ugolino,* one critic wrote:

The people portrayed by Mr. Polevoy are not people with form, or they are forms without personality; they are pale features of men who lived somewhere, once upon a time, made love, used trickeries, cut one another's throats, prayed, and passed away. . . . Polevoy's Ugolino at times resembles a tiger or a bloodthirsty villain, at others an easily duped simpleton, or, again, a weak coward.

The actors, however, appreciated *Ugolino* as suitable material for tragic declamation.

In a number of subsequent plays Polevoy paid ample tribute

to "official nationalism." An outstanding example was *The Grandfather of the Russian Fleet,* which dealt with Russian history. Emperor Nicholas I was particularly pleased with this play. On a number of occasions he attended its performance with his children; and he expressed to the author his special appreciation, telling him that he should be writing just such plays rather than publishing magazines. Naturally, therefore, the play used to be given several times a week, and soon it was even brought out in a German version.

Khrapovitsky explained this success of *The Grandfather of the Russian Fleet* in the following notation in his diary: "The piece is nonsense, but inasmuch as it is the product of a patriotic mind it was received with extraordinary enthusiasm."

Polevoy's one-act play *Merchant Igolkin,* based on an anecdote. told by Golikov, and eulogizing a Russian's devotion to his Tsar, is in the same style. *The Soldier's Heart, A Russian Remembers the Good, Kostroma Forests,* and *Yelena Glinskaya* belong to this category, too. The last made Belinsky exclaim:

Oh, rhetoric! Oh, string of words, taken and brought together at random from a dictionary! Oh, hero, with neither face nor expression, with neither character nor force, with neither majesty nor sense! Oh, drama in which everybody talks—talks much, protractedly, in a watery fashion, sentimentally, in a drawn-out manner, pithlessly, in chopped-up prose—and where no one is doing anything! Oh, drama where there are neither characters nor action, neither nationalism nor verse, neither language nor plausibility, yet in which there are many Russian words, many grammatical and linguistic errors; in which there is a world of boredom, boredom, boredom! Oh, miserable parody on a great creation of a great genius, shocking one's sensibilities!

Polevoy's favorite piece was *Parasha the Siberian Girl,* written on the subject of the well known novel of Count de Maistre. He used to complain that his plays, although very popular with audiences, were badly received by the literary critics. The critics accused him of having plagiarized all of the great foreign writers for his works, and of having no aversion to the works of Russian authors. He was reproached for the fact that he had brought about the return of "Kotzebuism" to our stage.

Chapter XVI

ACTORS OF THE SECOND QUARTER
OF THE NINETEENTH CENTURY
(1825–1855)

ON THE DEATH of Tsar Nicholas I, Vera, the daughter of the writer S. T. Aksakov, wrote in her diary: "No one, if he be candidly questioned, would wish that he be resurrected. He acted in good faith in accordance with his convictions. These convictions were the heavy burden which Russia bore for her sins."

Artists particularly suffered during Nicholas's long reign. The Emperor considered himself as an infallible judge in every field, and was encouraged by a crowd of flattering courtiers. Frightened by the Decembrist movement at home and by two revolutions in the West—in 1830 and, particularly, in 1848—he mercilessly suppressed every germ of an idea resembling freedom of thought, which he hated.

Although his predecessor had rarely visited the theatre and had manifested virtually no interest in it, Nicholas I was a habitué, his very appearance causing apprehension and fear. There was no limit to the money he spent to give the theatre an outward brilliance and to engage foreign celebrities. But his taste was very indiscriminating, and this in itself was disastrous for theatrical progress. His passion for subordinating everything to Chancery supervision led to the enactment of a large number of regulations dealing with all aspects of the theatre.

On September 23, 1837, the Director of the Theatres, A. M.

Gedeonov, approved "regulations on the duties of the artists of the Imperial theatres, and on fines for their violation." This enactment was divided into eleven chapters: on parts, rehearsals, costumes, performances, carriages, stagehands, orchestras, and on artists' illnesses, deportment, leaves of absence, and fines. In substance, the rules differed little from those of the eighteenth century. The management was authorized to punish actors for violation by fine, arrest, cancellation of contract, and retention of salary. Four years earlier, in a display of hypocrisy, Gedeonov had ordered that the salaries of unmarried pregnant actresses should be withheld, pending their "recovery," and also those of actors, dancers, and musicians "who because of their depraved mode of living contracted venereal diseases." How little the authors of these regulations understood of dramatic art is apparent from the fact that they required an actor to learn twenty-five lines of his part daily. The regulations remained in force up to Emperor Alexander III's reign.

The Statute affecting the artists of the Imperial theatres, approved on January 16, 1839, is especially significant. All theatrical employees were divided into three groups. Artists of the first category who had served ten years were granted the right to First Class Rank after six years of civil service, while artists of the second category were entitled to the same after twelve years of service. In addition, artists of the first category were granted the right, both while they were serving in the theatre and after retirement, to acquire honorary citizenship—personal citizenship after having honorably and diligently served in the theatres not less than ten years, and hereditary citizenship after not less than fifteen years of service.

On November 13, 1823, a decree by the Tsar dealt with "the remuneration of authors and translators of dramatic pieces and operas if these be accepted for production at the Imperial theatres." It remained in force until 1882. Many factors combined to encourage playwrights to produce plays in verse—the stipulated lump-sum payments, royalties on a percentage basis of the gross receipts, and particularly the high remuneration for such plays.

The outstanding actor in the Petersburg theatre during the reign of Nicholas I was Vasily Andreyevich Karatygin (1802–1853), who came from a theatrical family. Although his parents had not intended that he go into the theatre, his natural passion proved irresistible, and on May 3, 1820 (his father's benefit performance) he made his debut as Fingal in Ozerov's famous tragedy. At first he studied for the stage under the direction of Prince Shakhovskoy, and while still a student, gave private performances at his father's home. Shakhovskoy's system of instruction did not appeal to him, however, and he turned to Katenin, who was very proud of his Basil,[2] whose acting he considered similar in many ways to Talma's.

The young tragedian's début was extremely successful; but before long he was burdened with the ill will of his superior and of those who were envious of his stage achievement. His fellow actor Bryansky was most envious of all, because he foresaw that he would soon have to turn over to Karatygin all the roles which he inherited from Yakovlev, and be relegated to second place. The management obviously did not favor Karatygin, even though it engaged him on very lucrative terms, giving him a contract for three years with an annual salary of 2,000 paper rubles, a lodging provided by the crown, and one benefit performance during the contract period. In 1822, Karatygin, who was sitting with his brother at a rehearsal, did not notice the arrival of the Director of the Theatres, A. A. Maikov. Maikov reproached him bitterly for remaining seated in the presence of his superiors. Notwithstanding his truthful explanation, he was seized by the police three days later and locked up in the Peter and Paul Fortress; and it required energetic intercession by his mother and the influential ballerina Kolosova, whose daughter he subsequently married, to bring about his release from prison after two days. His family explained the unreasonably severe punishment as Shakhovskoy's vengeance, because of his preference for Katenin. This incident is convincing proof of the unenviable position at that time even of prominent actors.

Karatygin soon succeeded in overcoming all obstacles, however, and through work and talent became the leading actor of the Petersburg theatre. And when his wife, Aleksandra Mikhailovna, Kolosova (1802–1880), began to perform leading women's parts, the Karatygin couple reigned on the Petersburg stage.

Tall, with a handsome figure and an exceptionally strong and expressive voice, Karatygin was made for the heroic repertoire of those days, appearing both in classical tragedy and in melodrama. Kukolnik and Polevoy found him a most desirable actor for their

[2] French form of Vasily.—Ed.

plays, and usually tried to adapt the leading part to his special style, knowing that his popularity would ensure lasting success. Indeed, Karatygin was beloved by all Petersburg, including the Emperor himself, who did not cease to bestow his graces upon him.

Karatygin attained his success by a most painstaking preparation of his roles and constant work to improve his natural gifts, which he had perfectly mastered. In his acting there was nothing accidental or unexpected: everything down to the most minute detail was considered and appraised beforehand. He was also better educated than his fellow actors: enthusiastically and conscientiously he read everything he could get hold of to aid in the comprehension of his role.

The extent of his thoroughness may be realized from his attitude toward the part of Louis XI in the translation of Casimir Delavigne's melodrama. He studied it for over a year. In his study he set up a small stage with a light in front, and opposite the stage he placed a large mirror. Every evening, when he was not acting in the theatre, he used to arrange the furniture and all properties, put on a full Louis XI costume, arrange his make-up by looking at the king's portrait, and rehearse the entire part as though he were acting before a crowded theatre. Professor D. Kryukov considered it as Karatygin's best role:

His great art consists in his brilliant reconciling of all this character's capricious inconsistencies. In the effusions of fatherly tenderness he does not cease to be heartless; in jest, stern; in hilarity, superstitious; and in his soulless baseness, full of the proud realization that he has created France's greatness. Note how he embraces his daughter: this is not Lear's or Belisarius's love; you feel that the heartless old man sees this love as his morality and finds in it the salving of his conscience. This is the love of a man whose heart no longer throbs for anyone in the world. How inexorably he ridicules youth's love and the lunatic's despair, and with what pride he utters the words before long, 'I am blessed with heavenly bliss, and so on,' and confesses his conviction that he has established France's glory. Fatherly love and heartlessness, gayety and harshness, meanness and pride—all these components are perfectly blended in the single character of Louis XI, who by the magic of the artist appears before us as a living being.

With equal praise Kryukov commented on Karatygin's impersonation of Shakespeare's Coriolanus:

He grasped and correctly portrayed that giddiness of pride, that high-handed self-centeredness standing so in contrast with the essential morality of the people. He was haughty—haughty in the extreme. Each of his words, each of his gestures, breathed with this sentiment.

All the other actors were so poor, however, that they disturbed the wholeness of the impression of Karatygin's acting.

He also played the role of Louis XI in *The Enchanted Castle* with invariable success. And, in addition to that, from Delavigne's play he himself wrote the tragedy *The Plessy-Letour Castle*. In Kony's opinion, "Had Karatygin in all his life created no character other than that of Louis XI, his name would live forever in the annals of the Russian theatre."

One of his best roles was that of Belisarius in Eduard Schenk's drama, translated by P. G. Obodovsky, which was staged for the first time at the Aleksandrinsky Theatre on November 2, 1839; subsequently, this play reached the provincial theatres and became part of the tragedians' favorite repertoire.

Belinsky wrote of this role:

Karatygin created the part of Belisarius, and Belisarius, whom he portrayed, was a great man, a hero who, before he was blinded, was a menace to the Goths and Vandals and the protector of Christian peace against its foes; and, after he was blinded, he

> In his memory beholds
> The lands, the peoples, and the ages.

I am an enemy of effects, and it is difficult for me to fall under their sway. No matter how elegant, noble, and clever, they always arouse a strong revulsion in my soul, but when I saw the people carry Karatygin-Belisarius onto the stage in a triumphal chariot, when I saw that laurel-crowned old hero with his white beard in his modest kingly greatness, I was completely seized and mightily shaken by solemn rapture. The theatre thundered with applause. And yet the artist had uttered not even a single word, he made not even a single gesture—he sat in silence. . . . Whether Karatygin removed the crown from his head and laid it at the feet of the Emperor, or whether he thrust his head forward in order that the Emperor might again place the crown upon it, in every movement, in every gesture, one beheld the hero Belisarius. Briefly, in the course of the whole role noble simplicity and heroic majesty are apparent in every step, are audible in every word and every sound of Karatygin; constantly one beheld greatness in affliction, the blinded hero who

> In his memory beholds
> The lands, the peoples, and the ages!

Contemporaries noted the remarkable modulations in Karatygin's voice and admired the way he handled them. Indeed, his voice was exceptionally well adapted to the stage, and, with his deep basso, he was able to perform operatic parts.

While possessing unusually rich dramatic gifts which he perfected by assiduous labor, Karatygin lacked the profound inner power and ardor requisite for the impersonation and complete understanding of tragic parts; for that reason, although his acting was completely finished, he did not have the gift of moving the audience by depth of feeling. This constituted a handicap in the performance of roles—Hamlet, for example—which demand a particularly strong emotional quality. Parts requiring only technical mastery and outward effect, however, brought him well earned success. By the whole nature of his talent he conformed to the general pattern of outward polish and formal stateliness characteristic of art during the Nicholas period, which produced Karl Brullow in painting and Nestor Kukolnik in the field of drama.

Hertzen used to call Karatygin "a Guards' tragedian in whom everything was so memorized, studied, and ordered, that even passion arose in him in tempos; he had learned the ceremonial march of despair, and, having correctly slain somebody, he buried him in a masterly fashion." He dedicated all his art to serving the public, whom Belinsky defined as: "Gentlemen officers and government officials, a menagerie of orangutans and monkeys, disgrace and insult to humanity."

It is true that according to Belinsky "this toiler of the stage knew how to show what artistic form means." Belinsky categorically rejected the opinion, however, that "he was an actor with an all-embracing talent, a Goethe of stagecraft," crediting him with

an accidental, but not a God-given talent, whose success depends upon his outstanding natural features, that is, stature, carriage, figure, strong chest; after that upon erudition and intellect, more often upon shrewdness, but principally upon boldness. Decorativeness, elegance, noble posture, picturesque and graceful movements, mastery in declamation—

such are his habitual weapons. It is useless to accuse him of excessive
theatricalism: his acting is inconceivable without it. Inflated, unnatural, declamatory roles—in these he scores his triumphs. He makes
one forget their incongruity and absurdity. I believe he would be excellent in the part of Dimitry the Impostor in Sumarokov's tragedy, and
in those of all the glorious personages in Kheraskov's tragedies. Karatygin is the Marlinsky of dramatic art.

Karatygin himself translated many melodramas, and, owing to
his influence, had no difficulty in having them produced. This
enabled him always to create advantageous roles both for himself
and for his wife. For many years Mrs. Karatygin shared with her
husband the leading parts in a number of plays. Playing the part
of Esther under her maiden name Kolosova, this pupil of Katenin
prompted Pushkin to write a mischievous epigram. Later, her culture, exceptional among actresses of those days, and her diligence
secured her a prominent place in the company. Griboyedov chose
the part of Sophia for her; instead she was made to play that of
Natalie Dmitriyevna. Her portrayals of Mary Stuart and of Clytem-
nestra in Racine's *Iphigenia in Aulis* were popular. Outliving her
husband by many years, she left the theatre while still at the height
of her career, and wrote her valuable memoirs (published in the
Russky Vestnik, 1881, Nos. 4 and 5).

Almost simultaneously with Karatygin's triumph in Petersburg,
Mochalov rose to fame in Moscow. Among theatre lovers and
journalists of both capitals there were lively debates as to which
of the two was better. Paul Stepanovich Mochalov (1800–1848)
was born in an acting family. His father, who was not an outstanding actor, probably came to the Moscow theatre from Demidov's
serf company. He played in operas, tragedies, and comedies, as
most actors did in those days. After 1812, his popularity began to
grow. Director of the Theatres Kokoshkin used to say of Stephen
Mochalov: "Verily, he has talent, a big one, but he possesses little
skill." In his acting he had one particularly successful device: in a
highly emotional passage he would leap to the proscenium and,
with genuine feeling and ardor which sprang from the depths of
his soul, would speak lines which deeply moved the audience.
In the course of frequent repetitions, however, Mochalov began
to use this device in the wrong scenes. Even so, this counterfeit
inspiration did appeal to the public, and, in spite of it, certain of

Stephen Mochalov's roles—including some rather responsible ones, such as that of Misanthrope—pleased even such connoisseurs as S. T. Aksakov. The comment of his son's biographer that Mochalov senior was a gifted man in whom "the utter absence of skill and the misinterpretation of the characters he impersonated killed all talent," seems justified. The future celebrity of the Moscow stage, Paul Mochalov, was trained under the direct supervision of an actor of this type, the negative aspects of whose influence were apparent throughout his whole life. It may be said that the tragedian's youthful environment contributed little to the expansion of his intellectual horizon.

The youth's début on September 4, 1817, in the part of Polynices in *Oedipus in Athens* was enthusiastically greeted by both press and theatre habitués. Soon thereafter verses were composed in his honor, a form of recognition given only to the most renowned actors. For example, a certain poet wrote in eulogy:

> Mochalov! how beautifully thee
> The part of Tancred hast revealed to me!
> Thy magic gift all carpers will outlive,
> And to thy genius will enduring glory give.
> Proceed in thine own way, for talent does not fade,
> It shines as moon doth shine o'er waters deep.
> Immortal laurels' crown for those is made
> Who by their acting make spectators weep.

Even Catherine Semyonova, who was least likely to praise other actors, acknowledged young Mochalov's talent. Certain theatre lovers conceived the idea of providing him with a trip to Paris, in order that he might acquire technical perfection, but this plan never materialized.

Like most of the actors of the period, Mochalov had to perform extremely diversified parts. In addition to drama and tragedy, he frequently played in comedies. He played the part of Aristophanes in Shakhovskoy's comedy of that name, a role in which S. T. Aksakov liked him very much. It is said that as the Prince in *Negligent Housekeepers,* by the same author, Mochalov at times "was inimitably fine, astonishing and delighting the audience by his naturalness, truth, simplicity, and subtlety in the most minute details, and in the slightest nuances of human sentiment and speech."

The critics and the theatrical management of those days had so little comprehension of the role of Chatsky that at the first performance it was given to Mochalov. One critic did, however, comment as follows:

Mochalov, who it would seem was born for the role of Chatsky (?!), played it very unsatisfactorily. He represented not a fashionable man, differing from others merely by his attitude toward things, but a queer fellow, a misanthrope who even speaks in a manner different from others and rushes straight into altercations with the first comer, whereas in Griboyedov he unwittingly quarrels with everybody because he is unable to control the indignation of his noble soul, which is out of harmony with those whom he sees around him.

Another critic also expressed the belief:

This part is suited to his talent and aptitudes: one cannot say that Mochalov does not understand it, and yet he performs it very poorly. In the transitions from humor and inspiration, he is good—at times even excellent. But where he has to be calm and restrain his witticisms, he is decidedly poor. Continuously slipping into platitudes, he becomes a sober Repetilov. We do not wish to impose on him useless demands of cleverness and ease, inherent in an educated man of fashion; still we cannot but regret that in the part of Chatsky he, as though purposely, discarded all conventions prescribed by society.

Mochalov by no means considered himself to be suited for Chatsky's part, and confessed that he had never felt more nervous over a role. He said to the actress Lvova-Sinetskaya:

Here, for example, beginning with the very first act, I feel myself not properly cast, not in my correct role. The ease of Chatsky's manner, the casual chitchat, his laughter, his biting sarcasm sparkling with wit, his genuine hilarity and banter—why, I have never played such parts, and I am incapable of playing them. I am especially at a loss when it comes to the second act. What if I should be tempted to deliver that tirade, "Who are the judges, who?" in a tragic tone! The same is true of the other acts, particularly the fourth, where Chatsky thrashes about like one possessed, cursing everything and everybody. With my tragedian style and habits, I am apt to distort Griboyedov's immortal creation.

These comments indicate that he understood the part much more correctly than the theatre management, which continued to assign it to tragedians. He realized that by introducing the tragic tone he would tend to distort Griboyedov's scheme; and therefore he felt it to be his duty to refrain from performing the part.

Mochalov appeared most frequently in either classical tragedy or melodrama. He produced particularly strong impressions in the French melodramas *Thirty Years, or The Gambler's Life* and *Countess Clara d'Auberville*. In the latter piece he played the part of the husband, who is passionately in love with his wife, and is poisoned by an invisible hand. (In Petersburg this role was performed by V. A. Karatygin.) Contemporaries have provided no account of the impression which Mochalov produced in that particular role.

This melodrama, which at one time was frequently given on capital and provincial stages, is devoid of artistic merit. George Maurice, a shipyard owner, saves the ruined Count d'Auberville from misery, and in return proposes to his daughter Clara. She accepts, despite the fact that she loves a young physician, Carl d'Arbeille. George soon begins to realize that his wife does not love him, but this merely intensifies his love for her. Antony Cassad uses every means to create discord between them in the hope of becoming George's sole heir. He accuses her of betraying her husband with Carl and, when George's health begins to fail, sees to it that he suspects Clara of administering poison to him. At the eleventh hour, George discovers that none other than Antony Cassad has poisoned him; and he dies convinced of the innocence of his wife, whom he entrusts to Carl's care.

According to Glakhov:

Mochalov was always even and effective in Kotzebue's bourgeois drama *Misanthropy and Repentance*. In fact, this was one of his favorite plays, and his portrait was appended to the Russian version. He played the part of a deceived husband who went into seclusion and became a misanthrope. The best scene was the one in which he met a friend to whom he told the story of his misfortune. He would begin it calmly, almost indifferently; but little by little his emotion rose to a pitch that seized the audience. Every added word expressing the accumulated bitterness of his soul moved their hearts the more strongly, till, finally, they were unable to surpress their tears—those "unexpected and long forgotten acquaintances of theirs." By the end of the narrative, everyone, both in the audience and among the actors, began to weep, and many ladies could not refrain from sobbing.

In the opinion of Apollon Grigoryev, "His interpretation made of the trivial Meinau a figure of almost Byronic melancholy."

Virtually no patriotic piece of Kukolnik or Polevoy was staged without the participation of Mochalov, who made their heroes living men. "What did Mochalov fashion out of Lyapunov in *Skopin-Shuisky?*" asked Apollon Grigoryev. Here is his answer:

He caught the one poetic strain of this wild gentleman—I am speaking of Lyapunov of the play and not of the great historical Prokopy Pyotrovich Lyapunov—and on that one note built his role. That note is the verse: "Suffer till thy very death. . . . And keep thou suffering after death!" And so a poetic image arose, one that was probably never dreamed of in a drama so completely dependent on different effects.

In Polevoy's plays Mochalov played the parts of Nino (*Ugolino*) and the merchant Igolkin with particular success.

In Schiller's repertoire Mochalov performed the roles of Don Carlos (the tragedy in Obodovsky's translation was given on his benefit performance, January 3, 1830), Karl and Franz Moor in *The Robbers,* Ferdinand and Miller in *Wile and Love,* and Mortimer in *Mary Stuart.* He was at his best—though not always—in the part of Fernando. Of one of his performances, Belinsky wrote:

Mochalov appeared in the uniform of a garrison battalion commander—an unbuttoned uniform which, moreover, fitted him like a sack. And the acting, God, what acting! Of course, there were a couple of passages, but these two passages lasted two minutes, while we sat in the theatre more than three hours.

A traveler, who later saw a German actor play the same role in Berlin, however, recalled Mochalov's acting with reverence and delight.

He played the part of Miller at the performance in which his daughter made her début in the role of Louise. Actors themselves, in later days, used to say that they had never seen the equal of his Miller.

In Shakespeare, Mochalov played Othello, Lear, Richard III, Hamlet, Romeo, and Coriolanus, thus including almost the whole group of Shakespearean roles which still constitute the repertoire of every outstanding European tragedian. V. I. Rodislavsky maintains:

Richard III was the crowning achievement of Mochalov's Shake-spearean roles. His acting was particularly inimitable in the scene where Richard seduces Lady Anne at the grave of her husband. Filled with hatred and flinging bitter reproaches against his murderer, Anne fol-lows the coffin of her Henry; yet the scene ends with her consenting to become Richard's wife. One had to see Mochalov in the part of Richard III to believe in the possibility of such a scene. Only his voice, a voice commanding every nuance and directly touching one's heart, could make those words with which Richard captivates Anne so attractive, so alluring; and, after that, what a terrible transformation, when she goes away!

Mochalov began to play Shakespeare at a time when he was given on the Russian stage in translations of French adaptations. And even later, when Shakespeare began to be produced in Mos-cow, in translations from the original, Mochalov used to fall back on the adaptations from the French on his provincial tours. Among the Shakespearean parts, Mochalov was least successful as Romeo, perhaps because he started to play this role only in 1841, at the age of forty-one. His real triumph was as Hamlet in Polevoy's translation, which was first presented at his benefit performance on January 22, 1837.

Belinsky, who analyzed his Hamlet in great detail, devoted an enthusiastic article to it:

If in Mochalov's acting we did not find a rounded and perfect Hamlet, this was only because in his generally exquisite performance there were several defective spots. Still, in our opinion, he cast a new light upon this creation of Shakespeare. Only now do we comprehend that in the whole world there is but one dramatic poet—Shakespeare; that his plays provide a great actor with a worthy arena, and that only in parts created by Shakespeare may a great actor prove that he is a great actor.

In another passage Belinsky wrote:

We saw Hamlet artistically developed by a great actor, and, con-sequently, a live, real, concrete Hamlet; but not so much the Hamlet of Shakespeare as of Mochalov, because in this case the actor, willfully deviating from the poet, endowed him with much more force and energy than could be manifested by a man struggling against himself and oppressed by the burden of an unbearable calamity, thus investing in him much less melancholy and sorrow than Shakespeare's Hamlet ought to possess.

According to P. I. Weinberg's account, Mochalov recited Hamlet's famous monologue in the following manner:

He did not enter in a slow step, sunk in deep meditation, but he came almost running in a state of extreme nervous excitement, and then, stopping, he shrieked; "To be, or not to be—" and after several minutes of contemplation he threw himself into an armchair and uttered in despair, "that is the question." And then he recited the remainder of the monologue, at times leaping from the armchair, or again throwing himself into it, with the same pathological nervousness. Finally, with particular artistic effect he arose briskly, and when he came to the words, "To die, to sleep; to sleep: perchance to dream," it was as though he were shaken by horror at the very thought.

Everything in Mochalov's performance of Hamlet, according to Belinsky, except for the monologue and one scene, "was beyond any possible conception of perfection." But at the subsequent performance, Belinsky had to admit a great many unfortunate details. All witnesses agree that Mochalov gave a strident tone to the vague anguish, the evasive presentiment, and, later, the perilous determination of Hamlet to avenge his father's death.

Even in this role, however, he was unable to control himself. His acting was not determined by a strictly conceived plan but by momentary mood. For this reason the same part was performed brilliantly at times, and rather poorly at others. Even in the course of one performance his moods frequently changed, and he would either sink to a very mediocre level of acting, or suddenly rise to the height of dramatic perfection.

Such unevenness in Mochalov's acting made many enemies. For this reason he did not please A. I. Khrapovitsky, who in his diary said of Mochalov in the play *Thirty Years, or the Gambler's Life*: "Disgusting, abominable, good for nothing." And referring to Chatsky: "Mochalov portrayed some inn lackey, and when he pronounced the last words of his part, 'My carriage! Quick, my carriage!' loud applause broke out as if to show that the public was anxious that he promptly depart." Khrapovitsky also disliked his acting in *Wile and Love*, but he had to admit of his favorite role in *Misanthropy*, however: "Mochalov was good, that is, he created his role better; but he did not quite polish his performance, for which reason the best portions were lost, and the audience not fully satisfied."

Mochalov's gift was correctly evaluated by A. Shakhovskoy, who, better than anyone else, knew the nature of his undisciplined talent:

It is a misfortune [he used to say] when Paul Stepanovich begins to reason: he is good only when he does not reason, and I always ask one thing of him—not to try not to act, but to try not to think that the public is looking at him. His is a genius of instinct. He has to learn a part and perform it; if he hits the mark, it will prove a miracle; but if he doesn't, it will be trash.

Hertzen observed, "Mochalov is a man of impulse and of unruly inspiration."

An episode connected with Shakhovskoy's *Negligent Housekeepers* may serve as an illustration. At one performance the author unexpectedly arrived in the theatre, and remained out of sight in order not to embarrass Mochalov. Mochalov was relaxed and inimitable, and Shakhovskoy alternated between rapture and tears. After the performance, in Mochalov's dressing room, the delighted author almost threw himself at his feet, embracing and kissing Mochalov, who was puzzled and dissatisfied with his own performance. In a voice trembling with joy Shakhovskoy kept repeating: "Talma! What's Talma? Talma is not worthy to be your servant! Today you were a god!" Several days later, while he was still in a state of ecstasy over Mochalov's performance as Radugin, a rather influential connoisseur and theatre lover arrived in Moscow from Petersburg and in conversation spoke disparagingly of Mochalov's acting. Shakhovskoy became incensed and began to praise it to the skies; then, in order to prove his point, he persuaded the management to arrange a special performance of *Negligent Housekeepers*. Knowing Mochalov, people concealed from him the purpose of the performance; but rumors concerning the forthcoming examination before the severe, influential—and prejudiced—theatre lover reached him. He "tried his best," and played badly in the extreme. His attempt to play well for Griboyedov resulted in a similar failure.

In the opinion of Professor D. Kryukov:

Mochalov is endowed with too great a natural gift not to realize the tastelessness of the French manner, but his own naturalness does not quite attain the ideal. Where it is necessary to express natural impulses he is superb: how a misanthrope feels indignant; how a youth dreams; how to express passion and despair. Still these are not art, but merely imitations of nature! The taste, refined decorum, and ideal expressiveness, those qualities which render grief interesting and joy noble, throwing a light poetic veil over every living situation, are all lacking: nor is there that enticement which shields one from the prosaic nature of life, luring one into the ideal realm of artistry. Here art is stripped of its ideal dignity, and made a mere mirror of nature.

Mochalov's natural qualities were very good: a handsome figure, a powerful chest and a well set, large head gave him a majestic appearance. His voice, according to Belinsky, was a

superb instrument by means of which the artist at will produced all of the most variegated and contrasting notes of human sentiment and feeling. One heard in it the thunder of despair, the impulsive shrieks of rage and vengeance, the low whisper of concentrated indignation, the melodious lisping of love, the sarcasm of irony, and the calm and exalted word.

Owing to the mobility and expressiveness of his face, Mochalov's mimicry was admirable, and therefore his pantomimes had unusual power and artistic perfection. He paid no attention to make-up and costumes, however, neglecting his stage appearance to such an extent that he played the part of Mortimer without shaving off his whiskers, thereby making this role, which required a youthful countenance, appear senescent. In his style of acting, he was the direct opposite of Karatygin. As a matter of fact, they were alike in only one thing: they learned their parts thoroughly and did not require the prompter's assistance. Mochalov was similarly punctual for rehearsals.

The inability to control himself and, when necessary, completely to master the mood required for good acting, greatly oppressed him and was acutely painful for him. He could not fail to realize that his performance often fell far short of the ideal which he carried in his mind, but which he was able to express only in moments of inspiration.

Mochalov experienced many bitter hours because of his unhappy family life. The members of his family were incapable of understanding and satisfying all the demands of his complex soul. This prompted him to seek outlet for his feelings elsewhere, and, like many Russian men of genius, to drown his sorrow in liquor, which destroyed him.

It was Mochalov's misfortune that he had no close friends to give him moral support and to help him lead his perplexed soul out of the impasse. He was surrounded by drinking companions whose friendship was expressed only in adoration. They gladly treated him to liquor; they listened with delight to his declamation of his own verses or fragments from his favorite roles; but it was not within their power to help him direct his feelings into a more worthy channel.

Mochalov's passion for liquor, and his uneven acting, which made it impossible for his superiors ever to trust him and to praise him to influential connoisseurs or to people in whom the management happened to be interested, "grieved" the authorities. Like all actors of those days, Mochalov was, generally speaking, afraid of men of high social standing, especially those of military rank; but at times he lost his diffidence and conversed with his superiors in a manner offensive to them.

It is said that A. M. Gedeonov, having been appointed Director of the Theatres, came to Moscow and wished to see Mochalov in *Hamlet*. Informed that he was in the middle of one of his not uncommon bouts of hard drinking, the Director proceeded to his apartment, expecting to produce the impression of an incensed Jupiter descending from Olympus. Mochalov was seated with a deacon, drinking; and on learning who had come to see him he gave the Director no time to deliver the prepared rebuke:

"You, Gedeonov! How dare you call on Mochalov knowing that he is drinking? You, the Director, are beholding for the first time in your life Mochalov, the pride and fame of the Russian theatre—not on the stage at the moment of his triumph, when he excites, animates, and congeals the blood of thousands of people, when the theatre is shaken with shrieks and sobs. But you come to look at Mochalov when he is drunk and dirty . . . not when he is a genius, but when he ceases to be a human being. Shame on you, Director Gedeonov! Get out! Get out quickly!"

In order to evaluate this prank correctly, if the account is true, one has to recall another story told by Aksakov. On one occasion Mochalov played a difficult and long role in a translated play. He played the part not at all as it was written, but the public was enthusiastic, and called him back for many curtain calls at the end of the performance. Noticing Shakhovskoy on the stage, he came up to him with deep bows and said:

"Your Excellency, even though the public bestowed on me their flattering approval, yet the opinion of your excellency is to me dearest of all. Perhaps I did not play the entire role correctly. Please be good enough to give me your observations."

Mochalov's immediate superior, A. N. Verstovsky, had no use for him at all. In a letter to Director of the Theatres Gedeonov, after reporting that Mochalov had been drinking steadily for over a month, Verstovsky wrote: "It will be a pity if by wintertime we do not have a big tragedy for the merchants' holidays." We have evidence that Mochalov was particularly popular with merchants. It is difficult to believe Karatygin's brother's comment that the actor's Moscow neighbor, a merchant, watching Mochalov in the role of Fernando, kept repeating: "And how he plays, the rascal! Marvelous! Marvelous!" Perhaps this comment was made up to refer to Karatygin's own brother, the court favorite, whose rival could please no one but completely ignorant merchants. There is more accurate information, however: merchants collected 3,500 rubles for his journey abroad, and on the day of his burial they closed their stores and trading ceased, not by order of the authorities but on a decision of the merchants themselves. It is most significant that, in the opening scene of *The Abyss*, Ostrovsky shows merchants and students strolling in the Neskuchny Garden, both enthusiastically praising Mochalov's acting in *Thirty Years or The Gambler's Life*. All of this justifies the assumption that Mochalov, not highly regarded by the nobility or the theatre management—which was part of the nobility—was the idol of merchants and plebeian students and men of letters, for whom Belinsky was the most eloquent spokesman.

We have some interesting notes on the art of acting written by Mochalov. He maintained, "In the first place, the actor must proceed with the analysis of the author's thinking and intentions, that is, with the discovery of what he meant to express by such and such words, and what his aim was." Conversations with enlightened men and the actor's own education help in this task. "Depth of soul and a lively imagination are the two faculties constituting the basis of talent, however. Only then does the actor possess the gift to convey to the audience what he feels in his soul, that is, to make his imagination picture vividly the action, whether described or taking place—in brief, only then can the actor make the spectator forget himself. This great gift, it would seem, may be called both the most important aspect and the embellishment of talent. As a diamond shares its luster with other precious stones and by its delightful glow improves them, so this sublime gift gives life to the other aptitudes."

Mochalov's opinions confirm his propensity for melodramatic or purely romantic roles, such as Yaromir in Grillpartzer's *The Ancestress*. It is significant that Polevoy recast even Hamlet into a strictly romantic figure for Mochalov. His almost pathological power of imagination helped him to reincarnate in himself images completely remote from the actuality around him. S. A. Yuryev, who used to know him intimately in his youth, recounts how, once on a winter night as Mochalov was strolling through the Kremlin with some friends, he suddenly stopped in the midst of a conversation about the capture of the Kremlin by the Poles, pointed to the Red Staircase, with a changing expression on his face, and said: "Do you see these two boyars on the steps of the staircase and a Pole on the upper step? How impudently he looks and twists his mustache!"

Mochalov's inherent emotional sincerity enabled him, in suitable roles, to be sufficiently natural, and one may well believe those who were astonished at the naturalness and convincing quality of his acting in *Negligent Housekeepers*, for example.

The weltschmerz, which characterized the romantic poetry of that period, found in Mochalov its most profound and gifted interpreter in the theatre. This was due in large measure to the circumstances of his personal life. Much in the same way as Yakovlev, whose talent was comparable to his, he expressed his gloomy mood in verse. Here is one of his poems:

> Ah, thou Sun, thou golden Sun!
> All men dost thou warm and gladden,
> Only me thou dost not bask,

Even not when thou shin'st bright.
Be the day dark, dull, and gloomy,
Be it bright—'tis naught to me:
I feel weary here and chilly.
Nay, it seems that no joy wilt thou
Ever bring me, golden Sun,
And that only art thou destined
To make warm my somber tomb.[3]

In addition to lyric poetry, he wrote a three-act drama, *The Circassian Girl*. This romantic play depicted Caucasian mountaineers, a subject in vogue at the time, and dealt with the love of an Austrian officer Leopold for Mila, a Circassian girl. Mochalov himself played the part of her brother, the mountaineer Dzhembulat. The play is artistically neither better nor worse than others of the same period, and it merely shows that Mochalov did not escape the fashionable Byronism.

Like most artists of those days, he frequently played in provincial towns—for instance, in Kiev, Odessa, Kharkov, Voronezh, and Oryol, and at the Nizhny-Novgorod, Kursk, and Tomsk fairs. These tours and Mochalov's influence promoted the classical repertoire of Shakespeare and Schiller in provincial districts, in which, after the departure of the guest artists, provincial tragedians began to appear. The performances were also instrumental in developing a number of provincial tragedians, headed by the famous N. K. Rybakov (1811–1876), who was the prototype of Neschastlivtsev,[4] and who supposedly belonged to "the Mochalov school"—although this style, allowing the actor to proceed on his natural faculties, required no school.

Mochalov died as the result of a cold which he contracted on his way back from his performances in Voronezh. His death deeply saddened Moscow society, which was very fond of him. His burial was attended by huge crowds. Later a monument was erected on the artist's tomb bearing the following epitaph:

"Insane," men used to call you here,
And penniless you passed away,
And only 'fore the great Shakespeare
Bliss cast on you its golden ray.

[3] The Russian original is in blank verse and broken meter.—Tr.
[4] "The unhappy one."—Ed.

> So, sleep, great Shakespeare's friend insane!
> Our Lord has vindicated you:
> He has declared both empty and inane
> What men believe sagacity to be.

The editor of the *Pantheon* wrote in Mochalov's obituary:

Nature gave him a beautiful face capable of recording the impress of every passion, and a decidedly musical voice. When Mochalov, using this voice, spoke of love, it was a melody which, as a gentle tide, flowed into one's heart; when he whispered, that whisper shook the audience, because it was an ominous precursor of an approaching storm; and when the storm broke in thunderous, mighty sounds of his voice, the spectators' hair stood upright, since everybody beheld not an ordinary man but an enraged tiger or a Nero seized with wrath.

In conclusion, he wrote the following rhymed characterization:

> Mochalov is our Talma great,
> Our stage's fame and decoration,
> Much wit on him bestowed has fate,
> And he is blessed with inspiration.
> Our souls' unchallenged potentate,
> To us his art is ever dear.
> To him our thanks—but none as great
> As that which offers him our tear.

According to Belinsky, the public's devotion to Mochalov had temporarily threatened the success of Karatygin's tours. Karatygin's relationship with the public, he continued, was "not that of a proud potentate who laid down laws to it and swayed its wavering will by his own mighty will, but that of a flattering servant who, for a momentary success in light-minded applause and calls, sought to divine its idle whims." Charmed by Karatygin's skillful and effective acting, however, the public began to express the view that Mochalov was "a commonplace actor in every way: what faculties, what a stature, what manner, what a figure, and the like." His performance in the role of *Hamlet*, however, restored him to the good graces of the more intelligent theatregoers.

Comparing his acting with Karatygin's, Belinsky admitted that Mochalov rarely managed to sustain his role from beginning to end; he was good only in certain parts which, as it were, had been written especially for him, and in almost all other parts he was decidedly bad. Karatygin, on the other hand, was uniformly good, and was at his best in declamatory roles. Nevertheless all Belinsky's sympathies were with Mochalov. He extolled him for those moments of rare delight which his uneven, yet brilliant acting gave to the audience, writing:

I saw him in the part of Othello. The role, as usual, was poorly sustained, but there were nevertheless several scenes which lifted me from my seat, so that I neither remembered where I was nor knew who I was; scenes in which all subjects, all ideas, the world at large, and I myself merged into something indeterminate, forming one indivisible whole; scenes in which I heard horrible shrieks evoked from the innermost soul, and in which I read a dreadful story of love, jealousy, and despair—and these shrieks still echo in my heart.

Belinsky continued:

Karatygin . . . accepts any role whatever, and in each one of them he is the same; to say it in a better way, in not one of them is he unbearable as often happens in the case of Mochalov. But this is due not so much to the versatility of his talent, as to the lack of genuine talent. Karatygin cares nothing about the role. Yermak, Karl Moor, Dmitry Donskoy, Ferdinand, and Oedipus—these are all the same to him. So long as there is a role and words in that role, monologues, and, above all, declamations and rhetoric, with sentiment or without it, with sense or without it—I repeat, it is all the same to him. I understand very well that an actor may be excellent in the parts of Othello, Shylock, Hamlet, Richard III, Macbeth, Karl and Franz Moor, Ferdinand, Marquis Posa, Carlos, Philip II, Tell, Wallenstein, and so on, no matter how different these are in their spirit, character and coloration. But it is quite impossible for me to understand how one and the same talent can shine equally in the mad, intense role of Karl Moor, the declamatory, bombastic part of Dmitry Donskoy, the natural, animated role of Ferdinand, and also in the stiff part of Lyapunov. . . . Here I see, not talent, not art, but an extraordinary skill in overcoming difficulties. This kind of ability, highly rated by the French critics of the eighteenth century, reminds one of the skill of a juggler who casts peas through a needle's eye.

In an article on Belisarius, Belinsky again compared the two artists:

Mochalov's acting, in my judgment, is at times a revelation of mystery, a revelation of the very essence of dramatic art; but frequently it is also an insult to that art. Karatygin's acting, I believe, is the norm of the outward aspect of acting, always true to itself, never cheating the spectator, giving him everything he expects and even more.

A similar opinion of Karatygin was expressed by Gogol in a letter of May 30, 1839, to M. P. Balabina:

Karatygin is one of those actors who quickly, from the very first, attract one, forcibly seize one round the body and carry one away, so that one has no time even to recover and come to his senses. There are roles that suit him perfectly. But most of the parts created by Shakespeare, including that of Hamlet, require virtues which are lacking in Karatygin.

Apollon Grigoryev contrasted these artists with vivid imagery:

Karatygin is a gracefully laid-out garden with clean walks, gorgeous flower beds, and velvety lawns, rather subordinated to the norms of art, cleanly washed, trimmed, and neatly dressed. Mochalov is a thick forest: here are the enormous pine tree, the weeping birch, and the giant oak tree growing alternately, with roots and twigs twisted together—in short, this is Mother Nature.

D. V. Grigorovich, in his *Literary Reminiscences*, wrote:

I adored V. A. Karatygin. I did not notice his shortcomings. Because of my youth and zeal, critical sense gave way to spontaneous enthusiasm. Generally, it must be said that critics were very unjust to him. The tuning fork of malevolence was struck by Belinsky, who to the last preferred Mochalov. Belinsky called Karatygin only a boring declaimer, an actor without imagination. It is true that Mochalov, whom later I saw many times, was capable of inspiration, but inspiration came to him in waves, as though by whim. . . . Karatygin, who was less inspired, at least represented from beginning to end the character of the person whom he portrayed. He studied every role with equal conscientiousness. The spectator always left satisfied. In *King Lear, Hamlet, Louis XI,* and *Clara d'Auberville* he was excellent. It was not his fault that he had to play mostly in Kukolnik's, Polevoy's, and Obodovsky's repertoire, which was then popular. Karatygin's remarkable talent is proved by the mere fact that having begun his career with classical training, playing Ozerov, where, above all, projected declamation and conventional gestures were required, he soon mastered the manner of the romantic drama, acting in it with full ease and not less naturally than it is performed at present. His attitude toward himself and toward art was very demanding. I remember meeting him once on the street with a bundle of books under his arm. When I asked him what they were, he replied enthusiastically that they were the *History of the Dukes of Burgundy*, by Barante, which he needed in order better to familiarize himself with the period of Louis XI.

After Mochalov's death his repertoire was turned over to L. L. Leonidov (1821–1889). This artist, who served fifty years in theatres sponsored by the government, belonged to the same dramatic school as V. A. Karatygin, whom he very much admired. Hamlet was the most successful of the roles which he inherited from Mochalov. To his performance of that role Apollon Grigoryev devoted an enthusiastic article. Yielding to the spirit of the times, Leonidov adopted a somewhat simpler and more natural manner of acting. This was noted in 1852 in a letter to him from his fellow actor, I. V. Samarin:

Lyonya! Yesterday I saw you in a foolishly patriotic piece. One could have merited much applause in it, a great many curtain calls, by concocting a number of effects, to make the phrases more vivid and to put on a hero's garb. This you refused to do. Thank you! You were simple, natural, and excellent! You made up for the shortcomings of the author, who obviously relied on words and situations. You confined yourself to business. Once more—thank you!

Having served ten years in Moscow, Leonidov, by the wish of Emperor Nicholas I, was transferred to the theatre in Petersburg, where, after the death of Karatygin, he took over his roles.

Mochalov's permanent partner was M. D. Lvova-Sinetskaya, who played opposite him in all the plays in the repertoire. According to contemporaries, she acted with correct understanding of the roles with warm feeling and a noble manner. Her constant contact with outstanding men of letters who used her house for a meeting place when visiting Moscow, helped to develop her natural talents. She served on the Moscow stage from 1831 till 1860.

Mochalov's successor on the Moscow stage was Kornily Nikolayevich Poltavtsev (1823–1865). He had received an excellent education and had mastered the French language in childhood. For this reason, when in 1843 he enlisted in the service of the Moscow Crown Theatre, he acted from the very beginning in both Russian and French plays. He was confined to minor roles for a long time, and this prompted him to leave the Crown stage and go on tours of the provinces, mainly in the South. There he had to play widely diversified parts, until his unexpected success in the role of Ferdinand (Schiller's *Wile and Love*) revealed to him the true nature of his talent. From that time on, he concentrated on tragic parts, and soon became the outstanding tragedian of the provincial theatres.

On August 17, 1850, he reappeared on the Moscow stage in the role of Lyapunov in the tragedy *Michael Skopin-Shuisky* which, before that time, Mochalov had performed with such success. Later he played Mochalov's best roles in *Hamlet, Keyne, Death or Honor, Devilkin, The Bigamous Wife, Clara d'Auberville, The Gambler's Life,* and so on. For his first benefit, in 1851, he selected *Ugolino* in which, again, he appeared in Mochalov's prize role of Nino.

In addition, he played the parts of Othello, Coriolanus, and Lear, and, according to contemporaries, succeeded best as Lear. In the words of V. I. Rodislavsky:

Poltavtsev was endowed with a distinctly good face; a very pleasant voice, capable of expressing the most different intonations and nuances, in a clear, somewhat singsong diction; and also a good deal of naturalness, feeling, passion, acting skill, and diversity. It is to be regretted that he did not make the best use of his faculties but merely placed firm reliance on them, and that he did not sufficiently polish his roles; because of this, he played worse than his rich natural aptitudes would have permitted him—aptitudes so comprehensive that they enable him to perform a great variety of roles.

Among the female personnel of the Petersburg company during the Nicholas period, Barbara Nikolayevna Asenkova (1817–1841) particularly distinguished herself. A pupil of I. I. Sosnitsky, she was at her best in vaudeville, in which she played opposite N. O. Dyur, so that theatre lovers of those days thought of Asenkova, Dyur, and vaudeville as inseparable. Her stage triumphs began with the performance of the part of Cadet Officer Lelev in *The Hussar Quarters*. A contemporary wrote:

In this role she brought art to perfection: no one would have suggested that it was a modest and even timid maiden. No, this was a boy, a rake in the full meaning of the word; all her movements, all her ways. Asenkova was so much a part of her character that had it not been for the program, no one would have believed such a complete metamorphosis. In this role, as in all other roles of the same type, she was superb.

Asenkova enjoyed the special graces of Emperor Nicholas I, who liked her best in roles in which she had to dress like a man. This is why one vaudevillist after another, eager to please, hastened to write pieces in which she could appear in men's roles. Thus, the nature of the actress's talent and the beauty of her figure, which appeared to best advantage in men's clothes, produced a peculiar result in our repertoire. *The Marriage of Figaro* may be cited among serious plays of this kind; there, she performed the part of the page Cherubino delightfully. But Asenkova had to expand her horizons beyond this specialized type of part. She performed most diversified parts, including in her repertoire Marya Antonovna in *The Inspector-General;* Esmeralda in the melodrama adapted from Hugo's novel; Parasha, the Siberian Girl; Helen, daughter of Belisarius; and even Ophelia, in which, according to a contemporary, she

proved that there was decidedly a dramatic element in her talent. In Ophelia, Asenkova was poetically beautiful, especially in the insanity scene, which she rendered correctly and with precision. This was Shakespeare's Ophelia—sad, insane, yet gentle and therefore, touching, not as one possessed of the devil, as some critics would have her. Pallid, with an immobile face, with her hair falling loose, and with a fixed downward gaze, Asenkova sang in a heartbreaking voice:

> Larded with sweet flowers;
> Which bewept to the grave did go
> With true-love showers.

As she sang, the audience was completely enchanted, and even wept, the highest reward an actress can receive. The part of Ophelia was one of her favorites among all her roles, especially among her dramatic ones.

Nevertheless, the biographer had to admit that "in drama, for the most part, she was weaker than in comedy and vaudeville, even though she was tutored for her dramatic parts by Mrs. Karatygin."

Asenkova's vaudeville partner, the talented actor N. O. Dyur, died prematurely on May 16, 1839, having made his début in Petersburg only in 1828. Upon being graduated from school he began first to train for the ballet; and he became one of the ballet master Didlo's favorite pupils. Later, when in Shakhovskoy's first play *Phoenix* he had to dance a real *pas de deux*, he was able to display this talent, too. At times, he also appeared in operas; but he was at his best in vaudevilles, performing the parts of shrewd domestics.

N. V. Repina (1816–1867) was Asenkova's counterpart on the Moscow stage. Upon graduation from dramatic school she was admitted to the company, having participated in several performances while she was still a student. Youth, intellect, animated acting, and a genteel outward appearance made her an outstanding actress. She was most successful in comedies and vaudeville, in which she played leading roles, invariably sharing her triumphs with Shchepkin. According to V. I. Rodislavsky, she combined Kositskaya's sensibility, Orlova's intellect, and Schubert's naïveté. He considered that her best roles were Liza in *Sinichkin* and Suzanne in *The Marriage of Figaro*. Because of her ties with an official of the theatre management, A. N. Verstovsky, the well known composer, whom she subsequently married, she had a great deal of influence in the company; fellow actors and playwrights always tried to enlist her good will, because much depended on her. Some people believed she quit the stage so early (1841—at the age of twenty-eight) because of her marriage; others ascribed it to the fact that she herself did not wish to play roles which no longer suited her age.

In the early fifties, critics considered E. N. Zhulyova as a worthy successor to Asenkova on the Petersburg stage. Zhulyova, too, although officially cast as the leading vaudeville actress, had to play Ophelia, which she did with greater success than her predecessors. Even at the beginning of her career she revealed a wealth of talent, which at times made one forget the lack of the necessary technique.

For her benefit performances, Zhulyova used to select *Adrienne Lecouvreur* (1858), in which her success was very much lessened by comparing her performance with that of Rachel, who had recently made a guest appearance in Petersburg. She later played in *Macbeth* (1861), but without success. In her old age, Zhulyova specialized in the type of "dramatic old woman," having no rival in such roles as Murzavetskaya (*Wolves and Sheep*) and Mavra Tarasyevna (*Truth's Good, yet Happiness Is Better*).

The talented Samoilov family assumed a prominent place on the Aleksandrinsky stage during the second quarter of the nineteenth century. The first theatrical Samoilov began his career early in the century, but the most distinguished member of the family was Vasily Vasilyevich Samoilov (1812–1887). He made his début on October 5, 1834, in the part of Joseph in Méhul's opera *Joseph.* Beginning in January of the following year, he appeared regularly in operas and vaudevilles. He turned to the theatre accidentally, after resigning from the Mining Institute. He had an inimitable talent for mimicry and, in one vaudeville, could alternate between impersonations of a Greek, an Armenian, and a Finn, creating by his accent and his whole outward appearance a complete illusion. He became a popular performer for all authors of costume vaudevilles.

The Tsar favored pieces of this kind, and, moreover, especially patronized the talents of one of Samoilov's sisters, so that his good graces extended also to Vasily Vasilyevich. As a result he succeeded more quickly than would otherwise have been possible in assuming a prominent place in the company. When costume vaudevilles were removed from the repertoire (partly as a result of the fact that Samoilov had grown too old for them, and did not insist on their revival), playwrights began to write pieces adapted to his special talents. Among these plays Victor Dyachenko's *The Tutor* was the most typical. The whole interest in this play is centered on the role of the French tutor, George Dorsey. Samoilov managed perfectly to imitate the tutor's broken Russian, and to portray his peculiar appearance. Aristocratic manners and stately deportment made him a good Krechinsky as well, and his performance of that part won the praise of the author himself. When someone was needed for the character of an aristocrat on the crown stage, Samoilov proved the most suitable.

He came into his own in 1839, when, owing to Dyur's illness, he performed the part of Gubkin in *The Student-Artist,* in which, with inimitable talent, he imitated the singing style of two prominent operatic stars of the period. Later, in Kulikov's comedy *Strangers' Invasion,* he played the part of the old princess so skillfully that no one would believe it was a man. Neither manner nor intonation betrayed him even for one moment. Subsequently, he played with marked success the roles of Pekhteryev (*Luncheon with the Marshal of Nobility*), Count Lubin (*The Provincial Lady*), Lyubim Tortsov (*Poverty Is No Disgrace*), Agafon and Peter (*Thou Shouldst Not Live as Thou Pleasest*), Ivanov (*Bearing Another's Trouble*), Krechinsky (*Krechinsky's Wedding*), Arkhip (*Who's to Evade Sin and Ill Luck?*), Shalygin (*The Provincial Governor*), Rostakovsky (*The Inspector-General*), Flor Skobeyev and Opolyev (*Old Gentleman*), Ivan the Terrible (*Vasilisa Melentyeva* and *The Death of Ivan the Terrible*), and Obroshenov (*Jesters*).

P. M. Svobodin wrote:

Samoilov used to appear fully prepared even at the first rehearsal. At home he had a color sketch—often a finished portrait—of the character he was to impersonate. He had already thought out the entire play to the most minute detail, informing the director straight away how the character should be portrayed, how, in his opinion, scenes should be played, how one was to be dressed, where one was to stand, and so forth. Moreover, Vasily Vasilyevich paid attention not merely to his own part, but took equal care of every person in the play. And many actors were indebted to him for artistic guidance, and acted upon his pertinent observations and advice. A play in which Samoilov played was much better than those which were staged without him, notwithstanding the supervision of an excellent director.

P. P. Gnedich admits that the artist was incapable of performing Shakespearean parts; but the fact that he was the first actor to stop playing Hamlet as a marmalade romantic goes to prove what an outstanding and intelligent actor he was. It is particularly noteworthy that

when working on a role, Samoilov constructed a kind of graph of the performance. He would take the highest point of tension in the play and make it the climax, or highest point on the graph, while the rest of the play would be acted with less intensity. In each act the gradations of crescendo were analyzed in the same manner, as were the one or two outstanding sentences in each monologue. There were scenes, however, which remained completely in the shadow. . . .

Samoilov certainly understood stage perspective far better than his contemporaries. The illusion which he created was by no means dependent on layers of make-up on the face or a wig, but in the general rhythm of his whole figure, his movements, stride, and glance. His make-up was simple in the extreme. He made up few putty additions, seeking rather to impress the spectator by the general mood of the figure, the forcible speech, intonations, and even by his voice, which differed from role to role. He hoped to perform the part of Peter the Great, and used to say: "Believe me, for this I need no heels or toes; give me a door reaching only to my shoulders, give me a low ceiling and furniture two verchoks lower than the usual kind, and let the actor playing the part of Tsarevich Aleksey be short—and I will appear as a giant one sazhen [5] tall."   •

One of Samoilov's best creations was the part of the Old Gentleman in A. I. Palm's comedy of the same title. The whole role was wonderfully worked out to the most minute detail, and was sustained from beginning to end. F. P. Gorev later performed it with outstanding success.

Of Samoilov's performances as guest artist in Moscow in 1866, Bazhenov, the dean of the local dramatic critics, wrote:

He approaches his parts above all from their outward aspect, and in his performance he supplements them with everything he deems expedient, paying much attention to make-up and costume. This formal and artificial attitude by its very nature entails certain shortcomings: in polishing the form of the roles the actor at times overlooks certain facts relating to the real meaning of some part, even though it is not too complicated; or again he will overpolish to the point of mawkishness.

The Samoilov sisters, Mariya and Nadezhda Vasilyevna, were engaged in the same type of roles as Asenkova. Mariya Vasilyevna appeared on the stage first; she proved a first-class actress in Goldoni's comedy La Locandiera. Later, she specialized in vaudevilles, in which she excelled because of the simplicity of her acting. When she played, everything appeared natural and true, as though she spoke not the author's words, but her own thoughts which had just come to her. Her career was at its height in 1837; shortly thereafter she married a wealthy merchant and left the stage. One year after her retirement from the theatre, the younger sister, Nadezhda (1818–1899), made her début in one of the best parts in Mariya's former repertoire. At her début critics maintained that Nadezhda's acting was like a continuation of her sister's gifted performance.

Nadezhda's pert and vivacious character seemed made for vaude-

[5] Seven feet. Two verchoks = four inches.—Tr.

ville. Like her sister, she possessed a beautiful voice, so well cultivated that both could have performed in opera.

Having appeared on the stage when she was only seventeen,
Nadezhda Vasilyevna at once became the public's favorite and one
of the leading actresses in the company. Her acting served further
to consolidate vaudeville in the repertoire of that period. N. I.
Kulikov decided to take advantage of her gift for mimicking other
actresses, and wrote a vaudeville, *Mischievous Girl,* in which a
girl from the provinces, having visited Petersburg theatres, gives
an account of the capital, and acts out everything she has seen
there—the performance of the French actresses Plessy and Volnis
and even the dances of Fanny Elssler, whose fame was just then
at its peak in Petersburg. Samoilova scored a great success in the
part. In another vaudeville, *The Gypsy Woman,* she emulated most
wonderfully the manner of singing of the famous gypsy Katya—
from whom she took lessons specially for the occasion. She played
with overwhelming success in Nekrasov's melodrama, *Mother's
Blessing,* which was replete with musical numbers, while Samoilova of her own accord added many songs of Schubert, Varlamov,
and others.

Just at that time, Donizetti's Italian opera, *Daughter of the
Regiment,* was exceedingly popular. Samoilova succeeded in having it produced on the Russian stage for her benefit performance,
merely substituting the recitative for a dialogue in prose. The
success was complete. The play was repeated many times, and the
management arranged to alternate the Italian and Russian versions
at the Bolshoy Theatre. The public was especially captivated by
Samoilova's aria, "This is it, our native regiment," and it was sung
all over Petersburg.

The management valued Nadezhda Vasilyevna's singing highly,
and gave her the very good role of Lyubasha in Mey's tragedy
The Tsar's Bride. Like Asenkova before her, she had received the
part of Ophelia, for the same reason: "Ophelia sings couplets;
couplets are a vaudeville actress's specialty; and so Ophelia's part
must be assigned to a vaudeville actress"—that was the way the
theatre management reasoned in those days.

The third sister, Vera Vasilyevna Samoilova (1824–1880), was
melancholy and contemplative, and was, therefore, not suited for
the roles which made her sisters famous. She concentrated on play-

ing fashionable women, which she mastered with rare perfection. For example, she played Tatyana in scenes from Pushkin's *Eugene Onegin.* Turgenev wrote *The Provincial Lady* and *Where It's Thin It's Apt to Tear* especially for her. It was only because of her acting that Zhemchuzhnikov's comedy *The Strange Night* met with success. Theatre lovers long recalled Vera Vasilyevna's rendition of the part of Sophia in *Woe from Wit.*

The enthusiasm over the Samoilov sisters was far from unanimous. F. A. Kony, with obvious sympathy, reprinted in his journal the following comment from the *Odessa Messenger:*

Nadezhda Vasilyevna Samoilova undeniably revealed talent in roles requiring briskness, ease, and fluency, and, besides, she sang Russian couplets charmingly; but in parts full of deep feeling, or strongly marked by tenderness and femininity, we believe that even Odessa has actresses who would hardly prove inferior to the famous guest artist.

He found that in tragedy Vera Samoilova was physically poorly equipped, that her acting was often cold and monotonous, but that she was free from these defects in comedy:

Here, one is apt to admire her fine woman's instinct, the charming and natural coquetry, the simple yet graceful turns, the clever temperance in excesses, the unconstrained dexterity, and the dignity which characterize her acting.

Both the melodramas and the translated classical plays which filled the repertoire of the 1840's actually called for magnificent production—a requirement which was never met. In the production of *Coriolanus* (Rome), for example, side sets displayed Venetian palaces, whereas the back drop represented a nondescript Indian landscape. Nor were contemporary plays staged any better: all interior scenes at the Moscow Bolshoy Theatre were shown by side sets. The first attempt at introducing pavilion sets was made in the middle of the 1830's, and it was heralded as a great event by the newspapers. Pavilions came into regular use at the Maly Theatre, but they were confined to that stage. The innovation had not been adopted at the Bolshoy Theatre; there, side sets continued in use, their sole advantage being that they lent themselves easily to scene changing.

The following instruction issued by the Minister of the Imperial Court, Prince Volkonsky, to the Central Management Committee, is noteworthy:

I have observed that in many plays produced in the local theatres, stage sets and costumes do not conform to the period in which the action takes place; for example, in the drama *The Fortress of Magdeburg*, soldiers wore white uniforms, whereas in the Prussian Army there were no uniforms other than blue ones; likewise in the French vaudeville, which was given yesterday, Prussian costumes and uniforms in no manner conformed to the period. For this reason I suggest to the Committee: henceforth, when new plays are staged, more attention should be paid both to stage sets, which must harmonize with the period and the place of the action, and to costumes, in which the strictest exactitude must be shown.

With costumes, however, more care was devoted to the exactness of the military uniform, the idol of the time, than to the interests of the theatre.

Chapter XVII

SHCHEPKIN

IN THE NINETEENTH CENTURY serf theatres continued to exist in Russia, and they differed little from the serf companies of the preceding century except that, as the nobility grew poorer, the splendor of these private companies deteriorated. Some land-owners were compelled to transport them to cities, where they exhibited their artists' performances for money, while others sold their actors to the administration of the crown theatres; thus, in the beginning of the nineteenth century the crown purchased Stolypin's troupe. Sometimes serfs joined free companies, serving their masters on a quitrent basis; and such actors were distinguished from the free ones by the omission of the word "mister" before their names on the programs.

The status of serf actors, and especially actresses, continued to be as bad and as lacking in rights as in the eighteenth century, furnishing material for a number of literary works. One need mention here only Hertzen's novel *The Magpie-Thief*, which was based on true facts (communicated to the author by the actor M. S. Shchepkin) and also Prince Kugushev's story *Cavalry Sublieutenant Otletayev*, which truly depicts what used to occur behind the scenes of such serf theatres. N. S. Leskov in his story *The Toupée Painter* portrayed the fate of a serf actress with terrible, realistic truth. It was based on his reminiscences of a serf actress of the Oryol theatre of Count Kamensky. "She knew all her roles by sight" and danced the first *pas* in *The Chinese Gardener Woman*.

The existence of these serf theatres continued till the abolition of serfdom itself, on February 19, 1861.

In serf troupes many talents were hidden which, under different circumstances, could have assumed as prominent a position on the Russian stage as that which was the lot of the serf actor Michael Semyonovich Shchepkin (1788–1863). He was born in the province of Kursk in the family of a house servant of Count Volkenstein. The father was one of the count's most trusted servants, and the boy, from his early days, had access to the Count's house, where at the age of seven he saw a performance of the opera *The New Family*. Sent to the Sudzhin district school, he took part in school plays, and performed the role of a servant in Sumarokov's comedy *The Shrew*. After moving to Kursk he attended public school, and used to spend all his leisure hours in the theatre. There in November, 1805, he appeared for the first time on the stage of a public theatre, taking by chance the part of the postman Andrey in the drama *Zoya* on the benefit night of the actress Lykova.

Even before that time, during his vacation from school, he had played the leading part of Firulin, in Knyazhnin's comic opera *Misfortune from the Coach*. This performance was given at Count Volkenstein's serf theatre on the Countess's Saint's day. His acting won the praise of the Count himself who, stroking the boy on the head, said, "Good, Misha, good!" and let him kiss his hand. The success of the performance heightened the passion for the theatre which had long been stirring in the boy's soul; and so, as he admitted to his master's house the actress Lykova, bringing the benefit tickets, and heard her say that as yet there was no assurance that the benefit would take place because the actor Arepyev had gambled away all his clothes in an inn and was reduced to a shirt, he offered to help by performing Arepyev's role, which he fortunately knew. Lykova's situation was, indeed, a delicate one, since she had already distributed part of the tickets throughout the town; and she accepted the offer.

Having listened to Shchepkin in rehearsal before the performance, she advised him not to read so hastily and showed him how individual sentences should be pronounced. His visits to the theatre at Kursk, already mentioned, had been made easy by the fact that one of his schoolmates was a relative of the theatre manager. With his assistance, Shchepkin was able not only to go backstage but to help the actors by copying their parts, serving as a prompter, and so forth. Now, for the first time, he was to appear as an actor. The début proved so successful that Count Volkenstein "rewarded" him with a knitted vest.

After that, Shchepkin began to appear on the stage whenever an actor was sick, or there was a scarcity of performers. In 1808, while still a serf, he became a full-fledged professional actor. From Kursk he went to Kharkov and joined the local company; after that he proceeded to Poltava, Romny, Kremenchug, and other southern cities.

Before long he had won a prominent place in the company. Two years after he entered the theatre (i.e., in 1810), he was already receiving the maximum salary of 350 rubles.

The description by Shchepkin's colleague Sadovsky of the provincial actor's way of life applies to Shchepkin:

The provincial actor possesses nothing stable or secure—neither fame, which to him is literally smoke, nor property (about wealth, he dare not even dream), nor even a piece of daily bread. His renown does not extend beyond the boundaries of the city in which he happens to play, and even there it is dimmed at times by the fame of a traveling ropedancer or juggler. He always carries along with him all his belongings, since, shifting from place to place, he is in no position to settle down and provide himself with a home.

Frequently, his daily bread is dependent upon daily receipts; if these are good, he is not hungry; if there are no receipts— Pray forgive us. In provincial theatres it is not customary, or perhaps it is impossible, to pay salaries to artists at a fixed time, for instance, at the end of a month, and in specified sums. An actor, let us assume, agrees with the theatre manager to an annual salary of 600 rubles. But he does not get paid by the month. Rather, as need arises, or as opportunity presents itself, he receives now a silver ruble, now half a ruble—sometimes even less than that. Rarely does he receive money in advance. Almost invariably what he gets is on account of moneys earned during one or two previous months.

Shchepkin's situation was made worse by the fact that not only was he a serf but, having married a free girl, he made her also a serf. True, he himself in his *Diary* emphasized the "kindness and humaneness" of his masters; nevertheless, the higher his artistic, and therefore intellectual, achievements, the more painful it was to endure the yoke of serfdom.

Meanwhile Count Volkenstein, having been informed of the successes of "his" artist, because of pride (so common in the property-owning class) prized Shchepkin highly and refused to part with him at a low price. Only the efforts of the Ukrainian Governor-General Prince Repnin made it possible to free the artist. By means of a subscription list 1,000 paper rubles were raised "as a reward of the talent of the actor Shchepkin, for the assurance of his fate." However, Repnin deceived Shchepkin: having redeemed him from Count Volkenstein, he did not emancipate him, but acquired title to him and to his family. Not until 1821 did Repnin set him free, having kept him three years in his ownership; even after that he kept several members of the actor's family in his possession. In proportion to his means, Shchepkin had to pay a very large sum to free his relatives.

Shortly thereafter Shchepkin made his début on the Moscow crown stage (January 20, 1822) where he transferred on March 9, 1823.

In an obituary of F. F. Kokoshkin, V. Golovin tells how that director of the Moscow theatre instructed him, with a view to replenishing the personnel of the Moscow company, to look for suitable actors in the provinces:

Upon my arrival at a Kursk country estate I proceeded to the Ilyinsky fair, and because I had nothing to do I went to the theatre; there, among the idle talkers of Entrepreneur Stein's company, whom should I behold on the stage? . . . Michael Semyonovich Shchepkin. I could not believe my eyes. And in what setting? An ugly cart shed, a curtain all in tatters, carelessly painted sets, a dirty, uneven floor, an orchestra, not always paying attention to the trifling details of naturals and flats, ladies and gentlemen—to use Griboyedov's verse, "indeed, some monsters from the world beyond"—and Michael Semyonovich Shchepkin among them. Alpha and Omega together! Michael Semyonovich in *Experiment in Art* played a difficult role—now of a male, now of a female. In thousands of aspects this Proteus began to sparkle before me, as a precious diamond displaying all its facets! Upon returning to my apartment—to my little whitewashed peasant cottage—I was unable to fall asleep the whole night, and early at dawn I sent word to Shchepkin asking him to call on me. Michael Semyonovich came; we got acquainted. I began talking about his remarkable talent; on behalf of

Kokoshkin I invited him to join the Moscow company . . . and the devoted artist, though promised but a very modest salary (I doubt if it was one thousand rubles per year), out of mere love of art and the honor of belonging to the personnel of the Imperial actors, agreed to proceed with my letter to Kokoshkin, despite the fact that he had certainly been receiving from Stein, including benefits, more than six thousand rubles.

Soon Shchepkin won a prominent position not only among the members of the company, but, generally, among those who, by reason of their culture and the loftiness of their ideals, constituted the élite of Moscow society in the 1840's.

Humble descent and lack of systematic education did not prevent Shchepkin from becoming a close friend of the Aksakov family; he was on intimate terms with the circle of Stankevich, Belinsky, Hertzen, and Granovsky. He became acquainted with all the outstanding men of letters of that period; he became a close friend of Pushkin, Griboyedov, Lermontov, Shevchenko, Pogodin, Shevyrev, the Botkins, Turgenev, and others. How important Pushkin considered Shchepkin may be seen from the fact that he wrote in his own handwriting the first two lines of the artist's autobiography, as though inviting him to recount in these memoirs the instructive story of his life. Michael Semyonovich did this, having succeeded in giving an account of the first half of his life. But the closest friendship developed between him and Gogol, to whom Shchepkin was attracted, all else aside, by their common love of the Ukraine. Having met Gogol at the Aksakovs', Shchepkin, until the great writer's death, accompanied him hand in hand on life's journey.

Such a circle of friends tends to indicate the high level of intellectual and artistic development which Shchepkin had attained. Naturally, the proximity to such persons must have exercised a most beneficial influence both on his dramatic talent and on his general world outlook. It explains why his conception of dramatic art was on a much broader scale than his theatre colleagues.

This social position, advantageous to Shchepkin himself, proved to be beneficial also to all strata of actors. With his good luck, artists became equal members of the intelligentsia composed of scientists, men of letters, and musicians. Prior to him this was true only of I. A. Dmitrevsky. Shchepkin had won social recognition. The fact became particularly apparent in April, 1853, when Moscow society, in Pogodin's house, paid tribute to Shchepkin before his departure abroad. All of cultivated Moscow was represented at the celebration—the first in Russia to be organized on so large a scale—which was not an occasion for fraternizing by theatre lovers with a professional entertainer at a moment of spiritual enthusiasm, but a tribute by workers to a worthy confrere; not generous patrons alone, but friends and colleagues in a common work were honoring a collaborator.

At this celebration Shevyrev pointed out in verses that Shchepkin's acting was "the simplicity of nature"; and he wrote in a letter: "Simplicity—this is your motto, and under its banner you have contributed to the general progress of our thought."

During the first years of Shchepkin's career, vaudeville and melodrama reigned on the stage. However far these plays failed in aesthetic perfection, however alien their characters were to Russian reality, he succeeded in eliciting artistic meaning from them. Owing to his acting, plays insignificant of themselves commanded interest.

During his first year on the Moscow stage, Shchepkin played the part of the cook, Soufflé, in the Russian version of the vaudeville *The Secretary and the Cook*. In the preface to the printed edition of the play, with a portrait of Shchepkin, the translator wrote:

The trivial bagatelle *The Secretary and the Cook* owes most of its success to the delightful acting of the artist of the Moscow theatre Michael Semyonovich Shchepkin: it is being published with his portrait as a token of gratitude to him. I do not venture to guarantee the semblance, but I do vouch for the fact that I am not the first one who has been enchanted by Shchepkin's talent.

Later too, the popularity of this or that play was ascribed to the merits of his acting. Such was the case of a vaudeville entitled *The Tutor and the Pupil*, which A. I. Pisarev adapted from the French original. These vaudevilles did not satisfy Shchepkin, and, according to Aksakov, he constantly longed for Molière.

For an idea of what he had to play in those days, the list of roles he himself considered best, which he gave to Sosnitsky in 1831 before leaving for Petersburg, where he was to appear as guest artist, is most valuable: Lubsky in *The Noble Theatre*, by Zagoskin; Famusov in *Woe from Wit*; Dosazhayev in *The School of Slander*; Captain Cock in *Henry's Youth*; Danville or Benard, or at different times both, in *A Lesson to Old Men*; the title role in *Bot*; Arnolphe in *The School for Wives*; Harpagon in *The Avaricious Knight*; the vaudevilles; *The Tutor and the Pupil*; *The Secretary and the Cook*; *Busybody*; *An Uncle for Rent*; and *Old and Young*.

Shchepkin was very fond of the role of Simon, the orphan in Solovyov's vaudeville bearing the same title. The action of this one-act vaudeville takes place in a maritime section of France, where an orphan by the name of Simon lives. He falls madly in love with a beautiful girl, the farmer's daughter Louise, and later he saves her father's life. The latter wishes to reward Simon adequately by making his daughter marry him and appointing him heir of his entire estate. There is no end to Simon's happiness and joy; but Louise, not wishing to conceal anything from him, tells him that she has long been in love with another man. At that very moment Leroux, the lucky rival, appears after a long absence. Simon receives him in a very hostile manner and quarrels with him, emphatically refusing to give up Louise. Presently Leroux falls into the sea. Simon forgets everything and, risking his own life, rushes to the rescue. Having saved his enemy's life, he regards him as a brother; he does not wish to be a cause of suffering and, therefore, magnanimously relinquishes Louise to him.

In that vaudeville, devoid of any truth, the role of Simon is most sympathetically drawn. The entire action is centered on the role, which gives leeway for lively and diversified acting, replete with transitions from one mood to another. One could make a real display by the mere performance of numerous new couplets interspersed in the role. All this prompted Shchepkin to include it eagerly in his repertoire.

Continuous handling of such material made it difficult to act in artistic plays of real literary merit. As N. S. Tikhonravov has observed, Shchepkin, educated on a strange repertoire and on Zagoskin's and Shakhovskoy's comedies, was unable to master at once the part of Famusov; and only after many years did he bring it to the state of perfection which in the 1840's so delighted the audience. At least, those who saw him in Griboyedov's comedy in 1832 found noticeable defects in his acting, and considered Arnolphe in Molière's *School for Wives* the best role of his repertoire in those days.

Generally, Molière was among his favorite playwrights, and translators sought to adapt his plays to Russian life. For example, one of Shchepkin's most successful parts, Orgon in *Tartuffe*, was converted in Kokoshkin's adaptation into Count Znatov, while Jourdain in *Le Bourgeois gentilhomme* was transformed into Durman. Aksakov translated for Shchepkin *The School for Wives* and *The Avaricious Knight*. Both plays were selected by him for his benefit night performance. In the former he played Arnolphe; in the latter, Harpagon. As early as the 1850's he produced for his benefit night *George Dandin*, in which he played the leading part.

Of his performance of the role of Harpagon, a spectator wrote:

Observe how dexterously he approaches Marianne, how rightly he observes the manners of a decrepit old man who, to appear vigorous, draws up his shoulders; who seeks to please and is sugar-tongued. All these gestures are expressed as cleverly as if by a real miser. But presently Frosine begins enthusiastically to describe Marianne's charms. The old man is all excited, and his mouth waters; but at this very moment Frosine asks him to give her a tip for her labors, and he is torn by two antithetical feelings. How does Harpagon express them? He keeps silent; his lips move spasmodically as though shivering; his eyes, which only a moment ago sparkled and glittered with delight, now gaze fixedly into the distance; leaving his arms, from shoulders to wrists, in a hanging position. Thus Harpagon, with the tips of his fingers on both hands, quickly fans Frosine away—now from the right, now from the left, depending on the side from which she tries to approach him.

Shchepkin also enriched our repertoire by introducing Ukrainian plays by Kvitka-Osnovyanenko, Kotlyarevsky, and others on the Russian stage. Among these pieces was Kotlyarevsky's amusing vaudeville *The Muscovite Enchanter* (*Moskal Charyvnik*). Shchepkin's acting in it reached an exceptionally high level of excellence, and for this reason he readily included it in his repertoire on his tours as guest artist. The production of plays of this kind broke the ground for that triumph of the realistic-folk tendency in our drama which originated with Gogol's play and worthily culminated in a long series of Ostrovsky's plays.

Shchepkin's work was of enormous educational importance for the Moscow state. He brought with him a hitherto unknown careful and conscientious attitude toward art. Regarding the theatre as a sacred thing, he demanded that the actor discharge his duties with veneration, and in this respect he himself set a most instructive example. Never, not even once, did Shchepkin come to the theatre either late or without having completely studied and polished his role. Regardless of his broad stage experience, he paid full attention to rehearsals; and, no matter how often a play had been given, he would not appear in it without a preliminary rehearsal. He used to say: "To the actor the theatre is a temple. It is his sanctuary. Thy life, thine honor, everything belongs undividedly to the stage to which thou hast dedicated thyself. Thy fate is dependent upon these boards. Serve or get thee out." In these words he expressed precisely his own attitude towards art.

Having soon won among his stage colleagues a high degree of authority both in dramatic art and in professional ethics, Shchepkin was able to exercise his influence upon the company—all the more so as a considerable part of it consisted of his pupils at the dramatic school in which, beginning with the autumn of 1832, he was instructor in declamation. Here, too, he introduced the same painstaking and assiduous attitude towards work: even though no fixed hours had been set for studies, he hardly ever missed a lesson, taking as the basis of his teaching the simplicity which distinguished his acting.

In a letter to the artist Shumsky, Shchepkin outlined very interesting views on the nature of dramatic art:

Take advantage of the occasion; improve to the best of your understanding the faculties bestowed on you by God; do not reject advice, but seek to grasp it as firmly as you can; in order to check yourself and the counsels given to you, always bear nature in mind; get, so to speak, into the skin of the person in the play; study his social environment, his educational background, any peculiar ideas he may have, and do not overlook even his past. When all these have been analyzed, you will without fail act correctly. Remember that perfection is not given to man. Yet, working conscientiously, you will be drawing closer to it in the measure of the ability accorded to you by nature. Only, for God's sake, do not seek to make the public laugh, since both the droll and the earnest, after all, are derived from the correct view of the thing, and, believe me, after two or three years you will recognize a difference in the performance of your parts: with every added year the role will emerge in a smoother and more natural fashion. Watch yourself vigilantly: let the public be pleased with you, but be stricter with yourself—and cherish the belief that inner reward is more gratifying than all the applause.

Try to mingle with society as much as time permits; study man *en masse;* do not neglect a single anecdote, and you will always discover the antecedent cause—why something happened this way and not that. This living book will take the place of all theories, which as yet, unfortunately, are non-existent in our art. Therefore, observe all social strata without the slightest prejudice to any one of them, and you will find that everywhere there is both the good and the bad. This will enable you to do justice in your acting to every social set; that is, in the part of a peasant, when enraptured with joy, you will be unable to preserve fashionable decorum, while, in that of a gentleman who is angered, you will not start shouting and swinging your arms like a peasant. Do not neglect to polish theatrical situations and the various details observed in life; but remember that these are merely auxiliary means, and not the main object. They are useful only when that object has been studied and grasped.

In addition to the pupils registered at the school, Shchepkin had many others who lived at his house and, as it were, became members of his family. These students on entering the theatre submitted, like his colleagues, to his authority and gradually inculcated upon the Moscow Maly Theatre the principles of dramatic art which, in Russia, were first formulated by Shchepkin and Gogol. There emerged traditions which not only pertained to certain devices of stage technique, but—more important—gave the whole atmosphere of theatrical life an earnest and strictly artistic aspect, raising the Moscow Maly Theatre to a comparatively very high level. This gave the Maly Theatre considerable importance not only as an artistic but also as a cultural institution, comparable to Moscow University, and freed its personnel from the stigma of professional and moral slovenliness which had attached to other, particularly provincial, playhouses.

During the numerous tours as guest artist which Shchepkin

used to make in order to supplement his income, he brought the same principles to provincial theatres, and by his lofty example improved the quality of their performances even if only for a short time, thus contributing as best he could to their artistic perfection. As the result of his example, the Moscow company gradually acquired the habit of a conscientious attitude towards work. A minor actor, Stepanov, spending his last pennies, ordered in one of the vaudevilles a historically authentic dress coat for the insignificant part of Frederick the Great; he also sat two days, without straightening his back, in order to make a sheepskin wig characteristic of Tugoukhovsky. The administration itself paid no attention to "such trifles."

Shchepkin was concerned with the entire ensemble, going far beyond the limits of his own role. Karatygin and Mochalov, however great their individual talents, based the whole success of the performance upon their own parts, believing that their task was fully accomplished if they themselves impersonated a role in accordance with their design. Actors of lesser caliber clung to such a view even more tenaciously, and for this reason the performance broke up into a series of individual actors' endeavors, each independent of the others, and not bound into an organic whole.

Not only did Shchepkin polish his own role, but he sought, to the best of his ability, to make the performances of individual actors subordinate to the general style of the performance. He insisted on constant rehearsals, requesting even minor performers to study their parts with him. He also emphasized the importance of preliminary readings in plays with which he was quite familiar. Thus he laid the foundation for the ensemble about which Gogol was the first to speak in Russia. This made the Moscow Maly Theatre famous in the middle of the nineteenth century, and it is the very quality which became the distinguishing mark of our new theatre.

Shchepkin rated the general harmony of the performance so highly that for its sake, at times, he refrained from potential effects in his own part. In this connection, he wrote to Annenkov:

Several days ago *Woe from Wit* was given; in the last scene where Chatsky expounds his bitter views on contemporary social prejudices and trivialities, Samarin acted very well indeed, and I, in the role of Famusov, became so excited and so permeated with his thoughts that each one of Chatsky's utterances confirmed my belief in his insanity.

Having unwittingly convinced myself of this, I frequently smiled looking at Chatsky, and, finally, I could hardly refrain from giggling. It was all so natural that the audience, caught by the mood, burst into a roar of spontaneous laughter, and the scene suffered from it. At this point, I realized that it was a mistake on my part, and that I should give way to sentiments cautiously, especially in a scene where Famusov did not stand in the foreground. My daughter and I merely constituted the background, whereas Chatsky was the center of it all.

At present it is difficult to determine who was the progenitor of this idea, Gogol or Shchepkin. Was it the artist who had applied on the stage a theory elaborated by his friend, the writer? Or was it the writer, who with his pen had set down an idea which originated with his exceedingly gifted colleague, the actor? It is even possible that in this matter equally dear and close to both of them, the unanimity of their views, which may have arisen independently, tended to cement their friendship all the more strongly.

Belinsky wrote:

In the part of the Town Mayor [in *The Inspector-General*] one should see no one but Shchepkin, although his acting is not uniformly satisfactory. It is noticeable that he is weaker in the first act than in the other four. The opening scenes of the fifth act, with his wife and the merchants, are the triumph of Shchepkin's talent. In the role of Kochkarev [in *The Marriage*] he reveals more skill than genuine naturalness; be that as it may, it is his acting in this part alone which demonstrated to the Petersburg public what a play *The Marriage* actually is. In Burdyukov he lacks coarseness, bearish naturalness, and even voice; notwithstanding this, he is wonderful. In Famusov, Shchepkin lacks the noblesse that would make his acting perfect. The part of the Sailor in the play of that title is an added triumph of Shchepkin's art; there he is excellent, despite the fact that his physical faculties were beginning to fail somewhat, and that in this play he acts completely as an individual. Gorlopanov's story in the comedy *Bridegrooms* reveals the scope of Shchepkin's versatility. But if his acting attains perfection anywhere, it is in the part of Chuprun in *The Muscovite Enchanter*. No wonder he played it thirteen times in the course of some six weeks.

In another passage Belinsky observed:

Shchepkin is one of the few genuine priests of dramatic art who comprehend that an artist should not be exclusively a tragic or exclusively a comic actor, and that his distinctive function is to represent characters, regardless of their tragic or comic stamp, merely taking into account his external means, that is, refraining from playing young men if he be senescent and obese, and so forth.

According to Hertzen, "Shchepkin's acting, from beginning to end, was permeated with a warm naïveté; his work on a role did not restrain a single sound or a single gesture that would tend to give it firm support as well as firm soil." In his opinion, Shchepkin "created truth on the Russian stage; he was the first to become non-theatrical in the theatre."

Shchepkin gave a detailed account in his *Diary* of the style of acting which prevailed in the Russian theatre during the first years of his dramatic career. He wrote:

Acting was considered excellent when no one spoke in his natural voice and when acting consisted of extremely distorted declamation, words being pronounced as loudly as possible and nearly every one of them being accompanied by gestures. Especially in lovers' parts they used to declaim so passionately that even the memory of it is funny. Some words, such as "love," "passion," "perfidy," were screamed as loudly as strength permitted; yet the play of facial expression did not aid the actor, his face remaining as stiff and unnatural as when he first appeared on the stage. And again, for example, when in those days an actor was finishing an impressive monologue, after which he had to make his exit, it was customary to raise the right hand, and keep it raised, while leaving the stage. By the way, in this connection I recall one of my colleagues. On a certain occasion, having finished a tirade, as he was leaving the stage he forgot to raise his hand. And—imagine!— when halfway off, he decided to correct the error and solemnly raised that sacred hand.

The external impulse which prompted Shchepkin to question the entire purpose of this traditional manner of acting was his acquaintance with the enlightened amateur, Prince Meshchersky. He met this old theatre habitué (who in days gone by had been at the court of Catherine, and who remembered all the European theatres) in 1810 in Kursk, where he had been playing the part of the miser Salidar in Sumarokov's comedy *Dowry by Fraud*. As distinguished from all other performers, Meshchersky played almost without gestures, and "he spoke simply as everybody speaks." At first, this did not please Shchepkin:

Only it was strange that despite the simplicity of the acting—which I attributed to inability to act—in the course of the whole part one could see, whenever money was involved, that this was the sore spot in his soul. At such moments one would forget all other actors. Fear of death and the dread of parting with his money were strikingly real and horrible in the Prince's acting, while the simplicity with which he spoke in no way impaired his performance.

In the long run Shchepkin, too, began to adopt this method of acting; but that naturalness of speech which had fascinated him in the Prince remained for a long time beyond his reach, despite all his assiduous endeavors. In time he did succeed in speaking as though he were uttering a phrase not from the stage but in everyday life. Therein lay his principal innovation in the technique of Russian dramatic art.

Of course, it was not a mere coincidence that prompted Shchepkin to become Prince Meshchersky's disciple. Already many people had heard the Prince's natural delivery; but, according to Prince A. A. Shakhovskoy, the majority, headed by Dmitrevsky, adopted a hostile attitude toward this style. Shchepkin must somehow have been prepared for such an innovation, and his own aesthetic instinct must have led him, even though unconsciously, toward that path which was pointed out to him by Prince Meshchersky; otherwise he might have passed it by with utter indifference.

Professor D. Kyukov wrote:

The extent to which aestheticism in body movement is important in dramatic art may be understood from the living example of our own incomparable Shchepkin when, in performing the part of the old Cossack in *Natalka Poltavka*, he dances on the stage to the accompaniment of a song. How much simplicity and good nature in that dance! What an animated expansiveness of soul is revealed in every gesture; and how much dignity in every pose! Despite one's self, one has to admit that this dancing Cossack is more graceful and expressive than many a well bred hero in tragedy and all the vaudeville gentlemen in our midst.

Some witnesses asserted that Shchepkin the elocutionist was even more excellent than Shchepkin the actor. Referring to his delivery, he wrote to Annenkov:

I found declamation introduced in Russia by Dmitrevsky; he adopted it during his journeys in Europe as it then existed in European theatres. It consisted of loud, almost pedantic accentuation of every rhyme, with a slight emphasis on the mid-dividing point of the verses. All this rose louder and louder, so to speak, until the last line of the monologue was uttered as deafeningly as one's voice permitted. And I even heard declamation of this kind in the rendition of a great contemporary master, Prince Porfiry Vasilyevich Meshchersky.

Thus it continued till the advent in Russia of Mademoiselle George who, for a time, captured all of Europe. Her singsong manner, coupled with an enchanting voice, captivated all theatres as though it had grown into them. But God saved us: we, too, started singing; we sang for a little while and then gave it up. All Europe adopted her manner intelligently, that is, having given thought to the matter; she fashioned her singing out of popular sounds which permeated her native tongue; but we stupidly, and following our Russian "random fashion," without thinking or ruminating, took the purely French strain and applied it to our own peculiar phonetics.[1] It was wonderful! Even now the nonsense sounds in my ears! And for this reason, as we began to grow older and as, with the years, we began to advance in wisdom, we realized this folly and rejected it.

Elsewhere, however, Shchepkin himself pointed to Prince Meshchersky as a resolute opponent of Dmitrevsky's declamatory manner.

S. T. Aksakov emphasized that Shchepkin's talent was mainly made up of sensitiveness and ardor. To this he added animation, humor, and cleverness. Shchepkin perfected his pronunciation to such a degree of purity and clarity that, despite his thin three-note voice, his whisper was heard throughout the large Petrovsky Theatre.

In the summer of 1853 Shchepkin went to Paris, where he succeeded in seeing the then famous actress Rachel, and in familiarizing himself with the art of his French and German colleagues. Upon his return to Russia, he shared his observations with his friends.

The producer-director * S. P. Solovyov distinctly recalled the following counsels of Shchepkin:

[1] "Tuerdoert" and "Kakoert," coined words to describe Russian phonetics. —Ed.

* *régisseur*. Sometimes translated as producer-director and sometimes simply as director as the context indicates.—Ed.

Remember, my dear friend, that the stage is averse to carrion: give it a live man, and one not merely physically alive—one who lives with his intellect and with his heart. When stepping on the stage, leave behind its threshold all your personal cares and troubles; forget about your past, and think only of what you are at present. Never learn a role without having first attentively read the entire play. In real life, when one wishes to become well informed about somebody, one makes inquiries concerning his domicile, his ways of living and his habits, his friends and acquaintances; in our business we must follow the same tactics.

You are assigned a role, and, in order to find out what kind of bird it is, you must look into the play itself. It will unfailingly provide you with a satisfactory answer. When reading a part, by all means try to compel yourself to think and feel in the manner in which he whom you have to represent thinks and feels. Try, so to speak, to chew and swallow the whole part so that it may become part of your flesh and blood. If you succeed in this, genuine intonations and gestures will come to you of their own accord; whereas without this, no matter how much you may juggle, no matter what springs you may bring into action, the thing will be no good. You cannot deceive the public; they will forthwith sense that you are fooling them, and that you do not feel at all what you are uttering.

Remember that on the stage there is no absolute silence, save in exceptional cases when the play itself may warrant it. When you are spoken to, you listen, but you are not silent. Nay every word you hear you must answer with your glance, with every line of your face, with all your being. You will have, say, a scene without a speech which sometimes is more eloquent than words themselves, and may God help you at this moment, lest you glance sidewise for no good reason, or gaze at some strange object that has nothing to do with the scene. If you do, then everything will be lost!

Here, in a simple and generally accessible form, are expressed all the principles of impersonation and transformation which became the foundation of our school of dramatic art. This doctrine found its complete incarnation only at the end of the nineteenth century in K. S. Stanislavsky, who used to say: "Shchepkin established the bases of genuine Russian dramatic art—he is our great legislator." The succession of Stanislavsky to the art of Shchepkin can be directly traced through G. N. Fedotova, who always emphasized the enormous influence which Shchepkin had exercised upon her; for it was he who had watched her first steps on the stage and guided her with his advice.

According to N. M. Kulikov's account, once

at P. V. Nashchokin's house, after dinner, the topic turned to Karatygin's acting—and, as usual, in comparison with Mochalov's. At first, the matter was discussed quietly; but, after a while, an animated and even quarrelsome argument ensued. Shchepkin, who grew quite excited, persisted in his orations and, leaping from his seat, ran back and forth about the study. Finally he exclaimed in a solemn voice, as though uttering an incontestable truth: "Mochalov possesses warmth, ardor, a spark—a divine spark! Do you understand—a divine spark!"

Nashchokin, half jestingly, remarked: "I am not arguing about the spark. I agree. . . . But you must in turn concede, esteemed Michael Semyonovich, that there are occasions when that spark in Mochalov is either extinguished, or when it becomes buried under the ashes, and he plays very poorly the very role in which he had been superb! Now, Vasily Andreyevich is always the same: as he learned a role, as he acted it at the first performance, he continues to play it without deviating even a trifle from the tone which has been worked out.

And it comes down to this: Your Karatygin is clad in a St. Petersburg uniform, laced up, buttoned up on all buttons, stepping upon the stage as though on parade, unfailingly with his left foot: left-right, left-right, without ever daring to change his step to right-left.

In Shchepkin's time the Moscow theatre company became the leader in the Russian theatre. Far from its bureaucratic superiors, the company was in a position to devote more attention to artistic requirements than to official subordination. Here, the attitude towards work was ardent and earnest; in this the actors were also encouraged by the aspirations of a highly cultivated public which, by its love of art and enlightenment, distinguished the Moscow audiences of the 1840's from those in Petersburg.

We find in Belinsky a pithy characterization of both the repertoire and the public of the Aleksandrinsky Theatre of that period:

The Aleksandrinsky Theatre has its public with its own countenance, with its peculiar conceptions, requirements, and understanding of things. The success of the play consists in calling for the author, and in this connection only excessively senseless and boring pieces, or else excessively lofty artistic creations, are doomed to failure. Consequently, there is nothing easier than curtain calls at the Aleksandrinsky Theatre, and, in fact, recalls are loud and numerous there: at virtually every performance actors are called back—on some occasions as often as two, three, five, or even ten times. From this it may be seen what patriarchal customs prevail among the majority of the Aleksandrinsky Theatre public.

Plays which delight the bulk of the Aleksandrinsky Theatre audiences are divided into the poetic and the comic. The former are either translations of monstrous German dramas composed of sentimentalities, trivial effects, and false situations, or homespun compositions in which inflated phraseology and soulless exclamations degrade time-honored historical names. Songs, dances, opportunely or inopportunely providing a favorite actress with a pretext for singing or dancing, as well as insanity scenes, are inevitable components of this kind of drama, which evokes clamors of delight and rages of applause. Comic pieces are invariably either translations of, or adaptations from, French vaudevilles. These plays altogether stamped out both stagecraft and dramatic taste in the Russian theatre. In France vaudeville is a light and graceful child of social life. There it has its reasons and its virtues; there, it beholds for itself abundant material in everyday life and in domestic customs. Vaudeville fits Russian life and our Russian customs as much as sledge driving and sheep pelts fit inhabitants of Naples.

Among the actors of the Petersburg company only I. I. Sosnitsky (1794–1871) can be compared with Shchepkin. Sosnitsky was a pupil of the famous Dmitrevsky, from whom he inherited his attention to the technique of dramatic art. Even as a student in dramatic school, he played a juvenile role in the ballet *Medea and Jason*. The ballet master Didlo considered him one of his best pupils among the drama students. Sosnitsky made his début in 1811, and at first played madcaps, snobs, and gay vaudeville servants; in 1815, he came to the fore as a result of his performance of the role of Count Olgin in *The Lipetsk Spa*, in which he produced the impression of a genuine aristocrat. Prior to that, he began to develop his talent under the supervision of Prince Shakhovskoy. The elegance of his manners and his good looks gave him access to Petersburg society, where he frequently appeared in amateur productions.

There he also became intimate with Krylov, Griboyedov, and Khmelnitsky, whose counsel contributed much to his progress, one evidence of which was that, lacking real feeling, he substituted a polished role. He distinguished himself in Griboyedov's comedy *The Young Couple*, in which he appeared with E. Y. Vorobyova, whom he subsequently married. Among the outstanding parts of his later repertoire are: Figaro (*The Marriage of Figaro*), Chatsky (at the first performance of the comedy), Repetilov, the Town Mayor (this role he developed following Gogol's instructions), Ruggiero (*Ugolino*), Polonius (*Hamlet*), Kochkarev, Uteshitelny (*Gamblers*), Würm (*Wile and Love*), Sganarelle (Molière's *School of Wives*), Balagayev (*Luncheon with the Marshal of Nobility*).

On March 22, 1861, representatives of literature and of the theatre, with rare unanimity, celebrated the golden jubilee of "the grandfather of the Russian stage," the stage which he had also served by training a number of students. The most prominent of these students is Asenkova.

I. I. Sosnitsky exercised a great influence in the company, not only as an outstanding artist but also as an exemplary teacher. Belinsky said of him:

Sosnitsky is an unusually intelligent artist: an intelligence about the theatre, coupled with experience and familiarity with the theatre, at times efface a conspicuous lack of inspiration and creative talent, a shortcoming which is particularly noticeable in artistically created roles such as the Town Mayor in *The Inspector-General*. In this Sosnitsky is as bad as Shchepkin is superb.

According to the former director of the Petersburg company, N. I. Kulikov:

In France, the gifted Talma was the first to shake off tradition and to begin speaking like a human being; with us (in Petersburg) it was Sosnitsky. Handsome, graceful, with an expressive and playful face, with a pleasant and cunning smile, with animated, clever eyes, he played excellently the parts of young men, dandies, officers of the Guards, eminent grandees, and incurable madcaps. Following the example of contemporary outstanding personalities, Ivan Ivanovich, by reason of his fine military and fashionable manner and the elegance of his attire, became an authority in dress, manners, and dexterity to young men of fashion and of the Guards. And how inimitably he danced the mazurka! Many aristocrats used to take lessons from him. He was a favorite of the Petersburg public at large, and a friend of eminent men of letters—Pushkin, Khmelnitsky, and others.

At the close of his stage career Sosnitsky felt depressed because his superiors ignored him in the assignment of roles. He was also displeased with the new repertoire, and complained in a personal letter of 1862:

Our repertoire is still controlled by the sheepskin coat and vodka set. This is sad, very sad. But it will continue for a long time. Every week new authors spring up, each one more vile than the others, and they all busy themselves with realism. . . . In truth, Karatygin [P. A.] is right when he says: "We lack only public baths on the stage—an excellent idea and one that will yield large receipts." The stage set is inexpensive; artificial steam can be produced; tubs and bast-switches;[2] gorgeous realism; costumes are not needed; and the success will be overwhelming.

However, when the rumor spread that Kukolnik had written a new play, the old man's spirits were greatly cheered.

According to contemporaries, Sosnitsky was a very conscientious artist in his work, which undeniably exercised an ennobling influence upon those around him, serving as an excellent example of what may be achieved by assiduous labor coupled with native gifts.

[2] Used in public baths in Eastern and Northern Europe as part of the bathing ritual.—Ed.

Chapter XVIII

GOGOL

EVEN IN EARLY CHILDHOOD Gogol (1809–1852) may have gathered many impressions which contributed to the development of his passion for the theatre: his father Vasily Afanasyevich wrote several comedies in the Ukrainian language—good by the standards of those times—which were staged at the theatres of the neighboring landowners. Two are known: *Dog-Sheep* and *Roman and Paraska,* otherwise called *Simpleton, or Woman's Cunning Outwitted by a Soldier.* The contents of the latter closely remind one of I. P. Kotlyarevsky's famous vaudeville *The Muscovite Enchanter.*

Having matriculated at the Nezhin Lyceum, Gogol had the opportunity of taking part in school performances. Here is what one of his schoolmates tells us about these performances: "We played Fonvizin's comedy, *The Minor,* best of all. I have seen it at Moscow and Petersburg, but I always maintained that no actress played the part of Prostakova as well as the sixteen-year-old Gogol." He also played excellently the part of the nurse Vasilisa in Krylov's comedy *A Lesson to the Daughters.*

This unquestioned dramatic success during his school years was probably one of the principal reasons why later, when he despaired of the possibility of an immediate and brilliant career in Petersburg as a clerk, Gogol remembered the stage, and tried to join the crown company. The attempt was a failure; the administration suggested that he be subjected to an examination, and he was given two excerpts from Khvostov's plays to read. The government official who conducted the examination found that he was reading too naturally, without any expression, and submitted to the director of the theatres a memorandum in which he asserted Gogol's utter inability to act; he considered it possible to engage his services in the event that the authorities should grant a special favor, "only for parts without speeches."

It seems probable that the sad outcome of the examination was caused merely by the fact that Gogol's natural and unaffected reading had not yet been recognized by the directors of the Petersburg theatre. Not without reason, one of his school friends said: "If he had been accepted for the stage, he would have become a Shchepkin."

Subsequently, Gogol turned to the theatre, no longer as an actor but as a playwright. Ever since 1831 the creation of a comedy had been his cherished and guiding purpose. In his notebooks of that period are outlines of whole plays as well as sketches of individual scenes which he later utilized.

Gogol's dramatic conceptions were closely related to his theoretical views on the theatre, in which he was far ahead of his time. These have considerable interest for us. The lofty social and educational role of the theatre—the theatre as a "school," as a "professorial chair"—was his fundamental postulate.

"The theatre," Gogol maintained, "is in no sense a trifle, and by no means a vain thing, if one considers that a crowd of five or six thousand men at once fill it, and that the people composing this crowd, having nothing in common with one another, may, if broken up into units, suddenly be shaken, may burst into tears, and break into spontaneous laughter. This is a chair from which much good may be imparted to the world." "The theatre is a great school," he reiterated in another passage, "and its significance is momentous; in one breath it preaches a vital and useful lesson to a whole crowd, to thousands of men."

Hence Gogol's profound dissatisfaction with the insignificant and empty repertoire prevailing on the Russian stage, a repertoire which, by promoting "all sorts of ballet leaps, vaudevilles, melodramas, and those tinsel shows that appear magnificent to the eyes but only gratify depravity of taste or corruption of the heart," in no manner helped the theatre fulfill its important mission. "What was being given on the stage?" he asked. "Melodrama

and vaudeville, these illegitimate children of the mind of the
nineteenth century, complete deviations from nature."

Gogol considered the unnatural and misleading tendencies of
the contemporary repertoire as the reason for the lack of outstanding talents in the theatre:

Complaints about the scarcity of talent among actors are unanimous.
But where are talents to develop? On what are they to develop? Do
they happen to come across even a single Russian character which they
are capable of representing to themselves graphically? Whom do actors
impersonate? All kinds of infidels, men who are neither Frenchmen nor
Germans, but God knows who—all sorts of giddy persons. It is difficult
to describe otherwise the heroes of melodrama, possessing no specific
passion whatsoever, and still less a countenance. Is it not strange? Even
though we speak about naturalness more than about anything else, the
highest degree of distortion is being thrust under our noses.

In order to restore health to the theatre and to lift it to the
level of its lofty aims, Gogol suggested giving it free access to
classical drama in lieu of "rotten melodramas" and "ultramodern
vaudevilles":

The stage should benefit by the whole splendor of all the loftiest
creations of every age and of every nation. These creations should be
given more frequently, as often as possible, and one and the same play
should be continually repeated. It is nonsense to say that they have
grown too old and that the public has lost taste for them.

Among the great classics whose works should be restored to
the contemporary stage Gogol named, in the first instance, Shakespeare, Molière, Schiller, and Beaumarchais. At the same time he
most decidedly set as the aim of the Russian theatre the creation
of its own original, national repertoire, one that would comprise
highly artistic contemporary plays reflecting the life of Russian
society and the character of Russian men:

Russians—this is what we need! Give us our own! What are Frenchmen and all other people beyond the seas to us? Do we lack our own
people? Russian characters? Our own characters?—Give us our own!

Gogol extended his insistence on a national tendency in the
repertoire beyond drama. Observing the prevalence of foreign influences in opera, he meditated: "What an opera, what music

could be composed from our folk tunes!" Thus he was one of the earliest partisans of that school in our music which created the Russian national opera, taking advantage of the wealth of our folk songs which he so pointedly appraised.

The same progressive and fresh character distinguished his ideas on the organization of the theatre, the part of the actor in it, the ensemble, and the technique of the theatre.

Unhesitatingly asserting that the first place in the theatre rightly belongs to the actor-artist, and to him alone, Gogol strongly protested against a situation in which actors, regardless of their talents, found themselves subordinate to aristocratic theatre habitués, such as Kokoshkin, Zagoskin, and Shakhovskoy. During Gogol's time these theatre lovers were headed by Nicholas I himself with his excessive partiality for pseudo-romantic tragedy and vaudeville. The influence of "the august sergeant major" both on the repertoire and on the fate of the actors was boundless. This produced dreadful dramas in the soul of many an actor.

Mercilessly condemning the prevailing lack of coordination, mismanagement, and the thoughtlessness concerning the general plan of the performance, Gogol emphasized the importance of the ensemble in the performance of plays. "There is no effect more crushing," he wrote, "than that produced on man by a perfectly coordinated harmony of all mutually interrelated parts; thus far, however, man has been able to experience such an effect only when listening to a musical orchestra."

From the actor Gogol demanded "truth and naturalness both in speech and in bodily movement," a complete assimilation with the figure "so that the thought and aspirations of the impersonated character be appropriated by the actor himself, and that these stay in his mind during the entire performance of the play."

Acutely aware of all the vices of the contemporary theatre, Gogol even in his earliest plays refused to follow the beaten path, seeking new themes, new images, and novel forms of dramatic expression which would enable him to realize his artistic principles as completely as possible. He wrote to M. P. Pogodin, February 20, 1833:

I am possessed by the idea of a comedy. While I stayed in Moscow on my journey, and also when I arrived here, it did not leave my mind. However, thus far I have written nothing. Lately, the plot gradually began to take shape; the title *The Order of St. Vladimir, Third Class* is already inscribed in a thick white copybook. And how much bitterness! How much laughter and sting!

This play is said to have been Gogol's first attempt at playwrighting. It was conceived as a bold social satire on bureaucratic customs; the hero was to be the careerist government official Barsukov, seeking by hook or by crook to obtain the decoration of St. Vladimir, third class, and becoming insane because his solicitations come to naught. However, Gogol never carried out this scheme; we have only the several scenes which appeared in print at different times (*The Morning of a Government Official, The Lawsuit, The Cloakroom, Sobachkin*). The principal reason why he did not complete his first comedy was obviously that he realized the impossibility of saving it from censorship. In the same letter to Pogodin he confessed, "I stopped when I noticed that my pen kept knocking against such passages as would never be permitted by the censorship," and added with bitterness: "There remains nothing else for me than to invent a most innocent plot to which even a police precinct officer will take no offense. Yet what is a comedy without truth and indignation!"

Having cut short his work on *The Order of St. Vladimir, Third Class,* Gogol turned to another comedy, with a more "innocent" plot. This was *The Marriage.* On the text—it has five versions— he labored almost nine years (1833–1842). In its original form the comedy was entitled *Bridegrooms.* The action took place in the country, in the landowners' milieu. The fiancée Avdotya Gavrilovna and her fiancés—a retired subaltern officer Yaichnitsa, Zhevakin,[1] and others—were all landowners. Instead of the professional matchmaker Fyokla Panteleimonovna, that wonderful progenitor of Ostrovsky's gallery of matchmakers, there was Marya Savvishna, a lady's companion, who was being sent to a fair for the procurement of bridegrooms. Among the dramatis personae, there was, as yet, no Podkolesin,[2] who subsequently became the central figure in the play.

The theme of the comedy was reminiscent of the Ukrainian novels which Gogol had recently written: *The Sorochinsky Fair, Christmas Eve,* and *Ivan Fyodorovich Shponka and His Auntie.*

[1] Yaichnitsa = Scrambled Eggs. Zhevakin is from *zhevat,* to chew.—Ed.
[2] That is, Under the Wheel.—Ed.

The whole work bears an obvious farcical stamp in the dramatic situations, in the author's remarks, and in the dialogue.

In the subsequent versions the action of the comedy was transferred to the city. The fiancée was converted into a merchant's daughter, and the fiancés into government officials. The characters of Podkolesin and Kochkarev were emphasized, while the number of vaudeville and farcical episodes steadily decreased. The plot acquired a psychologically justified motivation. The folk quality became more pronounced. One of the most recent research students has made the pointed observation that Gogol's play was converted from a comedy of dramatic situations into a comedy of characters and customs.

In the final variant, which was published in the first collection of Gogol's works (1842), *The Marriage* was a strictly realistic play with a vivid synthetic satirical characterization of the life and the types of the bureaucratic merchant world, in many respects presaging Ostrovsky's portrayals.

The Marriage was first produced on the stage of the Aleksandrinsky Theatre in December, 1842, on I. I. Sosnitsky's benefit night. Notwithstanding the artist's excellent acting, the play was cruelly hissed. Critics who apparently were on the same intellectual level as the audience at that first performance, reproached the author for having written a trivial farce that violated the rules of elegant style and employed coarse words such as "swine" and "scoundrel." Gogol was accused of having presented such government officials as never existed in real life.

Of the fiasco of the play, one of the magazines stated:

The principal and sole condition of the stage is elegance and decorum. Where this condition is violated, there awakes in the soul of every not altogether perverted man some incomprehensible aesthetic feeling which revolts against this violation and repudiates coarse and filthy nature. Yes, Messrs. Authors, nature and naturalness are requisite to the stage—but in a purified form, in an elegant guise, expressed with delicacy and from a pleasant aspect. However, all of trivial and filthy nature is repugnant. And the public which unanimously hissed down Gogol's play revealed its refinement and its instinct for decency. Honor and praise to it!

The Marriage provided the artists with ample material. In Petersburg, Martynov was particularly fine in the part of Podkolesin, and Guseva in the role of the matchmaker. On Martynov, contemporary critics commented: "The hollow voice in which, with no strain and—it seemed—reluctantly, he speaks, was admirably adapted to the apathetic and indolent figure of Podkolesin." Regarding Guseva we read in one of the reviews:

Observe how she laughs at Kochkarev when he finds a bridegroom who jumps out of the window. In this somewhat hoarse laughter of the old woman, which blends with the healthy laughter of Kochkarev, there is something original and wicked: you can hear that Kyokla, who has spent a lifetime as a matchmaker, laughs not foolishly or merely in vain, but with a note of anger.

In Moscow the production of *The Marriage* brought no particular laurels to Shchepkin as Kochkarev. According to Belinsky, he revealed in this role "more skill than genuine naturalness." In later days, the part was more effectively taken by Shumsky, whose acting prompted one critic to make the following comments:

Until now we had seen only M. S. Shchepkin in that role, and we were convinced that it could not be performed better. Everybody was familiar with the type created by this artist. However, having seen Shumsky in the part of Kochkarev, many people have thoroughly revised their opinion: they found that Kochkarev is not an intriguer, not a sly person as he was represented by Shchepkin, but simply a very inconsequential man, an idler, a bustler, a chatterbox, as he was conceived by Shumsky.

Gogol's attempt to write the drama *Alfred*, relating to Anglo-Saxon history, dates from 1835. N. S. Tikhonravov expressed the view that "the idea of writing *Alfred* and the material for the play were suggested to Gogol by his university course on the history of medieval England." This play has survived only in excerpts. N. G. Chernyshevsky's opinion on it is most interesting:

As far as may be judged by its opening passages, in the drama we should have had something similar to Pushkin's beautiful scenes from the period of Knighthood. In this case simplicity of language and mastery in the unaffected handling of the scenes, ability in portraying characters and the characteristics of the way of life did not fail Gogol. Historical truth is strictly observed.

In a letter to Pushkin on October 7, 1835, Gogol made this request:

For mercy's sake, give me some funny, or not funny, but genuinely Russian anecdote. Meanwhile my hand shakes with the desire to write a comedy. . . . For mercy's sake, give me a plot: a five-act comedy will be ready in a jiffy, and I swear it will be much funnier than the devil.

It has been suggested that the plot of the brilliant comedy *The Inspector-General*—the zenith of Gogol's playwrighting creative power—was actually based upon an anecdote he had heard from Pushkin. This was to the effect that Pushkin on a journey for the purpose of gathering data on the Pugachyov uprising had been taken by Buturlin, the governor of Nizhny-Novgorod Province, for a government official who had received "a secret commission to collect information concerning irregularities."

It is possible that Pushkin communicated to Gogol the scheme of a play on an analogous theme which he originally meant to write himself, and which was reflected in the following sketch:

"Svinyin (Krispin arrives in NB for the fair) province—he is taken for an ambass(ador). Govern(or) is an honest fool, the govern(or's wife) plays pranks with him. Krisp. proposes to the daughter."

Besides, cases similar to the one depicted in *The Inspector-General* were a frequent occurrence during the Nicholas period, in the atmosphere of utter arbitrariness and irresponsibility of provincial officialdom. Even without Pushkin, Gogol might have known many an episode of this kind.

Molière's remarkable comedies, which Gogol so much admired, were of the greatest importance in the creation of *The Inspector-General*.

The character of Khlestakov closely reminds several critics of Mascarille in *Les Précieuses ridicules:* Molière's hero is as trivial, light-minded, and vainglorious, and he likewise brags about his connections with the *beau monde* and his literary achievements. The scene of the reading of the letter in the last act of *The Inspector-General* is similar to one of the scenes in *The Misanthrope* (Act V, Scene 7). In the behavior of the officials there is something in common with the comic situations in *Scapin's Deceits*.

In *The Inspector-General* (as well as in other Gogol comedies) we find a kinship not only to Molière, but to the playwrighting technique of the Italian comedy, particularly that of Goldoni; every

dramatic situation develops with the participation not of one but
of many persons (officials in *The Inspector-General,* fiancés in *The
Marriage,* sharpers in *The Gamblers*), and this enables the playwright to paint full character sketches including all the nuances.

It has been long observed that the plot of *The Inspector-General*
is similar to that of the comedy of the Ukrainian writer G. F.
Kvitka-Osnovyanenko, *The Newcomer from the Capital* or *The
Bustle in a County Seat.* This play, written in 1827 but published only in 1840, probably was known to Gogol in manuscript
form. His comedy, however, is so superior to its predecessor both
from the ideational and from the artistic standpoint that it is impossible to speak of his imitating Kvitka. Kvitka's style fully conforms to the method of comic ridicule which was prevalent in the
didactic plays of the eighteenth century. He heaps up a series of
droll figures, resorting at every step to exaggeration and caricature;
the characters of his comedies are extremely primitive; social satire
is lacking. Gogol transferred the handling of the same plot to a
new and infinitely higher level; thereby Kvitka's comedy was removed from *The Inspector-General* by nearly the same distance
that separates Shakespeare's dramas from Holinshed's chronicles.

The first version of *The Inspector-General* appeared in December, 1835. The comedy subsequently underwent many revisions,
which continued until 1842—long after its first production on the
stage. The elimination of the vaudeville element; the deepening
of the psychological motivations; the emphasized intricacy in characterization; the sharpening of the satirical motif; the marked emphasis on a faster pacing and tension in the development of the
action; the adoption of maximum terseness and expressiveness in
the text—that was the course Gogol followed in the improvement
and polishing of his comedy. Concerning its theme he wrote to
Zhukovsky in 1847: "I made up my mind to put together everything bad I knew, and in one breath to ridicule it all." Such was
the origin of *The Inspector-General.*

With enormous power Gogol revealed in *The Inspector-
General* the complete abomination and rottenness of the police-
bureaucratic regime of the Russia of the period of Nicholas I: the
"swine snouts" of the Skvoznik-Dmukhanovskys, the Lyapkin-
Tyapkins, and Derzhimordas; the dreadful power of the criminal
bureaucratic gang sitting on the people's necks; the unbridled orgy

of graft and embezzlement of public funds; the monstrous despotism; the insolent trampling on the most elementary human rights; the coarseness and ignorance. Such was the world that emerged from the pages of Gogol's comedy.

No one prior to Gogol, wrote A. I. Hertzen,

has given such a complete pathological and anatomical course on the Russian bureaucrat. With laughter on his lips, he pitilessly penetrates to the very depths of the corrupt, wickedly bureaucratic soul: Gogol's comedy *The Inspector-General* . . . is a horrible confession of contemporary Russia, reminding one of the revelations of Katoshikhin in the seventeenth century.

Notwithstanding all its sharpness of delineation and the richness of its colors, and despite its passion for hyperbolism and the grotesque, Gogol's comedy remains one of the greatest examples of realism, mirroring with extraordinary truthfulness social actuality in its most typical manifestations. The satirical genius of Gogol and the mighty synthesizing power of his realistic method are unfolded with particular vividness in his comic characters—the heroes of *The Inspector-General*. Along with the Prostakovs and Skotinins, the Famusovs and Skalozubs, the Town Mayor, Khlestakov, and all the other people in Gogol's comedy—including the sergeants' widow and the police precinct officer Ukhovertov—still retain their significance as artistic symbols with an enormous sociopsychological content. The mere mention of their names evokes in every man a whole complex of ideas and feelings.

As for the skillful development of the comedy intrigue, the symmetry of the dramatic structure, the cohesiveness and rightness of all the constituent parts, *The Inspector-General* has no rivals in all Russian literature. The action in it develops with the naturalness of an organic creation of nature, so that nothing could be either omitted or added without substantial damage to the play.

Equally unsurpassed, from the point of view of artistic power, colorfulness and expressiveness is the language of Gogol's comedy.

Belinsky placed *The Inspector-General*, together with *Dead Souls*, among those "profoundly true creations, by which Gogol so potently contributed to Russia's self-consciousness, enabling her to look at herself as if through a mirror."

It was not easy to obtain permission for the production of *The*

Inspector-General. Its appearance on the stage was made possible
only by the persistent solicitations of Gogol's influential friends
and patrons (Zhukovsky and Vyazemsky). Its first performance
in Petersburg, at the Aleksandrinsky Theatre, took place on
April 19, 1836. According to P. V. Annenkov, even after the
first act

perplexity was written on all faces: it seemed that no one knew what
attitude to take towards the scenes just witnessed. With every new act
confusion increased. As if finding relief in the assumption that a mere
farce was being given, the majority of the audience—led astray from all
theatrical expectations and traditions—embraced this interpretation with
unshaken resolve.

It is known that the Minister of Finance, Count Kankrin, remarked
after the performance: "What was the use of coming to see this
foolish farce?"

Vyazemsky reported:

The comedy was acknowledged by many people as a liberal manifesto, similar, for instance, to Beaumarchais's *The Barber of Seville,*
a political bombshell flung at society under the guise of a comedy.
Of course this impression, this prejudice, was apt to divide the public
into two contending groups, into two camps. Some people acclaimed
the play, were gladdened by it, seeing in it a bold, though veiled, attack
upon existing authority. In their opinion, although Gogol had chosen
as his battleground a small provincial town, he was in fact aiming
higher. Others regarded the comedy as an attempt against the state;
they were agitated, frightened, suspecting in the unlucky—or lucky—
playwright almost a dangerous rebel.

It was claimed by several eyewitnesses that Nicholas I, who was
present at the performance, applauded it and laughed heartily;
and he is alleged to have said, when departing from the theatre:
"Well, this is quite a play! Everybody got his due—I more than
the rest!" The "liberalism" of this comment by the Emperor is
nothing more than the hypocrisy and political intrigue habitual
in Nicholas.

Gogol himself thus summed up his impressions of the first performance:

The Inspector-General was just performed, and now I am so dazed
and perplexed. . . . I knew beforehand how the thing would develop,

but with all this, a sad, vexing, and burdensome feeling absorbed me. My own creation appeared to me repulsive and odd, as though it were not mine at all.

Of all the actors only Sosnitsky, in the part of the Town Mayor, satisfied him.

In Moscow the production of the play was fraught with even greater difficulties. To begin with, it was seriously impaired by the fact that Shchepkin, who, in compliance with the author's wishes and quite rightfully, was to have taken charge of it, remained away from it altogether in the end, owing to the stupid interference of the administration. This was apparently the fault of Zagoskin, who at that time was in charge of the Moscow theatres. As a result of the careless staging of the play, only Shchepkin as the Town Mayor, Potanchikov as postmaster, and Orlov as Osip proved satisfactory. All the others were very bad.

The press marked the appearance of *The Inspector-General* by a series of bitterly hostile comments. In *The Reading Library,* which zealously sought to convince the public that the talent of Baron Brambeus far exceeded that of Gogol, it was asserted:

In *The Inspector-General* there is no picture of Russian society; there are no characters; there is neither intrigue nor denouement; much is unnatural and contrary to truth; while the play *in toto* is nothing but an old anecdote which has been utilized many times in other literatures.

Bulgarin, reiterating all accusations catalogued in *The Library,* added that "everything in the play is implausible"; that "both the officials and the landlords are represented as greatest cheats and fools"; that "coquettes, such as the Town Mayor's daughter and wife, are nowhere to be found"; that "it is incredible that the whole town should be worse than Sodom and Gomorrah"; and that "it is altogether incomprehensible by what miracle this small town, without a single honest soul, can survive on the terrestrial globe." Furthermore, he declared that officials did not at all accept bribes as described in the play, and reproached the author for having used expressions which were not tolerated in good society.

Likewise Polevoy maintained that Gogol's reputation was being inflated without justification. He considered *The Inspector-General* as a mere farce, without discerning in it either drama or purpose, either intrigue or specific characters.

A worthy rebuttal to these accusations was made by Vyazemsky who, in the opening part of his article, placed *The Inspector-General* side by side with *The Minor, The Brigadier, The Slanderer,* and *Woe from Wit.* But Gogol's play was reviewed with particular sympathy in the magazine *Rumor* by an anonymous critic (it is now supposed to have been Belinsky) who wrote:

Copies of *The Inspector-General,* received at Moscow, have been read through, reread, memorized; they have been converted into proverbs, and out they went far and wide among the people, becoming transformed into epigrams and branding those to whom they were applicable. The names of the dramatis personae in *The Inspector-General,* the very next day, changed into proper names: the Khlestakovs, the Anna Andreyevnas, the Marya Antonovnas, the Town Mayors, the Zemlanikas, the Tyapkin-Lyapkins, arm in arm, started marching along with Famusov, Molchalin, Chatsky, and the Prostakovs. And all this happened overnight, even prior to the performance. Look! They—these ladies and gentlemen—are strolling along the Tverskoy Boulevard, in the Park, throughout the city; and everywhere, everywhere, wheresoever a dozen people are assembled, one among them unfailingly merges from Gogol's comedy. Now why is this so? Who has made this creation come alive? Who has made it so akin to us? Who has corroborated all these nicknames, these phrases, these droll and clumsy expressions? Who? This was accomplished by two great factors: the author's talent and the timeliness of the creation.

The cold public reception of the play at the first performances and the wicked press attacks produced on Gogol's pathologically sensitive soul a most painful impression. This probably explains his departure abroad following the production of *The Inspector-General.* Even though he asserted, "My play disgusts me," still for many years he did not cease pondering over it, revising it, and interpreting its contents to both actors and audiences.

The Inspector-General was followed by *The Departure from the Theatre,* which was so highly regarded by Belinsky; he regarded this polemical play as "a profoundly conceived theory of social comedy"; "a notice of warning to those who would seek properly to perform *The Inspector-General,*" which contained a number of remarkable ideas on the realistic art of acting; and finally *The Dénouement of The Inspector-General.* The latter dates from 1846, that is, from the period when *Selected Portions from the Correspondence with Friends* were written. The pathological crisis in Gogol's ideology which had developed by that time resulted in a most unfortunate interpretation of *The Inspector-General,* suggested in *The Dénouement of The Inspector-General,* an interpretation which assumed a mystical aspect.

In that play the leading comic actor says:

The Inspector-General is our awakened conscience, which will suddenly and spontaneously compel us to look attentively at ourselves. Khlestakov is the giddy-brained fashionable conscience—a venal, deceitful conscience: Khlestakov will be bribed exactly as our own passions dwell in our soul.

The abrupt change in the attitude of the author towards his play was painfully felt by the same Shchepkin into whose mouth he sought to put this labored and morbid interpretation. The great actor wrote to Gogol:

In the course of our ten-year friendship, I became so used to the Town Mayor, to Dobchinsky, and Bobchinsky, that it would be a dishonest act to take these and all others away from me. With what are you going to replace them? Leave them alone as they are. I love them. I love them with all their infirmities, as I do all men in general. Do not insinuate to me that they are supposed to be, not bureaucrats, but our passions: no; I do not wish such a transformation; they are genuine persons, live men in whose midst I have grown up and have almost grown old. Do you see what a long-standing acquaintanceship this is! From the world at large you mustered several men to one rallying spot, uniting them in one group; I became closely related to them; and now you try to take them away from me. No; so long as I live, I will not. I will not surrender them to you. After my passing, turn them even into goats, but until that time I will not cede Derzhimorda [3] to you because he, too, is dear to me.

At the first production of *The Inspector-General,* the part of the Town Mayor was performed more successfully than the others, perhaps because in both capital cities it was assigned to artists who were on intimate terms with Gogol, and who for this reason were in a better position to grasp the author's intention. In Peters-

[3] Based, like all the characters' names in *The Inspector-General* on onomatopoeia. Derzhimorda is formed from *derzhat,* to hold or grasp, + *morda,* mug, thus extortionist.—Ed.

burg the part was played by I. I. Sosnitsky, and in Moscow by Shchepkin.

We have on record a comparative description of the acting of both artists in that role. The eminent critic D. V. Averkiyev wrote:

Both artists played with equal excellence, while the difference in their performance was largely due to the difference in the nature of their individual talents. One of them (Shchepkin) was preeminently a comic, while the aptitudes of the other (Sosnitsky) came within the compass of the so-called *emploi* of first character parts. With one of the actors the Town Mayor appeared simpler, more cowardly, and wherever there was room for comic rage and anger, for example in the fifth act, Shchepkin performed miracles; in Sosnitsky's impersonation the Town Mayor was more reserved, more shrewd: his very roguery was, one may say, cultivated; it was not, it seemed, a natural appurtenance of the man but reminded one of something acquired through long experience.

Another critic wrote:

Shchepkin, owing to his southern temperament, his diction, figure, voice and his whole type of talent, based completely on realism, produced a strictly Russian Town Mayor—a carnivorous, cunning blade, and a rascal with the somewhat coarse countenance of a small provincial bureaucrat; one who knows well how to oppress and crush his inferiors, and how to crawl before his superiors. Sosnitsky, brought up on types of the French comedy in adaptations to pseudo-Russian customs of Khmelnitsky, and simply in translations, presented a more common appearance of a shifty and subtle, but cold, swindler with the voice and character of a fox, sweet as honey and bitter as gall.

Each was excellent in his own way. Of course Shchepkin was more typical; he was, as stated, an ignorant Russian man, ignorant in everything save in the art of outwitting anyone at his discretion. Shchepkin was able to discover one or two almost tragic notes in his role. Thus the words: "Don't ruin me! . . . Wife, children!" were uttered by him with tears in his voice, with a most miserable expression, and with his chin trembling; in fact it seemed that he was about to burst into tears. And for one moment this rogue evoked a feeling of pity. In Sosnitsky the Town Mayor was rather amusing, like that cunning trapped beast which he resembled. Nor were the physical features of the two actors identical; Shchepkin was of small stature, with a broad face; Sosnitsky tall, with elongated features.

After Shchepkin's death, the role of the Town Mayor was given to I. V. Samarin, who was thus faced with a most responsible task—that of appearing before the public which was still under the vivid impression of Shchepkin's brilliant performance. Therefore, strictly adhering to Shchepkin's interpretation of the part, he confined himself to the reproduction of his predecessor's acting in so far, of course, as his physical characteristics permitted. Later, the part of the Town Mayor was played with exceptional brilliance by V. H. Davydov, the successor to Shchepkin's talent, whose traditions he preserved. Prov Sadovsky utterly failed in this part; but, on the other hand, he distinguished himself by the remarkable performance of the role of Osip. In Apollon Grigoryev's words:

When Osip is on the stage everything lives, but without him it seems empty. One is apt to believe that he continues to live and act behind the stage even when he does not appear before one's eyes. Not even a needle can be stuck under this mask. One feels that it might prick the living body, to such an extent have mask and body grown together. Osip, when he is on the stage, obliterates everything else, even the Town Mayor himself.

Contemporaries have related that Sadovsky in the part of Osip became the character, as it were. By every glance and gesture he inimitably represented Osip's mood; for instance, his resentment against his master in the well known monologue; in brushing back and forth while shining his master's boots and spitting on them in such a manner that all the spectators were fully aware how vexed and irritated he was; his announcement to his master of the Town Mayor's arrival, his joy over the cabbage soup and gruel after a prolonged hunger; and his only too natural urging that the master depart from the town—all these were in truth a triumph of stagecraft. Hence critics were right when they maintained that "in his gestures, sighs, whimperings, and body positions the spectators sensed a whole drama."

The part of Khlestakov was played much less successfully both at the first performance and afterward. Dyur, its first performer on the Petersburg stage, failed to satisfy Gogol because he brought to the role a purely vaudeville interpretation; this was probably due to the rigidity of the theatrical tradition. "The leading role was lost," wrote Gogol, "and this I had expected. Dyur utterly failed to grasp what Khlestakov is. Khlestakov became something in the order of Alnaksarov, similar to a whole range of vaudeville scamps who came to us from the Parisian theatres."

Also, in the course of the subsequent stage history of *The Inspector-General* the actors who played Khlestakov only rarely conveyed correctly Gogol's intentions. In the interpretation of some actors Khlestakov appeared too sedate and too dandyish; in others, too insignificant. According to contemporaries, Samarin was guilty of the former extreme, Maksimov the latter. The role seems to have been best performed by S. V. Shumsky, who acted the scene with the waiter and at dinner particularly effectively. However, he could not at all master excessive bragging, and he had an altogether inappropriate mischievous expression which did not leave him even when he walked restlessly back and forth on the stage, tormented by pangs of acute hunger. But the part of Khlestakov was well performed subsequently by M. P. Sadovsky. Gogol himself realized the great complexity of the role, and wrote to Shchepkin:

In the whole play the most difficult part is that of Khlestakov. I do not know whether you will succeed in selecting an actor for it. God forbid that it be played in the usual farcical style in which braggarts and theatrical rakes are now impersonated. He is simply stupid: he babbles only because he sees that people are ready to listen to him; he lies because he has lunched heartily and drunk good wine; he is nimble only when he cottons to the ladies. I am very much afraid for this role.

The exact date when Gogol wrote his comedy *The Gamblers* has not been determined. It has been produced on the stage with marked success, though only on rare occasions. Among the performers, critics particularly praised Prov Sadovsky (Zamukhryshkin), Shchepkin (Uteshitelny), Samoilov (Zamukhryshkin), Sosnitsky (Uteshitelny), and Martynov (Ikharev).

N. A. Kotlyarevsky has called *The Gamblers* one of the most perfect dramatic works from the standpoint of technique: "The comedy is not invented but based on stories of actual tricks practiced by different sharpers and crooks. Stories about such stratagems frequently occurred in the literature of Gogol's period. Almost no novel of manners omitted them. Gogol's merit consisted in that he developed this traditional theme with extraordinary realism and inimitable wit: that he alone succeeded in expressing with equal truth a general tone in several variations; and—most important—

that he evaded all didacticism by excluding from the dramatis personae the former hero, the "victim"!

Belinsky considered *The Gamblers* to be "fully worthy of its author's name."

A passionate lover of the Ukraine, Gogol one time thought of becoming his father's successor and writing a Ukrainian play. While living abroad, he worked diligently on it, utilizing the historical data which he had gathered earlier, and ordering for study collections of Ukrainian songs. As was his custom, he also took liberal advantage of the counsels given him by his acquaintances. He contemplated writing a play of the Cossack epoch, which, no doubt, would have been a contribution to our drama as valuable as *Taras Bulba* is to another field of poetry. It is to be regretted that nothing came of these labors, and that the preliminary sketches of the play have been burned.

There remains for mention the comedy *The Tutor in a Difficult Position,* translated by Gogol from the Italian. (The original was from the pen of Giordano Giraud.) This play, in which Shchepkin and subsequently V. N. Davydov played with marked success, bears witness to Gogol's interest in the foreign repertoire.

Because he worked on his plays with rare industry, he was unable to produce a large volume of material for the theatre. Neither his sojourn abroad, where it was difficult to keep in contact with the Russian theatre, nor the shockingly unjust attitude of the shortsighted and unimaginative critics, encouraged him to concentrate on the drama. Nevertheless, in *The Inspector-General* and *The Marriage,* Gogol created the best examples of Russian comedy. These plays introduced realism to the Russian stage. Bringing to a close the entire preceding period of our dramatic development, Gogol became in Russia the progenitor of the realistic theatre, of the theatre of mighty social satire, which in its subsequent phases produced Ostrovsky, Sukhovo-Kobylin, and Chekhov.

"One must ascribe exclusively to Gogol," maintained Chernyshevsky, "the merit of firmly introducing in Russian belles-lettres the satirical, or, to use a more correct term, the critical style."

Gogol also established the same critical tendency in drama, thereby rendering his people an enormous service in their ideological struggle against the sociopolitical regime based upon the autocracy of the Derzhimordas.

Gogol's dramaturgy, replete with profound humanity, genuinely popular and utterly truthful, is also close to us contemporaries of the great socialist epoch—close "through those ideas of Belinsky and Gogol which made these writers dear to Nekrasov, as to every decent man in Russia" (Lenin).

THE THEATRE OF THE
SECOND HALF OF THE
NINETEENTH CENTURY

THE Sebastopol debacle revealed the utter bankruptcy of the government and the complete falsity of its policies. The "emancipation" of the peasants on February 19, 1861, disillusioned all honest people in the country, prompting them to join that struggle which was waged by the common people up to the reaction of 1881. Ostrovsky was the greatest playwright of that period to identify himself with popular circles. His plays were a sharply critical portrayal of aristocratic society. The best actors emerged from Shchepkin's school, while the actress Yermolova, who was close to progressive youth, combined artistic mastery with the power of social influence upon the audience. A stubborn struggle began against Italianism in opera, where a number of composers of a strictly Russian school came to the fore. The inability, and the refusal, of the government to take into account the growing aesthetic aspirations of the audience, and to mold conditions requisite to the work of the actor and the playwright, brought forth the first endeavors to organize theatres free from bureaucratic control.

The greatest figure of the theatre of that period was A. N. Ostrovsky.

Chapter XIX

OSTROVSKY

ALEXANDER NIKOLAYEVICH OSTROVSKY (1823–1886), passed his childhood and youth in an environment which left an impress upon the character of his creative work. His father was a government official in the Moscow Senate, and his mother was the daughter of a baker of sacramental wafers. He was born in the Malaya Ordynka,[1] in the very center of Zamoskvorechye, whose inimitable chronicler he was destined to become. By the time the future playwright was grown up, his father had resigned from government service and had begun to conduct private affairs, mostly of merchants, who for this reason used to visit his house.

Even in his early years Ostrovsky had occasion to observe many of the aspects of merchant life which subsequently served him as literary material. Upon graduation from the Moscow provincial gymnasium, he matriculated in the law division of the Moscow University; however, owing to a conflict with one of the professors, he did not complete the course. Having left the University in 1843, he became a clerk, first in the Arbitration, and later in the Commercial, Court. He remained in government service eight years. There, by the very nature of his work, he had to mingle constantly with most divergent people, thus coming in direct contact with the customs and interests of Moscow merchants. In the course of his service, Ostrovsky was able to study intimately the heterogeneous types of pre-reform Moscow officials. He later readily in-

[1] Famous street in the south-central section of Moscow; derives its name from the fact that the representatives of the orda (horde) were in residence there.—Ed.

cluded them among the characters in his plays, supplementing by personal observations those portraits of our bureaucracy which, by that time, Gogol had painted with rare mastery.

Ostrovsky had personal connections as well as business relations with merchants, and this brought him into still closer contact with their milieu. Several representative younger merchants, especially I. I. Shanin, were his most intimate friends. Their friendship left a lasting impression upon his world outlook, and provided him with inexhaustible material for his literary work, which he began while still in government service.

On January 9, 1847, in the *Moscow Municipal Messenger* there appeared over the signature "A. O. and D. G." sketches from the comedy *The Bankrupt*. These became the first scenes in the later famous comedy *It's a Family Affair—We'll Settle It Ourselves*.

Subsequently he himself wrote that he considered February 14, 1847, as the beginning of his literary career. "From that date on, I began to regard myself as a Russian writer, and with neither doubt nor hesitation I placed confidence in my vocation." On that day, at the home of the Moscow professor S. P. Shevyrev, Ostrovsky who by that time was already connected with literary circles, read his first dramatic scenes in the presence of the critic Apollon Grigoryev. Embracing the young author with sincere admiration, Shevyrev greeted him as a man of talent destined to write for his native theatre.

In 1849 at the home of Pogodin, Ostrovsky, alternately with Prov Sadovsky, read his comedy *The Bankrupt*, which was the original title of *It's a Family Affair—We'll Settle It Ourselves*. The reading was extraordinarily successful. Thereafter, he read it almost daily during the whole winter—now at the home of the poetess Rostopchina, now at the Princes Meshcherskis', now at the Sheremetevs'. Everywhere, the play produced a strong impression; and his renown spread rapidly throughout Moscow.

The play appeared in print in 1850, in the March issue of the magazine *Moskvityanin*,[2] signed "A. Ostrovsky." Censorship did not permit its production on the stage, however; and the Moscow governor, General Count A. A. Zakrevsky, put the author on the list of those of doubtful loyalty.

The success which accompanied the first steps of Ostrovsky's

[2] That is, *Muscovite.*—Ed.

literary career must have partly alleviated these disappointments. Before long he assumed a prominent place among men of letters, and the most competent judges rated him among our most outstanding playwrights. The broadly educated Prince V. F. Odoyevsky, having read *It's a Family Affair—We'll Settle It Ourselves,* wrote to a friend:

Have you read Ostrovsky's comedy, or rather tragedy, *It's a Family Affair—We'll Settle It Ourselves,* the real title of which is *The Bankrupt?* It is time to expose spiritually the class of people whose spirit is most corrupt. If this is not a momentary flash, not a mushroom, saturated with rot of every kind, springing of its own accord out of the earth, he is a man of enormous talent. In Russia there are in my judgment three tragedies: *The Minor, Woe from Wit,* and *The Inspector-General.* I am betting on *The Bankrupt* as number four.

Ostrovsky's success had been particularly assured from the time when he joined the Pogodin circle, the "Young Moskvityanin." Members of that very compact group gravitated toward the Pogodin magazine, *Moskvityanin,* and because of their militant views they sought, to the best of their ability, to push their partisans into the foreground. To the circle belonged, among others, the critic A. A. Grigoryev, the actor P. M. Sadovsky, the writer and storyteller I. F. Gorbunov, the novelist A. F. Pisemsky, the belle-lettrists S. V. Maksimov and P. I. Melnikov-Pechersky, the playwright A. A. Potekhin, the poets Mey, Edelson, and Almazov, and the eminent amateur of folksong Terty Filippov.

The distinguishing characteristic of the circle was its ardent love of folkways, with their poetry and ritual. This enthusiasm—in general, largely of an aesthetic character—conformed to the spirit of that period, which was marked by an awakening of interest in the observation and study of folk life. Ethnographic and historical studies which began at that time produced ardent collectors of folk poetry. The interest in the merchant way of life revealed in Ostrovsky's early creations was but a form of the general enthusiasm for the common people. The merchant mores of the first half of the nineteenth century were still closely linked to those of the peasants, and he directed his main attention to the merchant class not because he shared the narrow aristocratic view of Prince Odoyevsky that, spiritually, merchants constituted the most corrupt class of the population, but because of the interest in the popular ways of life which he shared with his sponsors, the Young Moskvityanin.

Even though Ostrovsky grew up in Moscow, with its living residues of the peculiar, strictly Russian style of life, he had Western tendencies before he joined that circle, and would make mocking comments on the odd architecture of the ancient Kremlin buildings. However, influenced by his friends' enthusiasm, he soon developed a love for the people's life, with its poetry and beauty.

Having renounced his former ideas, Ostrovsky promptly went to the opposite extreme. On one occasion, thrilled by Terty Ivanovich Filippov's rendering of folksongs and Sadovsky's stories, he exclaimed, "With Terty and Prov we will undo Peter's entire work."

The circle began in every way to extol its gifted member, even perhaps somewhat exaggerating his artistic and historical importance. Pogodin took a more reserved attitude than the other members of the editorial staff toward Ostrovsky's talent, which, however, did not prevent him from appreciating his gifts. Therefore, he enlisted Ostrovsky's close participation in the magazine work by having him make preliminary examination of articles and read proof. Collaboration with Pogodin may have partly influenced the creative work of the young author, whose plays reveal a certain kinship with Pogodin's novels on the customs of the Moscow merchant class.

Still, this work gave Ostrovsky no economic security, leaving him in an extremely difficult financial position. His letters of the period are full of complaints of oppressive poverty. However, he was destined soon to see his plays produced on the stage. His first production was staged in Moscow on January 14, 1853, the benefit night of the actress L. P. Kositskaya: the comedy *Don't Seat Thyself in a Sledge That Isn't Thine,* in which she selected for herself the part of Avdotya Maksimovna. The play had a great success, largely due to the excellent performance of the part of Rusakov by Sadovsky. Rumors about it reaching Petersburg provoked animated comments, in consequence of which the administration produced it on the stage of the Aleksandrinsky Theatre on February 19 of the same year.

Ostrovsky worked and created exclusively in the field of drama. The only exception is his *Diary of the Zamoskvorechye Resident,* anonymously published in 1847, which is in the form of a letter to his readers. On April 1 of that year he had begun a written description of a journey to an unknown land, Zamoskvorechye; and allegedly on the basis of this manuscript he wrote his *Diary,* the first portion of which, entitled "Ivan Yerofeyevich," was submitted to the readers. In a narrative full of humor and keen observation, Ostrovsky depicted the peculiarities of the same Zamoskvorechye to which he later devoted his best comedies. In this odd setting he portrayed the life of an irresolute petty government clerk Ivan Yerofeyevich and his stern friend Marfa Agurevna Kozyrina. Ostrovsky's life among government officials seems to have made an impression upon him, and their peculiar habits are vividly described in his sketch.

The *Diary* leaves no doubt that Ostrovsky would have acquired an eminent position among our belle-lettrists had he also explored the field of the novel.

Another nondramatic work by Ostrovsky is his description of the journey along the Volga which he undertook in 1856 in company with other prominent Russian men of letters, at the request of the Ministry of the Navy. It appeared in the *Navy Magazine* under the title "Journey Along the Volga from the Source to Nizhny-Novgorod." Complying with the Ministry's wishes, he paid particular attention to the customs and labor conditions of the ship workers and fishermen, and sought in every instance to give a precise picture of the status of their pursuits. He corroborated his personal observations by statistical data which he gathered with particular care, and he did not overlook other more or less noteworthy aspects of the localities which he studied. He studied the historical traditions of the different regions, revealing a very sound knowledge of the roots of our national history. He also inquired into economic conditions, presenting a picture of the industrial life of the country and carefully recording all the peculiarities of individual and family ways of living.

In his plays, Ostrovsky reflected the impressions of his journey. The meeting with an innkeeper who trafficked in his daughters gave him the plot of the comedy *A Much Frequented Spot.* The description of Torzhok was used in *The Thunderstorm.* The words with which the police inspector Razvadovsky introduced himself in Tver—"A man with long whiskers and limited ability"—were used by Ostrovsky in *The Girl Without Dowry* (Paratov introducing himself).

Ostrovsky borrowed different words from the materials published in newspapers, which he put in the mouths of his characters. He listened attentively to living speech. For instance, Gavrilikha, the matchmaker in the comedy *A Holiday Nap Before Dinner*, describes herself in the words, "Feet with a swing, head with a fling, tongue with a sting," which he borrowed from local Volga inhabitants. It is supposed that two Volga songs gave him the impulse to create *The Provincial Governor*.

Exceptional attention to our native speech, which was revealed in one of Ostrovsky's early works, was quite typical of him: the wonderful pointedness and power of the language of the dramatis personae, and the historical and folk authenticity were the fruit of his persistent studies and observations. We have evidence that in later days Ostrovsky was also engaged in compiling a special vocabulary of rare proverbs and expressions peculiar to various social strata. Such catchwords, scattered throughout nearly all of his plays, add much to their merit. He did not complete this important work.

Despite its businesslike character, Ostrovsky's article on his Volga journey has a very light and easy style, a language which is at once colorful and animated. All along, he paints rather curious folk scenes, considerably enlivening the narratives.

During the trip Ostrovsky had opportunity to study closely the customs of the remote provincial towns, one of which is depicted in his drama *The Thunderstorm*. The folk quality of this is so powerful and vivid that it unquestionably is derived from the author's direct observations. It was published in 1860 and had a success among virtually all literary groups unmatched by any of his previous plays. In the same year, it was submitted to the Academy of Sciences in the contest for the Uvarov prize, on which the decision was entrusted by the Academy to I. A. Goncharov and A. D. Galakhov. The former wrote:

By way of drama in our literature there has been no work equal to it. By its lofty classical beauty it indisputably occupies, and probably will long occupy, a leading place. No matter from what angle it be viewed— from the standpoint of the plan of its construction, or its dramatic dynamics, or, finally, its characters—everywhere it bears the stamp of creative power, or a fine power of observation, and elegance of finish.

And further:

Every person in the drama is a typical character snatched directly out of the life of the people, poured with the bright coloring of poetry and artistic finish, beginning with the rich widow Kabanova, who personifies the blind despotism bequeathed by tradition, a distorted conception of duty, and the lack of any trace of humaneness, and ending with the bigot Feklusha. The author exhibits a whole world of diverse live and real human beings found everywhere.

This flattering opinion was wholeheartedly seconded by Galakhov, who added: "The appearance of such an outstanding dramatic creation is particularly significant at a time of general decadence of dramatic literature, observable not only in Russia but also in the West." In conclusion he pointed out, "By the nature of his talent Ostrovsky is closely linked to the school of Gogol, to whom he is a worthy successor." But, in addition, "in his plays there is something original which, even after *The Inspector-General* and *The Marriage*, has weight of its own." Even so, certain voices were raised against this play, too. They protested against the substance of the plot, the delineation of the characters, and even against specific expressions.

Among the comments in defense of the play particular mention should be made of a short article by M. I. Pisarev, then a modest amateur and subsequently an eminent actor who created a number of important parts in Ostrovsky's gallery of characters. It appeared in a now forgotten Moscow periodical, *Wrapping Paper* (Numbers 19 and 20, 1860). Defending *The Thunderstorm* against the attacks of hostile critics, he gave a pointed evaluation of the acting of the artists of the Moscow theatre and a general analysis of the play. This review from the pen of a man with a complete understanding of the essence of stagecraft should be especially noted by persons intending to act in the play.

Among other things, here is what Pisarev wrote about its title:

Here, the heavenly storm serves merely as a parallel to the still more dreadful moral storm. The mother-in-law is storm, and the struggle is storm, and the realization of the crime is storm. And all these painfully affect Katerina, who, even without that, is inclined to meditativeness and impressionability. To this is added the storm in the sky. Katerina hears the news that storms do not come as a gift. And right away she begins to believe that the storm will kill her, because her soul is again troubled both by a real sin in the image of the old lady, and by a blind, not yet expiated sin. The latter has been arrested by old age, venting envious, poisonous wrath on everything bearing the impress of youth and beauty. "Why dost thou hide? There's no point in hiding! Probably thou art afraid—not eager to die? Thou long'st to live! Why wouldst thou crave for life? With thy beauty down into the abyss? Why, the sooner—the better!" And when suddenly Katerina beholds the Last Judgment painted on a wall she can no longer bear that inner storm, the storm of conscience, accompanied by the heavenly storm and by the dreadful folklore and by the ominous words of the old woman. She publicly confesses that she spent ten nights with Boris. In that troubled mood which echoed her early enraptured, visionary up-bringing amidst women pilgrims, when every minute she used to expect that thunder would crash and kill the sinner, it is natural that she neither saw nor heard people around her. Thus, if she confessed, she did so in a state of delirium.

The Thunderstorm was analyzed in detail in the article, "The Kingdom of Darkness," of N. A. Dobrolyubov, who was then a militant progressive critic. He gave a vivid and hate-filled definition of the "Kingdom of Darkness" depicted here by Ostrovsky; at the same time, better than anyone else, he explained the reason for the unfading importance of Ostrovsky's creative work:

Considering vital truth the principal merit of an artistic work, we thus define the standard which determines the merit and the significance of every literary phenomenon. By evaluating how deeply the author penetrates the very essence of a phenomenon, how broadly he encompasses in his images the various aspects of life, we become able to determine the greatness of his talent. Faithfulness to reality, to living truth, is invariably observed in Ostrovsky's works; it stands in the foreground above all aims and behind all thoughts. . . .

Ostrovsky knows how to look at man's soul; he knows how to distinguish nature from all deformities and abnormalities assumed from the outside. It is for this reason that outward oppression, the burden of environment weighing upon man, is felt in his works much more strongly than in many stories, which, though most revolting from the standpoint of their content, hide the inner, human aspects by the extrinsic, formal side.

According to Dobrolyubov, Ostrovsky was a folk writer because in his works two types of things, "family and property relations," are exhaustively and graphically treated. "In Ostrovsky's plays all dramatic conflicts and catastrophes originate as a result of the conflict of two parties: the old and the young, the rich and the poor, the despots and the oppressed." In Dobrolyubov's opinion, Ostrovsky's folk quality consists in the fact that he objectively reflects the people's hopes and aspirations for freedom: from the tyranny of the rightly filled purse; from the oppression of the Tsarist chanceries; from the humiliations of the parasitic bureaucrats; from obscurantism and ignorance. In the characters of Katerina and other heroines and heroes, Ostrovsky with profundity and talent revealed the rising, though still unrealized, protest against the "Kingdom of Darkness." In his plays the new life and new ideas dear to the broad masses paved their own way.

In the article "The Kingdom of Darkness" Dobrolyubov wrote:

We do not wish to make any general deductions concerning Ostrovsky's talent. We have sought to show how and what he embraced in Russian life by his aesthetic sense, in what form he expressed the things he had seen and felt, and what significance in our judgment should be attributed to the phenomena treated in his works. In Ostrovsky we have found a complete delineation of Russian life with its old Podkhalyuzin frock coat, Vikharev's gloves, Nadenka's handkerchief full of tears, Zhadov's swagger stick, and Tortsov's stupid, ugly hat.

Russian life of that epoch was shown through the typical characters portrayed by Ostrovsky. Dobrolyubov thus concluded his article "A Ray of Light in the Kingdom of Darkness":

If our ideas are in accord with the play, we ask that one more question be answered: Is it true that in Katerina vital Russian nature found its expression; is it true that the Russian background, with everything surrounding it—the need of the rising movement of Russian life— is revealed in the content of the play, as it is understood by us? . . . If after thinking over our article our readers should find that it is true that in *The Thunderstorm* Russian life and Russian strength have been mustered by the artist for decisive action, and if they should recognize the lawfulness and import of this movement, we shall be satisfied, no matter what our men of learning and literary judges may say.[3]

[3] N. A. Dobrolyubov, *Collected Works*, Vol. II, p. 366.

The movement to which Dobrolyubov referred was the dawning revolution. In the strong character of Katerina (despite all the contradictions and even inconsistencies in some of her actions) he saw the beginning of the protest of the weak, the oppressed, the afflicted; with her image he connected the revolutionary awakening of the people. A keen judge of Russian life gifted in describing human psychology, and a master of characterization, Ostrovsky was in his view a writer of the people not only because he had mastered the popular speech, but also because the very themes of his dramas were popular; their characters in most instances were popular, and the situations in which the author placed them were profoundly typical and objectively realistic.

The attention which was accorded to *The Thunderstorm* by the most divergent literary circles was commensurate with its stage success. The part of Katerina, first performed in Moscow by L. P. Kositskaya, soon assumed an honored place in the repertoire of Russian dramatic actresses. For a long time the play continued in the repertoire of St. Petersburg and Moscow and private theatres. The composer V. P. Kashperov wrote an opera dedicated to the theme of the play; but the prose text of the drama, when converted into verse, was very considerably distorted.

The Thunderstorm was translated into French and performed in Paris. There it did not meet with great success, as may be judged both from its relatively short run and from the review by Jules Lemaître, a typical exponent of the tastes of the Parisian public. He proved to be utterly unable to grasp the true beauty of the play, primarily because *The Thunderstorm* is linked by such strong bonds to Russian soil, and knowledge of this is needed for comprehension of the play. However, in Russia it enjoyed the great and lasting success which was accorded to the majority of Ostrovsky's other works.

Still, the administration of the crown theatres looked upon the playwright with great suspicion. Even in 1850, the Minister of Public Education wrote of Ostrovsky's first comedy:

In the author's orientation there is nothing reprehensible or ill-meaning, because, while permitting vice to triumph, he paints it in such dark and repugnant tones that they in themselves inspire disgust. However, the impression produced by this comedy is a most sorrowful one.

On this ground he suggested that

it be explained to Ostrovsky that the noble and useful aim of talent must consist not merely in the graphic portrayal of the ridiculous and the evil, but equally in its just denunciation . . . in the contrast between evil and virtue; that the picture of the ridiculous and the evil should contain such ideas and deeds as elevate one's soul; in the affirmation of the conviction, so important in public and private life, that even on earth crime meets with deserving punishments.

Obviously the authorities sought to compel the young writer to convert his plays into a eulogy of the existing order of things, allegedly meting out punishment for every crime. Ostrovsky did not take this slippery path, but retained independence during all his life.

His comedy *The Girl Pupil* (1859) was, within the limits of the permissible in the theatre of those days, one of the most vivid pictures of all the abominable aspects of serfdom. Even after 1861 he consistently portrayed the nobility in offensive colors: *The Forest, The Girl Without a Dowry, The Handsome Man,* and *Wolves and Sheep* include a striking gallery of parasites, idlers, fortune-seeking knights who, in their race for money, either marry rich old women or openly accept their support. No wonder that the militant standard-bearer of nobility, the writer Boleslav Markevich, in his novel *The Abyss,* deemed it necessary to express sorrow over the fact that the stage had become infested with "girl pupils with their protesting whimperings." These words are uttered by the director of the Moscow theatres.

The theatrical administration, instead of facilitating the production of Ostrovsky's plays, which were immeasurably better than anything playwrights whom it patronized had ever produced, raised all sorts of obstacles. This doomed him to poverty, and compelled him to endure the humiliating fuss with which the crown stage accepted every one of his new plays. In the end, the continuous struggle with bureaucratic delays became so painful that Ostrovsky admitted utter defeat, and considered abandoning his difficult career and turning to the writing of historical chronicles—not for the stage. Fortunately for the Russian theatre, he did not carry this out. In time his historical plays appeared on the stage, thus adding marked variety to the current repertoire.

Aesthetically Ostrovsky's historical plays are not of equal value. *Tushino* in some places degenerates into melodrama. *Kozma Zakharich Minin-Sukhoruk* inadequately represents the enthusiasm of the people seeking to protect their country against aggressors. Still, *Dmitry the Impostor and Vasily Shuisky* in many respects reaches the level of Pushkin's *Boris Godunov,* the form of which he adopted for these plays.

N. P. Kashin's careful comparative analysis of the literary background of Ostrovsky's historical plays fully demonstrates the fact that the dramatist sagaciously and assiduously studied all accessible historical works and such primary sources as had then been published. Having grown into them, he skillfully translated their colors into vivid speech whose theatre and folk quality rang true. Such, for instance, is Basmanov's magnificent monologue in the sixth scene of the second part of *Dmitry the Impostor and Vasily Shuisky.* Here, through the dead letters of the ancient chronicles and the faint sounds of oral folklore, the author succeeded in discerning bright and live images, and in finding the required hues for their portrayal. He was fortunate in divining the true nature or "spirit" of the events he pictured, while their exponents are most typical characters. These include, in the first place, the wonderful figure of Vasily Shuisky himself as well as the white-bread baker and the clerk Osipov.

Side by side with historical happenings forming the background, Ostrovsky at times produces very typical episodic figures in whom the characteristics of the given period are fully reflected. Such, for example, is Nastasya Dyuzhaya in *The Provincial Governor.* Sometimes, again, whole scenes introduce the audience into the very heart of the epoch. Such are the scenes before the cathedral in *Dmitry the Impostor,* and the preparations for the night's lodging of Shalygin in *The Provincial Governor.* Scattered among these there are a number of individual poetic episodes permeated with the gentle lyricism characteristic of Ostrovsky; the appearance of the Hobgoblin in *The Provincial Governor* may be mentioned.

Excellent knowledge of Russian history enabled Ostrovsky to reveal in this play the secular injustice and boundless despotism which reigned in Russia prior to Peter the Great, to which many influential Slavophiles of those days strongly urged us to "return." As a result, we have a play in which the vividly delineated images

of the fighters against authority—such as Roman Dubrovin, whose
wife was abducted by the provincial governor, and who joined the
"robbers' bands"—are shown amidst the skillfully developed action.
The action is aided by such colorful characters as the rich townsman Vlas Dyuzhoy, his boastful, foolish wife, and her daughters,
especially the youngest, the bold, untamable Marya, who narrowly
escapes becoming the old provincial governor's wife. The full depth
of popular despair is revealed in the old woman's lullaby (Act IV,
Scene 3):

> God has forsaken us, the Tsar shows us no mercy,
> Men have deserted us, and hard they are on us;
> We have to live among them, we have to serve them all,
> And so we're doomed forever to cater to their whims.

Because of well drawn characters *Vasilisa Melentyeva,* based on
the scenario of the director of the theatres S. A. Gedeonov, enjoyed
a marked success. In the course of its rearrangement by Ostrovsky,
however, not a single scene, not a single verse, of Gedeonov's
original sketch was left intact. All the parts in this play—those of
Vasilisa, her meek rival Anna, the Terrible Tsar, Malyuta, and
Vasilisa's lover—have provided our best actors with most gratifying
material.

If in another play, *Kozma Zakharich Minin-Sukhoruk,* Ostrovsky failed somewhat in his female parts, he succeeded in showing with great skill the environment in which his title character
grew up. "I grew up," Minin says about himself,

> On squares, 'midst crowded popular assemblies;
> I early wept o'er people's grief and sorrows;
> Though still quite young, with eagerness I carried
> The load of public service on my shoulders,
> And power never lured nor tempted me,
> But as a brood-hen watches o'er her chicks,
> So I protected my hard-favored brethren
> Against the rich and haughty potentates.

He says about the people:

> Not for their own, but for the sins of others
> They must endure their heavy punishment.
> They're flogged and robbed. Today they may be sated,
> Yet tomorrow may deprive them of the last

Dry crusts which they've been saving for their children.
Today thou'rt home; tomorrow to the woods
Thou hast to flee in an attempt to save
Thy soul, and hiding as some beast 'midst bushes,
Behold how thou art robbed of sweet-earned chattels.
If thou be caught, they'll make thee take an oath
Of loyalty to the accursed thief.
Yea, countless are all dev'lish sufferings,
All tortures, all past-bearing tribulations.
And yet, resignedly and patiently
These are endured. The people wait for something. . . .
Lo, fires 'long the shores are being kindled;
Forgetting their oppressive labor, haulers
Begin to cook their scant and wretched supper.
And presently a song is started. Nay,
Not bliss but slavery conceived that song,
Yea, slavery, and hard, excessive toil,
Destruction wrought by war, those villages
Aflame, and life with neither food nor shelter.

These beautiful verses, which appeared in 1862 in the columns of the *Contemporary,* accurately depicted the conditions in which the people were then living.

The great merit of the plays is also derived from their language, which at times is wonderfully pointed, full of color and grace and power.

Among Ostrovsky's works a special place must be assigned to the three-act comedy *The Comedian of the Seventeenth Century,* which was based on material gathered in connection with the two hundredth jubilee of the Russian theatre. The play is a narrative in dramatic form of the beginnings of the first Russian theatre at Moscow, during the reign of Tsar Aleksey Mikhailovich. On this theme Ostrovsky had a precursor in the person of A. A. Shakhovskoy, whose comedy *Fyodor Grigoryevich Volkov, or The Birthday of the Russian Theatre* presented the establishment of the Russian theatre in Yaroslavl, in the middle of the eighteenth century. Between the two plays there is a good deal of similarity in construction and in elaboration of the general plan. This theme, dear to the heart of the playwright, had the advantage of enabling Ostrovsky to express many of his cherished ideas on the theatre and its purpose. Depicting the initial phases of the theatre in a society which was not accustomed to spectacles of this kind, he necessarily portrayed a number of persons bitterly prejudiced against the theatre and was prompted to put into the mouths of the partisans of the innovation—for instance, Artamon Sergeyevich Matveyev—ardent orations in defense of the theatre and its high social significance.

In the same year (1873) the spring tale *The Snow-Maiden* was published, simultaneously with P. I. Tchaikovsky's music (later, Rimsky-Korsakov composed an opera on the same theme). This play constitutes Ostrovsky's only abandonment of the world of reality for the realm of creative fancy. Here his familiarity with the poetic conceptions and folk tales of the Russian people proved very helpful. He was also greatly assisted by his natural gift for gentle, warm lyricism. Thus there emerged a play permeated with enchanting grace and genuine poetry. The monologues of Spring, the laments of Kupava, and her dialogue with Berendey are among the greatest treasures of our dramatic literature. Ostrovsky's skillful hand introduced popular entertainments, festivities, and customs which provide necessary animation; but even within the framework of a tale he managed to present images full of inner truth and purely humane sentiments. Kupava, whose name was derived from apocryphal records, is deceived by the handsome Mizgir in the same manner that Dunya Rusakova, in the comedy *Don't Seat Thyself in a Sledge That Isn't Thine,* is offended by the nobleman Vikhorev; and she finds the same support in Lel that Dunya found in Vanya Borodkin. The colorful figures of Bobyl and Bobylikha are portrayed as possessing purely folk traits.

The entire play, which reveals the author's exceptional knowledge of Russian popular poetry, is written in a colorful and stylized language that transports the audience into the world of folksongs and proverbs. Maksim Gorky's observation that "the merger of romanticism with realism is particularly characteristic of our major literature" is fully applicable to *The Snow-Maiden.*

Such a masterful blending of the truthful delineation of the folk quality with the most delicate hues of poetic fancy is also peculiar to Ostrovsky's other plays. Without resorting to any stratagems he raised individual phenomena to the level of generalized symbols. This is proved by the very title *The Thunderstorm.* And Tsar Berendey in *The Snow-Maiden* closely resembles the modest dreamer, Kuligin, who is able to overhear and to feel the beauty of every little herb, of every flower:

Not a storm but a blessing, this is. . . . You always think of storm! . . . When a comet appears, I would rather keep looking and looking at it! In truth, one gets used to beholding stars. They are always alike, but here is something new; and so I would gaze at it and admire it. But you are afraid to lift your eyes to the sky; you are seized with shuddering! You have made scarecrows of everything! [Act IV, Scene 4.]

Obviously the last words, as well as Kuligin's whole speech, are colored with symbolism of the highest order.

All of Ostrovsky's plays, according to the social strata portrayed in them, may be divided into four groups. The first, and largest, comprises plays dealing with merchant customs. It includes: *A Family Scene* (1847); *It's a Family Affair—We'll Settle It Ourselves* (1850); *Don't Seat Thyself in a Sledge That Isn't Thine* (1853); *Poverty Is No Disgrace* (1854); *Hang-over from Other Folks' Wine* (1856); *A Holiday Nap Before Dinner* (1857); *The Thunderstorm* (1860); *An Old Friend Is Better Than Two New Ones* (1860); *When One's Dogs Fight—Strangers Keep Away* (1861); *One Finds What One Is Looking For* (1861); *It's a Good Horse That Never Stumbles* (1863); *Difficult Days* (1863); *Jesters* (1864); *An Ardent Heart* (1869); *Even a Cat Has Lean Times* (1871); *Truth's Good, Yet Happiness Is Better* (1877); *The Last Sacrifice* (1878); and *A Heart Is No Stone* (1880). The principal virtue of these plays is in their wonderfully delicate genre painting; it revealed to the majority of readers a hitherto unknown world which strongly impressed them with the originality of its forms and its inner arrangement.

It is interesting to compare Ostrovsky's plays portraying the merchant milieu with those of contemporary Western playwrights (for example, François Ponsard) who were concerned with the same social strata. Ponsard scored his initial success as a result of his plays dealing with the history of Rome and the revolution of 1789 (*Charlotte Corday*). However, seeking to adapt himself to the new order and customs which came into being in France after the *coup d'état* of "little Napoleon," Ponsard turned to the portrayal of the world of stock-exchange mongers, just then beginning to gain power. Such are his plays *Honor and Money* (1853) and *The Stock Exchange* (1856). In fact, these cannot be compared with Ostrovsky's plays both because Ponsard, with no justification whatever, retained in them his pet verse form, and because —even worse—in depicting reality he "varnished" and idealized it. For this he was politely reproached in the welcoming speech at the time of his election to the Academy. On the contrary, if Ostrovsky had been accused by his enemies of anything at all it was excessive negativism in the delineation of the "Kingdom of Darkness" of the Kabanovs and Podkhalyuzins. This is the best proof of the fact that he learned his realism not from the masters of contemporary Western drama. In him there is not the slightest hint of "bureaucratic heroism" and that "poetry of trade" with which all plays of Scribe are tainted, and which A. I. Hertzen so scornfully ridiculed.

The second group is of plays depicting "popular customs." These include *Thou Shouldst Not Live as Thou Pleasest* (1854) and *A Much Frequented Spot* (1865). Here, however, is portrayed that stratum of peasantry which forms, as it were, a transition to the burghers and petty merchant classes. The former play, by its characters, especially in the most successfully executed portrayal of Grunya, closely resembles the popular folksong creative style; it gives the picture of the ancient butter-week entertainments. A. N. Serov adapted it in the opera *Hostile Power*.

The more numerous third group is of plays devoted to the world of petty government clerks. It includes: *The Poor Fiancée* (1852); *A Profitable Business* (1857); *The Abyss* (1866); *There Was No Grosh—and Now a Whole Altyn*[4] (1872); and *The Rich Fiancée* (1876).

The action in Ostrovsky's plays of the fourth group takes place in the milieu of so-called "fashionable society." To this group belong the following: *Unexpected Incident* (1851); *The Girl Pupil* (1851); *Incompatible Characters* (1858); *No Wit Is Exempt from Foolishness* (1868); *Wild Money* (1870); *The Forest* (1871); *Hard-Earned Bread* (1874); *Wolves and Sheep* (1875); *The Girl Without a Dowry* (1879); *Talents and Their Admirers* (1882); *Handsome Man* (1883); *Guilty Without Guilt* (1884); and *Not of This World* (1885).

[4] Grosh—an old coin equal to half a kopeck. Altyn—three kopecks.—Ed.

It is necessary to note a few of Ostrovsky's plays portraying the peculiar milieu of actors. These include, in the first place, his comedies *The Forest, Talents and Their Admirers, Guilty Without Guilt*, and partly *The Girl Without a Dowry*, in which we meet our old acquaintance from *The Forest*, Arkashka Schastlivtsev,[5] who appears here under the name of Robinson. In the course of his constant dealings with the theatrical world Ostrovsky had ample opportunity to become thoroughly familiar with actors.

Ostrovsky made an enormous contribution to Russian drama by the creation of a long series of well drawn female characters, revealing in this respect exceptional diversity; these ranged from the gentle Snow-Maiden to the ferocious Kabanikha; from the chaste Katerina to the depraved wife of Kuroslepov (*An Ardent Heart*) or Yevgeniya (*A Much Frequented Spot*); from naïve Verochka (*Jesters*) to the mercenary and grasping Lydiya (*Wild Money*); from the noblewoman of ancient standing Murzavetskaya to the old peasant woman in *The Provincial Governor*. With equal mastery he embraced all nuances of characters and all social strata. He succeeded best in the portrayal of the bold Parasha (*An Ardent Heart*), bravely choosing the path of a working girl. No other Russian playwright has produced as great a variety of female characters as Ostrovsky. He thus unquestionably contributed greatly to the growth of our actresses.

It was his lot to experience at an early stage the sweetness of literary success; but likewise from the very beginning of his career he encountered hostility, specifically that of A. Bazhenov, an eminent Moscow critic and editor of the theatrical magazine *Intermission*. A connoisseur of foreign literature, freely embellishing his articles with quotations from the Western theoreticians of drama, Bazhenov attached particular value to the production on the Russian stage of Shakespeare, Calderón, Molière, and so on. He mercilessly condemned certain of Ostrovsky's plays; for instance, *The Abyss*, and was critical of Ostrovsky's historical chronicles.

Moreover, Ostrovsky was destined to encounter serious enemies even in those circles where, apparently, he least expected them. Actors, educated on translations of melodramas and vaudevilles

[5] That is, the Happy One.—Ed.

which in the 1840's almost inevitably reigned on the stage, felt incapable of coping with the Russian folk comedy; among them were many of outstanding talent who stubbornly opposed the infiltration of Ostrovsky's plays to the stage. This movement was headed by Samarin, Shumsky and—particularly important—Shchepkin.

However, other artists, led by Sadovsky, found in Ostrovsky's works real material for their exceptional talents, and sought by every means to strengthen his standing in the theatre. They fully realized the fact that they were thereby enhancing their own success, since their gifts had been nurtured on these plays and through them they advanced to the front ranks of the company.

Finally, the supporters of the new folk repertoire prevailed, and Shchepkin was the first to admit defeat. Referring to his attacks, one of the actors remarked: "For Michael Semyonovich and Shumsky, Ostrovsky tailors peasant coats that do not fit them, and he makes his blacked boots too tight; and so they are angry."

Still, these internal theatre difficulties in no way handicapped Ostrovsky's success in society. He at once found his public, which understood and valued him.

A number of minor episodes in his private life tend to show his widespread fame among the most diverse strata of Moscow society, which finally found in him its truthful and skillful chronicler. He was the first to examine closely the spiritual quests of that social stratum which had been ignored by earlier playwrights. Hence there is nothing surprising in the fact that even with his first plays, Ostrovsky imparted a love for the theatre to that public which heretofore had no notion of it. Subsequent productions merely tended to consolidate his theatrical reputation.

The opinion of the members of the Young Moskvityanin circle on the significance of Ostrovsky's dramatic work was best expressed in Apollon Grigoryev's enthusiastic articles. In his ardor—which, by the way, was quite sincere—for the genius of his friend he went so far as to allege:

Ostrovsky alone possesses, in the present literary period, his own stable, new, and at the same time idealistic world outlook, with a peculiar nuance conditioned by the character of the epoch, and, perhaps, by the distinguishing characteristics of the poet's nature itself.

This nuance we unhesitatingly declare is the fundamental Russian world outlook, sane and calm, humorous without morbidity, straightforward without deviations to one or the other extreme, and, finally, idealistic in the true sense of idealism, without false leanings towards the grandiose and, equally, without spurious sentimentalism.

In contrast to such excessive praise, Ostrovsky's plays were subject to unjustified attacks in the press by critics who, during the last years of his work, used to meet every new play with bigoted complaints about the deterioration of his creative faculties. However, two or three years later, the very play which was supposed to have been a manifestation of decadence began to be hailed as exemplary by the same judges. Dobrolyubov himself had to defend Ostrovsky against assaults of his kind, and wrote:

It has been asked why Ostrovsky portrayed in the person of such a bad man as Zhadov a representative of honest aspirations; people complained even about the fact that in Ostrovsky grafters are so trivial and naïve. It was maintained that it would have been far better to expose publicly those men who with cunning and deliberation engineer, promote, and support graft and slavish principles, and who in every possible manner oppose the penetration of healthy elements into the state and social organism!

Such a desire [he said in rebuttal], which is justifiable abstractly, proves, however, that the critic utterly fails to understand that Kingdom of Darkness which is portrayed by Ostrovsky . . . He would have sinned against truth and he would have falsely attributed to Russian life such phenomena as are altogether alien to it, had he ventured to represent our grafters as a regularly organized and well defined party. . . .

Even so, in the comedy a false note is sounded in the person of Zhadov; but it was recognized by the author himself before any critic discerned it. In the middle of the play he begins to lower his hero from the pedestal on which he has stood in the first scenes, while in the last act he reveals him as utterly incapable of the struggle which he had taken upon himself. . . . No doubt, he was in sympathy with those beautiful things about which Zhadov speaks; yet he felt that had he compelled Zhadov to perform them, he would have been guilty of distorting genuine Russian reality. At this point the demands of artistic truth put Ostrovsky on guard against the exaggeration of an outward tendency. . . . It is not at all difficult to produce a little mechanical puppet and present it as an honest bureaucrat; but it is difficult to breathe life into it and compel it to speak and to act like a human being.

Dobrolyubov also answered the reproaches of representatives of the opposite camp, who were dissatisfied on the ground that Ostrovsky had failed to endow Peter Ilyich, in *Thou Shouldst Not Live as Thou Pleasest*, with the generosity of nature, the powerful sweep which, supposedly, is inherent in a Russian, especially when in a state of debauch. However, he argued, the author's instinct had made him cognizant of the fact that his Peter, who recovered his senses as a result of the pealing of bells, is not an example of mighty Russian nature, that he is not a bold self-oblivious fellow, but merely a petty, tavern idler:

In order to restrain a man from drunkenness Ostrovsky, unquestionably, might have used a more effective incentive than the pealing of bells. Still, what is to be done if Peter Ilyich was the sort who could not yield to reason? One's own intellect cannot be instilled into a man; nor can popular prejudice be made over. To convey to a man a sense which he does not possess would be to distort him and bely the very life in which that sense is manifested.

Perhaps A. M. Skabichevsky came closer to the interpretation of Ostrovsky's world outlook. He defined the fundamental moral philosophy permeating all his plays in the following words of Platosha Zybkin, in the comedy *Truth's Good, Yet Happiness Is Better*:

Every man—whether he be great or small—is alike if he lives up to truth; and if in pursuing his business decently, honestly, honorably, working hard, as befits one—he also acts for other people's benefit, he is a patriot of his fatherland. But he who lives merely for physical survival, he who fails to comprehend reason and education, he who, with a feeling of outrage and derision against humanity, ignorantly acts only for his own enjoyment—he lives a debased life.

In truth [continues Skabichevsky], all the dramatis personae in Ostrovsky's play may be divided into two categories: they are either patriots of their fatherland in the sense that they seek to live according to truth, honestly and honorably; that they work hard, pursuing their labors—even if these be petty and inconspicuous—unfailingly for the benefit of others as well as themselves; or else those whose lives are based on "mad money," accumulated by more or less hidden and unlawful means, but who still cling to the belief that money constitutes man's whole dignity and pride. They regard working people with disdain; they regard work of every kind as the greatest humiliation to themselves; they live for absolutely nothing but their own enjoyment, with a feeling of outrage and derision against humanity, scorning it with conceited stupidity when they belong to culturally inferior social strata, or adopting an attitude of blasé arrogance if they happen to be anointed with a gloss of outward enlightenment; and, in the long run, they are truly worthless scamps in their lives.

Ostrovsky, having founded his own life on "dray labor," as he liked to call it, invariably sympathized with those whose lives are based on work; on the contrary, he had no mercy for idlers who, evading work themselves, in every manner oppress those who seek to balk them in their willful ways of living. Gordey, Tortsov, Korshunov, Dikoy, Berkutov, Paratov, Dulchin, Koprov, Kuchumov, and many others of the same stamp—such are the characters in the creation of which the playwright reveals now an angry, now a disdainful and mocking attitude toward those contemporary social strata, which stubbornly sought either to preserve or to win for themselves a dominating position. Thereby he became closely identified with the progressive forces of our literature, in the publications of which his plays used to appear.

In 1857, in the second issue of the *Contemporary*, Ostrovsky's comedy *A Holiday Nap Before Dinner* was published. Thereafter he was a faithful contributor to that progressive magazine. This fully bears out the sincerity of his statement in a letter to one of its publishers that he was "wholeheartedly devoted" to the *Contemporary*; in turn, the editorial office sought to monopolize him for that periodical. In 1868 his plays began to appear in the *Fatherland Diary*, to which the editorial staff of the *Contemporary* had moved. In letters to him its editor, M. E. Saltykov-Shchedrin, on several occasions expressed the desire to begin the new year with a play by Ostrovsky. In addition, Ostrovsky printed works in the *Messenger of Europe*. This fixes his place among our men of letters, while his plays have many points in common with the creative work of Nekrasov and Shchedrin, the editors of the *Fatherland Diary*.

In the latter part of 1869, Ostrovsky wrote to Nekrasov: "You and I are the only two popular poets. Only we two know the people, know how to love them, and feel with our hearts their needs without conventional Westernism and without childish Slavophilism." In content and power of censorious satire, *No Wit*

Is Exempt from Foolishness, Hard-Earned Bread, and other plays of the same kind are akin to the creative work of Saltykov-Shchedrin, Nekrasov's successor as editor of the *Fatherland Diary*.

The view has been expressed that "Gogol begat Ostrovsky." In fact, Ostrovsky went farther in the delineation of Russian folkways, adding to the gallery of bureaucratic types created by Gogol characters belonging to many other social strata. At the same time, however, in the content of his plays Ostrovsky drew closer to melodrama. For instance, the play *Guilty Without Guilt* exhibits such a kinship with typical melodrama, both by its plot and by the manner of delineation of certain characters. Having borrowed from Gogol exceptional mastery of folk portrayal, Ostrovsky retained in many of his plays the division of the dramatis personae into villains and virtuous victims characteristic of melodrama, as well as the custom of concluding the play with the unfailing triumph of virtue and the punishment of vice, even if for this purpose it became necessary to introduce inadequately motivated outside force.

Ostrovsky's attitude towards his predecessors should be defined thus: Having retained in several plays the distinguishing traits of melodrama, he followed Gogol's realism in the typical portrayal of the patterns of Russian life which are reflected in its characteristic representatives. He thereby expanded the portrait gallery of Russian comedy and the scope of Russian drama. Primarily a writer of everyday life, Ostrovsky invariably stood above its dictates, remaining its master. Excellent grasp of man's soul and of its moving passions enabled him at once to portray individual characters vividly and sagaciously, and to present consummate pictures of specific social strata. In vividness, the masterful pictures of the merchant class are fully matched by that of the bureaucratic world in *A Profitable Business,* and that of nobility in *Wild Money* or in *No Wit Is Exempt from Foolishness.* No one better than he had represented the milieu of actors. However, with absorbed attention to the most minute and vivid delineation of individual types and characters, he devoted much less attention to the development of the theme, which therefore tends to be defective in his plays.

In his dénouements Ostrovsky frequently resorted to purely artificial devices, abruptly cutting short the action. Such, for example, is the appearance of the noncommissioned officer Groznoy in the comedy *Truth's Good, Yet Happiness Is Better,* in which

one recognizes a variation of the classical *deus ex machina*. Often
a seriously raised problem is reduced in the concluding part of the
play to an anecdote, as in the comedy *Women Slaves,* where the
last act is in no way motivated by the preceding course of the play.
In his finales Ostrovsky generally attributed too much importance
to chance, thus considerably detracting from their vitality and strict
truthfulness. This peculiarity of Ostrovsky's plays is closely related
to his views on dramatic plots. According to D. V. Averkiyev, he
used to say:

The playwright does not invent plots; all our themes are borrowed
ones. They are supplied by life, by history, by our friend's story, or,
at times, by a newspaper article. At least, in my own case, all plots
have been borrowed. The thing that has happened cannot be invented
by the playwright; his business is to describe how it happened or could
have happened. Therein lies his whole task. When he pays attention
to this aspect, live men will come to him and begin to speak of their
own accord.

Whereas Gogol was a poet of visual perceptions, attaching particular significance to the attire of his characters and their positions
on the stage (either independently or with the assistance of the
artist Ivanov, he drew three sketches of the final scene of *The Inspector-General*), Ostrovsky, on the contrary, much as Pisemsky,
heads the realists—virtuosos of "aural sensation." This observation of
I. F. Annensky is confirmed by Ostrovsky's own admissions: "Why
is it easy to learn my parts? In them there is no contradiction between substance and sound: when writing, I am speaking them
aloud." It is known that at the end of his life he avoided watching
his plays from the auditorium, but listened to them with delight
from the wings.

How exacting he was in this connection even toward his favorite
actors may be appreciated from a notation in his diary dated February 6, 1886, referring to the rehearsal of *Mary Stuart*: "Everybody
sings: Fedotova now sings, now speaks in a bass; generally, the
reading was unintelligent." Here, then, special significance attaches
to that passage in *The Forest* where Arkashka complains that the
new actors are unable to play proficiently, and Neschastlivtsev,
confirming this statement, says: "In the capitals I myself witnessed
how plays are produced: the lover is a tenor, the raisonneur is a

tenor, and the comic is a tenor, so that there is no foundation to the play" (Act II, Scene 2). Possibly, here Ostrovsky also reflected his own predilections.

As an indication of Ostrovsky's views on speech in the theatre, his address at a dinner in honor of the actor A. E. Martynov is very significant. After pointing out that, beginning with Gogol's time, our dramatic literature had stood on the firm foundation of reality and had progressed along a straight path, he thanked Martynov for the fact that his soul "always looked for truth in the part, often finding it in mere hints. Out of a few traits you molded finished types, full of artistic truth. . . . Never have you resorted to farce in order to evoke from the spectators empty and useless laughter which leaves one neither warm nor cold." It is clear, then, that it was not in the indifferent "art for art's sake" that Ostrovsky saw the task of the theatre and of its mastery.

The same striving for truth prompted him to assert in his address that "despite all conscientiousness in the performance of translated plays our artists will never rid themselves of the mixture of the French with the Nizhegorodsky." [6] While admitting that it was impossible to get along without translated works, he candidly stated that translations were but a secondary matter, and not at all an essential requirement of the repertoire.

He adhered to these views to the end of his life. It has been reported that he commented on the production of Schiller's *Mary Stuart* at the Maly Theatre, which was acted very well with Yermolova and Fedotova in the parts of the queens: "How such plays spoil the Russian actor!" And this was said by a playwright who had translated several plays of Shakespeare, Plautus, Terence, Machiavelli, Gozzi, Goldoni, Cervantes, and contemporary Italians and was planning to undertake the translation of some of Molière's plays. He did not publish many of the translations, and obviously he made them only in order better to master the technique of the dramatic structure of the Western classics. Traces of these studies are clearly visible in the construction of his prologues, monologues, and so forth.

However, realizing that in this field actors, with very few exceptions, would be unable to "rid themselves of the mixture of the French with the Nizhegorodsky," he sought to present the

[6] That is, with the Nizhny Novgorod patois.—Ed.

characters of Western drama in their Russian versions. Thus, being aware of the unfitness of his friend Prov Sadovsky for the part of Shakespeare's Othello, he truthfully and profoundly portrayed an analogous gamut of sentiments and feelings in the character of the simple shopkeeper Lev Krasnov in the drama *It's a Good Horse That Never Stumbles;* thereby paving the way for the actor's brilliant success. *There Was No Grosh—and Now a Whole Altyn* masterfully transplants Molière's Harpagon to the milieu of the inhabitants of the remote districts of Moscow. As an outline for one of his most popular plays, *Guilty Without Guilt,* he borrowed Dumas fils' melodrama *Seamstress's Son,* which several years prior to that had been performed without success. But these adaptations were always made so skillfully, with such a fine appreciation of native folk conditions, that, at first glance, traits appropriated from predecessors are quite indiscernible.

Just before his death, Ostrovsky was engaged in correcting his version of Shakespeare's tragedy *Antony and Cleopatra.* This translation was made by him with the assistance of an Englishman by the name of Watson (stage name Dubrovin). In a letter to A. D. Mysovskaya dated July 28, 1885, he alluded to his intention to translate in collaboration with her all of Molière's works. He intended to undertake the translation of the prose pieces, while Mysovskaya was to translate the plays in verse. According to him, "This will be a most precious gift to the public, and you and I will erect an everlasting monument for ourselves." But Ostrovsky was not destined to fulfill this plan.

Many of his translations did find their way to the stage; thus, *The Criminal's Family* was for a long time in the repertoire of both the crown and provincial theatres. These translations are important, among other things, in that the selection of the plays reveals Ostrovsky's own tastes and views on the interests of the Russian repertoire. In passing, it may be interesting to note Averkiyev's observation to the effect that Ostrovsky, by the nature of his talent, most closely resembled Goldoni:

Both writers have many traits in common: the same good-natured humor, the same wonderful penetration and absorption of the popular idiom; and in both we see an abundance of characteristic traits, the same inexhaustible supply of pithy words and expressions, and, finally, the same inclination to sentimentality.

Side by side with Ostrovsky's original plays, it is necessary to note a number of those which he wrote in collaboration with other playwrights. In addition to *Vasilisa Melentyeva,* he wrote with P. M. Nevezhin the comedy *Whim* (1881), and with N. Ya. Solovyov *Belugin's Wedding, The Wild Girl* (1880), and *It Shines but Does Not Warm One* (1881).

Careful study of the rough drafts of his manuscripts reveals his literary methods. It has been ascertained that even in the first draft of a play, when listing the dramatis personae, he indicated the actors he had in mind, later modifying the tentative casts, apparently because he became convinced that some other actor would better cope with a given role. Here we have added proof that Ostrovsky, when writing his plays, always took into account the theatrical possibilities of the company for which he wrote a play. This was not the least important reason for the success of his works.

In the course of the work itself Ostrovsky frequently changed the first and last names of individuals, transposing scenes, shortening or elaborating cues. Often he also changed the titles of his plays. Thus, *Poverty's No Disgrace* was originally entitled *God Opposes the Haughty; Hang-over From Other Folks' Wine* was *Learning Is Light—Ignorance Is Darkness;* and *Incompatible Characters* at first bore the title *The Dowry.*

The preliminary work on the last play is particularly noteworthy. Having sketched several of its scenes, he made up his mind to elaborate the same theme into a novel, of which three chapters are still available; these represent Ostrovsky's second work in belletristic form. Had it been completed, it would have differed little from the average novel of those days in most of its scenes. Only where he turns to the intimately familiar world of bureaucrats and petty merchants does his innate talent flash brightly. The banal and hardly interesting description of a rich government official's widow who decides to marry a dandy to whom she has taken a fancy is followed by a vivid picture of the poor clerk who sees her pass in a carriage drawn by a pair of horses:

Nothing happened on the road. Only the hard-working clerk, engaged in copying some papers, noticed her through the window from behind the geraniums; and it occurred to him how pleasant it would be for such a rich and pretty lady to fall in love with him and marry him. He would then buy a racing droshky and ride in it, driving it himself, or—even better—he might order a sky-blue cloak with a black velvet lining. And he sat long pondering over what he should do first: buy the droshky or order the cloak. After that he looked long at the mirror, winking, smiling, and assuming different poses.

Critics justly regard this clerk as the earliest sketch of the future Misha Balzaminov.

Still better is the end of the chapter describing the home of the widow's parents, the merchant Tolstogorazdovs, and their pastimes. Here Ostrovsky is in his native element, and these pages would do credit to any of our classical works of fiction. In two short pages he gives a complete picture of a merchant's home, with the family and the servants, portraying the master as follows:

Karp Karpych, in a red shirt with collar unbuttoned, was sitting in the corner room before an open window; a door to the veranda stood open, so that a light draft blew on him, moving his sleeves. Hideously rolling his eyes, red with sleep, he twisted his mouth now this way and now that, blowing off flies that alighted on his face. In his right hand he held a smooth stone weighing some fifteen pounds, and beside him on the window sill lay a bag full of nuts. He took two or three of them, placed them on the sill, and cracked them with the stone. Suddenly, he cried out in a loud voice: "Matryona!" Around the corner a passer-by squats down, and slowly gasps for breath. Why should a good wealthy merchant be scaring passers-by in such a frightful manner!

Ostrovsky was very much a part of the theatrical world. According to A. Ya. Golovachyova, the daughter of the eminent actor Ya. Bryansky, he "read his plays with wonderful mastery: each person in the play, whether male or female, stood out in relief, and listeners to his reading felt as if excellent actors were performing their parts before an audience."

Ostrovsky had many disappointments and troubles before he succeeded in the stage production of his first comedy. Subsequently, however, each one of his new plays produced on the Aleksandrinsky stage came as an event to the artists and the public as well as to the administration, because the house was always sold out. When his plays were staged, Ostrovsky would travel from Moscow and spend much time with the actors helping them grasp their parts. He was almost moved to tears whenever an actor or an actress endeavored to comply with his suggestions. For Martynov he felt a kind of reverence. In his indulgent attitude toward the actors, Ostrovsky was an exceptional playwright. He never scolded them, as others did; moreover, whenever some artist was censured before him he would come to the defense. "No, truly, he is not as bad as you say," he would admonish the stern critic. "He tried his best, but what can he do if he has little dramatic talent!"

A thorough knowledge of the stage enabled Ostrovsky to create parts with which gifted actors could easily cope. Frequently he would introduce words and additions made by the actors themselves: this he did in the part of Arkashka in *The Forest,* while in *The Thunderstorm* he added for Katerina a monologue founded on a story told by the first performer of this role, Nikulina-Kositskaya.

In 1881, he formulated his views on the theatre in a memorandum on dramatic schools. Fearing the collapse of the theatre as a result of the intrusion of amateurs, he considered the shortcoming of amateurs to be that their audiences saw on the stage something that did not resemble life. In order to be satisfied the spectator had to forget that he was in a playhouse. It was necessary that actors be able to live on the stage; and that could only be achieved by training,

assiduous labor and rigorous study of technique. An actor is a plastic artist. But can one be either an artist or even a skillful artisan without having mastered the technique of one's art or trade? As a good calligrapher has no handwriting of his own, but has all styles, so the actor should have on the stage no manner of walking or posture of his own, but should have different ones, those which are required by the particular role and the given situation.

Thus, Ostrovsky's conceptions of acting fully coincide with those of Dobrolyubov, who considered "the principal virtue of an artistic production to be its living truth."

In March, 1885, the Meiningen company visited Moscow. Ostrovsky went to see some of their performances, and in his diary he admitted that they were instructive. He was thrilled by the last scene of the third act in *Julius Caesar,* of which he said: "But this is a pleasure not much greater than that which we derive from well coordinated movements of disciplined troops in a parade, or from a well trained *corps de ballet.* We see in them not art, but skill." In *Julius Caesar,* he "saw neither Caesar nor Shakespeare. I saw an excellently disciplined company of mediocre actors and disgustingly wailing actresses make a display of themselves." The defect of the company was in the fact that "everywhere one sees the stage director. The leading player acts by command and according to pattern." For this reason the principal artists lagged behind the stage mob and proved inferior to it. However, "the grouping on the stage of the leading artists and of the mob, both in the state of calmness and in motion, is good. The mob lives, is agitated, indignant, and thrills the public more than the oration of Antony. The height of perfection is the feast at Tertsky's."

If Moscow residents wondered about the hitherto unknown devices of stage lighting, and so forth, Ostrovsky remained indifferent to them, believing that "thus it should be in every well organized playhouse where there is more or less competent administration"—which in his view we did not have at that time. Equally, he maintained that with our enormous expenditures for the theatre we could have had scenery and properties better than those of the Meiningen company; yet he did not like the fact that because of their excessive naturalism Julius Caesar himself seemed to "form part of the properties." By reason of outward semblance to the portrait of Caesar that part was assigned to an actor altogether unsuitable for it; the result was that one beheld "a wax figure." It is quite noteworthy that this external authenticity and pomp of the stage setting "surprised the wealthy but unsophisticated public." [7]

The performances of the Meiningen company made Ostrovsky still more conscious of the shortcomings of the Moscow crown theatres, the administration of which was entrusted to him during the last year of his life.

His connection with the theatre was by no means confined to dramatic writing. Having himself experienced the difficulties encountered by a playwright with no income whatever from the production of his plays on private provincial stages, he founded the Society of Dramatic Authors and Composers, the activities of which soon spread over all of Russia. The Society guaranteed to each

[7] *The Theatre,* No. 1, 1939, pp. 75–81.

of its members certain remuneration for every production of his plays, even on the most remote provincial stages.

During his last years Ostrovsky was preoccupied with organizing a popular theatre in Moscow with private funds which, because of its admission prices, would be accessible to the broad masses of people, and whose repertoire would satisfy their artistic requirements. In a memorandum on this subject, he pointed out that workers from remote villages were coming to Moscow, necessarily experiencing there the influence of the general educational level. In this connection the greatest influence was exercised by the theatre, for which the toiling masses craved.

Russian authors [he wrote] are eager to try their hand before a fresh public whose nerves are not very pliable, and which looks to powerful dramatic effect, to broad humor, to ardent and sincere sentiment, to vital and strong characters. Dramatic poetry has more immediate appeal to the people than all other literary forms. Any other composition is written for the educated classes, whereas dramas and comedies are designed for the whole people. This proximity to them in no way minimizes dramatic poetry; on the contrary, it doubles its strength, preventing it from vulgarization and triviality: only those works have outlived centuries and ages which were genuinely popular at home. Such creations, in time, became comprehensible and valuable to other nations, and, ultimately, to the world at large.

The important point here is that plays are written (it would be more correct to say "should be written") for the whole people. Ostrovsky himself acted accordingly; this explains the particular success of his works immediately after the Great October Socialist Revolution, when they attained a leading place. Among our classical playwrights, he occupies the first place on the Soviet stage; he is also produced in translation in the Ukrainian, Yiddish, White Russian, Armenian, Tartar, Mordvinian, Mari, Chuvash, Komi-Nari, and other languages. It has been ascertained that since 1917, he has been played in seven hundred theatrical centers of the U.S.S.R.

In 1886 Ostrovsky was appointed director (of the artistic department) of the Moscow Imperial Theatres. This appointment had a far-reaching significance: it was a rare occurrence—unfortunately not always followed in later times—that at the head of the foremost of our Russian theatres a man was placed who possessed adequate training for the post. Being familiar with all the shortcomings of our theatre, Ostrovsky, without sparing his already impaired health, eagerly began to work for its improvement. This appointment greatly gladdened the artists who, partly at least, got rid of the incompetent tutelage of the court and bureaucratic circles. However, death prevented him from realizing the things he strove to accomplish, and for which he was better qualified than anyone else.

In his address at the Pushkin celebration in 1880, Ostrovsky emphasized the service rendered by the poet, in that he "had revealed the Russian soul, leaving in his wake both a school and successors." Among the latter, in the field of historical drama the first place undeniably belongs to Ostrovsky. The best pictures in all his chronicles emerged from the incomparable "Inn Scene on the Lithuanian Border." About Ostrovsky, too, it may be said that in a large measure he revealed the Russian soul. He was not destined, however, to originate a school, and numerous attempts to imitate him went no further than the adoption of his outward methods.

Chapter XX

ACTORS OF THE SECOND HALF
OF THE NINETEENTH CENTURY

IT IS EVERY PLAYWRIGHT'S greatest good fortune to meet a master who, by the very nature of his talent, is able to give a precise impersonation of the most typical roles in his plays. In the case of Gogol it was Shchepkin, whose name was associated with all his plays. In the case of Ostrovsky it was Sadovsky that proved such a priceless treasure. He performed Ostrovsky's most important roles; his acting unquestionably contributed to the success of the plays. However, Sadovsky himself found them a most fertile soil for the display of his talent. Thus, they helped each other, the two constituting one indissoluble whole.

Like Shchepkin, Prov Sadovsky Yermilov, 1818–1872, emerged from the wretched depths of the provincial theatre. Having lost his father—an insignificant member of the Ryazan middle class—at an early age, he was brought up by his uncle, a provincial actor from whom he inherited his stage name. Living with his actor uncle, he soon was able to go backstage; and he grew so attached to the theatre that he made up his mind to become an actor himself. At the age of fourteen, he joined Turchaninov's company in Tula, and made his début in Scribe's vaudeville *Vatel, or The Descendant of a Great Man*. During the first year, he played about fifteen roles of the most diverse character and also copied hundreds of parts for various actors. For all this he received from the manager at the close of the season an honorarium in the amount of one ruble.

It was at this time that his roamings with different companies began. He visited Tula, Kaluga, Ryazan, Yelets, Lebedyan, Voronezh, Tambov, until fate brought him to Manager Pivato in Kazan, where he chanced to play with Shchepkin. By then his talent had already developed considerably, and in provincial districts he was regarded as an actor of such outstanding ability that managers, one after another, sought to lure him into their services. Shchepkin appreciated the talent of the young actor and aided him with his counsel and suggestions. Possibly, too, he had a pleasant memory of Sadovsky's acting because it revealed one of the most characteristic traits of his own manner; namely, absolute simplicity. In any event it is known that, on his return to Moscow, Shchepkin spoke to his superior about the young artist to whom he had taken a liking, and thus facilitated his début on the Moscow crown stage.

In March, 1839, at Moscow, Sadovsky's examination took place. He played the part of Jeannot Bijou in a vaudeville, *Love's Poison, or The Barber-Versifier,* translated by Lensky. Superiors approved of his acting and engaged his services in the company as an actor of the third category with an annual salary of 800 paper rubles. At first, he played mostly the roles of simpletons in vaudevilles, which in those days reigned supreme. Critics compared him sometimes with Zhivokini and sometimes with Lensky, but, generally speaking, they were not too generous to him.

According to friends, during the first years of his Moscow service Prov Mikhailovich continually brooded, because he was unable to find suitable roles and unwilling to pester his superior, Verstovsky, who was not well disposed towards him.

However, connoisseurs soon discovered his real value. As early as 1843, the *Repertoire* and the *Pantheon,* opening the gallery of Russian artists, began their series of biographies with an article on Sadovsky. Its author highly praised the simplicity and complete independence of the twenty-five-year-old actor, predicting a brilliant future for him if he should work under Shchepkin's guidance.

M. P. Pogodin, publisher of the *Moskvityanin,* greeted Sadovsky in the following terms:

I deem it my duty to call attention to this young actor who, I may say unhesitatingly, before long will become a favorite and a Moscow celebrity if, faithful to art, he gives thought to it, labors, and learns to perfect his talent. His animation, simplicity, and dexterity are such as are rarely found. He has a very great deal of naturalness. One discerns sincere tenderness. It is a pity that one rarely sees him on the stage! Among our actors, as among scientists and medical men, there is a kind of respect for rank. For example, should there appear a new talent for the parts of Shchepkin or Repina, he or she would not readily be given work. Yet, under whose guidance could they be trained better than under that of our famous veteran and our charming—we will not use the word "lady veteran"—ever youthful and graceful actress. Sadovsky, too, could replace in many parts our old lover Zhivokini, of course without any reflection on the latter's well earned merits. Let us express the hope that the administration will give the public the opportunity of beholding Sadovsky more frequently by offering him a chance to appear more often on the stage and practice the most difficult of all arts.

In this case, too, Pogodin proved his astuteness.

With every new role Sadovsky's success had grown steadily. He played simpletons so well that connoisseurs had to admit they had never seen anything to equal them. He played the part of Filatka in the popular vaudeville *Filatka and Miroshka—Rivals* with particular brilliance. That role was more or less akin to the character parts which in later days brought him well-deserved fame throughout Russia.

For the first two or three years Sadovsky invariably appeared in parts that were insignificant as art. Only the secondary role of the Fool in Shakespeare's *King Lear,* which he performed with superb mastery, and which he managed to bring to the foreground, furnished genuine material for his great talent.

In 1843 he performed Podkolesin in *The Marriage* and Zamukh-rishkin in Gogol's *Gamblers.* According to his biographer, "this irresolute clerk weighing the question whether or not to marry, as Hamlet ponders over the question 'to be or not to be,' was excellently portrayed by Sadovsky. His mere speechless scene with the fiancée invariably evoked thunderous applause." It was also then that Sadovsky began to appear in the Molière repertoire, in which Shchepkin enjoyed such deserved fame. He played Jourdain in the Zotov adaptation of *Le Bourgeois gentilhomme,* Argan in *Le Malade imaginaire,* to whom Polevoy gave the name of Shched-ushin, and Sganarelle in *The Forced Marriage,* adapted by Lensky who chose the new title, *Burst but Marry.*

In the Russian dramatic repertoire Sadovsky at that time played

Skalozub in *Woe from Wit* and Osip in *The Inspector-General,* and his masterful performance of the later role at once placed him in the forefront of stage artists. Still, as heretofore, he had to appear in melodramas and vaudevilles, or even in translated classical pieces which did not always suit his talent. With the exception of Molière, he rarely played foreign classics with success.

Of his performance of the part of Benito in Calderón's comedy *Under One's Own Arrest,* Bazhenov wrote:

Sadovsky was decidedly excellent in the role of Benito, since we can point to nothing in his acting that was inexpressive or superfluous. Profound naïveté, which permeated each word and each gesture of the artist, all the more impressed the audience by its humor, and evoked all the more irresistible laughter, the less it seemed deliberate or designed to make people laugh—a rather common aim among performers of such parts. Quite in accord with the spirit and character of the role, Sadovsky said and did the drollest things with imperturbable seriousness, not even for a moment making the spectator sense the presence of the actor playing Benito, instead of Benito himself.

However, in many other foreign pieces Sadovsky's acting hardly satisfied the artist in him. Sadovsky the Russian transformed himself into a foreigner with difficulty. For example, he was not quite satisfactory in the part of the gravedigger in *Hamlet,* simply because there he smacked too much of a Russian Muzhik. Apparently this was the prime reason for his utter failure in the part of King Lear. He wanted the part so much that he had selected the Shakespearean tragedy for his benefit night. Yet he performed it so poorly that subsequently he refused to appear in it.

Sadovsky found his real material in Ostrovsky's plays. He eagerly seized upon his first comedy while it was still in manuscript form, and by reading it in private homes throughout the entire season he brought fame to the young author. It was through Ostrovsky that he established intimate contact with the members of the Young Moskvityanin circle. All his life he remained faithful to this circle, shunning the Westerner groups in his own household as well as in his political views and personal sympathies.

At that time, censorship did not permit the stage production of *The Bankrupt,* so Ostrovsky's comedy *Don't Seat Thyself in a Sledge That Isn't Thine,* with Sadovsky in the part of Rusakov, was the first to appear on the stage. It is difficult to determine whose was the greater triumph on the day of that first performance, Ostrovsky's or Sadovsky's. In any event, the most glorious phase of the actor's work began then, and it was marked by the creation of a whole gallery of character parts. In virtually every one of Ostrovsky's new plays the best role was reserved for Sadovsky, and he therefore selected Ostrovsky's plays for his benefit night.

According to S. V. Maksimov,

After the light and merry parts, such as that of the officer in *We Don't Keep What We Possess*, the highly comical talent of Prov Mikhailovich, greeted like heavenly manna, the parts of Benevolensky; that of the rich and sedate merchant Rusakov, a man of a purely Russian stamp; the homeless and utterly ruined idler Lubim Tortsov, and so forth. After Osip in *The Inspector-General*, Sadovsky's portrayal of the vital, thoroughly familiar persons in Ostrovsky's dramas and comedies was also wonderful, and specifically his performances appeared as an altogether unexpected and new event; it was as if the actor had been merely awaiting this new word, which made the nerves tingle and moved one to inspiration.

Intimate acquaintance with all strata of the Russian people enabled Sadovsky to achieve such realism in acting that it always seemed to the spectator that he beheld a person whom he had met somewhere, with whom he had dealt, but whose name he had temporarily forgotten. It was difficult to imagine that a given part could be performed in a manner different from that in which he played it. The artist's acting coincided so closely with the author's conception that the spectator felt the author's character must have spoken and acted precisely in that way. Perfection of the performance in large measure was achieved by the chiseling of the most minute details of the role.

This may be perceived, for example, from Bazhenov's description of Sadovsky's acting in the part of Benevolensky:

The grandiose walk in his first appearance on the stage evoked loud applause. What a wonderful bureaucratic importance he managed to assume, from head to toes! How skillfully he maneuvered before Marya Andreyevna! With what cunning he sipped his drink and nodded his head, as though keeping time, while listening to her playing—meanwhile furtively glancing at the hors d'œuvres that had just been served! How appropriate that pressing of the knees and little tapping of the foot as Benevolensky tried to appear clever! Why, it is impossible to enumerate all the nuances in Mr. Sadovsky's acting! Here, we have comedy of the purest and highest quality.

Having created a part, Sadovsky was not satisfied with its success, but continued to work assiduously to perfect his interpretation. Thus, having played with outstanding success the part of Krasnov (*It's a Good Horse That Never Stumbles*), Sadovsky by the end of the season radically changed its interpretation, and unexpectedly began to perform it from beginning to end in an altogether new light, without leaving intact a single detail of the original rendition.

In Ostrovsky's repertoire Sadovsky played the following parts: Podkhalyuzin and, later, Bolshov (*It's a Family Affair—We'll Settle It Ourselves*); Smurov (*The Morning of a Young Man*); Benevolensky (*The Poor Fiancée*); Puzatov (*A Picture of Family Bliss*); Lubim Tortsov (*Poverty's No Disgrace*); Peter Ilyich (*Thou Shouldst Not Live as Thou Pleasest*); Tit Titych Bruskov (*Hang-over From Other Folks' Wine*); Yusov (*A Profitable Business*); Neuyedenov (*A Holiday Nap Before Dinner*); Coachman (*Incompatible Characters*); Gustomesov (*An Old Friend Is Better Than Two New Ones*); Potapych (*The Girl Pupil*); Dikoy (*The Thunderstorm*); Bruskov (*Difficult Days*); Krasnov (*It's a Good Horse That Never Stumbles*); Kozma Minin (*Kozma Zakharich Minin-Sukhoruk*); Khrykov (*Jesters*); Shalygin (*The Provincial Governor*): Vorontsov (*The Abyss*); Bessudny (*A Much Frequented Spot*); Osipov (*Dmitry the Impostor*); Vorotynsky (*Vasilisa Melentyeva*); Mamayev (*No Wit Is Exempt from Foolishness*); Kuroslepov (*An Ardent Heart*); Vosmibratov (*The Forest*); and Akhov (*Even a Cat Has Lean Times*).

From the above list it is apparent that Sadovsky was also successful in dramatic roles: Krasnov, Rusakov, and so forth. This is further confirmed by his great success in the part of Anany in Pisemsky's *Bitter Fate*. He likewise appeared in Turgenev's plays (*The Provincial Lady, Luncheon with the Marshal of Nobility, A Month in the Country*), as well as in those of Potekhin and Sukhovo-Kobylin (Rasplyuyev in *Krechinsky's Wedding*). In Petersburg, too, he met with brilliant success; he appeared there as guest artist in 1857 and in subsequent years. To begin with, he played the part of Lubim Tortsov, which had been performed by

Samoilov. However, whereas Tortsov in Samoilov's interpretation was a kind of fool, Sadovsky "produced the character of a man of purely Moscow stamp, inconceivable anywhere else than in the ancient Zamoskvoretsky merchant milieu." After that he performed the parts of Osip, Podkolesin, Rasplyuyev, Rusakov, and Mordoplyuyev (*The Bridegroom from the Cutlery Market*). He was at his best in the roles of Podkolesin and Rasplyuyev. Theatre lovers maintained that only Sadovsky's acting revealed the genuine Rasplyuyev. On his next arrival he played with exquisite mastery the role of Benevolensky (*The Poor Fiancée*); however, his performance of the part of the Town Mayor, after Shchepkin and Sosnitsky, was of little interest.

On his acting in the part of Osip, Apollon Grigoryev observed: "So to announce the arrival of the Town Mayor, so to express delight with sour cabbage, soup, and gruel, and so to approach Khlestakov, urging him to depart—one has to renounce altogether one's own personality and crawl into Osip's skin." On this basis the critic made the following comparison between Sadovsky's and Shchepkin's acting: "Shchepkin portrays passions independently of the individual; Sadovsky plays the individual himself." A. N. Serov also emphasized the difference in their acting: "In Shchepkin there are a great many schools, a great many routines, and, therefore, a greater or lesser number of appendages. In Sadovsky all is naturalness and truth in a genuine, artistic realization."

Still more precisely V. I. Rodislavsky explained the difference between Sadovsky and his predecessors:

Shchepkin and Mochalov have been merely striving for simplicity and naturalness; in the performance by the best actors of those days— for instance, Shchepkin, Mochalov, Saburova, and Repina—there was still apparent what might be called acting. Sadovsky, even at the beginning of his career, may truly be considered as the one who was principally responsible for the fact that simplicity and naturalness began to reign supreme on our stage, having subdued all other tendencies.

The talent of I. F. Gorbunov (1831–1895) developed under Sadovsky's wing. The parts of Kudryash and Afonya (*Thou Shouldst Not Live as Thou Pleasest*) were his most successful dramatic roles. As a performer of scenes of his own invention and as a story-teller he was unrivaled. His mastery of all the linguistic nuances of Russians belonging to every stratum and milieu, as well as those of foreigners, enabled him by mere sounds to portray the many-countenanced and many-colored human throng. His exceptional familiarity with people's way of life as well as a rare faculty for observation enabled him, by means of two or three features, pointedly to reveal the pathological aspects of contemporary life. The mask of General Dityatin, which he made, enabled him in the person of that fragment of the Nicholas epoch to react to current life. In addition, his stories, not intended to be spoken, show an excellent mastery of divergent literary styles, while his sketches dealing with the history of our indigenous theatre are valuable because of his keen understanding of its conditions.

The full artistic superiority of the Moscow company over the one in Petersburg was demonstrated in 1870, when P. M. Sadovsky, S. V. Shumsky, G. N. Fedotova, and others played there as guest artists. According to A. I. Wolf:

Ostrovsky's plays were performed with an extraordinary ensemble, never seen before on our stage. Both profound evaluation of all details and the serious attitude of the guest artists toward their task deeply impressed the spectators, who were accustomed to the careless acting of our artists. Rehearsals began to be conducted in a wholly different manner. The guest artists insisted that all actors and actresses learn their parts, and that they not only think about themselves, but also contribute to the general effect of the play. These comments did not please our leading artists; and they pleased even less the head director and the supervisor of the repertoire.

In addition to Sadovsky, one other talent of the Moscow company came to light in Ostrovsky's plays. Prior to that time S. V. Vasilyev (1827–1862), who played vaudeville simpletons, had in no way distinguished himself. True, he did perform with marked success the roles of the billiard scorer Sharov in Kulikov's vaudeville *The Crow in a Peacock's Feathers*, and of Yemilya in Lensky's *The Simpleton and the Good-Mannered*; yet his real success began with the part of Vanya Borodkin (*Don't Seat Thyself in a Sledge That Isn't Thine*), which he played with genuine feeling. This was followed by the roles of Razlyulyayev (*Poverty's No Disgrace*) and Tikhon Kabanov (*The Thunderstorm*). He succeeded particularly in the latter, in which he managed to convey, instead of a simpleton, a man possessing sentiment that, though stifled by family oppression, revealed its true nature in grief. In his interpretation of this role Vasilyev was joined by Martynov, with whom he played Mishenka in Potekhin's play *Another's Wealth Does Not Aid Me*. He was also very good as Khlestakov.

Vasilyev put himself completely into the character he impersonated, combining high comedy with sharply dramatic situations. While impressing the audience by his variety of shadings, the talented actor played with great ease and without strain. His early blindness prevented him from creating for himself the honored name which he fully merited. He was long remembered by Moscow theatrical habitués, who highly prized the simplicity and sincerity of his acting.

Vasilyev's wife, Yekaterina Nikolayevna Lavrova (1816–1877), was a most gifted actress in a variety of *emplois*. Ophelia and the Queen (*Hamlet*), Anne Page (*The Merry Wives of Windsor*), Bélise (*The Learned Women*), and especially, Viola in Shakespeare's *Twelfth Night*—these were her best parts in the foreign repertoire. In Russian plays, during her youth, she played particularly well the roles of Marya Andreyevna in *The Poor Fiancée*, Anna Pavlovna in Ostrovsky's *Jesters*, and Laura in Pushkin's *Stone Guest*. She played the first part so well that even such an exacting critic as Bazhenov maintained, "It could not be improved upon." Apollon Grigoryev praised her very highly for her performance of the part of Sofya in *Woe from Wit*. In addition, she performed with marked success the roles of fashionable women in French plays and melodramas. She also paid her tribute to the vaudevilles which were popular at that time.

Three of Lavrova's daughters also became actresses: for example, in her time, Nadezhda Sergeyevna was a wonderful performer of Molière's soubrettes; subsequently she played with distinction the difficult *emploi* of *grande dame*.

One of the most gifted performers of women's parts in Ostrovsky's plays was Lyubov Pavlovna Nikulina-Kositskaya. The fate of this actress, who left very valuable memoirs, was by no means common, and it deserves special notice. Kositskaya (1829–1868) came from a family of peasant serfs, and was destined to experience the horrors of slavery. At an early age, having become a chambermaid to a Nizhny Novgorod merchant woman, Lyubov Pavlovna went with her mistress to the local theatre; and from that very evening she became obsessed with the dream of a stage career. After a long struggle with her parents, she succeeded in joining Nikolsky's troupe in Nizhny Novgorod. In that city was something in the order of a school for future actors of the company; not only did Kositskaya play there—at first, of course, small parts—but she also acquired training requisite to a future actress. Special attention was paid to the development of the voice, and, generally, to singing. Parts were studied under the guidance of more experienced actresses.

At Nizhny Novgorod young Kositskaya received only fifteen rubles per month and free lodging, even though she appeared in somewhat responsible parts—for instance, in that of Nadezhda in Verstovsky's opera *Askold's Tomb*. Later, she played for a while in Yaroslavl. Soon she was admitted to the Moscow Dramatic School, and only two years after her graduation she became a recognized favorite of the public.

The Moscow reviewer of the *Pantheon* wrote in 1848 that Kositskaya was a very useful acquisition for the Moscow stage, and that for this reason she had promptly won the public's affection:

This, she fully deserves. Depth of sentiment, soul, and a sense of responsibility, coupled with a charming stage presence and a sweet little voice—all these, which she possesses in abundance, ensure a great deal. Even so, she still has to study much; she has yet to become used to the stage and master its requirements. In those passages where sentiment, soul, and passion are needed, she is excellent: she forgets herself, her acting is natural, and she reveals a lofty, poetic nature. However, where the dramatic situation or the role calls for artistic refinement, observation, and graphic expression that will enable her to adjust herself in a weak scene, it is at once noticeable that she lacks so-called theatrical shrewdness; in short, where sentiment is silent, she too has nothing to say. This means that she still has to acquire skill and master a manner expressive of her individual outlook, a manner that will not fail her in any situation. Kositskaya is now what Mochalov used to be—she delights but does not satisfy.

He believed that one of her best roles was that of Marya in the melodrama *Mother's Blessing*, in which supposedly the peculiarities of her gifts were fully revealed. Of her performance of the part of Parasha the Siberian girl, the reviewer wrote: "Miss Kositskaya possesses a beautiful voice which is clear, pleasing, penetrating, one that is apt to move and delight us by mere modulations. In my judgment, the mysterious power to her success lies precisely in that voice."

But the success of Nikulina-Kositskaya was not in character plays alone. For instance, in 1866, on her benefit night, she produced a translated tragedy *Jane Grey,* in which she performed the part of the ailing King Edward. In the opinion of Bazhenov, she coped with her role rather well, and her costume on that occasion was very becoming.

Apollon Grigoryev would hardly have shared these views. He did admit:

She has an inner flame which, at times, flashes brightly—now in a heart-rending moan, now in an astounding gesture, now, again, in a striking glance; she is endowed with a tender speech blazing into one's soul such sounds as no one can resist. . . . However, no role in which she fails to act naturally has been adequately analyzed by her. She is wont to give way to whims of impulsive imagination. She does not overcome the unevenness of her manner.

As an example of such uneven acting he mentioned her part of Argolina in the drama *The Sea Wolf;* but he considered that almost no artist was so capable of passionate ecstasy. "It would be strange to think of her in the parts of Juliet or Desdemona," and he counseled her to confine herself to the roles of Russian women. Her stage tears, the oddity of her manners, and the sentimentalism of her diction made him decidedly challenge those who spoke about her likeness to Mochalov.

Kositskaya's natural gifts found worthy material in Ostrovsky's plays. In them she created such parts as Avdotya Maksimovna (*Don't Seat Thyself in a Sledge That Isn't Thine*), Katerina (*The Thunderstorm*), Grusha (*Thou Shouldst Not Live as Thou Pleasest*), and Anna Markovna (*Poverty's No Disgrace*). Critics of that epoch enthusiastically commented on her acting in these roles.

Kositskaya enjoyed both the affection of her colleagues and family happiness, having married the actor Nikulin. Only the theatrical administration hardly ever favored her. To a certain extent, Nikulina-Kositskaya's memoirs enable one to get a glimpse of her personality.

The best Varvara in Ostrovsky's *Thunderstorm* on the Moscow stage was Varvara Vasilyevna Borozdina (1813-1866). Having graduated from the dramatic school, she played with general approval in vaudevilles, where her success was enhanced by her exceptional beauty. However, it was only after Ostrovsky's plays made their appearance that she found dramatic material worthy of her talent. It was said by contemporaries that she was the best Lepochka ever to appear in the comedy *It's a Family Affair—We'll Settle It Ourselves*.

In 1852 the reviewer for the *Pantheon* wrote about Borozdina:

Her first début—a successful one in *Fra Diabolo* in 1847—showed that the actress had been preparing for the opera; but later she developed a preference for vaudeville, where triumph awaited her. Her acting was almost always characterized by simplicity, absence of affectation, and the desire not to act but to appear a genuine, living personage, conforming to her natural characteristics without imitating anybody. Miss Borozdina is undeniably endowed with talent—but special talent. A very attractive countenance and a good voice contribute to the success of the young actress.

An invaluable performer in vaudeville was I. V. Zhivokini (1808–1874), the permanent favorite of both the Moscow and the provincial public. His talent was little suited for plays requiring a cautious respect for the text. Witnesses say that

he was particularly fond of resorting to unexpected sallies: he would stop an officer making his way to the exit before the end of the performance of a vaudeville, and by a good-natured and inoffensive request prevail upon him to remain in his seat to see and listen to what was to happen at the very end of the play. At times, noticing that his colleagues, actors and actresses, tarried in their dressing rooms, he would begin telling anecdotes of his journeys in the provincial districts.

On other occasions, he would stop the orchestra, which had already begun to play the accompaniment to the concluding couplet, mimicking the contrabass and reproaching the violin for prematurely starting the music before he had told everything he meant to tell. He would then go on to recount his meeting on the Tverskoy Boulevard with Tarnovsky, the author of the vaudeville, who, according to his story, had submitted to him for choice two concluding couplets: one on behalf of the author praying indulgence for the composition, and the other on behalf of the artists praying indulgence for their present acting; now, he, Zhivokini, wished to sing the latter couplet, and not the one the orchestra began to play.

Again, at times, he would amiably advertise new plays, and then, following the text of the vaudeville, he would invite the public to attend his daughter's wedding; when, naturally, the public met his invitation with silence, he would begin to complain in his peculiar snuffling voice: "See, they shun our wedding, yet there is a regular onrush to *Krechinsky's Wedding*"! He also used to question those seated in the orchestra pit, for instance, as to how they liked the play; or, appealing to the gallery, he would ask the theatre critics seated there to give a favorable account of his acting in the newspaper reviews.

"Zhivokini," says A. D. Galakhov, "was an exceptional buffoon —one in a thousand. At the first sound of his voice, which could sometimes be heard from the wings, the public experienced pleasant emotion which created a responsive mood. But when he appeared, hilarity and laughter swept over the stage, leaving room for nothing else. To behold him and remain indifferent or in a bad frame of mind was simply impossible. Everything in him was full of fun: expression of the face, gestures, diction. He could manage, without speaking, by merely turning his eyes this way and that, or by movements of his hands, to draw loud applause."

Such comments suggest that Zhivokini must have possessed all the attributes which were requisite to actors of the Italian *commedia dell' arte*. This is the reason why vaudeville gave him much more leeway than Ostrovsky's pieces, in which he played Rizpolozhensky (*It's a Family Affair—We'll Settle It Ourselves*), Tolstogorazdov (*Incompatible Characters*), Mudrov (*Difficult Days*), Kuritsyn (*Thou Shouldst Not Live as Thou Pleasest*), Shilokhvostov (*Jesters*), Pereyarkov (*The Abyss*), and so on.

In the Petersburg company Y. N. Linskaya (1820–1871) distinguished herself in the parts of old merchant women in Ostrovsky's plays. She was a pupil of Shakhovskoy, and she made her début in the role of Parasha the Siberian girl. However, she scored real success only when she turned to comic parts. Arina Fedotovna (*Don't Seat Thyself in a Sledge That Isn't Thine*), Khorkova (*The Poor Fiancée*), Kukushkina (*A Profitable Business*), Kuroslepova (*An Ardent Heart*), Cheboksarova (*Wild Money*), and, particularly, Kabanova (*The Thunderstorm*) were among her best roles. She was equally successful in the plays of Gogol, Griboyedov, and other authors of recognized eminence. In no two roles was she the same; invariably the characters which she created breathed life.

Among the best actors of the Moscow company was also S. V. Shumsky (1821–1878), whose real name was Chesnokov. He received his pseudonym for his admirable childhood performance of the role of Shumsky in Khmelnitsky's play. He was among Shchepkin's most gifted pupils. As early as 1852, a critic in the *Pantheon* wrote of his guest artist performances in Petersburg:

He is preeminently a contemplative and reasoning actor. Such are the characters which he creates; he imparts to them a typical coloring; he expresses nuances with great care; he weighs and prepares the transitions from one passion to another, from the stage of calm to emotional agitation; he especially points up portions of the role highly important for the portrayal of the entire character.

Shumsky's stage career is excellent proof of what an intelligent man can achieve by industry and perseverance. Not only were his physical resources deficient, but his diction was impaired by a basic defect; namely, indistinct pronunciation. He pronounced *s* as *sh,* and *z* as *zh,* but managed to rid himself of all this by strenuous work. Even in later days, those who saw him several times in the same part, always observed an improvement and greater polish in its performance.

Because he based his acting not on natural aptitudes but on work, Shumsky appeared with almost equal proficiency in both comic and dramatic roles. Suffice it to mention that he played equally well both Zhadov and Arkashka Schastlivtsev.

At first, he specialized in the roles of fashionable young men in melodramas. Subsequently, when these were replaced by the "social plays" of Dyachenko, Chernyshev, and others, which assumed a leading place in the repertoire, Shumsky found in them a rich harvest of successes. In the classical repertoire he played during his career the parts of Figaro, Franz Moor, Würm (*Wile and Love*), Ivan the Terrible (in Aleksey Tolstoy's trilogy), Khlestakov, and Chatsky. According to contemporaries, in the last role he emphasized the sense of dignity and the intellectual aristocracy inherent in the character. In his interpretation, Chatsky was no longer a youthful man, but one who, while still possessing a youthful heart, had acquired maturity of mind and the faculty of sound judgment. Everything he said seemed to be the fruit of experience and reflection, something completely independent.

Shumsky's début as Kochkarev in Gogol's *The Marriage* was cordially received by the critic of the *Pantheon,* who compared his acting with Shchepkin's. Even though the author of the article, as other Muscovites, maintained that no one could be better in the role than Shchepkin, Shumsky caused him to change this opinion. Shumsky's portrayal of Kochkarev was not of "a ferreter and intriguer," as Shchepkin represented him, but "a giddy and hairbrained fellow, ready for everything, in glaring contrast with the calm, suspicious, and extremely irresolute Podkolesin. . . . Thus, I believe, Gogol created him; and thus was he represented on the stage by Shumsky."

He played admirably Krechinsky, and Count Lyubin in Turgenev's *Provincial Lady*.

Of Shumsky's performance of the role of Scapin, Bazhenov wrote: "Shumsky very correctly grasped and rendered the general tone of the part, that of a roguish, boastful domestic who practiced all sorts of knavish tricks, not so much out of mercenary considerations as out of love of art—as a matter of profession and habit." The translator of Molière's comedy wrote that it was impossible to express in words the artistic refinement with which Shumsky played Scapin.

Shumsky's attitude toward Ostrovsky's repertoire was more reserved than that of his theatre colleagues; yet this did not prevent him from performing with great success a great many roles in those plays, in which he impressed one again with the versatility of his talent. He alone was capable of impersonating the characters of Vikhorev (*Don't Seat Thyself in a Sledge That Isn't Thine*), Dobrotvorsky (*The Poor Fiancée*), Obroshenov (*Jesters*), Karpelov (*Hard-Earned Bread*), Chugunov (*Wolves and Sheep*), Groznov (*Truth's Good, Yet Happiness Is Better*), Arkashka, and Zhadov.

An attempt was made to assign to Shumsky the place which had been occupied by V. V. Samoilov. Such a comparison is an insult to the memory of the Moscow artist. The two were comparable only in the diversity of the roles which they undertook. However, Samoilov attained success in them by means of make-up and outward imitative devices, whereas Shumsky solved his problems by a remarkable penetration of the subconscious of the characters, so that the outward impersonation in no way overshadowed all other aspects.

A. I. Sumbatov-Yuzhin gave a detailed account of Shumsky's performance of the part of Cheremukhin in the adaptation of the French play *Woodcocks Are Not Destined to Fly over Trees*. Prior to the performance Shumsky had seen S. A. Palma in this little play at Tiflis. Unlike Palma, he played with reserve, and avoided grimace, winking, running about, and waving his hands; nevertheless, in the end the comic role, "by its many facets and psychological depth, grew into a living image worthy of Balzac or Dickens."

Like the majority of his colleagues in the Maly Theatre, Shumsky devoted special care to diction, giving far less attention to costume.

At the height of Ostrovsky's supremacy on the Moscow stage, melodramas were still given there, because they pleased the audiences. In addition, under the influence of men of letters headed by the eminent critic Bazhenov, Shakespeare and the Spanish classics were enthusiastically produced. Among the performers in this foreign repertoire the most prominent was I. V. Samarin (1817–1885). Brought up on melodramas, he found in them for a long time the principal material for his refined talent. Subsequently, his repertoire comprised the part of Chatsky, Ferdinand (*Wile and Love*), Mortimer (*Mary Stuart*), and Marquis Posa (*Don Carlos*). Among Shakespearean roles he was particularly good as Petruchio in *The Taming of the Shrew* (in his own production) and Benedick in *Much Ado About Nothing*. He succeeded brilliantly in the part of Crespo in Calderón's *El Alcalde de Zalamea*.

Samarin made his début in the role of Khlestakov. Belinsky wrote of the performance: "Mr. Samarin's features, manners, and tone are too intelligent and noble for the part of Khlestakov; for this reason he was unable either to perform it subjectively or to rise to its objective understanding and impersonation."

Of the part of Falstaff, another critic wrote:

Neither by his features nor by his acting was Samarin a Falstaff. The artist lacked Falstaffian animalism, which is the outstanding characteristic of this knight. Many of the various sentiments which Falstaff experiences in the course of the comedy, Mr. Samarin expressed too chastely and too sincerely, so that, in some places, they even bore a touch of genuine feeling, whereas they should have had the character of profanation of feeling, in the same sense that Falstaff himself is not so much a human being as the parody of a man. Again, Samarin's face in no way fitted the character: it shone with senile pleasantness and good nature; it was attractive, whereas it should have produced a repulsive impression by the manifestation of extreme sensuality and inflated arrogance, exhibiting the repugnant traits of a most vicious and unbridled mode of living.

Contemporaries maintained that

in his acting the artist did not transform himself into the character he impersonated. He admirably expressed tenderness, suffering, joy, offense, and so forth. But this he did to a certain extent impersonally, as it would have been done by an able elocutionist assisted by the illusions of costume and mise en scène. In all his parts such an artist is uniformly graceful and noble; he moves the spectator and evokes his smypathy in equal measure; yet, in point of fact, he always plays one and the same person, or—more correctly—he always reproduces very similar attractive or touching situations.

In his old age, Samarin played Famusov, Skvoznik-Dmukhanovsky, and even Ivan the Terrible in *Vasilisa Melentyeva.*

He readily tried his hand in the field of playwrighting. His plays *Morning Is Wiser than Evening, With Disagreements Gone All's Well Again,* and *Dmitry the Impostor* pleased the public.

Perhaps Samarin's principal importance lies in his pedagogic work. The system of training in declamation which he created still has its supporters.

About the middle of the nineteenth century, Alexander Yevstaf-yevich Martynov (1816–1860), a pupil of the talented teacher P. A. Karatygin, assumed prominence on the Petersburg stage. His talent was not at once apparent. He first trained for ballet dancing, for which his excellent physique delighted the ballet master Didlo. But at the same time he was severely criticized in Bryansky's dramatic class. "This brat," complained Bryansky, "studies painting, and he wants to be transferred to the dramatic class. I made him learn a part and listened to him; but it seems that he had better remain a color grinder: his pronunciation is bad, his voice is weak, and I believe little good will come of him." Karatygin took another view of the rejected Martynov, and developed him into such an artist that shortly after his appearance on the stage, Belinsky felt justified in writing in one of his reviews: "What a talent, gentlemen! If he studies and learns, not only vaudevilles but comedies as well, we will not be orphaned on the Aleksandrinsky stage for a long time."

He was at first made to play in very foolish vaudevilles: *Hail, Fellows—and Farewell! Tiger's Skin; A Recipe for the Correction of Husbands,* and so forth. These could provide no material for a refined and artistic performance, and Martynov was merely able to display outward comic effects. Since he did not value these insignificant roles, he treated them quite carelessly; failing to polish them beforehand, he would even appear in them without proper memorizing. Nevertheless, owing to his innate talent for comedy, he achieved outstanding success in these parts.

Ostrovsky remarked, "When Martynov appeared in the vaudevilles *I am a Traitor* and *Acquainted Strangers,* the public rushed to see him, no matter how often these were given." This fully corroborates D. V. Averkiyev's statement: "At times, Martynov was great in the most awful nonsense." And D. E. Grigorovich relates:

Martynov sometimes appeared on the stage after having had a chance merely to glance at the role: but even this was enough for him to create occasionally an original character. On one occasion he did not memorize the part at all. But having before his appearance provided himself with a long pipe, he entered the stage, and after each sentence (whispered to him by the prompter), he inhaled deeply, thus expressing by his face and by his whole figure a displeased air which produced, from head to foot, the typical obstinate and intractable bureaucrat. Instinct also prompted him to create a remarkable scene in Chernyshev's play *Money Is Not Happiness.* Representing a miser who had renounced his daughter, and who before death had unexpectedly become benevolent and pardoned her, Martynov introduced a nuance about which the author never dreamed. Embracing his daughter in a fit of repentance, the covetous father begins to fear that people will again seek to take her away from him: savagely he clasps her, dishevels her, and with a frightened air, looking around like a beast, he begins to emit wild, incomprehensible sounds. This whole scene as improvised by Martynov invariably produced a terrifying effect.

Eventually Martynov also began to include in his repertoire more serious parts: Bobchinsky and Khlestakov (*The Inspector-General*); Podkolesin (*The Marriage*); Ikharev (*Gamblers*); Bartholo (*The Barber of Seville*); Zagoretsky (*Woe from Wit*); Rasplyuyev (*Krechinsky's Wedding*); and Harpagon, Jourdain, Sganarelle, and Géronte in Molière's plays. If formerly critics most often compared Martynov with the Moscow comic Zhivokini, presently he assumed Shchepkin's *emploi*. Fortunately he guarded against any imitation of Shchepkin. An example of this was the part of Harpagon, in which he was particularly good and scored a great success at Kazan in the summer of 1845. His letters written there contain interesting information on the remuneration of guest artists from the capitals: he was paid 8,000 assignation rubles for his summer performances in Kazan and Nizhny Novgorod.

The new aspects of Martynov's talent were revealed with particular clearness when he appeared in the part of the daring coachman Mishenka, in Aleksey Potekhin's play *Another's Wealth Does Not Aid Me*. Martynov exhibited an equal wealth of sentiment and temperament both in the first act, with its colorful coachman's story, and in the last patricide scene. A whole drama unrolled before the public which had hitherto appreciated Martynov only in comic parts. His performance produced a similar impression in Chernyshev's one-act play *The Bridegroom from the Debtors' Prison*, an adaptation from Dickens. Gradually swerving more and more in the direction of drama, Martynov performed, by the end of his career, with exceptional perfection the part of Tikhon in Ostrovsky's *Thunderstorm*, into which he poured all his spiritual power.

A graphic characteristic of Martynov was presented by F. A. Koni: "In the play *Don Ranudo,* impersonating an old servant of an impoverished Spanish grandee, he used to appear in the rear of the stage at the end of a street; carrying a saucepan, he represented a man seized with laughter. Its sounds were not yet audible, but his very appearance made the entire audience laugh spontaneously. Even so, comedy was not his real métier. His performance of the part of Tikhon in *The Thunderstorm* revealed in him such a depth of dramatic talent, such a sense of reflection, and such an 'infectiousness' in the influence of his talent upon the spectators, that he reached tremendous heights. Somehow it even became strange to think that this artist who evoked tears from the audiences and potently moved their souls, had so recently jested and sung couplets on the stage. He, who in *The Thunderstorm* had heard Tikhon address these words to his mother, while standing by the body of his wife who had drowned herself, 'Mamma, it is you who killed her!' can never forget it." In later days, peculiarities of Martynov's talent were repeated by V. N. Davydov.

Martynov's success was foretold by Belinsky who, having made the reservation, "It's good to speak at an opportune moment and to keep silent at an inopportune one," wrote:

We perceive in him a gold nugget of dramatic talent; and if Martynov, without deceiving himself by his triumphs, will assiduously and disinterestedly labor with a view to mastering his art; if he will not stand on one spot but will move forward and forward, in due course something more substantial than more and more vaudeville plots of the Aleksandrinsky Theatre will come out of him.

And Gorbunov asserted that by his performance in *The Thunderstorm* Martynov "killed all the methods of the old Karatygin school."

Fanya Snetkova (1838–1929), a pupil of Vera Samoilova, first received recognition in vaudeville for the animation and grace of her acting when playing in Petersburg in 1855. Later she scored a real triumph in the part of Katerina (*The Thunderstorm*). Even though she little resembled the merchant woman, she put into her performance a great deal of ardor and sentiment. In the sixties she was one of the most outstanding actresses in Petersburg. She played the part of Mashenka in Turgenev's *Bachelor* with a marked success, which she shared with Martynov—a wonderful Moshkin.

Struiskaya I, who was noted for her performance of the role of Dunya (*Don't Seat Thyself in a Sledge That Isn't Thine*), was soon on Snetkova's level. Even in her début as Dunya, Elena Pavlovna Struiskaya (1845–1903) revealed much sincere warmth and genuine feeling. She won still greater fame as a result of her performance in the role of Katerina (*The Thunderstorm*). In the early seventies she became a favorite of the Petersburg public, appearing mostly in heartrending pieces which were then very much in vogue.

Broshel was the third noted actress of those days. Her acting was marked with nervous impetuosity in tragedy and charming gayety in comedy. The opinion has been expressed that, by the nature of her talent, she anticipated Savina. As early as 1864, she appeared with great success in *The Poor Fiancée*, and after that in the part of Annushka in *A Much Frequented Spot*. However, shortly afterward she left the stage for good, having been in the theatre only one and a half years. During that time she played the role of Verochka (*Jesters*) with particular excellence. N. S. Leskov, who had analyzed her acting in detail,[1] was enthusiastic over the credibility of her suffering, her grace, and the fluidity of her movements. L. N. Antropov said, "Lyrical, subjective talent, not theatrical, but intimate; sincerity; candidness bordering on naïveté—such are the traits which, first of all, impress one in her acting. Sentiment and nerves are dominant, and it is virtually with these alone that she performs."

Among the actors who appeared in the 1860's, a prominent place should, with all justice, be assigned to Modest Ivanovich Pisarev (1844–1906). Before graduation from the Moscow University, and through his high-school teacher Apollon Grigoryev, he became friendly with theatre habitués who grouped themselves around Ostrovsky. Having played several years on Moscow amateur stages, he began his career as a provincial actor at Simbirsk; after that he appeared in Orenburg, Samara, Kazan, and other provincial cities. Starting with a salary of 35 rubles per month, he soon became a noted actor, and won special fame by the performance of the part of Arbenin in Lermontov's *Masquerade*. During the Polytechnical Exhibition at Moscow in 1872 Pisarev appeared as guest artist in the Narodny[2] Theatre in the following plays: *Thou Shouldst Not Live as Thou Pleasest* (Peter), *Svat Fadeich*, and *It's a Family Affair—We'll Settle It Ourselves*.

The best role in his repertoire was Anany in *Bitter Fate*, in

[1] *Otechestvenny Zapisky*, No. 2, 1866, Dec.
[2] That is, People's.—Ed.

which he shared success with his wife P. A. Strepetova (1850–1903), our best Lizaveta. When Brenko founded the first private theatre in Moscow, Pisarev assumed one of the leading places in it. He occupied the same position in the theatre of F. A. Korsh, which grew out of the nucleus of Brenko's company. After 1885, when he joined the Aleksandrinsky Theatre, he came to the fore especially through his classic performance of the part of Neschastlivtsev. In general, the majority of Pisarev's most successful parts were in Ostrovsky's plays.

Pisarev was highly regarded by his stage colleagues for his culture and devotion to literature, and he maintained very close relations with a number of writers. His enlightenment made him a most valuable instructor of future artists.

The dominant trait of Pisarev's acting was his exceptional ability to express the intention of the author, to whose aims he always paid most scrupulous attention. He formulated his views on the actor's creative attitude toward the author's intention in an early article on Ostrovsky's *Thunderstorm*. There, he wrote:

A good actor playing in an original piece and seeking to divine the author's ideas, often stumbles upon certain expressions which are not in accord with the general character of the person; he stumbles upon all those irregularities and discrepancies which in his own judgment conflict with the character's generic traits. In such cases a good actor will, by his creative sense, screen the author's errors; thus clever staging will make even a poor play seem good.

On the other hand, a mediocre actor devoid of creative sense and aesthetic instinct, who is unable to transform himself with all his being into the role, who attacks it from the outside as a mere performer and not as a person brought to life in that part—especially if he has poorly learned it or if he wanders off on the beaten path of monotonous methods of acting and diction—such an actor, failing to understand the author fully, and being unable to master himself to the extent of a complete transformation, will inevitably deviate from the general tone and be powerless to render the speech and to impersonate the countenance of the character in constant accord with the author's intention. Consequently, his part either will be rendered incorrectly or will remain detached from the whole.

The actor translates the character from the world of words into the living world, gives to him the appearance, the flesh, the voice, the gestures, the expression. Thereby the inner world of the character, which the author delineates by mere hints, becomes more graphic and more distinct: a personage existing in word or only in imagination becomes genuinely alive on the stage, perceptible to both eye and ear. But it is precisely at this point that two good actors may disagree respecting the same part. They utter the same words; but the sound itself, the modulations of the voice, the whole appearance of the person expressed in his character, all this transparent exterior through which his spiritual nature shines—in brief, all dramatic acting—is colored with the unique pecularities of the performer. We note the difference in the same role, and we form opinions as to the viewpoint from which this or that actor has envisaged his part, to what extent it fits his aptitudes, the pattern of his mind, and his moral leanings.

A witness of P. A. Strepetova's acting in Moscow, when she appeared there for the first time as guest artist on the stage of the Narodny Theatre, wrote:

Even after the first performance, everybody began to discuss her extraordinary talent; and almost invariably the same judgment was expressed: "She is not pretty; she has a poor figure, but the moment she begins to speak—she is better than a beauty. What a voice! What eyes! What a face when, without uttering a word, she gazes at Anany from under her brows. One is afraid to look at her."

During her first season the repertoire of the young actress assumed definite form. She was at her best in character parts in Ostrovsky's and Pisemsky's plays: as Katerina in *The Thunderstorm* and as Lizaveta in *Bitter Fate*.

If on the question of Strepetova as Katerina opinions differed somewhat, certain particularly rigorous judges maintaining that in the part she lacked the mildness and dovelike tenderness inherent in Katerina, there was unanimous agreement with respect to Lizaveta:

Never was there such a performer of this role as Strepetova: it could not be better played. This was no longer acting: it was a complete illusion, an artistic incarnation of the figure of a tragic woman. When, in the first act, Strepetova, casting down her eyes, plucks the edges of her apron and then raises these wonderful eyes of hers and tells her husband, "What is there to say! I have no words against you," when in the third act, with disheveled hair, in a hemp sarafan, she comes running and screaming, "Nay, nay, you are not going to have it your way!" the audience is seized with that particular, inexpressibly terrifying mood which is familiar to all great artists. The entire audience, as one man, the souls of all those assembled, people so dissimilar and so heterogeneous, merges into one soul, and that soul surrenders to the power of the actress.

During the last years of her stage career, Strepetova created an extraordinary role, full of tragic expression—that of Nikita's mother in Tolstoy's *The Power of Darkness,* actually making the part the central one in the play.

The revolutionary movement of the 1860's was reflected in the theatre far less than in other aspects of Russian life. Owing to complete subordination to censorship, playwrights were practically deprived of every chance to portray the new men and the new tendencies, as these were revealed in novels of the same period. Only in rare plays—for example, *The Old Gentleman,* by A. I. Palm, a member of the Petrashevsky group—was it possible to reveal a faint outline of the new life. Palm, in most inoffensive colors, portrays a printing office organized as an artel by young people.

Unsuccessful attempts were made on the stage to ridicule "new men" by exhibiting them in the most unfavorable light. Thus, in 1866, Chernyavsky's very weak comedy *Civil Marriage* was produced in the Aleksandrinsky Theatre, after having been read by the Minister of the Interior in the Winter Palace, who gave it full approval.

The revolutionary movement failed to find as active partisans among actors as, for instance, among painters, who sharply renounced government control over art, and formed on a new basis an artel out of which the *peredvizhniky* [3] emerged.

However, it would not be correct to say that revolutionary tendencies did not touch the theatre. A colorful exponent of the new moods in the actor milieu was M. N. Yermolova (1853–1928). Daughter of a prompter at the Maly Theatre, she was brought up in very modest circumstances. As a child she entered the ballet class of the Dramatic School; but she was reluctant to serve in the ballet, and tried in vain to transfer to drama. The instructor in the dramatic class, I. V. Samarin, found her untalented; and, despite her wishes, she was compelled to return to the ballet.

[3] Exponents of realistic painting who formed a unified movement in the 1870's and whose pictures were on view at periodic showings arranged by the *"Peredvizhnik* exhibitions."—Ed.

However, selected by an influential actress, N. M. Medvedeva, she was given an opportunity on January 30, 1870, to perform the leading part in Lessing's tragedy *Emilia Galotti* in lieu of G. N. Fedotova, who had fallen ill. She at once attracted the attention of the connoisseurs. Nevertheless, for a long time the administration kept her in obscurity, stubbornly assigning only secondary parts to her for several years. Not until 1873 did she succeed in playing Nadezhda in Mey's *The Lady from Pskov*, Fair-Spring in *The Snow-Maiden*, Lubov Gordeyevna in *Poverty's No Disgrace*, and Katerina in *The Thunderstorm*.

During these years she became very close to progressive youth, absorbing with delight the verses of Nekrasov, the contemporary "sovereign of thought," and devoting much time to self-education. Her acquaintance with the translator and connoisseur of the drama S. A. Yuryev exercised a decisive influence upon her, and it was under his guidance that she created for her benefit performance on March 7, 1876, the character of Laurentia in Lope de Vega's tragedy *The Sheep Well*. There the depth of artistic refinement blends in harmony with the extraordinary social upsurge which converts a common girl into the inspired leader of a popular uprising against the oppressors. The actress managed to find for this shades and feelings akin to the moods of the progressives in the audience. The performance turned into a political demonstration, and for this reason the piece was soon forbidden for a long time to come.

Yermolova's fame was assured, however. From that time on, appearing by necessity in plays of the current repertoire, she zealously promoted at her benefit performances the best of the Western classics. Imogen in Shakespeare's *Cymbeline*, Estrella in Lope de Vega's *The Star of Seville*, Schiller's Joan of Arc and Mary Stuart, Grillpartzer's Sappho, Klärchen in Goethe's *Egmont*, Negina in Ostrovsky's *Talents and Their Admirers*—these were her best roles. Despite the diversity of the parts which she performed—there were about three hundred—she brought them all down to one general idea; namely, the renunciation of personal well-being and happiness for the sake of serving higher ideals. If her Maid of Orleans gives her whole self for the salvation of her motherland, Negina renounces life with her beloved and betrays him, because in those days the existence of an actress, serving art, often called for such sacrifices.

Emphasizing hatred of oppression with extraordinary power, Yermolova by the characters she created taught others to regard life as a heroic sacrifice. She regarded the world as a tragedy. No matter how empty the role, even in a most insignificant play, she succeeded in filling it with her soul, revealing the depth of her personality. She was admirable as Mary Stuart, portraying not a queen, not an ardent Catholic, but a sensual woman with all her charm and fascination. She portrayed her own self, revealing her longing for liberty, her anger and disdain for the oppressors, and her readiness to die for truth. Her encounter with Queen Elizabeth (Fedotova) was turned into an artistic contest between two women of altogether different types. When in *The Maid of Orleans* Yermolova as Joan of Arc rent the chains, the audience sank into reverent excitation and believed in the possibility of such a miracle.

The details of her performance of the part of Negina were reconstructed from memory by Y. M. Yuryev.[4] A. I. Yuzhin, who played with her in that play, observed:

Ostrovsky set before the actress an immensely difficult task: Negina must decide whether or not she should sacrifice her love for the stage. Nor is it only a question of sacrifice; she must become somebody else's mistress; she must resort to the barter of self in order not to quit the stage, not to renounce her creative work which she treasures more highly than honor, love, or even human dignity.

And amidst all this filth she must remain "purer than the purest and chastest maidens."

How serene and beautiful is Yermolova when, on the last night of her freedom, proud and invincible, she yields to her beloved, a humble, poverty-stricken teacher! How great she is when deliberately she deceives him, concealing from him that by this time on the morrow she will be alienated from him, and will have become a sold and lost woman! Those lovely and luminous eyes gleaming with a smile through lucid feminine tears! That fascinating amorous gesture, winding one arm around the neck of her beloved and resting her other arm on his shoulder, against which she presses her little head!

[4] *The Theatre*, No. 9, 1937, pp. 93–125.

Inner truth—incontestable truth—and the right of a woman's feelings vindicate that which the injustice of human hypocrisy condemns.

Another witness, N. E. Efros, adds:

Perhaps Yermolova was never so complex in the analysis of the mysteries of a woman's heart, in the delineation of the confusing and involved impulses of a woman's soul, as in the closing act of the comedy, when Negina bids adieu to Meluzov and says that she cannot be a heroine.

In this most difficult role she unfolded in all its brilliance the infinite perfection of her technique and the richness of a wonderful voice, which enabled her to express the faintest nuances of mood and feeling.

Off the stage, Yermolova exerted her influence upon audiences from the concert platform, where she recited Pushkin and Nekrasov. Every one of her appearances was received as an event of enormous artistic and social importance. It is known that she produced an extraordinary impression in her youth when, at the modest evening parties of students, she recited Nekrasov's verses "Green roar sweeps 'long and drones," which she made into a battle cry.

Blending in her creative work the brightest romantic colors with consummate artistic truth, Yermolova better than anyone else personified a harmonious synthesis of realism and romanticism. In her tremendous influence upon the audience she brought the stage back to the times of Mochalov. In her attitude toward art, on the other hand, she fully and faithfully preserved Shchepkin's tradition: she left nothing to blind inspiration, and assiduously prepared her part in the most minute detail. To that end, she gave herself completely to the theatre.

A. A. Yablochkina wrote in her reminiscences of Yermolova:

Not only was she without the desire to attract attention to herself, but she sought to stand aloof from everybody, to hide in her inner self, as it were—to become isolated. Inevitably, this created around her a peculiar atmosphere. Every happening behind the scenes, all theatrical joys and disappointments, arguments and quarrels, jests and witticisms, contests of ambitions—briefly, everything that boils and blusters within the actor milieu was remote from her; and any of these incidents that might reach her dressing room came as hardly more than a ripple.

However, this "desire to hide" has made it difficult to penetrate the inner world of the actress, which has been far from fully explored. She retired into the roles she created, and dwelt not in her private life but in the lives of those whom she impersonated. Everybody was afraid of disturbing her in any way or diverting her from her creative work, and this tended to bring about a state of isolation. It seems that she herself must have felt this condition, which probably was difficult for her to endure.

All this vividly illustrates Yermolova's attitude toward her work.

Circles friendly to her were sympathetic toward S. A. Yuryev, who, allegedly, at some evening party described the actress as "a perfect incarnation of Turgenev's Elena." And, in fact, of all literary characters the heroine in the novel *On the Eve* most closely resembles Yermolova; for, in her, rare spiritual beauty was blended with the determined desire wholly to dedicate herself to the realization of all the aspirations which inspired the best representatives of the period.

Stanislavsky called Yermolova "the heroic symphony of the Russian theatre." This aptly emphasizes the fact that, in addition to portraying with greater depth and power than any other Russian artist the entire heroic content of drama, her very service to the theatre constituted heroism, devoid of humiliation and compromises with the administration, in which so many of her colleagues indulged. The administration did not hold her in esteem. Indeed, at the end of her career it even sought to discharge her from the Maly Theatre, despite the fact that she embodied its best traditions. Only after the Great October Socialist Revolution did her anniversary celebration assume a character worthy both of the gifted actress and of a great nation. On that occasion all Moscow, headed by the staffs of all the theatres, paid solemn tribute to her who, according to her own admission, had always "longed for warmth and light for mankind." She was the first actress upon whom the honorary title of People's Artist of the Soviet Republic was bestowed.

Yermolova shared her success with Glikeriya Nikolayevna Pozdnyakova-Fedotova (1846–1925). A pupil of the Dramatic School, Fedotova developed under the influence of Samarin and Shchepkin. In 1862 she appeared in the part of Verochka in Boborykin's *Child*, promptly assuming a leading place, which she held until grave illness late in life compelled her stay at home. Even then, she continued to participate in the life of the theatre by counseling young artists whose successes gave her the greatest joy.

In Ostrovsky's plays she was the first to perform the parts of Larisa (*The Girl Without a Dowry*), Aksyusha (*The Forest*), Parasha (*An Ardent Heart*), Annushka (*A Much Frequented Spot*), Tugina (*The Last Sacrifice*), Snow-Maiden, Vasilisa Melentyeva, and Otradina (*Guilty Without Guilt*). In later years she played with unsurpassed mastery Murzavetskaya in *Wolves and Sheep*, in which she earlier performed the part of Kupavina, while in *Wild Money* she turned from the part of Lydia to that of Cheboksarova. Even this partial list is indicative of the versatility of her talent.

In the Western classics she played with equal facility parts requiring altogether different aptitudes; namely, Shakespeare's Cleopatra, Lady Macbeth, and Mistress Page, and Schiller's Queen Elizabeth. The mastery of her acting was in no way inferior to that of the best Western actresses. In her later years she created a splendid portrayal of Volumnia in Shakespeare's *Coriolanus*, and she produced a profound impression in Nevezhin's mediocre drama *Second Youth*, which, solely because of her acting, acquired artistic merit. Depth of feeling; the working out of a role in all its most minute details and the strict coordination of all of its features; ability by one restrained gesture, by one expressive glance, to give a finishing touch to a character—such are the principal characteristics of her talent. Without uttering a single word, by a provocative glance, and by a seemingly casual stroking of her ripe arms, her Vasilisa Melentyeva would entwine and enmesh Ivan the Terrible. The Snow-Maiden's tenderness and Queen Cleopatra's domineering passion were equally within her grasp. Ascribing all her triumphs to the influence of her teachers, headed by Shchepkin, who taught her to practice her art with reverence, the great Russian actress Fedotova, was a matter of fact not inferior to them, even in intellect or in talent. Infinitely rigorous toward herself, she tenderly nurtured the aptitudes of young actresses, guiding their first steps by her wise counsel. Through her the best traditions of the Maly Theatre reached K. S. Stanislavsky.

Pisemsky, the author of *Bitter Fate,* admitted that, having traveled all over Europe, having seen all the theatres and many good actresses, he had found nowhere such depths of feeling as in Fedotova.

However, even comparisons with such actresses did not dim the brilliant talent of N. A. Nikulina (1843–1923). Ostrovsky assigned to her the parts of Kupava, Verochka (*Jesters*), Poliksena (*Truth's Good, Yet Happiness Is Better*), Nastya (*There Was No Grosh—and Now a Whole Altyn*), Zhenya (*Hard-Earned Bread*), Tsarina Anna (*Vasilisa Melentyeva*), Korinkina (*Guilty Without Guilt*), Smelskaya (*Talents and Their Admirers*), and Glafira (*Wolves and Sheep*). She also inherited the role of Varvara in *The Thunderstorm.* She was very fond of the part of Glasha in Averkiyev's *The Antiquities of Kashirsk.* Gay, young, adroit merchant women—such was the beloved métier of her colorful, rich creative art. Vigor, inner power and faith in her good fortune permeated her portrayals, which were always truthful and fascinating.

As the years passed, the part of Glafira went to E. K. Leshkovskaya (1869–1925), who portrayed the same milieu in a more refined and magnificent way, with a touch of Western fashion. Her ways of artistic delineation were much finer and more complex. Her Glafira (*Wolves and Sheep*) and Lydia (*Wild Money*) were already worn-out women of the end of the century. In the brilliant attire of fashionable women, Leshkovskaya mercilessly exposed the utter hollowness of the female sex in the *beau monde* of the capitals. The plays of her stage colleague A. I. Yuzhin-Sumbatov—*Gentleman, Casting-Net,* and so forth—provided her with excellent material in such character roles.

In the Maly Theatre one of the leading actors was A. I. Lensky (Verviziotti, 1847–1908). An illegitimate son of Prince Gagarin by an Italian woman, he had a highly diversified education as a child. However, he became an orphan at an early age and was brought up in the family of the actor K. N. Poltavtsev. In 1865 he began to play vaudeville simpletons at Vladimir. He served in Smolkov's company at Nizhny Novgorod and at Samara, Murom, Saratov, Kazan, Astrakhan, and Tiflis. During the 1875–1876 season he met V. V. Samoilov at Odessa, and while playing with him learned his method of making-up by the use of the simplest devices. On April 26, 1876, following his début, he received an engagement in the company of the Maly Theatre, where he soon assumed a prominent position.

Originally he performed the parts of first lovers in comedy and tragedy, but later he turned to character roles. Among Russian classics he acted in the plays of Pushkin (the Impostor and Don Juan in *The Stone Guest*), Griboyedov (Chatsky, Famusov), Gogol (Ikharev and the Town Mayor), Turgenev (Rakitin, Stupendyev, Shpigelsky), and Ostrovsky (Glumov, Baklushin, Murov, Paratov, Velikatov, Dudukin, Pribytkov, Lynyayev, the provincial Governor and Mamayev). In Shakespeare he played Petruchio, Hamlet, Bassanio, Benedick, Romeo, Richard III, Iago, Othello, Falstaff, and Cardinal Wolsey; in Schiller, Franz Moor and Philip II; in Molière, Don Juan and Tartufe; in Hugo, Gomez de Silva in *Hernani* and Don César de Bazan in *Ruy Blas*; in Lope de Vega, Busto Tabera in *The Star of Seville*; in Gutskov, Uriel Akosta.

Among plays of the modern repertoire he was at his best in the parts of Stolbtsov (*The New Enterprise*, by Nemirovich-Danchenko, Count von Trast-Saarberg (Sudermann's *Honor*), and Bishop Nicholas (Ibsen's *The Pretenders*).

An admirable painter and sculptor, Lensky was an unsurpassed master of creating outward appearances in every role; however, believing that "form, no matter what it be, is good only if it stands with regard to its substance in the same relation as a nutshell to its kernel," he always combined that appearance with profound content. He fully complied with his fundamental precept to the actor "that the spectator behold everything, hear everything, and receive everything the stage can give him, without the slightest effort on his part." His manner of acting was based on the principle of artistic simplicity: "The better an actor, the nearer he is to that simplicity; however, the nearer he is to simplicity, the simpler, the more accessible seems his art." Lensky believed that the actor's eyes are the principal means of interpreting the author's intention.

His attitude toward the text of a role is apparent from the way he analyzed the performance by one of his pupils of Figaro's monologue in Beaumarchais's *The Marriage of Figaro*. Studying the gradual dramatic crescendo in Figaro to the last detail, he sought to discover the appropriate tone in which the monologue should be recited.

His portrayal of Famusov—in that role he had to appear after such masters as Shchepkin and Samarin—may serve as an example of the most conscientious extraction from the text of all hints and suggestions of the playwright concerning the various roles. He discovered in Griboyedov direct indications as to licentiousness, "animal interests," with regard to women; fear that Chatsky might propose to Sophia as well as joy when it proved possible to prevent it, and at the same time the desire to have Sophia marry as soon as possible a fiancé such as Skalozub. All these findings were based on the study of the "cross-characteristics" which Griboyedov gave when he had the various persons in the play describe each other.

In reciting Griboyedov's verses Lensky distinctly emphasized the rhymes, catching up those of his interlocutor. In his performance, the words at his final appearance in the fourth act, "Come, follow me, come quick—come quick!" by their wealth of color and diversity of nuance produced an extraordinary symphony in which every sound and every gesture were carefully weighed. Whereas Shchepkin described Famusov as a Molchalin who had achieved success, Lensky in his Famusov portrayed a Repetilov who in his old age attained "prominence in rank." By a number of details, beginning with the star on his nightgown, Lensky emphasized the aristocratic pride of his Famusov, to whom Khlestova herself is an equal. Famusov was his favorite part. By his own admission, he played it twenty years in succession with such ease that it was as if he were sitting at home in his nightgown.

The versatility of his acting, which was always distinguished by noble elegance, was remarkable. Silently, without uttering a single word, he managed to express the whole gamut of his psychic impulses, as he used to do it in the part of Benedick (*Much Ado About Nothing*), who having learned from the conversation of friends that Beatrice is in love with him, walks back and forth in a state of hesitation for a long time after their departure. Then, straightening his whiskers, full of pride and conscious of his victory, he makes his exit.

Suffice it to compare Lensky's attire and posture in the part of Lynyayev in the fourth act, when he is still proud of his bachelor freedom, with his metamorphosis in the fifth act, when he becomes Glafira's captive. This change clearly indicated Lynyayev's subsequent fate.

In *The Pretenders* Lensky created an all-inspiring image of a misanthrope, with a bald skull and lop-eared, and with a dimmed malicious look, dying in an armchair on the proscenium.

His analysis of Falstaff in the articles *Actor's Notes* is the best illustration of rare insight into the author's intentions. But this was not easily achieved. By his own admission, while working on the part of Demurin (*The Price of Life,* by Nemirovich-Danchenko) he did not sleep at night, trying to find the appropriate tone for the decisive scene with Yermolova. But this preparatory work, to him, was the most treasured part of the task, and at times his "quests" at rehearsals were more successful and more instructive than the performance itself.

The most cultivated actor in the company, Lensky better than any of his colleagues was suited for the guidance of young people. In 1889 he became a teacher in the Dramatic School; and a number of outstanding actors of the succeeding generation came out of his class. Ten years later, in 1898, he was entrusted with the instruction of the young actors in the Novy [5] Theatre, where he revealed his exceptional talent as stage director. His best productions were Ostrovsky's *The Snow-Maiden,* and Shakespeare's *A Midsummer-Night's Dream, Romeo and Juliet,* and *The Merry Wives of Windsor.* However, his endeavors to lift the Maly Theatre to an adequate level, and to give leeway to young talent proved unsuccessful: he was unable to overcome the ignorance and apathy of the administration. Having produced D'Annunzio's *Francesca da Rimini,* he found himself altogether isolated and compelled to quit the stage so as not to be "an impotent witness of the final corruption of the theatre by all kinds of robbers." With the latter he was destined to have a particularly sharp encounter during the staging of S. Yushkevich's *The King,* which was never produced. His free plans were smashed against the dead walls of the crown theatre.

However, Lensky's colleague A. I. Yuzhin-Sumbatov (1857–1927) did manage to adapt himself to the crown theatre. Shortly after the University he entered the Maly Theatre, having assumed

[5] That is, New.—Ed.

at the end of his life the position of artistic director. Apparently he considered himself capable of playing the tragic repertoire, and he tried his hand at Hamlet, Macbeth, Richard III, Egmont, Ruy Blas, Marquis Posa, and Mortimer. Yet, in these roles he lacked appropriate depth of feeling; moreover, his outward resources were not quite favorable. He was far better in comedy, and the parts of Figaro and, especially, of Telyatev (*Wild Money*) were among his finest creations.

In addition to articles on the history of the theatre and stage practice, he wrote many plays: *Hawks and Ravens* (in collaboration with V. I. Nemirovich-Danchenko), *Arkazan Chains,* and others. His comedies are noteworthy, mordantly and pointedly portraying the upper strata of the capitals: *Gentleman, Casting-Net,* and *The Irininsky Parish.* Trying his hand at historical drama, he portrayed Ivan IV. However, he was much more successful in *Treason,* in which he depicted the past of his native Georgia. He also dealt with the Caucasus in the play *The Old Cast,* depicting typical figures from the Caucasian army. The love intrigue of the play, however, does not go beyond a purely conventional pattern.

F. P. Gorev (1850–1910), who came from the provincial stage, possessed far greater natural aptitudes for tragedy. He was at his best in translated melodramas—in *The Fighter of Ravenna* and the like. In his mature years he created forceful and colorful images in Coppée's *Jacobites* and Sudermann's *Motherland* (Magda's father). In Russian plays he was equally successful both in Leskov's *Dissipator* and in Gogol's *Marriage*—in which he performed the part of the midshipman Zhevakin. Flagrant injustice from the willful director of the theatres, S. M. Volkonsky, compelled him to resign from the crown stage, the best actors of which he never was able to match, owing to a touch of provincial mannerism in his acting.

The comedian V. A. Maksheyev (1843–1901) also came to the Maly Theatre from the provincial stage. His performance of the parts of the Town Mayor, Rasplyuyev, and Rizpolozhensky was marked with mild good humor. Likewise N. M. Muzil (1839–1906) and A. O. Pravdin (1846–1921) came to Moscow from provincial Russia. The latter was an inimitable Kuchumov in *Wild Money.* He also played exceptionally well in Molière's plays, skillfully portraying the typical national traits of the French. At the same time he excellently impersonated the Germans, and in Erckmann-Chatrian's play he successfully competed with the eminent German actor Possart.

M. P. Sadovsky (1847–1910) continued the creative tradition originated by his father, Prov Sadovsky. Mikhail Provych found in Ostrovsky's plays the most fertile soil for his artistic work, which was marked with versatility beyond the limits of any particular *emploi:* Tikhon, Arkashka, and Meluzov, Andrey Belugin and Baraboshev, Murzavetsky and Mulin—for each of these dissimilar roles he was able to find right and appropriate shadings. In Nemirovich-Danchenko's play *The New Enterprise* he performed excellently the part of the ailing and submissive Andrey Kolguyev, in some scenes reaching the heights of genuine tragedy. He did not like to appear in the Western classics; yet even in them—for example, in Shakespeare's *The Winter's Tale*—he was quite successful. For many years he was the sole Khlestakov in the company at the Maly Theatre. Certain critics were enthusiastic about his acting in this role; however, with advancing age, it was not long before he ceased to be suited for it. Besides, his countenance and manners made it hard to see in him the pitiful government official that Khlestakov was in reality.

For a while he contributed to the press, and he wrote, in addition to translations, two little volumes of stories depicting the lives of the humble and downtrodden in the remote districts of his native Moscow. An excellent student of its customs, he gave in these a number of truthful sketches. However, some of them were spoiled by an excessively saccharine quality—all the more unexpected in the face of his bitter and mordant verses branding the ridiculous and hideous aspects of the work of his superiors.

Olga Osipovna (Lazareva) Sadovskaya (1846–1919), his wife, formerly an amateur in the Artistic Club headed by Ostrovsky, entered the Maly Theatre at an early age. Even in her youth she began to play the parts of old women. Her interpretation of matchmakers and lady companions in Ostrovsky's comedies was beyond praise; despite a certain monotony of characteristic traits and dramatic situations, she managed to find for each one altogether novel nuances, never repeating herself or resorting to the slightest exaggeration. It is impossible to conceive anything excelling her Domna Pantelevna in *Talents and Their Admirers.* Just as her husband, she was an incarnation of folk simplicity and truth. However, the particular force of her acting lay in an exceptional mastery of speech, the most minute modulations of which she utilized both for the expression of the different moods and for the coloring of the character parts. Very restrained in transitions and gestures, she used to arrest the spectators' attention by the mere mastery of speech, at times making even a small role (for instance, in *The Provincial Governor*) one of focal importance.

By the combined stage work of Yermolova, Fedotova, Lensky, the Sadovskys, and a number of other progressive Russian actors, the Maly Theatre in those days became the sole platform from which a considerable group of men were able lawfully to express, not their personal, but their public sympathies—their approval or disapproval of this or that author, of this or that tendency or ideal impersonated on the stage. In its beneficial influence the theatre far exceeded even the loftiest and finest recreations, and in many rsepects it rose above its neighbor, the Moscow University, in educational significance. Not without reason did the young people coin the apothegm, rampant in Moscow: "We studied in the University, but we were educated in the Maly Theatre."

During that period the Aleksandrinsky Theatre in Petersburg developed in an altogether different fashion. It was isolated from both the University and the progressive literary circles. At the same time, its proximity to the Ministry of the court had a most degrading influence, since the bureaucrats were its complete masters. The engagement of actors, their subsequent fate, and the selection of plays were in their discretion. This may be well seen, for example, from Ostrovsky's correspondence with the actor F. I. Burdin.

In Petersburg the public, too, was quite different. Students who, in the time of Mochalov and Yermolova, were irresistibly attracted by every performance in the Maly Theatre were quite indifferent to the Aleksandrinsky. It is quite noteworthy that V. V. Veresayev, who lived in Petersburg during his student years, does not say a single word about that theatre. However, the eminent representative of the Guard, Imeretinsky, openly confessed that, if wealthy Guard officers used to look for mistresses in the ballet and among French actresses, poorer officers were content with the more accessible actresses of the Aleksandrinsky. In addition to these officers, government employees and Gostiny Dvor[6] merchants formed the nucleus of its audiences.

M. G. Savina (1854–1915) reigned long on the Aleksandrinsky stage. She was the daughter of a provincial teacher of painting who became an actor. Even as a child living in Odessa, she began to appear in theatrical performances. Subsequently, she played in operettas and in comedy. In 1874 she joined the Aleksandrinsky company, promptly assuming the first place and acting in many leading roles of the Western and the Russian repertoire, both in comedy and in drama. She attained genuine perfection in *The Inspector-General,* first as the Town Mayor's daughter and later as his wife. Here she fully revealed her mastery of character delineation based on an extraordinary power of observation, coupled with an ability to polish every detail. However, her expression of deep feeling did not always exhibit the inner power and depth of synthetized thought which gave such a harmonious perfection to Yermolova's acting. Brilliant abilities helped her to overcome the inadequacies of her education and to acquire that outward gloss which enabled her to appear in the parts of fashionable ladies gushing French phrases.

Shrewd playwrights closely associated with Savina, such as V. A. Krylov and I. V. Shpazhinsky, were quick to grasp the peculiarities of her talent with its Bohemian touch, and they created for her— as a tailor models a dress "to fit one's figure"—parts in such plays as *The Scapegrace.* In these she was superb. Others began to mold into short scenes her own masterful stories about the various meetings which took place during her career. Thus, Shcheglov's short plays *Female Fiddle-Faddle* and *Female Chitchat* and A. M. Fedorov's play *The Woman Patient* came into being. Savina managed to fashion out of these trifles rich and true pictures.

Novels were assiduously turned into plays for her. One of these enabled her to glitter in the part of Nastasya Filippovna in *The Idiot,* adapted from Dostoyevsky's novel. In her youth she greatly impressed Turgenev by imparting to the role of Verochka, in *A Month in the Country,* a meaning which the playwright himself had not suspected. Subsequently, in the same comedy, she played with much force the part of Natalya Petrovna. However, despite all her fondness for the plays of Turgenev, with whom she

[6] St. Petersburg commercial quarter.—Ed.

was bound in friendship for many years, she failed to master the role of Liza in *The Noblemen's Nest*, which P. I. Weinberg adapted for her. By mere skillful acting Savina was unable to express the captivating lyricism and purity of that character.

The actress paid much attention to compliance with living truth, as may be seen from her portrayal of Akulina in Tolstoy's *The Power of Darkness*, where, with merciless boldness, she exhibited the utter wretchedness of that befuddled peasant girl.

An actress in her own life, with all the characteristic traits of her profession, Savina created a similar image of the actress in Chekhov's *Sea-Gull*, in no way concealing the intrinsic hollowness of that "priestess of art." Also in *Tatyana Repina* she skillfully portrayed the characteristic traits of an actress. With naturalism far exceeding permissible bounds, she represented the death agony of a woman who poisoned herself; nevertheless, even then she did not quite succeed in expressing the depth of her moral suffering. However, in such fabrications as *Matryona—the General's Lady*, through which Sardou's *Madame Sans-Gêne* was transplanted into the Russian scene, she felt completely at ease—all the more so as the proximity to the Mikhailovsky Theatre and frequent trips to Paris enabled her to learn from Frenchwomen. It has been observed that her style of acting more or less closely resembled Réjane's.

Unquenchable thirst for acting prompted Savina to rush about in tours of the provinces. In the spring of 1899, first among all Russian actresses, she proceeded with a company to Berlin and Prague; the latter city was chosen because of the sympathy of the Czechs of those days with everything Russian. In Berlin she played *Tatyana Repina, Vasilisa Melentyeva,* and *The Enchanter* (Shpazhinsky's drama). The second and third were designed to impress the Germans with the picturesqueness of the ancient boyar's ways of living.

However, not satisfied with the status of an "exotic" actress, Savina boldly entered into a contest with Western actresses as Marguerite Gautier in *La Dame aux Camélias*, and Magda in Sudermann's *Motherland*, particularly dear to the Germans. And in that contest she acquitted herself satisfactorily.

A brilliant mind, inclined to spitefulness, as well as inexorable will power in the attainment of a set goal, for many years enabled Savina to reign in "her" theatre; but, while occupying the first place in it, she did not forget the little people of the theatre. She devoted much time and labor to the Russian Theatrical Society, which was founded on her initiative; and by her influence and money she alleviated the lot of the old provincial actors and their orphans.

Among the rather mediocre actresses of the Aleksandrinsky Theatre, V. V. Strelskaya (1838–1915) stood out by her talent. In her youth she appeared in operettas, and in the latter half of her life she distinguished herself in comic old women's roles. Having mastered speech with exceptional skill, she successfully imparted a peculiar emotional warmth to every role in her simple acting.

The foremost actor of the company was V. N. Davydov (I. N. Gorelov, 1849–1925). Like Savina, having come from the provinces, he played equally well both trifling and classical roles. His Town Mayor, Famusov, Rasplyuyev, and especially his Podkolesin, were the finest creations of Russian stagecraft. Through Samarin, a continuer of the Shchepkin school, he also possessed the peculiar aptitudes of Martynov, with whom he competed quite successfully in the part of Mishenka (Potekhin's *Another's Wealth Does Not Aid Me*). By the power of its expressiveness, his mimicry in the last appearance of Podkolesin was amazing. His Harpagon in Molière's *Miser*, and his Shylock in Shakespeare's *Merchant of Venice* proved that he was also quite equal to Western classics. Strongly dramatic roles, too, such as Nedykhlyayev in Shpazhinsky's *Affliction*, the old man Muromsky in Sukhovo-Kobylin's *The Lawsuit*, were within the range of his talent. Chekhov's *Ivanov* found in him its first and most admirable performer. He was endowed with the powerful gift of revealing his talent also in short plays, for instance, in *The Bridegroom from the Debtors' Prison* (after Dickens), and particularly in Nekrasov's *The Boredom of Autumn*, where he gave a remarkably truthful performance as a uselessly vegetating landowner. He displayed all nuances of his gift in Turgenev's *The Bachelor*. Under proper direction he would have assumed an honored place among the best European actors; but, unguided, he dissipated himself on bagatelles and more readily appeared in plays not worthy of his talent. Numerous though his pupils were, and much as they valued his lessons, perhaps it was this lack of discrimination that prevented him from creating a school with a specific artistic stamp of its own.

K. A. Varlamov (1848–1915), Davydov's colleague, who also emerged from the provincial stage, soon became a favorite of both the Petersburg and provincial public, by which he was cordially nicknamed "Uncle Kostya." In operetta and trifling farce he was always an amusing and colorful performer. Extraordinary innate aptitudes of a genuine farcical comedian in the style of the Italian *commedia dell' arte* also enabled him to appear creditably in plays of the best dramatists: in Turgenev's *Luncheon with the Marshal of Nobility* and *The Bachelor*, in Ostrovsky's *Truth's Good, yet Happiness Is Better*, and in Gogol's *Osip*. He played all these parts admirably, refraining from risky devices of exaggeration which brought him such easy success in worthless plays. His Berendey in *The Snow-Maiden* captivated one not merely by his outward picturesqueness but also by his exceptional emotional warmth, while his Rusakov (Ostrovsky's *Don't Seat Thyself in a Sledge That Isn't Thine*) created a profound impression by the depth of his affliction and repentance.

The parts of dandies—Agishin in *Belugin's Wedding* and Telyatev in *Wild Money*—were excellently performed by V. P. Dalmatov (1862–1912), who left the provincial and private theatres for the Aleksandrinsky stage. By a fatal misunderstanding, he believed himself a tragedian and mutilated the parts of Hamlet and Macbeth.

Young dramatic roles were forcefully and colorfully performed by Mamont Victorovich Dalsky (1865–1918), who appeared with success in *Othello* and *Karl Moor;* but he was at his best in melodramas. An ungovernable disposition and deliberate unwillingness to be considerate with his colleagues made it impossible for him to serve in a properly managed theatre, and soon compelled him to retire to the provincial stage, where his performances amid a miserable company and mise en scène were enthusiastically received.

Of those who played side by side with these provincial products, only a few pupils of the Petersburg Dramatic School were successful. N. F. Sazonov (1843–1902) in his youth played in operettas the parts of Paris and Piquillo, while in his mature years he was a skillful performer of character roles—Andryusha Belugin in *Belugin's Wedding* and Rydlov in Sumbatov's *Gentleman*.

P. M. Svobodin (1850–1892), the most intelligent and conscientious actor in the company, steadily sought to improve his knowledge, notwithstanding the fact that neither his colleagues nor his superiors were disposed to assist him. The utter impossibility of piercing the wall of bureaucratic indifference to the problems of art tormented him and hastened his death (he died during the performance of Ostrovsky's *Jesters,* in which he played the part of Obroshenov). His fate graphically shows how difficult it was for a man devoted to art to live and work in the musty atmosphere of an "actors' bureaucracy" such as dominated the Aleksandrinsky stage, which was devoid of any social significance and hostile to every attempt to rejuvenate it. That theatre was also correctly depicted in the candid memoirs of A. Nilsky and in P. Gnedich's novel *Behind the Footlights,* based on the observations of many years.

Comparison of the Aleksandrinsky Theatre with the Moscow Maly Theatre demonstrates the fact that the latter attained artistic maturity and public influence not because, but in spite, of bureaucratic control. This brilliant page was inscribed in the history of the Russian theatre solely by the creative work of such artists as Shchepkin, the Sadovskys, Yermolova, Fedotova, and Lensky, who managed, without sparing their efforts, to protect "their home" and their work against the onslaughts of the bureaucrats. The obstinacy and arbitrariness of the bureaucrats were all the more dangerous because, up to 1882, the law forbade the organization of private theatres in the capitals, and as a result spectators were deprived of any means of comparison. The evil was eliminated only when the private theatres of A. A. Brenko and, later, of F. A. Korsh were founded.

Originally, Korsh organized a strong company including V. N. Davydov (who had temporarily left the crown stage), N. D. Rybchinskaya, G. I. Martynova, A. Ya. Glama-Mescherskaya, E. F. Krasovskaya, N. N. Kudrina, N. P. Roshchin-Insarov, P. F. Solonin, I. F. Kiselevsky, L. I. Gradov-Sokolov, and V. I. Valentinov. The enterprise was headed by M. V. Agramov, who, as director, produced *Woe from Wit* on October 17, 1877. To Moscow residents this production seemed insolent, since Griboyedov's comedy was regarded as the backbone of the repertoire of the Maly Theatre. However, Davydov-Famusov was in no way inferior to the actors of the crown stage, where, at the time, no one even remotely approached Kiselevsky (1839–1898) in the part of Skalozub. Here, all secondary roles were well acted, whereas in the Maly Theatre they were assigned to persons not at all suited for the stage. (This happens almost invariably when small parts are neglected.) As a result the performance lacked organic unity. Instead of a well worn and miscellaneous stage setting in which all periods were ignored and jumbled together and some roles were acted in virtually contemporary dress, the private theatre gave a strictly consistent and authentic production. Such a scrupulous attitude toward the task was new in Moscow, and it clearly demonstrated the backwardness of the crown stage. The excellent production of *Woe from Wit* was followed by several other successful ones. But Korsh, confident of success once he had firmly established his reputation, soon began to neglect all artistic problems and converted his theatre into a purely commercial enterprise.

Chapter XXI

PLAYWRIGHTS OF THE SECOND HALF
OF THE NINETEENTH CENTURY

IN MAINTAINING a hostile attitude toward Ostrovsky, the theatrical administration had at its disposal a sufficient number of its favorite playwrights, to whose mediocre work it accorded full leeway. Foremost among them were the author of *The Governess*, V. A. Dyachenko (1818–1876), and his successors V. A. Krylov (1838–1906), I. V. Shpazhinsky (1832–1897), and P. N. Nevezhin (1841–1919). The prevalence of their plays was "convenient" to influential actresses and actors alike, so that the plays of creative writers faced a hard uphill struggle and only in exceptional cases found their way to the stage.

Our literature of the 1860's was distinctly marked by social criticism. The foremost author of plays of this character was certainly Saltykov-Shchedrin, about whom A. M. Gorky said:

The range of his creative sweep was remarkable. He kept abreast of life, without remaining even a step behind it; fixedly he looked it in the face, and bitterly and prophetically he ridiculed everybody and everything. This was not Gogol's laughter—it was something far more deafening, truthful, profound, and potent. Without the aid of Shchedrin it would be impossible to comprehend Russia's history of the second half of the nineteenth century.

And N. G. Chernyshevsky wrote:

In no writer prior to Shchedrin had our ways of living been painted in such dark hues. No one chastised our social evils with greater mercilessness. Every decent Russian is Shchedrin's sincere admirer.

However, precisely because of the power of social criticism in his creative work, censorship and the theatre administration were extremely hostile to every attempt to produce his plays on the stage. Thus, in 1856 *Bygone Times*—the dramatization of one of the chapters of *Provincial Sketches*—was interdicted; and in 1857 *Petitioners,* an adaptation of the fourth chapter, suffered the same fate after having been designated for Linskaya's benefit-night performance of October 31. Instead she was compelled to use the producer-director N. Kulikov's adaptation *Mrs. Muzovkina's Story,* a play which was rarely produced on the stage afterward.

On September 8, 1857, scenes from the *Provincial Sketches* were produced on the benefit night of the actor Grigoryev. In 1880 A. A. Brenko's private theatre staged N. Kulikov's adaptation of the remarkable chronicle *The Messrs. Golovlev,* entitled *Little Judas.* Saltykov-Shchedrin himself called this adaptation "idiocy," and refused to see it when it was transferred to Petersburg. However, impartial judges took a different attitude, and particularly praised V. N. Andreyev-Burlak's performance of the leading part of Little Judas. This character in Shchedrin's delineation, by reason of its profound veracity and polish, is not inferior to the best creation of Molière and Dickens. In later days Little Judas was brilliantly impersonated on the stage by I. N. Bersenev in Sukhotin's play with the strange title *The Victor's Shadow,* in which he added to *The Messrs. Golovlev* excerpts from *The Tales* and *Messieurs et Mesdames Pompadours.* His well deserved success was shared by S. Birman, S. V. Giatsintova, Gotovtsev, and A. Cheban, the latter having created a profoundly truthful image of the new "life's master"—the merchant Kukishev.

Saltykov-Shchedrin was a close observer of theatrical life, as may be seen from his spiteful but most pointed articles in the magazine *The Contemporary* [1] Sardou's and Augier's comedies, which were then being given at the Mikhailovsky Theatre, furnished him with the pretext, in an article "Dramaturgists—Parasites in France," to portray the complete disintegration of France under Napoleon III, where "the feeling of the capon's satisfaction penetrated all social strata and the offsprings of all ages." His notes on Russian actors of both capitals demonstrate the fact that among dramatic critics of those days hardly anyone comprehended better than he the act-

[1] Nos. 1, 2, 1863—either unsigned, or signed "K. Curin."

ing of artists. Here, for example, is his definition of Samoilov's talent: "An actor of all lands and ages, but preeminently—of all costumes." He venomously observed that Samoilov was particularly admirable in—the ballet. Why actors refused to help stage the plays of so rigorous a judge will be readily understood.

Only on December 2, 1893, on Varlamov's benefit night, the Aleksandrinsky Theatre produced *Pazukhin's Death*, which had been prohibited by the censor since 1857. The beneficiary played the part of Furnachyov, akin to the covetous hypocrite Little Judas; Davydov, Pazukhin; Pisarev, Finagey Bayev. This fearful play exhibits a repulsive gallery of monsters who center all their thoughts and feelings on the heavy chest in which the old leaseholder Pazukhin has hidden the stolen capital. In order to extract and seize the property, his children and kinsmen wage a desperate struggle, revealing the turpitude of a family which conceals its unquenchable thirst for money under the hypocritical mask of ostentatious virtue. Long years of service in provincial Russia enabled Shchedrin to discover, in a well studied milieu, living originals for a drama which presents perhaps the most hideous picture of merchant life ever offered on our stage.

Pazukhin's Death did not long survive on the stage of the crown theatre. It was revived by V. I. Nemirovich-Danchenko on December 3, 1914, at the Art Theatre with B. Kustodiyev's colorful stage settings.

A genuine tragedy of serfdom was created by Ostrovsky's fellow townsman A. F. Pisemsky (1820–1881) in *Bitter Fate*. The two playwrights are similar in their mastery of a truthful portrayal of life around them, in their sensitive attention to local living conditions, in their penetration into the inner souls of their characters, and also in their delineation and the structure of their speech, which they elaborated with remarkable diversity in each separate character. But Ostrovsky created a whole cycle of plays outstanding from an artistic standpoint and mutually supplementing one another, whereas Pisemsky exhausted himself as a dramatist in the one play. It cannot even be compared with his other dramatic works, which left no trace in the history of the theatre.

Bitter Fate is based on an actual occurrence in peasant life which Pisemsky might have learned about as early as 1848 in his official duties. This correlation with an actual court episode is reflected even in the names of several persons in the play. True, he also could have made use of Kraszewski's novel of similar content, which was written in 1842 and appeared in a Russian translation in the columns of the *Library for Reading* one year before the appearance of the play.

Pisemsky's drama was submitted to the Academy of Sciences in the contest for Uvarov's prize, and there it was critically analyzed. I. F. Annensky pointed out that its tragic quality is derived wholly from the horror of unvarnished truth; its text is marked by no showy moments, and the final scenes of the acts are without the nerve-racking passages favored by French romantics of the mid-century. It is altogether devoid of idealization of the dramatis personae. It is a social tragedy because

its dramas, both those brightly flashing and those already extinct, wiped out, and suppressed, do not grow out of personal qualities, or complex spiritual life or conflict of one will with another, or a fatal sweep of passion proudly challenging the order of things, but out of a complicated and deeply imbedded pattern of life which has peculiarly crippled, effaced, and oppressed many human lives.

Annensky also shrewdly observed the enormous advantage of Pisemsky's tragedy over earlier plays, including L. Tolstoy's *The Power of Darkness,* in that it contains not even a hint of didacticism, and no *raisonneur* such as Tolstoy's Akim.

According to Pisemsky's original scheme, Anany was to become a robber who would return to the village and murder the mayor; but A. E. Martynov persuaded him to include Anany's penitence in the dénouement.

Among Pesimsky's other plays, *Self-Styled Law Enforcers* (*Samoupravtsy*) is historically accurate. In 1866 it was produced on the Aleksandrinsky stage, where V. V. Samoilov scored particular success in the part of the jealous old man. This tragedy was included in the repertoire of the first season of the Moscow Art Theatre, where the final scene of the people's movement was produced with unprecedented power.

The Narodniki movement [2] of the sixties found its representative in playwriting in A. A. Potekhin (1829–1908). His first—extremely

[2] Described by Ushakov as "a social and political movement of radical intelligentsia during the second half of the nineteenth century."—Ed.

naïve—play, *Men's, Not God's, Judgment,* appeared in the March, 1853, issue of the *Moskvityanin (Muscovite).* It was a sharp protest against serfdom, and overcame the censor's objections only with the assistance of M. P. Pogodin and Grand Duke Konstantin Nikolayevich. It was produced on the Moscow stage on November 29, 1854. Permeated with a sentiment which then inspired a certain part of society, it had a success enhanced by the superb acting of Nikulina-Kositskaya in the leading part of Matryona. Having personally experienced the delights of serfdom, she deeply and vividly absorbed her role, and her inspired acting greatly aided the author.

Potekhin's best play, *Another's Wealth Does Not Aid Me,* is important because he abandoned in it his former abstract and artificial representation of peasant ways of living and showed a real peasant. And this realistic image was destined to remove from Russian drama the earlier bookish peasant. In the carriage driver Mishenka, the involuntary villain of the piece, Potekhin managed, especially in the famous narrative, to depict the boldness of his broad nature, in which one perceives genuine strains of the driver's daring song. Here the author was assisted by the actor Martynov. In his memoirs Potekhin wrote: "From the first glance at Martynov's figure, from the first word he uttered, one could feel life and truth on the stage. Not an actor made up and dressed as a peasant, but a genuine, real, young peasant yamshik appeared on the stage of the theatre." Yet even here Potekhin did not escape tendentiousness. Depicting with finesse the course which brought the complacent lad to attempted patricide, he made his Mishenka a tool in the hands of the wretched house servant, seeking to reveal in this character the full strength of the degrading influence of the master's servants.

In 1867 Stebnitsky (N. S. Leskov, 1831–1895), the author of novels which in those days were too highly rated, produced in the Aleksandrinsky Theatre his play *The Dissipator.* A rich young merchant is declared a dissipator. He is victimized by his guardian, who after drowning his father and debauching him compels him to marry a woman at once wicked and foolish. He leaves his wife and goes abroad, where he studies factory management; on his return home, he endeavors to share with the workers the profits of the plant. His project arouses the indignation of all the other merchants. Taking advantage of the situation, the guardian, with a view to concealing misappropriations which he has perpetrated in the course of his duties, induces the merchants to declare his ward a dissipator, to establish custody over his property, and to lock him up in an insane asylum.

The villainous guardian, the old debauchee, who through persistence and craftiness manages to gain full control over the apathetic merchants and rule the town by decree, is well delineated. the old rake's other victim, the daring and beautiful Marina, is excellently conceived. These three characters provide the performers with gratifying material. Even early in the twentieth century, the tragedian F. P. Gorev liked to appear in the play. The frame for the principal characters was furnished by the horrible conditions of family and public life, and the entire picture is consistently painted with the powerful hues of the social satire of the sixties. For all the roles, even the minor ones, the author managed to find a rich language taken directly from life.

Leskov made a bold departure from the customary dramatic construction both by avoiding stereotyped figures and by discovering unusual methods for the delineation even of the love intrigue that was demanded in those days. Yet he did not escape the major vice of all of his creative work, the lack of a sense of proportion. In consequence he overloaded the play by introducing in the action scenes depicting the courtroom; the workers' drinking bout accompanied by songs and dancing; the siege of a cellar in which the heroine hides, as in any melodrama; the fire in the town, with alarm bells ringing, to the sound of which Marina and her lover, the ill starred "dissipator," die. The play has a full array of typical figures which, however, are altogether unnecessary. The main theme is obscured by witty, yet wholly superfluous, anecdotes. Leskov, who in his articles so cleverly analyzed other authors' plays, did not avoid their shortcomings in his own. He wrote nothing more for the stage, and therefore could not develop the novel devices of the strictly original dramatic elaborations which, in some scenes, so favorably distinguished his play from the stereotyped drama of the epoch.

The plays of A. V. Sukhovo-Kobylin (1817–1903), who belonged to the wealthy nobility and was a childhood friend of Herzen, are rather unique. From 1850 to 1857 he was kept under indictment, charged with the murder of his French mistress. Having, therefore, studied all too closely the setting of criminal investigations and court trials which prevailed during the epoch of Nicholas I, he filled his trilogy (*Krechinsky's Wedding, The Lawsuit,* and *Tarelkin's Death*) with these impressions. The first play, depicting the frauds of the fashionable sharper Krechinsky, was staged in Petersburg in 1856. The part of Krechinsky was brilliantly performed by Samoilov, who skillfully made his evil ways apparent through outward gloss. In the course of this he used his favorite device of coloring his speech with foreign accents, and thus gave to the whole part a touch of the Polish nobleman. The author was delighted with his acting and thought him superior to the Moscow performer Shumsky, who was "too elegant." In later days, the part of Krechinsky, in the style of Samoilov, was played by I. F. Kiselevsky, while V. P. Dalmatov was nearer to Shumsky's interpretation. Prov Sadovsky, as Rasplyuyev, roused the author's indignation because he made the character too vulgar, and played a petty filcher instead of a nobleman admitted to the exclusive English Club and received at the very proper home of the noble Muromsky. However, Sadovsky's example has been followed by the majority of the performers of the role, including V. N. Davydov and Stepan Kuznetsov.

Censorship took an unfavorable view of *The Lawsuit*. This tragedy depicts with exceptional force the "black injustice" of the old courts, and boldly brands both the petty and the big spoliators, such as Nightingale the Robber, for ruining and defaming honest people "under the protective shadow of a dreamy forest of laws, by means of traps, snares, and fishing rods of justice." The part of the ruined Muromsky was performed with outstanding effectiveness by V. N. Davydov, and in the eighties Andreyev-Burlak successfully played the role of the village mayor. In 1900–1901 the play was revived by the Moscow Maly Theatre, when the part of the chief of the bureaucratic gang, Varravin, was performed by Rybakov; that of Muromsky, by Lensky; and O. A. Pravdin appeared in the role of Tarelkin.

Tarelkin's Death takes place in a police station. Tarelkin, tied to a chair, is brought in for questioning by patrolmen. The tortures of the man subjected to the "third degree" are reproduced directly from life. However, they are portrayed within a frame of semi-

fantastic buffoonery, so that the performance becomes an applica-
tion to drama of the devices used by Gogol in his story *The Nose*.
Nevertheless, even within this unusual setting, all methods of
the old police investigations are reproduced with complete authenticity. Here Rasplyuyev appears in the guise of a police officer who,
in an outburst of inspiration, gives the command: "Arrest all
Russia!"

The play was first presented on October 15, 1900, at the A. S.
Suvorin Theatre under the title *The Merry Days of Rasplyuyev*.
In October, 1917, this most peculiar play was produced on the
Aleksandrinsky stage, and in November, 1922, it was given in
Moscow. Arbitrary efforts to make the performance strictly formal-
istic by means of circus tricks obscured the content. In 1902
Krechinsky's Wedding was shown in Paris. French critics gave
high praise to the extraordinary clarity of the comedy, finding in
its lightness and in the precision of its portrayals close resemblance
to the manner of Scribe, their master of dramatic technique.

I. S. Turgenev's plays occupy a place of their own. Perhaps because in them the tendency toward social criticism does not appear
so baldly as in Gogol and Sukhovo-Kobylin, they failed to win
appreciation among critics and the popularity on the stage which
they unquestionably deserved.

Turgenev, like the majority of young landowners of that period,
had an opportunity to familiarize himself with the theatre at a very
early age in his parents' home, where "noble" shows were staged.
Much later, he eagerly took part in such amateur entertainments.
Thus in 1855 Grigorovich, Druzhinin, and Vasily Botkin were his
guests at Spasskoye. In collaboration with them he wrote a farce
in which he played. In later days he used to recall this with pleasure. On several occasions he wrote French librettos for operettas to
the music of his friend Madame Viardot; and he himself appeared
in comic parts.

As a student Turgenev wrote the tragedy *Stenio* in five-foot
iambs and showed it to Professor Pletnyov; but it never appeared in
print. He began to occupy himself seriously with playwrighting
toward the close of the 1840's.

His first dramatic piece, *Indiscretion*, was based on Spanish life,
in which he was then keenly interested. It closely resembled Prosper
Mérimée's *Le Théâtre de Clara Gazul*, which Pushkin classed

among "unusually remarkable works," and borrowed from it all the names of its dramatis personae. Its only production on the stage was in 1884, when a German company in Petersburg gave it two or three times in a German version.

Turgenev wrote the majority of his plays while sojourning in France. Their chronological sequence is as follows: *Where It's Thin It's Apt to Tear*, 1847; *The Boarder*, 1848; *The Bachelor* and *Luncheon with the Marshal of Nobility*, 1849; *A Month in the Country*, 1850.

Turgenev made his stage début with the comedy *The Bachelor*. It distinctly shows the influence of Gogol's creative work in individual characters—particularly Shpundik; in the servants' habit of wallowing on sofas; and, even more, in the selection of the milieu, so vividly depicted in Gogol's Petersburg novels.

The Bachelor was brought to Petersburg by Shchepkin. At the termination of his tour as guest artist during the 1849–1850 season, the play was, as it were, sent to the archives, probably because no one ventured to perform the part of Moshkin after him. In the scene where he read the letter in which the fiancé of his pupil renounces her, Shchepkin was particularly successful, his reading being interrupted by genuine tears of indignation.

In 1899 the Aleksandrinsky Theatre revived *The Bachelor*. Davydov in the leading part astounded the audience by the masterful transitions from one mood to another, and by the meticulous presentation of the most minute details of a profoundly delineated character. Mashenka was played by Komissarzhevskaya, who revealed with captivating tenderness the helpless situation of an orphan. Along with Davydov and Komissarzhevskaya, Varlamov (Shpundik) and Strelskaya (Katerina Savishna) gave brilliant performances distinguished by their truthfulness and rich humor.

Luncheon with the Marshal of Nobility, which was produced simultaneously with *The Bachelor*, pleased the public, especially because of the landlady Kaurova, who busies herself with the division of property, refusing, however, to accede to any proposal. Meanwhile she continually complains about alleged offenses and persecution, regarding everybody as her enemy. According to contemporaries, "Sosnitskaya impersonated this character with striking accuracy." In the *Luncheon with the Marshal of Nobility*, aside from a masterful portrayal of the figures of the "defenseless widow" Kaurova and her brother Bezpandin, one is impressed with the characterization of county nobility at large, from the landowner Mirvolin, who has sunk to the level of a toady, to Pekhteryev, skillfully weaving his intrigues to secure the position of marshal of nobility. The scene of the division of the estate between Kaurova and her brother is indisputably one of the finest episodes of Russian comedy.

The Provincial Lady, which was staged in 1850, met with greater success than the first two plays.

The Boarder was produced in 1861. The leading part of Kuzovkin was played by Vasilyev II. He was particularly good in the scene where he was compelled to perform jesters' tricks in the presence of his daughter, uttering "What for? What for?" with such emotional appeal that the whole theatre was shaken by applause. Abroad, the Italian tragedian Novelli scored particular success in this play; his acting made it intelligible to a public which was not familiar with Russian customs.

Turgenev's longest play, *A Month in the Country,* was first produced in Moscow in 1872. In Petersburg it was given on the benefit night of Savina, who admirably performed the part of Verochka; subsequently, in 1903, she turned to the role of Natalya Petrovna and played it with equal success.

P. O. Morozov says:

In Turgenev's plays we see typical figures, now touching and now amusing, but always interesting because they reflect our life of those days, home life—intimate, family, and personal—with its little joys and sorrows, everyday "dull" preoccupations and troubles, good fortunes and misfortunes. These are in no sense heroes, but most ordinary, most mediocre people, portrayed with delicate humor and with deep understanding of their inner being which is not readily revealed to the superficial observer. Turgenev loves these people. By the strength of that love and of his talent he arouses in the reader and spectator both attention to and sympathy with their fate. Their existence, poor in outward circumstances, acquires a particular interest for us because the author throws light on all its inner significance, revealing to us even the slightest emotional impulses of the dramatic personae and making us virtual participants in their inner lives. The most valuable aspect of Turgenev's dramatic works is just this delicate psychological treatment and the masterful delineation of the characters—qualities which in a large measure compensate for the lack of specific dramatic action, of outward illusions, of seething life.

All this is particularly noticeable in *A Month in the Country,* where Turgenev

portrays life in his characteristic mild hues, without ignoring the most minute, scarcely visible details. The tender, graceful coloring of the life of the old "nest of gentlefolk" is disturbed now and then by the intrusion of pressing, always rather gross, reality, which under Turgenev's pen acquires a slightly humorous coloring. This provides the play with an original, vital background and a distinctive setting.

In comparison with his predecessors, Turgenev also made an enormous forward stride in the representation of the subjective world of his dramatis personae. Prior to him, dramatists solved the problem in a much simpler fashion by attributing to each character a specific passion, in the belief that the more strongly the passion dominated him, the more successful and the more vivid the character would be. The whole dramatic conflict was centered on the overcoming of obstacles which passions of other men created for the realization of the aims of the principal character.

But Turgenev transferred the strife to the subjective world of a single person, making the different tempers of his own soul struggle against each other. Natalya Petrovna, in *A Month in the Country,* lives through such a struggle, and for this reason the description of her inner life is particularly profound. She alone is responsible for her suffering, and if in former times the persons in every play were divided into villains and their victims, her villains and victims are united in one individual. Instead of a sharp, rectilinear portrayal of the sentiments and moods of his characters, Turgenev frequently made their emotions smolder in the depth of the soul, whence they would unexpectedly emerge, taking the person himself by surprise, and for that reason revealing all the more forcefully their power over him.

Likewise Turgenev's characters manifest their feelings in a far more delicate fashion: the spectator does not realize at the outset with whom he is dealing, since the real sentiments and designs are revealed only gradually. One must watch every word, for the key to an understanding of the temper of a particular person, of his swift transitions from one mood to another, may be given in a slight hint contained in a sudden exclamation slipping from his tongue. In this respect the one-act play *Where It's Thin It's Apt to Tear* is particularly good. Here, the characters of a young girl and her two admirers are portrayed with unsurpassed mastery. It is impossible not to delight in the perfection of the graceful dialogue, skillfully woven like fine lace. At the same time, the author, by cleverly grouping the details, gives a vivid conception of the milieu in which the action takes place, thus conveying to the audience its peculiar mood.

Where It's Thin It's Apt to Tear in many details resembles the novel *Correspondence* (1855), in which the last letter portrays Turgenev's own situation within Viardot's family. Together with *The Provincial Lady* and *An Evening in Sorrento,* this comedy reminds one of Alfred de Musset's dramatic *proverbes.*

Turgenev did not live much in Russia. He had neither time nor desire for the unceasing effort and insistent solicitation to obtain production of his plays. Besides, he lacked the support of an ardent literary group. He had also few actor friends. If some of them boldly embarked upon his plays, the majority, spoiled by melodramas and vaudevilles, were not equal to his exquisite, and—as they were called—"overdelicate" creations. This was specifically expressed in an epigram of P. Karatygin, a true echo of the opinion which prevailed backstage:

> Although Turgenev did attain great fame,
> The stage to him is far from being fair:
> His comedy's so thin that one can't blame
> Him who admits—where 'tis thin it's apt to tear.

To actors educated on Polevoy and Obodovsky, Turgenev's plays were too refined. They were devoid of the crude, garish colors of favorite playwrights; nor was there in them that gratifying tendency which saved the play and unfailingly rewarded the actor with applause, not for his acting but for the content of the words he spoke. Turgenev frequently wrote that in art "truth is that air without which it is impossible to breathe."

Where It's Thin It's Apt to Tear presents to the performers a most difficult problem because of the unique delicacy of the dialogue, which is based on scarcely noticeable transitions. In 1912 this problem was brilliantly solved at the Moscow Art Theatre, where V. I. Kachalov, in the part of Gorsky, produced an example of the loftiest mastery of speech. Neither spectators nor actors were used to such finesse in acting and such an exquisite artistic manner; they were accustomed to plays in which all *i*'s were dotted and all *t*'s crossed; in which an entire monologue was devoted to every impulse of the soul and every change in the individual's mood; and in which the spectator was told in the utmost detail everything he was supposed to know. Here, however, the monologue was replaced by terse repartee, at times only one line long. Of course, if the traditional manner of acting were adhered to, all of this would be meaningless and lost.

In 1909 the Art Theatre produced *A Month in the Country*, under the supervision of Stanislavsky and Moskvin. Stage settings by M. V. Dobuzhinsky presented an admirable picture of country life on an estate; every detail of the sets conveys the tender lyricism with which this exquisite psychological play is permeated.

In Turgenev's plays Martynov found fertile soil for his talent. Nekrasov wrote in *The Bachelor*, "Martynov performed the part of Shpundik successfully and artistically, which was the more remarkable since his role is one of the most insignificant." In 1859 he played the part of the bachelor Moshkin, and twenty-five years later Turgenev recalled with warm gratitude "the vivid and tender image" created by the actor just before his career came to an end.

Martynov also appeared in *The Provincial Lady* in the part of Stupendyev, which was played by Shchepkin in Moscow. The part of Count Lyubin was performed there by Shumsky, and in Petersburg by V. V. Samoilov. Turgenev himself noted in a letter that Samoilov was far inferior to Shumsky. "Samoilov's acting is wholly formal, and, essentially, quite monotonous."

Turgenev's plays were highly regarded abroad. The best Italian actors appeared in *The Boarder*. In Paris it was produced by Antoine. In Vienna, as well as in Germany, *The Provincial Lady* and *A Month in the Country* were often produced with the same success. The latter was regarded as an adaptation of Scribe's *The Ladies' Battle*; in point of fact, however, its plot is much more like that of Balzac's *Stepmother*. Even so, Turgenev introduced in his intrigue a wholly different milieu and quite distinctively delineated his characters. He likewise eliminated all traces of the melodramatic manner present in Balzac, and brought the mutual relations of the principal characters nearer to living truth.

The end of the sixties was marked by the appearance of many plays concerned with Russian history. Among them, the most significant from an artistic standpoint was the production on the Aleksandrinsky stage of the tragedy *The Death of Ivan the Terrible*, the first part of a trilogy by Aleksey Konstantinovich Tolstoy (1817–1875). The administration paid special attention to it and tried to make the costumes and properties both splendid and historically authentic, engaging an expert archaeologist to assist the directors. Such hitherto unheard-of care was due less to the literary prominence of the author—the administration both earlier and later often staged plays of even greater writers with inexcusable carelessness—than to his influence at court.

The first production of *The Death of Ivan the Terrible* failed to secure for it a leading place in the repertoire. This was partly the author's own fault, since in exercising his right to select the cast he mistakenly assigned the part of Ivan the Terrible to Vasilyev II, who specialized in the performance of comic roles. Poor judgment was likewise shown in the assignment of the role in Moscow to Shumsky.

The staging of the play was exemplary. Director Yablochkin showed much mastery in the mass scenes. After the first night Vasilyev performed the part of Ivan about five more times, and then Samoilov began to appear in it. One cannot say that he gave an adequate portrayal of the stern Tsar. The figure of Vasilyev Vasilyevich, though handsome and elegant, was not majestic, and did not suit the character he impersonated. This failure of both Vasilyev and Samoilov in the performance of the part of Ivan gave the eminent poet D. D. Minayev the pretext for this epigram:

> To thee I do address this lachrymose request:
> Pray tell, what did this acting mean?
> Vasily Vasil'ch and Vasilyev Paul [3]—they both were on the scene,
> But Ivan Vasil'ch the Terrible, where was he? That's my quest.

Despite the shortcomings inherent in the trilogy, especially its last part, it may be compared in artistic polish with Schiller's dramas. In his world outlook and psychic aspect, Tolstoy most

[3] That is, Vasily Vasilyevich Samoilov and Paul (Pavel) Vasilyev II.—Transl.

closely resembled Schiller, whose works he knew to perfection. For this reason it is not too bold to suggest that the character of the King in *The Maid of Orleans* exercised an influence upon the creation of the image of Tsar Fyodor and on the description of his attitude toward Irina; and Irina has certain traits in common with Agnès Sorel. The opening scenes of *The Death of Ivan the Terrible,* in their construction, are also quite similar to Schiller's.

The character of Ivan the Terrible, in the first part of the trilogy, reminds one in some respects of the portrayal of Louis XI in Delavigne's well known play, which was quite popular in the Russian repertoire of Karatygin's epoch. It seems that Aleksey Tolstoy appropriated from the French play certain devices and dramatic situations, of course substantially improving them and in many ways giving them a much more profound and refined treatment. The essential distinction between Ivan and the French hero lies in the sincerity of his conduct, which is particularly emphasized by Tolstoy in explanatory notes dealing with this character.

Boris Godunov is the least successful part of the trilogy. The play seems unnecessarily long-winded. This is particularly noticeable in the beginning—for example, in the scene of the ambassadors' reception, which is monotonous and, therefore, tiresome. Certain parts in the play are insufficiently elaborated, for instance, that of Semyon Godunov, who frequently appears on the stage solely to provide Boris with a convenient interlocutor to whom he expounds his hidden thoughts.

In a comprehensive analysis of the tragedy *Tsar Fyodor Ioannovich,* P. V. Annenkov shows that it and the first part of the trilogy are exclusively founded on the consummate psychological episode of the principal character, while all other elements of their content are mere supplements to the main theme. The critic emphasizes the poet's masterly treatment of the characters of both Tsar Fyodor and Irina. His merit is all the greater because the material for the characterization of the first focal personage in the play was very meager, and yet

out of this scanty and far from tragic material the author created Fyodor's character, which is remarkable for its inner substance. He made him a sick man, unfit for work, but possessing such treasures of the heart, such wealth of affection for men, and endowed with such angelic chastity with respect to himself and to others, that this impotent ruler often elevates himself to the comprehension of human characters; his decisions, by their wisdom, excel those expressed by everybody around him—by all those who voice their opinions and attempt to counsel him. The tragedy of his situation lies in the impotence of his physical and moral nature, contrasted with the noblest instincts and designs.

The critic pays tribute to Tolstoy's familiarity with history; however, he points out that this did not prevent him from introducing into the play details hardly conceivable in the milieu. Such, for instance, is Irina's conduct in the final scene, which is completely at variance with the Moscow ceremonial. Similarly, the behavior of both the conspirators and Boris himself rather smacks of acts and customs of Western men.

Scattered through the trilogy are a number of scenes of high artistic merit, such as: Ivan's negotiations with the boyars who implore him to assume power again; the reception of the ambassador Garaburda; the reading of Kurbsky's letter and of the obituaries of Ivan's victims; the last scene preceding Ivan's death; the reading to Fyodor Ioannovich of state papers; Prince Vasily Shuisky's toast at Romanov's feast and his speech about the Impostor. Some students compare these scenes, in their dramatic power of expression and stylistic mastery, with those of Shakespeare.

However, the trilogy has substantial shortcomings. For example, in the second part the love episode is an utter failure:

To begin with [critics maintain], it is altogether superfluous, because the boyars' petition for the divorce of the Tsar and the Tsarina could have reached the Tsar in some other—and more natural—way. Besides, the scenes with Princess Mstislavskaya and Shakhovskoy appear comic, instead of producing a tender effect. One really is inclined to doubt that in those days all girls in Russia were like Princess Mstislavskaya. In the person of Shakhovskoy love in general is ridiculed.

The following observations of P. P. Gnedich on Aleksey Tolstoy's trilogy seem quite correct:

He wrote his trilogy under the influence of Delavigne and Shakespeare, and also, perhaps, Bulwer-Lytton. It is of little import that simultaneously the traits of Macbeth and Minister of Interior Timashev are attributed to Godunov, and that Ivan the Terrible resembles Louis XI. Even so, after Pushkin's Boris, these are our best dramas.

Aleksey Tolstoy appended to the first two parts of his trilogy comprehensive plans for their production. In them he explained in detail his attitude toward the historical events depicted in his plays, defined the meaning of both, and suggested their general tone. Further, he analyzed each role separately, with most subtle and interesting psychological observations, stating the reasons why he had introduced the given role and defining its relation to other characters. He also issued a warning against dangerous errors of interpretation; likewise, he made suggestions as to costumes and manners, indicating the works in which respective illustrations might be found, and so forth.

The sketch concerning the role of Bityagovsky in the first part of the trilogy, and of Kleshnin in the second, may serve as specimens of his analysis of individual roles. The author also comments upon the scenery and properties to be used in the production of his plays.

In the plan for the staging of *Fyodor Ioannovich* one discerns a faint polemic note; it seems that the author elaborated his scheme also with a view to defending his literary methods from attacks by the too zealous partisans of Russian independent creative art.

The second part of the triology, *Tsar Fyodor Ioannovich*, the production of which had long been prohibited, was presented by P. P. Gnedich on October 12, 1898, in the Suvorinsky Theatre. P. N. Orlyonev played the part of Tsar Fyodor with the deliberate intent of giving to the spectacle (which was repeated many times) a direct political meaning.

That tragedy when it was produced by the Moscow Art Theatre with the part of Fyodor in the hands of I. M. Moskvin, who by his performance at once assumed a leading place among Russian actors, opened a new and brilliant page in the history of the universal art of the theatre.

N. A. Chayev (1828–1914) also wrote historical plays. A fellow townsman of Ostrovsky, he held the position of director of the Moscow Theatres for a short time after Ostrovsky's death. Among his plays *Kinsman Fadeich* (1864) is particularly interesting; it depicts the widespread movement of the people against landowners, and critics acclaimed it as "a genuinely popular piece."

Noteworthy also is *Mother-in-Law* (1867), adapted from the legend about Prince Mikhail, in which Glikeriya Nikolayevna

Fedotova masterfully played the young princess poisoned by her mother-in-law.

In addition, Chayev wrote *Dmitry the Impostor* (1866), *1613, or The Election of Mikhail Fyodorovich to the Throne* (1861), and *Tsar Vasily Shuisky* (1883). In the last, on the basis of original sources, the complex character of the eminent boyar received an altogether unique interpretation. Weaker are the plays dealing with contemporary life, namely, *The Lonesome* (*Biryuk*, 1874)— taking its name from that given to the professor of astronomy— and *The Snipe*. The milieu of zemstvo workers is depicted in the comedy *You Should Know Us* (1876). An observer of the life of the Maly Theatre over many years, Chayev was particularly close to Prov Sadovsky, whose influence is noticeable in his plays, written in animated and colorful language derived from a most scrupulous study of ancient records.

D. V. Averkiyev's (1836–1905) drama *The Antiquities of Kashirsk* (1872) depicts the outrages of the boyars against their poor neighbors and has many scenes advantageous to actors, so that our best actors of the seventies, eighties and nineties readily appeared in it. The comedy about Frol Skobeyev, adapted from a novel of the end of the seventeenth century, was given with similar success on the stages of the so-called "popular" theatres.

Noteworthy is Averkiyev's attempt to introduce the characters of Russian fairy tales into the frame of Aristophanes' comedy: *Wealth* (*The Golden Grandfather*). For many years he was one of the most prominent dramatic critics of both capitals. In 1895 he published an excellent translation of Shakespeare's *Hamlet*, and in 1893 a book *On Drama*, in which he revealed a good knowledge of Western classical drama and of Pushkin, whose *Boris Godunov* he ranked with the best dramatic creations.

By the last decade of the nineteenth century, the plays of L. N. Tolstoy (1828–1910) had become a most valuable contribution to our dramatic art. In his article "On Shakespeare and Drama," subjecting the dramatic works of Goethe, Hugo, Pushkin, A. K. Tolstoy, and Ostrovsky to most severe criticism, he adds: "Let the reader not think that I am excluding from evaluation of drama those theatrical pieces which I have accidentally written."

However, it is more than an accident that Leo Tolstoy throughout the greater part of his creative career (from 1856 to 1909) repeatedly resorted to the dramatic form, and dramatized sixteen plots with varying degrees of perfection: *Free Love; Uncle's Blessing; A Nobleman's Family; Practical Man; A Contaminated Family; The Nihilist; Aggey; Peter the Boarder; The First Distiller; The Power of Darkness; She Used Too Much Cunning; The Fruits of Enlightenment; The Living Corpse; And Light Shines in Darkness; Children's Wisdom;* and *All Qualities from Her.* His persistent tendency to write for the stage was predicated on his conception of drama as "probably the most influential province of art." Sharply criticizing the decadence of the contemporary bourgeois theatre and the "triviality and immorality" of bourgeois playwriting, he enthusiastically welcomed the idea of a people's theatre during the last decade of his life. To P. A. Denisenko, who was planning to start a magazine devoted to the popular theatre, he wrote with great sympathy: "The problem with which you are preoccupied—a people's theatre—is likewise of great concern to me. And I should be glad if I could be of assistance to it."

On peasants' theatrical shows, he commented: "This is a powerful means and, above all, a direct one."

The Power of Darkness (1886) and *The Fruits of Enlightenment* (1889), are Tolstoy's principal plays.

The plot of *The Power of Darkness* was derived from a court case of Yefrem Koloskov, which was communicated to him by a close acquaintance, the Tula prosecutor, who recalled:

This was a case of the murder of a peasant girl's newborn child by its father, a distant relative with whom she lived in the same family and in the same house. The peculiar characteristic of the case, aside from the dramatic setting of the murder itself, was the conduct of the murderer, who, racked by conscience, publicly confessed of his own accord to the crime. Later he craved trial and punishment, and, even though he was convicted and sentenced to hard labor, he was pleased with the penalty, considering it as the expiation of his sin, an alleviation, and a chance to continue life.

This topic enabled Tolstoy to paint with overwhelming effect a picture of the destitute, ruined, and ignorant village, agonizing under the yoke of Imperial and landowner exploitation, and to create a remarkable gallery of character types from the peasant life which he knew so well. The realism with which the great writer revealed the hopelessness of the people's life was so merciless that the government of Alexander III categorically prohibited production of the play under the hypocritical pretext that it was "immoral."

However, in this work, we see also graphically reflected those contradictions in Tolstoy's mentality which V. I. Lenin discerned with such gifted insight. His ideals are expressed in the righteous old man Akim, who, as with all Tolstoy's heroes of this pattern, is pictured as extraordinarily benign and meek. He advocates the preservation of the principles of natural peasant economy, and renounces everything connected with town and urban culture. This character serves as an excellent illustration of Lenin's well known words about Tolstoy:

An ardent protestant, a passionate accuser, a great critic, he at the same time revealed the kind of lack of understanding of the causes of the impending Russian crisis, and of the means of its solution, that is typical only of a patriarchal, naïve peasant, and not of a writer on European culture.[4]

The Fruits of Enlightenment was the outgrowth of a short comedy originally jotted down by Tolstoy for performance at home. According to a critic's pointed definition, he showed in it

the two-faced aspect of old Russia: on the one hand, the Russia of the nobility with spiritualistic séances and bourgeois liberalism—the Russia with silk lining; and on the other, the Russia shivering under a straw roof, the Russia ruled by darkness. In the latter, in lieu of spiritualistic séances, the practices of conjurers and charmers prevail; in lieu of choice liqueurs, vodka, of which there are "all qualities"; in lieu of thousands of dessiatines, everlasting toil in the face of scarcity of land, "with no room for even a chick."

In the rough drafts of the play Tolstoy specifically named those representatives of the idling and sporting Moscow nobility who served as prototypes for his Zvezdintsevs, that is, the Samarins, the Lvovs, and others.

"By birth and upbringing," wrote Lenin, "Tolstoy belonged to the highest stratum of landowning aristocracy in Russia; he broke with all traditional conceptions of that milieu."[5] Disdainful ridi-

---

[4] Lenin, *Collected Works*, Vol. XIV, p. 401.
[5] *Ibid.*, p. 405.

cule of disgraceful idleness, emptiness, spiritual wretchedness, and cultural degeneration of the nobility, as well as sincere sympathy with and compassion for the muzhiks, whose every word is permeated with intelligence and a serious businesslike attitude toward life, convincingly demonstrate Tolstoy's break with his class and his going over to the side of the people.

The Fruits of Enlightenment was first produced in Moscow on the stage of the Hunters' Club by a group headed by K. S. Stanislavsky. This was his earliest venture as producer-director. After many requests the production was permitted, in a private performance without programs. In addition to the future actors of the Art Theatre, V. F. Komissarzhevskaya, who shared their purposes, took part in the play. It met with enormous success, attracting to its performers the attention of all connoisseurs and friends of the theatre. Thereafter the performance was repeated many times.

On September 26, 1891, the comedy was given at the Aleksandrinsky Theatre, and on December 12 of the same year at the Maly Theatre on the occasion of N. V. Rykalova's jubilee. Aside from the author's name, the success of the play was predicated on the brilliant acting of A. P. Lensky as the Professor, G. N. Fedotova as Zvezdintseva, O. O. Sadovskaya as the Cook, and, particularly, of M. P. Sadovsky who, with infinite veracity, portrayed the first peasant. Subsequently the comedy was staged all over Russia.

As early as 1887, Savina received Tolstoy's consent to produce his tragedy *The Power of Darkness* on her benefit night. But even her influence was powerless to overcome censorship obstacles, and the play was first given in translation on the Paris stage in Antoine's Théâtre Libre on February 10, 1888. The French actors considered it a special honor to appear in it, even in minor parts. The role of Nikita was performed by Antoine as well as this could be done by a man who had no knowledge of Russian life. Among the spectators, Emile Zola was particularly delighted.

Parisian success prompted the production of the tragedy in Brussels, Geneva, Amsterdam, and Berlin (first, on the stage of the Free, and, later, the People's Theatre). In 1893 *The Power of Darkness* was staged all over Italy.

On October 16, 1895, *The Power of Darkness* was produced on the stage of the Suvorin Theatre, and two days later, October 18,

at the Aleksandinsky Theatre, where Savina distinguished herself
by her extremely realistic performance of the role of Akulina. Here
the acting was much inferior to that of the private theatre. Moreover, on the crown stage peasant life was shown in the conventional
manner of embellished theatricalism. On the other hand, Suvorin's
director E. P. Karpov (1857–1926), a connoisseur of the village
who himself had written a number of successful plays dealing
with peasant and worker ways of living, succeeded in producing the
authentic life of the destitute and ignorant village, displaying his
ability to stage mass scenes.

Among the individual performers on the private stage the following were above criticism: I. I. Sudbinin as Nikita; M. Mikhailov (died on February 14, 1914), who had earned the reputation of being the best Akim; and M. P. Domasheva, who delighted
the audience by her touching acting in the part of Anyutka. All
these were overshadowed by Strepetova in the role of Matryona,
who portrayed a horrible image of wicked criminality in the character of the wild witch. In contrast, on the crown stage V. V.
Strelskaya portrayed Matryona in a mild, good-natured manner.
The majority of the spectators accused her of failure to comprehend that monster; yet other opinions were voiced to the effect that
Strelskaya even more graphically revealed the boundless "power
of darkness" by emphasizing the fact that under its cover, not
pathologic monsters—like Strepetova's Matryona—but most ordinary
human beings are doomed to perpetrate horrible crimes, without
seeing in them anything abnormal. Tolstoy himself considered that
his tragedy was best produced by the Moscow Buffoon Theatre.

Chapter XXII

THE PROVINCIAL THEATRE

WE FIND in Ostrovsky's plays, either fully or partly devoted to the portrayal of theatrical life, the most authentic picture of the Russian provincial theatre in the middle of the nineteenth century, when the serf theatres were already passing out of existence. Impressarios, actors, actresses, and their admirers among the public —all these were completely portrayed. *The Forest, Guilty Without Guilt, Talents and Their Admirers,* aside from their dramatic merits, are valuable to the history of the Russian theatre as priceless material for the characterization of the generation of actors that was gradually passing out of existence.

Here we shall see, passing in review: Gennady Demyanovich Neschaslivtsev and Arkady Schastlivtsev, from year to year measuring by their accustomed footsteps the surface of Russia, from Kerch to Vologda and from Vologda to Kerch, with their opera hats, a pair of wigs, and a pair of pistols with broken gunlocks in their sacks—but with happy reminiscences in their hearts of acting *Belisarius* in the town of Lebedyan, when Nikolay Khrisanfovich Rybakov himself paid tribute to their performance; the tragedian Yerast Gromilov, lamenting the fact that he is decent only when drunk, which, however, does not prevent him from preaching decency to a rich merchant; the comedian Robinson, who ever since childhood has had a distinct dislike for being flogged, considering that the only obstacle to his journey abroad without a passport and the only goal of his life was getting drunk; the actor Shmaga, deriving his historical name from one of the earliest Russian artists,

"a comedian in life and a villain on the stage," professing the faith
that "the actor is proud," and that his place is in a refreshment
bar; the dandy Milovzorov, deporting himself on the stage like
a barber until he learns proper manners from one of those actresses
who claim that it is easy to play with him because he is endowed
with "much realism"; Neznamov, a pure soul but too impetuous
in his dealings with people, who entered the theatre because all
other careers were closed to him.

Heading these theatrical workers is the impresario Migayev,
who knows little, who judges the actor's talent by his pocketbook
("If he produces big box-office receipts he is a talent"), and who
declares himself "a materialist." In his theatre he arranges separate dressing rooms in order to provide enjoyment of the charms
of the talented actresses for such admirers as Prince Dulebov, who
thus explains his interest in the theatre:

Every one of us is occupied all day long—some with family and
business matters, others with public affairs; only in the evenings are we
free for a few hours. Now where, as with a young actress, is it so
pleasant to relax, so to speak from the burden of cares—in the case of
one from business troubles, and in the case of another from preoccupations with the department or locality entrusted to his administration?

And such young and congenial actresses happen to be available in
the persons of Korinkina and Smelskaya. The embarrassment of
Smelskaya merely comes down to this: she is courted by the Prince,
and yet she is also anxious not to let the rich Velikatov slip away.

Only in exceptional cases does this world of the theatre find in
its midst such enthusiasts as the assistant director Narokov, who
in days gone by was a wealthy landowner and says:

I love the theatre, I love art, I love artists. I sold my estate, received
much money, and became an impressario. Isn't this happiness? I rented
the local theatre, refurnished everything anew—stage scenery and costumes; I engaged a good company, and started living as though in
paradise. . . . I didn't mind whether or not there were receipts; I paid
large salaries to everybody punctually. Thus I enjoyed myself for five
years, and then I began to realize that money was coming to an end.
Upon the termination of the season I discharged all the artists, gave
them a farewell dinner, made an expensive present to everyone as a
remembrance . . . and after that my Gavryushka rented my theatre,

and I entered his service. He pays me a small salary, and little by little he pays for my installations.

No wonder that in such an environment Aleksandra Nikolayevna Negina finds it hard to live; she cannot exist without the theatre, but for the sake of stage success she is compelled to abandon her beloved and to seek protection from the crude public and the whims of the impresario under the wing of a wealthy admirer. And it is lucky if it happens that such a protector is some kind-hearted man like Dudukin, who, in order not to be altogether idle, specializes in the alleviation of the lot of actors and actresses. However, the stage reconciles its servants with life's misfortunes: Neschastlivtsev is quite sincere when he says: "I am a poor, miserable hobo; yet on the stage I am a prince. I live his life; I am tormented by his thoughts; I weep with his tears over ill starred Ophelia, and I love her as forty thousand brothers are powerless to love." Inviting Aksusha, whom he has saved, to the stage, he promises her: "Thou shalt appear a queen on the stage, and a queen thou shalt leave the stage, and thus thou shalt remain." Despite all trials and privations, even Arkashka, who is introduced in the play as a counterbalance to the enraptured Neschastlivtsev, is unable to part with the stage. And when he finds himself well provided at his rich relatives' home, he begins to ponder over the question whether it would not be a good thing to strangle himself; and in despair he escapes at night through a window, thus getting rid of his anguish—only to resume a vagabond's life.

Even the anecdotal aspect of these "actor" plays of Ostrovsky is highly valuable to the history of the provincial theatre. He did not invent the various episodes, but he included in his plays those actual happenings which he either personally observed, or heard told by the actors themselves. Thus, Schastlivtsev's account of the tragedian Bichevkin who "had already once killed himself to death" (*The Forest*, Act II, Scene 2) actually did take place in some provincial locality in the fifties; only the name of the incautious actor, so thinly disguised by Ostrovsky, was Veryovkin.

In his memorandum on dramatic schools Ostrovsky wrote:

There sprang into being an enormous number of provincial actors; however, among them the percentage of artists even slightly suited for the stage was very small—almost negligible. The others were riffraff composed of all sorts of idlers, belonging to all classes, and to every possible walk of life. The provincial stage was the final haven for men who had tried different professions and had failed—for those who had absolutely nowhere to go. It was a paradise for idlers and parasites evading all serious work and seeking not only to be sufficiently fed, but even to enjoy life and to occupy an eminent position in society.

An even more drastic picture of provincial theatrical life was given by Saltykov-Shchedrin in chapters of *Messrs. Golovlev* describing the ruin of the sisters who had entered the theatre.

The authenticity of these pictures is vouched for by the many reminiscences of actors of those days. Among them the memoirs of Peter Mikhailovich Medvedev (1837–1906) stand out by their animated style and wealth of detail. A pupil of the Moscow ballet school, he began his career at an early age in the provincial theatre, acting in many cities of central Russia. He played there at a time when old actors who had emerged from serf theatres were ending their careers. Therefore he was destined to witness the appearance on the stage of the young group of artists. Thus he had, in fact, observed the momentous meeting of two generations of Russian actors. Before long, leaving the actors' ranks, he became in the sixties and seventies one of the most noted provincial impresarios. During his last years he served in the capitals, first in Korsh's Theatre, and later on the Aleksandrinsky stage, where for a while he held the position of director.

The composition of the companies, in which Medvedev had to play during the early years of his career was variegated. Thus, in Tula the director and a prominent member of the company was a former government official who, having been discharged for abuses in alcohol and graft, somehow had become an actor:

His appearance, indeed, was beastlike, with a scarlet face, always punched and spotted with scratches; he used to hold his arms like a hoop; he spoke harshly and abruptly; both on and off the stage he indulged in the unfortunate habit of accompanying each sentence with ribaldries, uttering these as though to himself.

The impresario Azbukin, well known in provincial districts, was a police officer dishonorably discharged for fraudulent conduct. Another actor in the same Tula company was the son of serf parents; playing parts of raisonneurs, he was not particularly distinguished for his education. When a theatre habitué asked him what a raisonneur was, the poor actor began to puff and blush, and finally had to confess: "Forgive me, sir, I am a serf; I was told that I was a raisonneur, and I keep saying that I am one; but what this word actually means, only God knows."

Naturally, such actors could not claim large salaries; and, as a matter of fact, in some companies the highest salary did not exceed 35 rubles a month, while the lowest was 5 rubles. If the company worked a whole year the salaries were even lower: the highest was 15 rubles, and the lowest 3 rubles a month.

The overwhelming majority of provincial society regarded actors askance. This attitude in the merchant class, for instance, is evident in the following story from Medvedev. On one occasion he happened to be traveling with a merchant who had been squandering money:

It became necessary to hide his wallet, which was fully packed with assignation rubles, and to dole him small sums, or else to make payments on his behalf. As we were nearing Nizhny, he demanded that the wallet be produced. I returned it to him. He counted his money over for a long time; then he began staring at me; after that there was a protracted silence. Finally he asked me, "Who are you?" "An actor." "Go on! Go on! Don't lie! What kind of actor are you?" I tried to persuade him, but he refused to believe me. "Why don't you believe me?" "Well, what's the use of arguing? If you were an actor, you would have robbed me; but all my money is safe." As we were parting, he placed three rubles in my hand. I returned the money. "See! You claim you are an actor! But what actor will refuse a three-ruble tip!"

And yet actors had to maintain friendly relations with such a society; naturally, they were wholly dependent upon it. This was particularly true of actors receiving benefit performances, since in those days it was customary for actors and even actresses personally to deliver tickets for their benefit performances to eminent townsmen:

The beneficiary would engage an experienced theatre usher who knew the public; the actor would appear with a decent-looking cabman; the usher was supplied with programs printed on rice paper—for prominent citizens, on satin. The beneficiary, wearing full dress, seated himself in a coach, while the usher sat in the coach box, next to the cabman. Both would make the sign of the cross, and then depart. The beneficiary inquired on whom they should call first. "Here resides a kindly man; he often comes to the theatre. Perhaps, we shall be received." Presently, they arrive. The usher gets off his box, rings the bell either at the front door or at the delivery entrance in the back yard. He disappears for a long while, and the actor, sitting in the coach, keeps pondering who that merciful person may be. The usher returns, sadly shaking his head in the distance and mournfully taking his seat in the coach box. "What happened?" "Why, probably we came at the wrong time. He shouted at me, 'What do you want?' Here, I say, is a benefit actor. 'The devil,' says he, 'drives you around. Tell him that if I choose to come I know where the box office is, and I will buy a ticket myself!' "

Here is how Medvedev depicts the arrangement of a certain contemporary theatre:

Stage scenery was shabby: a forest, two chambers, and that's all. In the costume wardrobe there was something for *The Inspector-General:* one livery, civil service uniforms. In salon plays they were used for full dress suits, for which purpose brass buttons were covered up with black calico. There were also two marquis coats and twelve red hussar soldiers' pelisses purchased at bargain prices (these uniforms were the impresario's pride.) The rest was junk. Stage furniture: painted wooden chairs and one armchair. In aristocratic settings, red fustian slip covers were put on this furniture.

Nor could actors and actresses boast of their wardrobes. The leading lady's costumes consisted of a black, white, colored, silk, and calico dress, and several character costumes. The rest had even fewer. However, actresses managed to brighten this meager wardrobe with all sorts of adornments. Two men had full dress. Lucky fellows! And what an air they assumed when one was compelled to borrow a full dress from them. Nearly all of them had frock coats. In private they were decently dressed. The band was composed of six musicians (in view of the fact that in theatres of that time plays with singing numbers were frequently produced, the orchestra was important). Neither a tailor nor a hairdresser was on permanent staff. For the changes of scenery and the raising of the front curtain there were amateurs who performed these duties without remuneration. The functions of stage manager, and property man were attended to by actors, usually young actors. There was no director, and the actors themselves had to determine their places on the stage.

One of the essential reasons for this primitive state of provincial theatres, aside from the modest budget due to the low prices of the seats, was the fact that theatrical managers were mostly men altogether lacking in artistic interests who looked upon the theatre exclusively from a commercial standpoint.

The same picture is given in the memoirs of P. A. Strepetova; in *Things Lived Through*, by A. P. Lensky; and in "Reminiscences of the Nizhny Novgorod Theatre," by P. O. Morozov (*Ye Yezhegodnik*, No. 3, 1910).

One of the most typical owners of provincial theatres was the Nizhny Novgorod impresario Fyodor Konstantinovich Smolkov, who earned a wide reputation by his proverbial avarice, and his ability either to engage an outstanding actor at a low price or to reduce his salary under a more or less plausible pretext. His stinginess was also reflected in the production of historical plays, as may be seen from the following incident recounted by Medvedev:

Mary Stuart is being produced. The director tells Smolkov that it is necessary to order a hatchet. "Give me a ruble." "What for?" "Strelkova insists that in the last act she be beheaded by an executioner." "This is not necessary!" "Then what shall we do?" "Do we have a pistol?" "For heaven's sake! According to history Mary Stuart was beheaded!" "Well, that was in the case of the real Mary Stuart, whereas Strelkova may be shot with a pistol. This is unimportant!" And thus it was done: Mary Stuart was shot."

If such was Smolkov's attitude toward the historical aspects of productions, he was not less peculiar with respect to the assignment of roles:

The actor A. A. Ralph is given the part of Famusov, he refuses to take it. The matter is investigated: "Why don't you take the part of Famusov? I will penalize you," says Smolkov. "Why should I play Famusov? I always played Chatsky. You know my *emploi*. I am a lover." "But Famusov is also a lover!" "What do you mean? Good Lord! Famusov—a lover!" "Why not? Doesn't he flirt with Liza?" answers Smolkov imperturbably.

One must remember that, all in all, Smolkov was one of the most respectable entrepreneurs, whereas others, equally ignorant and miserly, did not have his business ability and innate shrewdness.

In those days there were not many big provincial theatres. P. A. Strepetova reported that in the seventies there were only eight good provincial playhouses: in Kiev, Kharkov, Odessa, Tiflis, Kazan, Voronezh, Rostov-on-Don, and Saratov.

From Strepetova's memoirs we shall cite only an excerpt dealing with costumes:

The Frenchwoman's gown of the eighteenth century consisted of nothing but a modern dress, which was worn with merely a white powdered peruke and one or two black "patches" (that depended on the whim and zeal of the actress) pasted to her cheek. The male attire was somewhat more elaborate. In addition to the powdered peruke, a black cloth cape was sewed to an ordinary modern black frock coat, oilcloth funnel-shaped bootlegs were fitted to one's own patent leather shoes—and the marquis was ready. And if, to top it off, on the right side of the actor's chest an abnormally large glass bead star was displayed, it meant that he intended to impersonate some prince or Somersetian duke, or, at least, the President in *Wile and Love*. Two such enormous glass bead lozenges signified that the wearer was a member of a royal family.

The hideous situation of provincial theatres did not escape the notice of contemporaries, who fully realized the defects both in the artistic aspect of the production and in the actors' status. This is clear from a humorous article entitled "The Fate of a Provincial Actor," which appeared in 1847 in the columns of the magazine *The Repertoire and the Pantheon* (No. 12), published by F. A. Kony. It is in the form of a letter from the actor Osip Boot. Sharply ridiculing the status of provincial theatres, he comes to the conclusion that the provincial actor is a lost man, in the precise sense of the term. Engaged in acting, he gradually forgets his former ability to do anything useful, either for himself or for society. His physical strength wanes because, at times,

> He does not sleep, or without food he fares—
> Indeed, a heavy cross he bears.

In the same year, *The Repertoire and the Pantheon* (No. 11) carried an article entitled "Physiology of the Provincial Theatres," by an author who concealed his identity under the pseudonym of Ippolit Bublik. This is a sketch of the organization of the provincial theatre of the period and a characterization of both theatrical habitué and actors, headed by their manager and impresario. It is enough to cite an excerpt pertaining to costumes:

Nothing is funnier than the sight on the stage of some Hamlet in a hussar's jacket, or a marquis of the period of Louis XV in a calico garment tailored after an illustration of last year's fashions. In some theatres costumes are tailored fairly well, but actors wear them altogether indiscriminately. If they have to appear on the stage in the guise of some Petersburg German, they will without fail consider it necessary to put on a French waistcoat and a three-cornered hat. Sometimes, the Roman military leader Belisarius appears on the stage in a camlet Almaviva and wearing a naval officer's hat. On several occasions I saw Veronica's shade (*Ugolino*) appear in a pink catafalque, wearing a bright-colored dress and singing to the tune "Go thou home, my little cow!"

The general deduction is that "provincial theatres are still on the lowest level of dramatic art." However, among provincial actors were persons who reflected credit on their milieu. Such, for instance, was the comedian K. T. Solyonik (1811–1851). A student of Vilna University, he went on the stage when he was still a very young man. He localized his work in the biggest companies of the South, and became so outstanding among his colleagues that on several occasions he was invited to the capital. However, he did not wish to leave his native Little Russia.[1] He was highly appreciated by Gogol.

Solyonik's best parts were Lev Gurych Sinichkin, Famusov, Repetilov, Khlestakov, Dobchinsky, and Kochkarev. In Ukrainian plays, especially *The Muscovite,* his acting in the role of Chuprun was superior to that of Shchepkin. According to one of his contemporaries, Solyonik "gave flesh, blood, and a live soul to the playwright's creations, supplying that which the author was unable to express in the dead letter; through him these creations were rendered clear and comprehensible to everybody."

In later times, too, eminent artists had to work on the provincial stage under conditions which did not measure up to their talents; for example, P. A. Strepetova (1850–1903), Nikolay Khrisanfovich Rybakov, Kornily Poltavtsev (1823–1865), and N. K. Miloslavsky (1811–1882), an inimitable performer of melodramas who represented in provincial districts the same tendency that V. V. Samoilov represented in Petersburg. In 1859 Miloslavsky made his début in the Aleksandrinsky Theatre. Of this event I. I. Sosnitsky wrote in a private letter: "He vividly reminds one of Karatygin. In my judgment, he is very good for the provincial stage. But for Peters-

[1] Ukraine.—Ed.

burg his stature and figure are good—and nothing else. His voice is composed of two instruments: the bassoon and the English horn. In his recital there is no sense but much bellowing."

There appeared in the provincial districts numerous dramatic talents who developed notably and later joined the crown theatre, where they became outstanding contributors to the progress of the Russian theatre. Among those prominent on the provincial stage were Ivanov-Kozelsky (1846–1898), a specialist in Shakespearean parts and an artist of enormous tragic temperament, and Andreyev-Burlak (1843–1888), the best Arkashka in *The Forest*.

Established theatrical companies began to come into being in the provincial districts in the latter part of the eighties. The best of these was headed by N. N. Solovtsov (1857–1902), who could not get along with Korsh in Moscow. Soon Solovtsov, with his wife M. M. Glebova, Roshchin-Insarov, and Kiselevsky, transferred his work to Kiev. They were joined by excellent local actors—E. Y. Nedelin, Chuzhbinov, and others. The "Solovtsovites" played in Kiev and Odessa for ten years (1892–1902), having organized in the provincial regions the first exemplary artistic enterprise. From their midst emerged a number of outstanding actors. Solovtsov's example influenced other impresarios; namely, M. M. Boroday and A. M. Dyukova, who began to form good companies in Kharkov and other large provincial cities, staging productions that bore witness to the growth of the provincial theatres.

After Solovtsov, the most noted and conscientious entrepreneur was N. N. Sinelnikov (1856–1939). An excellent actor in his early years, he became a director in Korsh's theatre. Subsequently he headed his own company in Kiev, Kharkov, and other southern cities. Endowed with the rare faculty of recognizing the genuine gifts of artists and guiding them, he became a distinguished teacher of a whole generation of actors; and his company always achieved a good artistic level.

But all these performances were inaccessible to the majority of peasants and urban proletarians: ticket prices were high, and poorly dressed people were not admitted to the theatre. Only tent shows were left to them; there, in cities, on holidays, most primitively staged plays, filled with bloody exploits, shooting, and the like, were given.

In the latter part of the eighties, the government decided to assume tutelage over popular entertainments. Instead of heeding the opinions of such experts as A. N. Ostrovsky and S. A. Yuryev, who understood the aesthetic tastes of the people, it quite artificially created a hypocritical network of "wardships of popular temperance"—a senselessly expensive enterprise. In Moscow, M. V. Lentovsky organized for the people a playhouse of his own, "The Buffoon." There, among other plays, he produced *The Power of Darkness*—in many respects better than it had been staged in the crown theatres. In Petersburg arose the Vasilevsky Island Society of Popular Entertainments, in which N. A. Popov worked for a while. E. P. Karpov successfully staged plays in factories in the Petersburg suburbs. The hands of these producers were tied by the stupid selection of plays authorized for such audiences, which resulted in the audience's indifference.

Meanwhile, the people, with their modest means, worked unceasingly to solve the problem of creating their own genuinely popular theatre, which grew and developed free from tutelage of any kind.

The historical play about King Maximilian and his disobedient son Adolf was the foundation of this repertoire. The question of its origin is both complex and controversial. Its nucleus is composed of scenes in which the heathen king orders his Christian son to pay homage to the "pagan gods." However, the other scenes, apparently, were borrowed from certain interludes (for instance, that "About Anik, the worrier, and his struggle with death"). Here also we find inserted scenes from the Nativity, Petrushka, and other popular plays, such as *The Sloop*, and *Nobleman*. In addition, the text is replete with excerpts from popular songs and romances, as well as with popular adaptations of the verse of Pushkin, Lermontov, and other poets. In the beginning of the eighteenth century the play could have conveyed to the audience sharp political humor, since contemporaries may have detected in it a satire on the attitude of Peter I toward his Lutheran wife and his son Tsarevich Aleksey.

The second among the most popular Russian people's dramas bears different titles: *The Boat*, *The Sloop*, *The Robbers' Gang*, *Ataman*, and *Mashenka*. It is derived from several robbers' songs, for instance, from those about Stenka Razin. It depicts a boat sailing down a river; robbers sit in the boat; in their midst stands the ataman, who asks his assistant what it is that is seen in the distance.

Episodes from the third popular piece, *The Self-Styled Nobleman*
or *The Naked Nobleman,* are introduced in the different variants
of this drama. The latter play is based on an anecdote about a
nobleman and a village mayor who reports to the landowner that
everything is all right "only your mamma has passed away, the
house burned down, the cattle died off," and so forth. The plays
The Nobleman, The Steed or *The Horseman,* and *The Horse
Doctor* deride the justice of noblemen, landowners in general, and
the various authorities. The play *Mavrukh* is a satire on Divine
service and the clergy's mode of living. The people also staged
little scenes which were adaptations from theatrical plays. Such
was *Parasha,* a revision of the actor P. G. Grigoryev's comedy
The Yamshchiks (produced during the 1844–1845 season on the
Aleksandrinsky stage). In *Parasha* almost all the dramatis personnae
are retained, although some of them appear under other names.
However, it omits altogether those spurious and completely boasting orations without which, during the Nicholas period, it was
impossible to gratify the authorities. Grigoryev's play was included
in the collection of performances for soldiers, and, on their return
home from service, the soldiers might have brought it to their
villages.

In the Trans-Onega region, the comedy *Pakhomushka* was quite
popular at "colloquies"; by change of dress and the simplest make-
up a parody on matchmaking and on a church wedding ceremony
is performed. After the nuptial night the newlywed husband leaves
home to seek a job; on his return, he finds his Pakhomikha with
a child whom she begat from a stranger. The deceived husband
thrashes his wife and her seducer, and, in a state of excitement,
begins to beat all his guests, who hastily run away with laughter
and screams. This little scene, full of *chastushkas* and animated by
almost constant play, now with a horse or a boat, now with a
bench or a child—all made out of a coat taken from somebody's
shoulders—gives ample leeway to everyone desiring to take part in
the play.

Conclusion

THE GENERAL DECADENCE of Russian culture at the end of the nineteenth century, produced by political and economic causes, also brought about a marked decline in theatre business, which, according to K. S. Stanislavsky, "in those days was controlled by restaurateurs on the one hand, and by bureaucrats on the other."

The lowering of theatrical standards was expressed with particlar vividness in the exercises of the first all-Russian convention of theatrical workers, which took place in Moscow in March, 1897. Permitted on condition that it refrain from discussing the situation on the crown stage, the convention devoted its whole attention to the provincial theatre, whose workers constituted the majority of those present.

Provincial delegates strongly insisted on prohibitory measures, including the forbidding of tours by the artists of the crown stages in provincial districts, inasmuch as "they had enough to eat anyway, and only deprived their hungry art colleagues of their crusts of bread."

Against a background of such statements, the voice of A. P. Lensky sounded lonely indeed when in his report he pointed out that actors themselves were to be blamed for the difficulties which they experienced:

Is it not a shame, is it not insulting to realize that the Russian actor's profession is the only one which does not regard education as a benefit to itself and to its art? Is it possible to degrade its work more strongly and more obnoxiously than the actor himself humiliates stagecraft when, speaking of his attitude towards it, he claims that, essentially, his art does not require any art at all; that, in order to acquire the right to be considered as an actor, it is enough merely to call one's self an actor and appear on the stage and begin to talk.

[427]

Lensky urged harmony between "the enlightened actor and the director-artist"; in their coordinated work he saw the assurance of the so badly needed improvement of the theatre. However, the majority of the delegates at the convention earnestly reiterated Arkashka's complaint in *The Forest*, "The educated ones have overpowered us," and derided the arguments relating to the elevation of the actor's artistic level.

It was difficult for those individual actors who understood the real cause of the degradation of the theatre to raise dramatic art as a whole, because of the complete absence of the necessary conditions. The newly organized theatres least of all vindicated the hopes which were placed in them. For example, on September 17, 1895, a theatre in Petersburg, headed by A. S. Suvorin, was opened with the production of Ostrovsky's *Thunderstorm*. In the days gone by Suvorin had written in the columns of *The Messenger of Europe* (1871, No. 1) about the shortcomings of the crown stage. Yet his own theatre, possessing considerable artistic and financial assets, sank after the good productions of *The Power of Darkness* and *Tsar Fyodor* to the level of a mediocre enterprise, in which everybody, including Suvorin himself, submitted to the whims of such altogether doubtful artists as L. B. Yavorskaya or B. Glagolin.

Nor was the situation any more promising on the crown stage, which had chained its actors with bureaucracy and routine. In the final analysis the Maly Theatre also, its growth having been so arrested that it failed to heed the new tendencies in art and, thus, to satisfy the tastes of its best spectators, retarded the progress of its young actors.[1] The Moscow opera likewise retreated to the background before its successful rival—the private opera.

During those years the outstanding event in the life of theatrical Petersburg was the entry into the Aleksandrinsky company (May 1, 1896) of V. F. Komissarzhevskaya after her brief service on the provincial stage. Having played with enormous success Rose in Sudermann's piece *The Butterflies' Battle*, and Klärchen in his *Destruction of Sodom*, on September 17, 1896, she appeared as Larisa in *The Girl Without Dowry*. Marya Andreyevna in *The Poor Fiancée* and Mashenka in Turgenev's *The Bachelor*, by reason of the depth of feeling and dynamic power in the acting

[1] See Sergey Glagol, *Life*, 1900, No. 12.

of Komissarzhevskaya, occupy an honored place among the women characters created on the Russian stage. The enchanting voice, sounding from her innermost self, a voice which she developed under the guidance of her father, an eminent opera singer, put the audience under the spell of Komissarzhevskaya, in whose creative work audiences found a reflection of their own feelings and moods.

However, "the actress of life," as P. D. Boborykin pointedly called her, was able to impersonate only characters similar to herself. Neither her cultural nor her social aspirations, very remote from those of the majority of her stage colleagues, found response in her environment. Before long, she began to feel a stranger on the Petersburg crown stage, which proved incapable of coping even with those few artistic plays which appeared in Russia in the years of theatrical impoverishment.

Such, for instance, was the fate of A. P. Chekhov's *Sea-Gull*. First produced on the Aleksandrinsky stage on October 17, 1896, it was withdrawn from the repertoire after the fifth performance.

Neither the crown stage nor the majority of private theatres at the end of the nineteenth century complied even with the most modest artistic requirements. Both the best actors and the dramatists began to feel dissatisfied and disillusioned. The most profitable and favorite show became the farce, which reiterated the most risqué and coarsest situations of operetta plots, differing from operetta only in that neither musical ear nor voice was required of the actor.

Such was the sad situation of the professional stage. The regeneration of dramtic art originated in the circles of genuine connoisseurs and devotees of art. Of such circles there were not a few in Moscow. As early as 1873, Lev Polivanov, in conjunction with the pupils of his private gymnasium and his friends, organized a Shakespearean society. Turgenev, who attended its production of *Henry IV*, declared that he had never seen a finer Falstaff on any European stage.

In 1888 there was organized on a far broader basis the Society of Art and Literature under the direction of the actor and playwright A. F. Fedotov (1841–1895), the singer F. A. Komissarzhevsky, and the amateur painter F. L. Sologub. Foremost among the actors was K. S. Alekseyev-Stanislavsky (1863–1938), a grandson of a French actress, and a factory owner who was taught singing by V. F. Komissarzhevsky and dramatic art by G. N. Fedotova. That circle produced *The Fruits of Enlightenment*. The part of Betsy was performed by V. F. Komissarzhevskaya, who then was not yet contemplating a stage career. In addition there were produced: *Uriel Akosta; Those Who Determine Their Own Fate; Bitter Fate; Othello; Much Ado About Nothing; Twelfth Night; Hannele; The Sunken Bell; The Village Stepanchikovo; George Dandin;* and *Wile and Love*. In the last the part of Ferdinand was played by Stanislavsky, and that of Louise by Perevozchikova (Lilina). The production of *Those Who Determine Their Own Fate* was directed by G. N. Fedotova.

The performances of that society constituted a real epoch in the artistic life of Moscow: in them, conscientious staging, which was thought out in every detail, and coordination in the acting even of the most insignificant parts, blended in harmony with strict historical authenticity—an aim which the crown theatres were both unwilling and unable to attain. In these productions there was not even a trace of that conventional theatricalism which the Society openly challenged.

K. S. Stanislavsky, who had gradually assumed leadership of the circle, finally came to the conclusion that it should be reorganized into a permanently functioning theatre. This he achieved in collaboration with Vladimir Ivanovich Nemirovich-Danchenko (born December 11, 1857). The outstanding dramatist of that period, whose plays *New Enterprise, The Last Will, Gold,* and *The Price of Life* are distinguished by a fine description of the lives of merchants' sons (such as were depicted by Ostrovsky), Nemirovich-Danchenko rightfully became Stanislavsky's worthy collaborator. The dramatic class directed by Vladimir Ivanovich in the School of the Philharmonic Society was the best dramatic school of the time, and a number of good actors were trained in it.

Stanislavsky and Nemirovich-Danchenko brought together the ablest participants in the performances of the Society of Art and Literature with the graduates of the Philharmonic School and, having succeeded through combined efforts in a perfect coordination of the actors' work, created the Moscow Art Theatre.

The production by the Moscow Art Theatre of the second part of A. Tolstoy's trilogy *Tsar Fyodor* on October 14 (27), 1898 (its opening performance), inaugurated a new era in the history of the Russian and the world theatre. Incarnating in its creative work all the best elements of the past life of the theatre, the Moscow Art Theatre at the same time became a laboratory in which new artistic methods were conceived, and these invariably exercised a dominating influence upon all forms of dramatic art, both in Russia and abroad.

The Russian theatre entered a new phase of its development, finding its way out of that impasse into which it was driven in the years of political reaction during the reign of Alexander III. It has been justly pointed out:

"The Moscow Art Theatre came into being during the years of the general popular awakening before the first Russian revolution. The Russian toiling masses, led by the worker class, were getting ready for decisive battles against the world of savagery, misery, and violence. The Art Theatre was called to life by a mighty wave of democratic upsurge." [2]

[2] See the address of the Union of Soviet Writers to the Moscow Art Theatre on its 1938 anniversary celebration.

RUSSIAN TRANSLITERATION TABLE

(Based on the new Russian orthography)

This scheme is designed for the convenience of readers who do not know Russian. It is intended primarily for the rendering of personal and place names — mostly nouns in the nominative case.

The aim is to produce words as "normal" in appearance as possible, without the use of diacritical marks, superscripts or apostrophes, but at the same time to approximate the sounds of the Russian words, so that if spoken by an educated American they would easily be identified by a Russian.

Names which are a part of English cultural tradition, such as Moscow, Archangel, Tolstoy, Tchaikovsky, are given in their customary English spelling.

Extended phrases or entire sentences involving verb forms and case endings, which occur in footnotes for the convenience of students who know Russian, are given in a somewhat more complex transliteration which is reversible.

Russian		English	
А	а	*a*	
Б	б	*b*	
В	в	*v*	
Г	г	*g*	{ except in genitive singular where it is *v*, as in Tolstovo.
Д	д	*d*	
Е	е	(1) *ye* { when initial, and after Ь, Ъ, and all vowels, except Ы, И: Yekaterina, Izdanie, Nikolayev.	
		(2) *e* elsewhere, as in Lenin, Vera, Pero.	
Е	ё	*yo*	but after Ж and Ш = *o*.
Ж	ж	*zh*	
З	з	*z*	

[432]

Russian		*English*	
И	и	*i*	but after Ь = *yi*, as in Ilyich.
Й	й	*y*	{ in terminal diphthongs, but *i* medially, as in May, Kochubey, Kiy, Tolstoy, but Khoz*y*aistvo.
К	к	*k*	
Л	л	*l*	
М	м	*m*	
Н	н	*n*	
О	о	*o*	
П	п	*p*	
Р	р	*r*	
С	с	*s*	
Т	т	*t*	
У	у	*u*	
Ф	ф	*f*	
Х	х	*kh*	as in Kharkov.
Ц	ц	*ts*	Tsargrad.
Ч	ч	*ch*	Chapayev, Vaigach.
Ш	ш	*sh*	Shakhta.
Щ	щ	*shch*	Shchedrin.
Ъ	ъ	Omit	
Ы	ы	*y*	Mys, Tsaritsyn.
Ь	ь	Omit	
Э	э	*e*	Ermitazh.
Ю	ю	*yu*	
Я	я	*ya*	

Adjectival Endings

Singular	ЫЙ,	ИЙ,	ый, ий	{ both simply *y*, as in Dostoyevsky, Grozny.
Plural	ЫЕ,	ИЕ,	ые, ие	both simply *ie*.

The English letter *y* serves both as vowel and as consonant (as it does in English): (1) as a vowel *within* words, as in Mys, Tsaritsyn, and also (2) as an adjectival terminal vowel, as in Khoroshy, Razumovsky, May, Kochubey, Tolstoy, and (3) with consonantal force to soften vowels, as in Istoriya, Bratya, Yug.

Index of Persons

Index of Works

E-E

F-F

Fâcheux, Les, by Molière, 130
Falcon of Prince Yaroslav Tverskoy, The, or, The Betrothed on the White Steed, by Prince A. A. Shakhovskoy, 180, 181
False Friend, The, by Mercier, 134
Family Scene, A, by Alexander Nikolayevich Ostrovsky, 334
Fashionable Incident, A, by Nicholas Ivanovich Khmelnitsky, 192
"Fate of a Provincial Actor," 422
Fausses Infidelités, Les, by Barthe, 200
Feast During the Plague, The, by Alexander Sergeyevich Pushkin, 213, 226
Fedia and Volodia, by N. A. Nekrasov, 196
Fedinka and Luka, 103
Fedul and His Children, 84-85
Feigned Infidelity, by Alexander Sergeyevich Griboyedov, 200
Female Chitchat, by Shcheglov, 387
Female Fiddle Faddle, by Shcheglov, 387
Fifteen Years in Paris, or Not All Friends Are Alike, by Alexander Ivanovich Pisarev, 194
Fighter of Ravenna, The, 384
Filatka and Miroshka—Rivals, 353
Fingal, by Vladislav Aleksandrovich Ozerov, 162-163, 165, 174, 185
Finn, by Prince A. A. Shakhovskoy, 181
First Distiller, The, by Lev Nikolayevich Tolstoy, 411
Forced Marriage, The, by Molière, adapted by Lensky, 353
Forest, The, by Alexander Nikolayevich Ostrovsky, 329, 335, 336, 342-343, 347, 356, 379, 415, 417, 424, 428
For the Russians, by Racine, 150
Fortress of Magdeburg, The, 277
Fra Diabolo, 362
Francesca da Rimini, by D'Annunzio, 383
Free Love, by Lev Nikolayevich Tolstoy, 411
French-Russian, by Ivan Perfilyevich Yelagin, 142

Friend of the Unfortunate, The, by Kheraskov, 140
Fruits of Enlightenment, The, by Lev Nikolayevich Tolstoy, 411, 412-413 430
Fyodor Grigoryevich Volkov, or The Birthday of the Russian Theatre, by Prince A. A. Shakhovskoy, 181, 332

G-G

Gamblers, The, by Nicholas Vasilyevich Gogol, 230, 296, 306, 314-315, 353, 369
Gapholia, see Athalie, by Racine
Gentleman, by A. I. Sumbatov, 380, 384, 390
George Dandin, or The Confused Husband, by Molière, 83, 121, 285, 430
Georgian Night, The, by Alexander Sergeyevich Griboyedov, 209-210
Girl Pupil, The, by Alexander Nikolayevich Ostrovsky, 329, 335, 356
Girl Without a Dowry, The, by Alexander Nikolayevich Ostrovsky, 324, 329, 335, 379, 428
Giulio Mosti, by Nestor Vasilyevich Kukolnik, 242
Gold, by Vladimir Ivanovich Nemirovich-Danchenko, 430
Good Soldiers, The, 99
Governess, The, by Victor A. Dyachenko, 393
Grafter, The, by Alexander Petrovich Sumarokov, 130
Grandfather of the Russian Fleet, The, by Nicholas Alekseyevich Polevoy, 245
Grandfather's Parrots, by N. A. Nekrasov, 196
Grandmother's Parrots, by Nicholas Ivanovich Khmelnitsky, 192
Greek Ravings or Iphigenia in Taruis, by Nicholas Ivanovich Khmelnitsky, 192, 193
Gromoboy, by A. N. Verstovsky, 197
Guardian, The, by Alexander Petrovich Sumarokov, 130
Guilty Without Guilt, by Alexander Nikolayevich Ostrovsky, 335, 336, 341, 344, 379, 380, 415

M-M